The Political Economy of Grand Strategy

A volume in the series

CORNELL STUDIES IN SECURITY AFFAIRS

Edited by Robert J. Art, Robert Jervis, *and* Stephen M. Walt

A list of the titles in this series may be seen at

http://www.cornellpress.cornell.edu

The Political Economy of Grand Strategy

Kevin Narizny

Cornell University Press

Ithaca and London

First published 2007 by Cornell University Press
First printing, Cornell Paperbacks, 2007

Printed in the United States of America

Library of Congress Cataloging-in-Publication Data

Narizny, Kevin, 1974–
    The political economy of grand strategy / Kevin Narizny.
        p. cm.—(Cornell studies in security affairs)
    Includes bibliographical references and index.
    ISBN 978-0-8014-4508-8 (cloth : alk. paper)
    ISBN 978-0-8014-7430-9 (pbk. : alk. paper)
    1.   National security—United States—History—19th century.
2.   National security—United States—History—20th century. 3.   National
security—Great Britain—History—19th century. 4.   National security—
Great Britain—History—20th century. 5.   International relations—Political
aspects. 6.   United States—Foreign relations—19th century. 7.   United
States—Foreign relations—20th century. 8.   Great Britain—Foreign
relations—19th century. 9.   Great Britain—Foreign relations—
20th century. I. Title. II. Series.
    JZ1480.N38 2007
    327.41009'034—dc22   2007010663

Cloth printing   10 9 8 7 6 5 4 3 2 1
Paperback printing   10 9 8 7 6 5 4 3 2 1

Contents

Acknowledgments   vii

1. Theory   1
2. The Political Economy of the United States, 1865–1941   39
3. American Grand Strategy toward the Periphery   72
4. American Grand Strategy toward the Great Powers   113
5. The Political Economy of Great Britain, 1868–1939   159
6. British Grand Strategy toward the Periphery   190
7. British Grand Strategy toward the Great Powers   235
8. Conclusions   301

Index   323

[v]

Acknowledgments

I am grateful to the many people who have lent their time, intellect, and goodwill to support the writing of this book. Foremost thanks are due to Aaron Friedberg and Ken Schultz. Not only did their guidance improve my work in countless ways, but they also had a profound influence on my development as a political scientist. In the early stages of the project, I also benefited from the generous advice of Peter Trubowitz, Ben Fordham, James Nolt, Jeffry Frieden, Andrew Moravcsik, Anne Sartori, Wolfgang Danspeckgruber, and the participants in the Princeton International Relations Graduate Field Seminar. My research at Princeton was funded in part by the MacArthur Foundation, the Center for International Studies, and the Research Program in International Security.

Since leaving Princeton, I have had many fruitful conversations with fellow scholars about political economy, grand strategy, and everything in between. I am particularly indebted to Arman Grigorian, Mark Haas, Deborah Boucoyannis, P. R. Goldstone, Colin Dueck, and Taylor Fravel. As friends and colleagues, they helped tide me over many critical junctures in the project.

As one who studies economic interests in matters of life and death, I cannot stress enough my appreciation for the financial assistance of the Olin Institute for Strategic Studies at Harvard University, headed by Steve Rosen and Monica Toft; the Belfer Center for Science and International Affairs at Harvard University, headed by Steve Miller and Steve Walt; and the Committee on International Relations at the University of Chicago, headed by Duncan Snidal. This book would never have been realized without their support. I can only hope that they view its publication as a positive return on their investment in my survival as an academic.

[vii]

Portions of this work were previously published in three articles: "The Political Economy of Alignment: Great Britain's Commitments to Europe, 1905–39," *International Security* 27, no. 4 (spring 2003): 184–219; "Rational Idealism: The Political Economy of Internationalism in the United States and Great Britain, 1870–1945," *Security Studies* 12, no. 3 (spring 2003): 1–39; and "The New Debate: International Relations Theory and American Strategic Adjustment in the 1890s," *Security Studies* 11, no. 1 (autumn 2001): 151–70. I acknowledge MIT Press and Taylor and Francis for granting permission to use them here.

Outside of the world of political science and publishing, I owe special thanks to Joel Shapiro, Nipada Ruankaew, and Matt Savare. Without their friendship, I might have finished this book sooner, but at a far greater cost to my sanity. Finally, I thank my family, and especially my mother, who encouraged me to take this path from the very beginning. If I believed in dedications, this book would be for her.

K.N.

Chicago, Illinois

The Political Economy of Grand Strategy

[1]

Theory

Throughout the discipline of political science, the state is seen as an object of contestation, or an arena for competition, between groups with differing interests, ideologies, and cultural values. To advance their particular agendas, societal actors organize themselves into coalitions, intent on providing their leaders with the electoral, financial, or coercive means needed to take office. Once such a coalition wins control over the state, it enacts laws that benefit its members at the expense of other groups. Politicians rarely follow through on all of their promises, but they do consistently favor the preferences of their supporters and benefactors. Thus, politics is inseparable from policymaking.

As obvious as this may sound, one isolated subfield of political science steadfastly refuses to accept it. In the study of international security, the vast majority of research assumes that the state is largely, if not wholly, independent of societal pressures. From this perspective, the state's role is to act in the interest of the entire nation, not to represent particular factions within it. If the state is forced to choose between policies that have different distributional implications, benefiting some groups and imposing costs on others, it will aggregate preferences as best as possible to maximize overall utility. The resulting social welfare function is known as the "national interest." Without a concept of the "national interest," the argument goes, the state would be unable to set clear priorities for its foreign policy, leaving it unable to respond effectively to external threats.

In this book, I argue that the dichotomy between the study of international security and the rest of political science is conceptually bankrupt. The assumptions that set the former apart—first, that the state can be considered a unitary, autonomous actor, and second, that it is the neutral arbiter of an objective "national interest"—have seriously distorted scholars' views of the origins of state behavior. I propose instead that foreign policy follows the same logic as domestic politics. Whenever it has distributional implications, as is almost always the case, those who benefit and those who do not will coalesce around opposing positions. Each group may believe that its favored approach to foreign policy represents the nation's best interests, but its conception of the "national interest" will invariably be biased by its parochial concerns. To ensure that its preferred policies are enacted, it will provide material support to politicians with views similar to its own. As a result, state behavior will reflect the interests of the ruling coalition, not an elusive "national interest."

These concerns are not merely academic; they also have great practical importance. Consider, for example, contemporary American foreign policy. Did it matter which party won the last presidential election? Does it matter which party wins the next? If so, the subfield of international security is in dire need of theoretical development, because there is very little in the literature, at least outside of specialized work on political psychology and public opinion, that would explain why partisan control over the executive should matter, much less predict what positions each party will take.

This chapter is divided into five sections. First, I explore how established perspectives on international relations deal with the "problem" of domestic politics. Next, I flesh out the concept of grand strategy, showing how it can be defined and operationalized for comparative analysis. I then present a theory of grand strategy that is based on the sectoral interests of domestic coalitions. In the penultimate section, I elaborate on the concept of interest aggregation, which makes the critical connection between societal preferences and executive behavior. Finally, I conclude with a discussion of the cases on which I will test the theory.

THEORETICAL FOUNDATIONS

Unlike international security, the subfield of international political economy has paid a great deal of attention to domestic groups' influence over policymaking. The classic statement of this approach is E. E. Schattschneider's *Politics, Pressures, and the Tariff*.[1] According to Schattschneider,

---

[1] E. E. Schattschneider, *Politics, Pressures, and the Tariff: A Study of Free Private Enterprise in Pressure Politics, as Shown in the 1929–1930 Revision of the Tariff* (New York: Prentice-Hall, 1935). See also Thomas Ferguson, "From Normalcy to New Deal: Industrial Structure, Party Competition, and American Public Policy in the Great Depression," *International Organization* 38, no. 1 (winter 1984): 41–94; Peter Gourevitch, *Politics in Hard Times: Comparative Responses to International Economic Crises* (Ithaca: Cornell University Press, 1986); Jeffry A. Frieden, "Sectoral Conflict and Foreign Economic Policy, 1914–1940," *International Organization* 42, no. 1 (winter 1988): 59–90; Helen V. Milner, *Resisting Protectionism: Global Industries and the Politics of International Trade* (Princeton: Princeton University Press, 1988); Ronald Rogowski, *Commerce and Coalitions: How Trade Affects Domestic Political Alignments* (Princeton: Princeton University Press, 1989).

sectors that compete with imports tend to be protectionist, while those that export more often favor free trade. Their preferences influence the policy-making process through the agency of local politicians, who have strong incentives to promote the parochial interests of their electoral base. When politicians with import-competing constituencies control the government, tariffs will be raised; when politicians with exporting constituencies control the government, tariffs will be lowered. Thus, foreign economic policy can be highly politicized.

Most scholars recognize that domestic factors can affect security policy as well. However, few attempt to theorize systematically about the strategic interests of societal groups. Instead, they focus on the structure of the state and the character of its leaders. Every decade or so, the field has produced a new conceptual "revolution" on the subject. In the 1960s, Samuel Huntington, Kenneth Waltz, and others examined the role of process and institutions in foreign policymaking; in the early 1970s, Graham Allison pioneered the study of bureaucratic politics in crisis diplomacy; in the late 1970s, Robert Jervis published a seminal analysis of decision makers' psychological biases; in the 1980s, Michael Doyle popularized the idea that regime type affects conflict behavior; and, in the 1990s, Alexander Wendt advanced a new paradigm, constructivism, to explore the role of social norms and state identity.[2]

Each of these "revolutions" makes an important contribution to the field, but none has gone far enough. The extant literature has two critical limitations. First, it views domestic politics as a constraint on the pursuit of the "national interest," not as the fundamental determinant of state behavior. It does not consider how societal preferences influence governments' overarching goals; instead, it simply assumes that policymakers pursue "security," an abstract ideal that can rarely be specified *ex ante*. Second, it has little to say about partisan politics, the natural product of societal coalitions' struggle for control over the state. As a result, it cannot explain why turnover in government should lead to changes in state behavior.

This book is not the first to raise these issues. The idea that divergent socioeconomic interests can lead to partisan conflict over security policy flourished in the early twentieth century, as seen in the writings of J. A. Hobson,

---

[2] Samuel P. Huntington, *The Common Defense: Strategic Programs in National Politics* (New York: Columbia University Press, 1961); Kenneth N. Waltz, *Foreign Policy and Democratic Politics: The American and British Experience* (Boston: Little, Brown, 1967); Graham T. Allison, *Essence of Decision: Explaining the Cuban Missile Crisis* (Boston: Little, Brown, 1971); Robert Jervis, *Perception and Misperception in International Politics* (Princeton: Princeton University Press, 1976); Michael Doyle, "Kant, Liberal Legacies, and Foreign Affairs, Part I," *Philosophy and Public Affairs* 12, no. 3 (summer 1983): 205–35; Alexander Wendt, *Social Theory of International Politics* (Cambridge: Cambridge University Press, 1999).

Eckart Kehr, and Charles Beard.[3] However, these works had little influence on the development of international relations theory after World War II. Instead, the discipline has taken a roundabout route to rediscover their insights. Building on Schattschneider's legacy, a small number of scholars have recently begun to import preference-based models of international political economy into the study of international security.[4] Unfortunately, their work has not yet gained widespread recognition as constituting a full-fledged alterative to systemic paradigms. Most scholars continue to work under the assumption that, because all individuals within a state have a strong interest in the defense of their borders, parochial interests and partisanship have little or no impact on the conduct of security policy.

I argue, in contrast, that there is far more to security policy than just shielding the homeland from attack. It also promotes trade, protects foreign investment, and generates income for actors involved in the provision of strategic goods. If different domestic groups have divergent preferences over these issues, security policy will become just as politicized as foreign economic policy. Even in polities with a high degree of consensus, the analysis of societal interests is still needed to explain why different parties are able to agree on one particular policy over all of its plausible alternatives. This pluralist view is less parsimonious than the standard statist perspective on international security, but it promises far greater explanatory leverage over issues of critical importance to the field.

Systemic Theories

The dominant paradigm in the study of international security, realism, is inherently maladapted to this challenge. According to realists, as well as most institutionalists and many constructivists, the analysis of a state's behavior

---

[3] J. A. Hobson, *Imperialism: A Study*, 3d ed. (London: Allen and Unwin, 1938); Eckart Kehr, *Economic Interest, Militarism, and Foreign Policy: Essays on German History*, trans. Grete Heinz, ed. Gordon A. Craig (Berkeley: University of California Press, 1977); Charles A. Beard and Mary R. Beard, *The Rise of American Civilization: America in Midpassage*, vol. 3 (New York: Macmillan, 1939), 442–58. A closely related literature, Marxist-Leninist theories of imperialism, is based on domestic economic interests, but it tends to elide partisan differences over foreign policy. See Anthony Brewer, *Marxist Theories of Imperialism: A Critical Survey*, 2d ed. (London: Routledge, 1990).

[4] Miles Kahler, *Decolonization in Britain and France: The Domestic Consequences of International Relations* (Princeton: Princeton University Press, 1984); Jack Snyder, *Myths of Empire: Domestic Politics and International Ambition* (Ithaca: Cornell University Press, 1991); Alan C. Lamborn, *The Price of Power: Risk and Foreign Policy in Britain, France, and Germany* (Boston: Unwin Hyman, 1991); James H. Nolt, "Business Conflict and the Demise of Imperialism," in *Contested Social Orders and International Politics*, ed. David Skidmore (Nashville: Vanderbilt University Press, 1997), 92–127; Peter Trubowitz, *Defining the National Interest: Conflict and Change in American Foreign Policy* (Chicago: University of Chicago Press, 1998); Benjamin O. Fordham, *Building the Cold War Consensus: The Political Economy of U.S. National Security Policy*,

in the international system should begin with its external environment, not its internal preferences. In this view, foreign policy is formulated not on behalf of particular constituencies within the state, but rather for the state as a unitary whole. Executive decision makers are autonomous, independent actors who have either few incentives or little desire to respond to the demands of parochial interest groups. To the extent that domestic considerations intrude on foreign policymaking, they are conceived as secondary, or intervening, variables that constrain governments' pursuit of "national interests." Realist studies of the role of domestic politics in international relations focus on institutional limits on the power of the executive, not preference formation.

A few scholars have nevertheless attempted to incorporate societal preferences into the realist paradigm. There are two methods of doing so. Neoclassical realists, who believe that domestic variables influence how decision makers perceive, mobilize, and employ instruments of power, sometimes categorize states into different types, most commonly "revisionist" and "status quo."[5] In analyses of strategic interaction, these labels can serve as valuable shorthand for states' preferences over situation-specific outcomes. However, it is dangerous to use categories like revisionist and status quo to explain broad patterns of state behavior. Without a microfoundational theory of preferences, scholars must infer states' types *ex post*, from their observed behavior.[6] The result is tautological theoretical claims: revisionist states do X, and state A is observed doing X, therefore state A is revisionist,

---

1949–51 (Ann Arbor: University of Michigan Press, 1998); Etel Solingen, *Regional Orders at Century's Dawn: Global and Domestic Influences on Grand Strategy* (Princeton: Princeton University Press, 1998); Steven E. Lobell, *The Challenge of Hegemony: Grand Strategy, Trade, and Domestic Politics* (Ann Arbor: University of Michigan Press, 2003).

Also relevant is a burgeoning literature on the ideological sources of partisanship. See James D. Morrow, "Arms versus Allies: Trade-Offs in the Search for Security," *International Organization* 47, no. 2 (spring 1993): 207–33; Sandra Halperin, "The Politics of Appeasement: The Rise of the Left and European International Relations during the Interwar Period," in *Contested Social Orders and International Politics*, ed. David Skidmore (Nashville: Vanderbilt University Press, 1997), 128–64; John M. Owen, *Liberal Peace, Liberal War: American Politics and International Security* (Ithaca: Cornell University Press, 2000); Eric Heginbotham, "The Fall and Rise of Navies in East Asia: Military Organizations, Domestic Politics, and Grand Strategy," *International Security* 27, no. 2 (fall 2002): 86–125; Brian C. Rathbun, *Contesting the National Interest: The Partisan Politics of Humanitarian Intervention in Britain, France, and Germany* (Ithaca: Cornell University Press, 2004); Mark L. Haas, *The Ideological Origins of Great Power Politics, 1789–1989* (Ithaca: Cornell University Press, 2005).

[5] Gideon Rose, "Neoclassical Realism and Theories of Foreign Policy," *World Politics* 51, no. 1 (October 1998): 144–72; Randall L. Schweller, "The Progressiveness of Neoclassical Realism," in *Progress in International Relations Theory: Appraising the Field*, ed. Colin Elman and Miriam Fendius Elman (Cambridge, Mass.: MIT Press, 2003), 311–47.

[6] Jeffry A. Frieden, "Actors and Preferences in International Relations," in *Strategic Choice and International Relations*, ed. David A. Lake and Robert Powell (Princeton: Princeton University Press, 1999), 39–76.

which confirms the assertion that revisionist states do X. Like a judge ruling on an obscenity case, a neoclassical realist may be tempted to derive preferences from the suspect methodology of "I know it when I see it."

The only way for neoclassical realists to avoid this trap is to make typologies dependent on states' relative power, not their internal characteristics. In this view, a state's preferences are defined by the differential between its material resources, especially its economic capacity and military capabilities, and its share of the spoils in the international system, like colonies or influence in international institutions.[7] "Revisionist" states are typically those that lost their last major war but are rising again, such as Germany in 1918–39, whereas "status quo" states are typically those that won the last major war but are in decline, such as Great Britain in the same period. There is nothing methodologically inappropriate about deriving hypotheses on states' behavior from their position in the international system, as long as it is done in a consistent, falsifiable manner based on objective criteria. However, this perspective cannot explain anything outside of the context of relative power. To account for partisan variance in domestic preferences, one must look elsewhere.

Another school of thought, defensive realism, takes a more nuanced view of preferences, but it nevertheless does not accord them analytic priority over systemic factors. Defensive realism is based on the assumption that states do not need to act aggressively to be able to protect themselves from their neighbors.[8] Whenever they deviate from moderate, security-seeking behavior, domestic "pathologies" must be responsible. In this view, a regime that represents all societal interests fairly and objectively, pursuing the true "national interest," will adopt rationally limited foreign policy objectives. Only when a regime favors certain societal interests at the expense of others will it need to provoke international crises, either to rally the public behind its unstable domestic coalition or to justify spending increases for its supporters in the military.

Defensive realism has come under a great deal of criticism in recent years, not only from proponents of preference-based theories, but also from realists who view the dilution of their paradigm with a proliferation of hypotheses on domestic politics to be methodologically unsound. As Fareed Zakaria writes, "defensive realism begins with a minimalist systemic assumption that explains very little state behavior, generating anomalies instead. It then uses auxiliary domestic politics theories to explain away these inconvenient cases—which comprise much of modern diplomatic history. Imre Lakatos

---

[7] Robert Gilpin, *War and Change in World Politics* (Cambridge: Cambridge University Press, 1981); Randall L. Schweller, *Deadly Imbalances: Tripolarity and Hitler's Strategy of World Conquest* (New York: Columbia University Press, 1998).

[8] Snyder, *Myths of Empire*.

terms such projects theoretically 'degenerative.'"[9] The more that scholars have tried to graft preferences onto realist assumptions about the nature of the international system, the more that the paradigm has come to resemble a Ptolemaic model of the universe. At its heart is a parsimonious, elegant conception of state behavior, but one which requires myriad ad hoc corrections to be reconciled to the empirical data. The epicycles of realism provide scant reassurance to those who believe that preferences lie at the core of the discipline.

Preference-Based Theories

The realist paradigm is unquestionably useful for generating insights about strategic interaction between states. However, its assumption that systemic pressures take analytic priority over domestic preferences leaves theorists without a firm foundation on which to build a general theory of state behavior. To remedy the problem, it is necessary to invert the standard method of analysis in the field. Before addressing external factors such as the distribution of power or the presence of threat, scholars must first examine how governments' fundamental objectives in the international system are shaped by the preferences of societal coalitions. In other words, they must treat the international environment not as the underlying determinant of "national interests," but rather as a constraint on the pursuit of parochial domestic interests.

Andrew Moravcsik fleshes out this alternative view of state behavior in his seminal article, "Taking Preferences Seriously: A Liberal Theory of International Politics."[10] Liberals believe that the construction of theories should start at the lowest level of interest aggregation, with individuals, whereas realists believe that it should start at the highest, with states. Thus, liberal theories are microfoundational, whereas realist theories are systemic.[11] This is, at essence, a claim about analytic priority, not causal weight: liberals do not assume that internal variables (e.g., regime type, ideology, or economic interests) always dominate external variables (e.g., power, threat, offense-defense balance), nor do realists necessarily assert the opposite. All but the

[9] Fareed Zakaria, "Realism and Domestic Politics: A Review Essay," *International Security* 17, no. 1 (summer 1992): 193. See also John A. Vasquez and Colin Elman, eds., *Realism and the Balancing of Power: A New Debate* (Upper Saddle River, N.J.: Prentice Hall, 2003); Jeffrey W. Legro and Andrew Moravcsik, "Is Anybody Still a Realist?" *International Security* 24, no. 2 (fall 1999): 5–55; Rose, "Neoclassical Realism."

[10] Andrew Moravcsik, "Taking Preferences Seriously: A Liberal Theory of International Politics," *International Organization* 51, no. 4 (autumn 1997): 513–53.

[11] Moravcsik complicates his argument with the claim that liberal theories are also systemic. While he is correct to note that the distribution of preferences within a system affects its stability, he does not conceive of the system itself as the prime mover of international politics, as is the case in true systemic theories. See Kenneth N. Waltz, *Theory of International Politics* (Reading, Mass.: Addison-Wesley, 1979), 80, 98, 121–22.

most religious partisans of the debate admit that the relative importance of international and domestic factors can vary significantly from case to case.

This does not mean that scholars' choice of paradigm is simply a matter of taste, however. Since liberals treat societal variables as fundamental, not secondary, they can analyze the domestic origins of a broad range of "inconvenient cases"—those that "comprise much of modern diplomatic history," in Zakaria's words—without sacrificing theoretical coherence. When a scholar employing a liberal methodology confronts a systemic causal factor, he need only layer it in as an intervening variable, one that constrains rather than determines preferences. In contrast, a realist who decides that systemic factors are insufficient to account for a state's behavior must take an ad hoc step backward, selectively unraveling the social welfare function (the "national interest") that she had initially assumed. Because the liberal paradigm is less likely to take shortcuts with preference formation and interest aggregation, it offers a more solid foundation on which to build theory.

GRAND STRATEGY

This book raises questions that are fundamental to the study of international relations: Why do some nations aggressively attempt to expand their international influence, while others refuse commitments that they could easily protect given their national resources? Why do some states seek military control over peripheral territories, while others declaim imperialism? Why do some leaders eagerly support internationalist initiatives, while others disdain them in favor of strict realpolitik? To get a handle on these "grand theory" issues, I examine a dependent variable that captures the essence of great powers' foreign policy: grand strategy.

The term *grand strategy* carries weighty connotations. To many, it evokes an image of statesmen, generals, and diplomats huddled around a tabletop map of the world, calculating how best to defend vital "national interests" from a hostile international environment. Though intuitively appealing, this classical archetype represents a set of assumptions about state behavior that is both conceptually limiting and analytically biased. In this section, I define and operationalize grand strategy so as to make it broad enough to be compatible with a wide range of theoretical perspectives and comparative case studies yet restrictive enough to be tested in a clearly falsifiable manner.

Defining Grand Strategy

Grand strategy can be defined most concisely as the general principles by which an executive decision maker or decision-making body pursues its international political goals. It is much like foreign policy, but at a higher level of abstraction, focusing on broad patterns of behavior rather than specific decisions. It is *strategy* in the purest sense of the word: a set of choices made to gain valued goods. It is not the outcome of those choices; a strategy is not defined in terms of whether it succeeds or fails. Nor is it defined by its flaws of implementation; an executive's strategy does not lose its essential character if it is blocked by insubordinate agents or an obstructive legislature. Finally, it is not the valued good in itself; strategy is about means, not ends.

This definition is somewhat at variance with accepted usage in the international relations literature. First, it does not make any claims about what purpose grand strategy serves. Many political scientists do not conceptually separate the ends and means of grand strategy. Instead, they adopt the realist assumption that the most important elements of a state's foreign policy are comprehensible in terms of only one goal, security. For example, Barry Posen writes that grand strategy is a "political-military means-end chain, a state's theory about how it can best 'cause' security for itself.... A grand strategy must identify likely threats to the state's security and it must devise political, economic, military, and other remedies for those threats."[12] Similarly, Thomas Christensen writes, "I define grand strategy as the full package of domestic and international policies designed to increase power and national security."[13]

The idea that grand strategy is motivated above all by the desire for security is an eminently reasonable assumption, but it is woefully incomplete. Security is not an object unto itself; it has no meaning in isolation from interests. Most obviously, states have an interest in protecting their homeland from invasion, but this will rarely be the only consideration influencing their behavior. They might seek to expand their territory, protect their foreign trade and investment, promote their political ideology, or pursue humanitarian causes. Unfortunately, realism has almost nothing to say about the process by which such interests are defined. The best it can do is to try to infer from states' actions, *ex post* and ad hoc, what concerns other than self-preservation might have contributed to their broadly conceived "national interest." A more balanced view of grand strategy can be found in Clausewitz's dictum that "the political object" of conflict will "determine both the military objective and the amount of effort it requires.... War, therefore, is an act of policy."[14] Whether in war or peace, strategy is a function of politics.

---

[12] Barry R. Posen, *The Sources of Military Doctrine: France, Britain, and Germany between the World Wars* (Ithaca: Cornell University Press, 1984), 13.

[13] Thomas J. Christensen, *Useful Adversaries: Grand Strategy, Domestic Mobilization, and Sino-American Conflict, 1947–1958* (Princeton: Princeton University Press, 1996), 7.

[14] Carl von Clausewitz, *On War*, trans. Michael Howard and Peter Paret (Princeton: Princeton University Press, 1984), 81, 87. See also Edward N. Luttwak, *Strategy: The Logic of War and Peace* (Cambridge, Mass.: Belknap, 1987), 182; B. H. Liddell Hart, *Strategy* (New York:

A second controversy over the definition of grand strategy is the question of whether it must be intentional—that is, governed by an explicit plan or guiding philosophy in which priorities are ranked and policy instruments are used in a coordinated manner. Some scholars imply that an unplanned grand strategy is, in fact, no strategy at all.[15] I believe a more sensible case can be made for the proposition that, as long as a clear pattern can be discerned in the executive's foreign policy initiatives, this pattern constitutes a grand strategy. There is little analytical difference between a plan (e.g., NSC 68) and a pattern of behavior that reflects consistent values, goals, and trade-offs (e.g., containment). It does not matter whether executive decision makers ever explain their reasoning, or even if they consciously think about how their various decisions over different foreign policy issues are related to each other.

Another reason to define grand strategy as a pattern, not a plan, is that it cannot always be attributed to a particular individual or source document. In some polities, the executive decision maker is not one person, like the American president, but rather a collegial body of politicians, like the cabinet in Great Britain. In the British government, the prime minister does not always get his way, nor does the foreign minister. Indeed, neither one may be able to obtain his ideal policy over any given issue if other members of the cabinet are willing to override him. In short, the grand strategy of parliamentary governments may be formed out of a continuous process of compromise-making between different cabinet factions. It may contain internal contradictions, but, as long as it is not random, it can still be analyzed as a meaningful pattern of behavior.

Operationalizing Grand Strategy

Most studies of grand strategy in political science and history have been limited to a single state, in a discrete time period, with a specific type of behavior in mind. As a result, the term is rarely operationalized for broad, comparative purposes. One scholar might characterize the United States' grand strategy during the Cold War as "internationalism," to differentiate it from isolationism; another scholar, looking at the same case, might describe it as "containment," to point out that the United States attempted neither to appease

---

Praeger, 1954), 335–36; Richard Rosecrance and Arthur A. Stein, "Beyond Realism: The Study of Grand Strategy," in *The Domestic Bases of Grand Strategy*, ed. Richard Rosecrance and Arthur A. Stein (Ithaca: Cornell University Press, 1993), 4–5; Alastair I. Johnston, *Cultural Realism: Strategic Culture and Grand Strategy in Chinese History* (Princeton: Princeton University Press, 1995), 115.

[15] John J. Mearsheimer, *Liddell Hart and the Weight of History* (Ithaca: Cornell University Press, 1988), 17; Michael C. Desch, *When the Third World Matters: Latin America and United States Grand Strategy* (Baltimore: Johns Hopkins University Press, 1993), 2.

the Soviet Union nor to roll back its existing gains. Neither characterization is incorrect; they simply refer to different aspects of an overarching whole.

The problem is that grand strategy is a multidimensional concept. It encompasses such diverse facets of a state's behavior as its willingness to provide public goods, cooperate in multilateral organizations, and support international law; its military strategy and force deployments; its predilection for territorial aggression, economic autarchy, and alliance-making; and its level of defense spending. Even if this list were exhaustive, which undoubtedly it is not, it shows that there are far more combinatorial possibilities of grand-strategic profiles than any analyst could reasonably address. Thus, most scholars simply operationalize grand strategy along the dimension that is most relevant to their research. This suffices for studies of individual countries, but a comparative analysis of grand strategy must deal with the fact that different dimensions of grand strategy may be more salient for some states than others. In this section, I propose a compromise solution, one which employs three dimensions and generates seven strategic types. I attempt to capture the elements of grand strategy about which scholars of international relations care most while creating a reasonably parsimonious, manageable, and well-defined concept to use as a dependent variable.

The first dimension of grand strategy is the level of activity, or assertiveness, in a state's foreign policy. It represents the state's willingness to pay the costs, whatever they may be, of following a particular strategy. States rarely devote all of their available resources to the pursuit of their international objectives; instead, they make an expected utility calculation about what level of investment will produce the most profitable returns. If a state has a very intense preference for a particular outcome, or if it perceives a "window of opportunity" in which short-term effort will produce exceptional long-term payoffs, it will act with a high degree of assertiveness. If a state is indifferent between outcomes, or if it perceives that its efforts will produce rapidly diminishing marginal returns, it will be less active.

Most strategies can become more or less active without losing their essential character. However, one strategy is defined solely by the position it occupies on this dimension: *isolationism*. This is a strategy of inactivity, in which the executive decision maker chooses not to devote resources to expanding and protecting the influence of the state outside of its borders. Such a strategy will typically be associated with relatively low levels of defense spending because only national borders and coastal waterways need be secured. Of course, when threats to the homeland increase, an isolationist executive might be compelled to spend more on the military or enter into defensive alliances. However, the military spending and alliance activity of isolationism should still be less than that of any other grand strategy, given the same level of international threat.

Figure 1.1. Grand Strategy toward the Great Powers

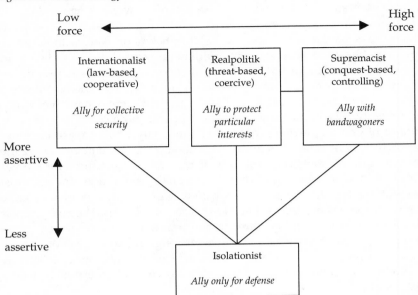

To differentiate between other, more active grand strategies, I employ two additional variables. One is the geographic locus of a state's foreign policy goals. Depending on its underlying preferences, it may choose to treat weak states, or those in the "periphery" of the international system, in a very different manner from great powers, or those in the "core" of the international system. This distinction, though crude, recognizes the critical point that the efficacy of any given strategy may depend greatly on the relative power of the state at which it is directed.

The last dimension of my operationalization of grand strategy is the extent to which a state is willing to use force to achieve its foreign policy goals. There are three basic levels of force: conquest, coercion, and cooperation. When subdivided by geographical locus, they generate six types of strategy in addition to isolationism (see figures 1.1 and 1.2). Half of them, those directed specifically toward the great powers, are associated with a particular alignment imperative. In the following pages, I discuss all six strategies in descending order of their reliance on force.

Conquest

At one end on the continuum of a state's willingness to use force is a strategy of conquest. It is premised on the idea that the most effective way to pursue the state's international goals, whatever they may be, is to seek

Figure 1.2. Grand Strategy toward the Periphery

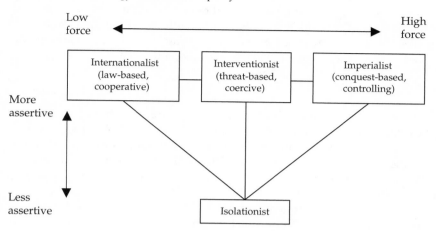

direct, long-term control over people and territory. When applied to the periphery, it is commonly referred to as *imperialism*. When directed toward one or more of the great powers, it might be called *supremacism* (for lack of a better term).

Since the rise of the modern state system, nearly every one of the great powers has attempted at some point to acquire territory in the periphery. Nevertheless, an imperialist strategy can be quite costly. First, there are myriad expenses associated with the acquisition and management of new colonies. Native rulers must be defeated or co-opted, nascent rebellions must be suppressed, and administrative structures must be created. Over time, some colonies may become fiscally self-sufficient, but others may be a constant drain on the resources of the imperial metropole. Second, great powers often have overlapping claims and divergent interests in the periphery. When one of them tries to alter the territorial status quo, conflict may result. To protect its overseas possessions, an imperial power will need to build a deep-water navy and acquire military bases along its lines of communication and supply. The larger its empire, the more points of vulnerability it will have to defend, and the more it will have to spend on defense.

The costs of imperialism pale before the burdens of supremacism, a strategy of the conquest of great powers. By definition, great powers are difficult to defeat, and they rarely surrender without a protracted struggle. Consequently, this strategy is rarely pursued. War between the great powers is not uncommon, but it is usually fought for limited aims and in a geographically limited theater of operation. Once a state adopts the more ambitious strategy of seeking control over large swaths of territory in the core of the international system, like Napoleonic France or Nazi Germany, it usually provokes a counterbalancing coalition.

[13]

Due to the sheer difficulty of conquering great powers, any state that follows a strategy of supremacism will have a clear alignment imperative: ally with any other state willing to bandwagon with it. Only with the help of like-minded partners, or at least unwitting dupes, will a supremacist state have a chance to overcome the combined might of its adversaries.

Coercion

In the middle of the continuum of force are strategies based on coercion. They do not employ conquest to achieve international objectives; instead, they rely on the use of threats, and resort to military force if necessary, to gain the compliance of other states. When directed toward weak states, a strategy of coercion is *interventionism*. When applied to the great powers, it is *realpolitik*.

An interventionist strategy requires a strong navy and a network of overseas military bases from which to project force and establish spheres of influence in the periphery. In that respect, it is similar to imperialism. However, interventionism is less likely to create conflict with other great powers, and it does not require the state to set up structures of colonial governance. For both of these reasons, interventionism should be less costly than imperialism. A clear example of interventionism is American foreign policy toward the periphery during the Cold War. The United States repeatedly sought to coerce weak states to do its bidding, but it did not impose direct rule through formal empire.

A strategy aimed at the coercion of great powers, realpolitik, is similarly moderate. Great powers are difficult to conquer, but their behavior can be influenced by the credible threat of war or other actions that will be detrimental to their security. The preeminent practitioner of aggressive realpolitik was Otto von Bismarck, who used a combination of diplomatic manipulation and military force to build a dominant position for Prussia at the center of Europe. He resorted to war on several occasions, but he did so only for the limited goal of unifying his country, not to subjugate neighboring great powers.

Realpolitik has a less rigid alignment imperative than supremacism. A state following a realpolitik strategy will ally against the greatest threat to whatever it values most in the international system. Its values might be ideological, cultural, or economic, and they might focus on either the periphery or the core. In this case, everything depends on the preferences driving the state's strategy, which cannot be assumed.

Cooperation

The least force-dependent form of international influence is diplomatic reciprocity. For this to be effective, a state must first convince its neighbors

[14]

to agree to rules that define the limits of acceptable conduct between them. The resulting strategy is *internationalism*. Among students of American foreign policy, the term is often used simply to describe behavior that involves the United States in "foreign entanglements" outside the Western Hemisphere. In this study, I adopt its classic comparative meaning: the set of principles and prescriptions designed to construct an international system governed by legal norms and peaceful cooperation.[16] It can be directed at just the great powers, or confined to a regional subsystem of states, but in its maximal form it recognizes the sovereign equality of all states.

The most critical policy elements of internationalism are multilateral decision making, through which laws are created and enforced, and binding arbitration, through which laws are interpreted. These two mechanisms constrain state behavior in different ways, but they serve the same ultimate purpose: to resolve interstate disputes through the application of general rules, not ad hoc contests of power. More than any other strategy, internationalism can be expected to require compromise. It is not pacifist, however; it dictates that states should form coalitions to stop aggressors, even at the cost of war. The best-known historical example of an internationalist leader is Woodrow Wilson, who codified many international legal principles and policies in the League of Nations Covenant.

Internationalism, like supremacism, has stringent requirements that give it a clear alignment imperative. As noted above, a state following this strategy will seek to uphold international law and treat all states, or a well-defined subset of them, as sovereign equals. To that end, it will try to avoid alliances altogether in favor of collective security. Under collective security, states pledge to band together to oppose all aggressors, regardless of what substantive issues are at stake in their conflicts.

Thus far, I have avoided any mention of military planning or wartime strategy in this framework of analysis. These concepts are intimately related to grand strategy; however, they are more often its functional product than one of its constitutive elements. For example, knowing whether Germany intended to follow the Schlieffen Plan in World War I gives one little insight about the general principles by which it pursued its international goals between 1871 and 1914. All it conveys is how the German military intended to accomplish the specific task of winning a war with France; it does not capture the broader dynamics of conflict between the two states. I am concerned only with the latter type of question, so I do not address military doctrine at length.

[16] Warren F. Kuehl, "Concepts of Internationalism in History," *Peace and Change* 11, no. 2 (1986): 1–10; Kjell Goldmann, *The Logic of Internationalism: Coercion and Accommodation* (London: Routledge, 1994), 2–5. See also the definition of "multilateralism" in John G. Ruggie, ed., *Multilateralism Matters: The Theory and Praxis of an Institutional Form* (New York: Columbia University Press, 1993).

[15]

I also exclude one of the most common forms of military deployment: small-scale, short-term interventions intended solely to ensure the safety of foreign nationals' lives and property in civil conflicts. These minor uses of force, which are sprinkled throughout the history of both the United States and Great Britain in the late nineteenth and early twentieth centuries, have few strategic implications.[17] Instead, they are one-shot operations, not intended to establish either precedent or political influence. While this distinction may be unsatisfying to those whose national sovereignty has been violated by an "apolitical" intervention, it is nevertheless necessary to delimit the concept of grand strategy. Thus, I address only interventions designed to change the policies or regime of the target state.

With these caveats, all of the strategic types described above are illustrated in figures 1.1 and 1.2. Having operationalized grand strategy as a serviceable dependent variable, I now turn to the independent variable, sectoral interests. In the following pages, I show how the preferences of societal groups determine executive decision makers' choices of grand strategy.

SOCIETAL PREFERENCES

Preference-based theories of international relations are, almost by definition, less parsimonious than realism. On opening up the black box of the state, one discovers a panoply of variables, actors, and levels of analysis that are orders of magnitude more complex than the elegant world of billiard-ball states. To construct a theory from this chaos of building blocks, I proceed in four discrete stages of analysis (see figure 1.3). First, I formulate initial hypotheses about linkages between the economic interests of domestic groups and their positions on grand strategy. Second, I discuss how these positions might be constrained by domestic and international circumstances. Third, I explain how I expect state leaders to aggregate societal preferences. Finally, I discuss the process of theory testing and point out some potential pitfalls in it.

Preference Formation

Individuals are affected in numerous ways by their state's involvement in international politics. Consider, for example, a state's decision to intervene

---

[17] Richard F. Grimmett, "Instances of Use of United States Armed Forces Abroad, 1798–2004," Congressional Research Service report RL30172, http://www.au.af.mil/au/awc/awcgate/crs/rl30172.htm (last accessed April 2006); Brian Bond, ed., *Victorian Military Campaigns* (New York: Praeger, 1967).

Figure 1.3. The Theory

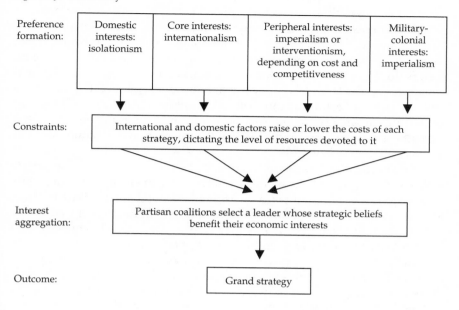

to protect one of its firms' investments in a foreign country. This action may have distributional implications for the firm's employees, its owners, its competitors, other firms with which it does business, all other firms that invest in or export to the target country, the military personnel that participate in the intervention, firms that supply equipment to the military, and taxpayers. A complete political-economic analysis would distinguish between and take into account every one of these groups' interests. The result, however, would be intractably complex.

The key, then, is to identify which interests are most salient. For the making of foreign policy, the relevant societal actors and their interests are difficult to theorize *ex ante*. However, the dependent variable of this study is not foreign policy; rather, it is grand strategy. My concern, in light of the previous example, is not whether the state chooses to intervene in a specific country, but rather the extent to which it is willing to protect its nationals' property in foreign markets. The particular interests of individual firms, owners, and employees may affect foreign policy, but they lie at too low a level of aggregation to have a consistent effect on grand strategy. Their concerns are too narrow, and their coalitional influence too weak, to determine the executive's overarching strategic behavior.

[17]

Only two types of economic interest are broad enough to sustain a theory of grand strategy: class and sectoral. In other research, I have demonstrated that class interests affect the *means* by which states respond to threats.[18] Class is not, however, the main determinant of states' *goals* in the international system. Classes do not compete for survival in the international economy; sectors do. The closure of foreign markets may have adverse distributional consequences for land, labor, or capital, but it does not threaten their existence as classes. Sectors, in contrast, risk economic "death," in the form of bankruptcy, in an adverse international economic environment. Given the different stakes of classes and sectors in the international economy, sectoral interests should be key.

More specifically, I focus on sectors that derive income from external markets. Exporters and owners of foreign investment are included; importers and recipients of inward investment are not. I make this distinction for two reasons. First, importers have less at risk in the loss of trade with individual countries. They may suffer from short-term adjustment costs, but most will be able to find alternative suppliers. (Those that import intermediate goods from their own facilities overseas are far more vulnerable, but they are owners of foreign investment and therefore are included in this study.) Exporters and outward investors, in contrast, often specialize in specific foreign markets and may be ruined if forced out. Second, importers may actually benefit from a disruption in supply when demand is inelastic. For example, uncertainty over the production of oil following the Iraq War of 2003 was a boon to American refiners. In contrast, the loss of foreign markets has strong, unambiguously negative effects on exporters and outward investors.

Sectoral interests, as they pertain to grand strategy, can be separated into four basic types. The first three are defined in terms of actors' exposure to the international economy. "Domestic interests" are largely autarchic, having little or no connection to the international economy; "core interests" depend on income from exports to or investment in the markets of great powers; and "peripheral interests" depend on income from exports to or investment in the markets of peripheral states. A fourth group, "military-colonial interests," does not rely on income from any sort of private market, international or domestic; instead, its members are the bureaucrats, diplomats, professional soldiers, and defense industry employees whose livelihoods depend on government spending on grand strategy. The four

---

[18] Kevin Narizny, "Both Guns and Butter, or Neither: Class Interests in the Political Economy of Rearmament," *American Political Science Review* 97, no. 2 (May 2003): 203–20. See also David M. Rowe, "World Economic Expansion and National Security in Pre-World War I Europe," *International Organization* 53, no. 2 (spring 1999): 195–231.

groups are not necessarily exclusive of each other; for example, any given individual could derive income from both the core and periphery, and therefore belong to both the core and peripheral interest groups. The purpose of these categories is not to classify individuals, but rather to facilitate analysis of the relative strength of each set of interests within political coalitions.

Domestic Interests

Domestic interests have no stake in the international economy. Consequently, they have little to gain from their government's involvement in international politics. For them, any strategy that tries to accomplish anything more than homeland defense will be a waste of their taxes. When faced with a threat of invasion, they should not hesitate to build up their military and form defensive alliances; however, their ideal strategy should be isolationism.

Core Interests

Core interests rely on income from the markets of other great powers. Their primary goal in international politics should be to maintain stable, peaceful diplomatic relations among states in the core of the international system. There are two reasons for this. First, friction between great powers is almost always injurious to core interests, even if their own state is not involved in the conflict. In the event of war, international trade will collapse, investments will be confiscated, and the repatriation of profits will be forbidden. Some sectors will be able to profit from the sale of arms and raw materials to the belligerents, but they will find it costly in the short term to shift from civilian to military production. To guard against these dangers, individuals employed in sectors that depend heavily on income from the markets of great powers should support internationalism, a strategy designed specifically to solve the problem of interstate conflict.

Second, core interests should seek to lay the "high politics" foundations for cooperation over "low politics" economic issues. Great powers cannot, by definition, be coerced without incurring enormous costs, so any rational attempt to foster trade and investment between them must be based on persuasion. Internationalism is particularly well suited for this task: all of its policy prescriptions, including the strengthening of international law, the creation of regimes, and the use of multilateral diplomacy, are intended to facilitate noncoercive bargaining. An internationalist strategy will not lead immediately to a world of free trade, but it may help clear a path for peaceful cooperation.

Peripheral Interests

Individuals employed in sectors that export to or invest in weaker, peripheral states should have a very different set of priorities. They will be

[19]

better served by a unilateral, antilegalist grand strategy, one in which their government reserves the right to make threats and undertake armed interventions at its prerogative. There are three reasons why this strategy should be more advantageous to peripheral interests than internationalism. First, small states in less-developed parts of the world tend to be less internally stable than great powers. They are more susceptible to coups, civil wars, and ethnic unrest, all of which disrupt commercial activity. Consequently, businesses that export to and invest in peripheral countries will be more likely to need the unilateral, "illegal" use of military force to protect their interests. Second, war with weak states is much less costly than war with great powers. Businesses that focus on the periphery will see coercive intervention as a viable option when diplomatic persuasion fails to meet their needs, whereas those that concentrate on the markets of great powers will not. Finally, internationalism limits states' flexibility in the defense of their interests in the periphery. It dictates that they respond in a principled manner to all violations of international law, rather than align with countries whose goodwill is needed to maintain the security of their most remote and vulnerable overseas trade and investment. Periphery-oriented sectors should be willing to see their government cooperate with other great powers for limited, well-defined purposes, but not for universal legal principles.

With internationalism ruled out, two choices remain: interventionism and imperialism. The trade-off between them is straightforward. A state that seizes colonies can restructure their institutions, control the enforcement of their laws, extract resources from them, capture their consumers, exploit their labor, and restrict access to foreign competition. Imperialism therefore promises many benefits to peripheral interests. At the same time, however, it can be very costly. In all likelihood, a state that adopts this strategy will need to increase the size of its military, and therefore raise taxes on its citizens, to defend its possessions from external threats, suppress resistance from its colonial subjects, and create infrastructure for economic development. Interventionism, in contrast, eschews conquest in favor of coercion. It does not seek direct rule over territory, but rather threatens the use of force against foreign governments that do not heed its wishes. While less costly, it also promises fewer benefits.

If individual firms could dictate when and where their state annexed colonies, they would probably have a strict preference for imperialism. While it might lead to higher taxes, they would be responsible for only a small fraction of the burden. The benefits of control over their markets would be concentrated on them, while the costs of conquest would be diffused throughout society. In reality, however, individual firms rarely have such direct influence over foreign policymaking. Instead, they must join a broad-based coalition that advocates the expansion of the empire in commercially valuable areas throughout the periphery. In the resulting logroll, each firm

[20]

improves the odds that its export markets will be annexed, but it also has to help pay for colonies that are of interest only to other firms. These costs can be extensive, as noted above. As the size of the coalition increases, the total cost of empire could eventually outweigh the benefits to individual peripheral interests.

Another limitation on an imperialist strategy is that it rarely provides firms with monopoly profits. It does not put them at an advantage vis-à-vis all of their potential competitors, just those from other countries. That is, even if firms can exclude foreign businesses from their colonial markets, they still have to compete with their own nationals. In this situation, they might conclude that the costs of empire are too high to justify a marginal increase in sales. Thus, peripheral interests should demand an imperialist grand strategy only when their circumstances are desperate—that is, when, to make a profit on their exports and foreign investment, they need the un-fair competitive advantages that colonial markets provide. Otherwise, they should be satisfied with interventionism. By relying on coercion rather than conquest, they will have the support of their government without taking on the burdens of empire.

This discussion is not intended to be an exhaustive account of all the fac-tors that might affect societal support for imperialism. Consider, for exam-ple, the diffusion of military technology to native insurgents. As the costs of repression increase, so too will the level of taxation needed to sustain an empire, and the sectoral coalition that initially favored imperialism will eventually unravel. Thus, an analysis of decolonization would require a much more detailed analytic framework than can be provided here.[19] Prior to the era of decolonization, however, societal opinion over the utility of empire could vary widely. Given that variance, the theory renders a clear prediction: sectors that were able to undercut their competitors and expand their market share in the periphery without acquiring colonies should have been interventionist, while those that were losing ground should have been imperialist.

Military-Colonial Interests

Societal actors that derive income from government spending in inter-national affairs, "military-colonial interests," should favor the strategy that requires the largest possible budgetary outlay at an acceptably low level of

---

[19] See Kahler, *Decolonization in Britain and France*; Jeffry A. Frieden, "The Economics of Intervention: American Overseas Investments and Relations with Underdeveloped Areas, 1890–1950," *Comparative Studies in Society and History* 31, no. 1 (January 1989): 55–80; Jeffry A. Frieden, "International Investment and Colonial Control: A New Interpretation," *International Organization* 48, no. 4 (autumn 1994): 559–93; Hendrik Spruyt, *Ending Empire: Contested Sovereignty and Territorial Partition* (Ithaca: Cornell University Press, 2005).

risk. In the late nineteenth and early twentieth centuries, that strategy was imperialism. (Supremacism, in contrast, too easily resulted in catastrophic failure.) For military contractors, it implied higher defense spending, which would increase profits. For officers, diplomats, and civil servants, the expansion of military commitments and colonial administration created new career opportunities. Furthermore, these individuals naturally wanted to succeed in their assigned tasks, so they sought to augment the resources at their disposal. Thus, a combination of profit motive, desire for personal advancement, and bureaucratic imperatives should have united these actors in favor of an imperialist grand strategy.

The domestic, core, peripheral, and military-colonial interest groups constitute the fundamental units of analysis in this study. If the hypotheses presented above are correct, different coalitions of societal actors will have radically divergent views on international politics. Their fundamental strategic goals will be determined by their domestic interests, not by some abstract conception of what "national security" demands. When one of the four groups is dominant within a political coalition, I expect its leaders simply to adopt that group's ideal strategy: imperialism or interventionism for peripheral interests, internationalism for core interests, isolationism for domestic interests, or imperialism for military-colonial interests.

Such internal cohesion is rare, however. Parties often unite voters for reasons that are unrelated to their material interests, much less their stake in the international economy. As a result, more than one set of sectoral interests can hold an electorally critical position within a political coalition. When this occurs, I expect to see the emergence of compromises between their preferences. There are two possible types of compromise. The first arises when domestic interests, who should favor isolationism, play an important role in the coalition. Domestic interests act as a brake on other actors' preferences over grand strategy, seeking to minimize foreign engagements and keep costs down. The more politically powerful this group is, the more isolationist the coalition should become, regardless of what qualitative type of grand strategy its other members would like to follow.

The second type of compromise emerges from a coalition that is closely divided between core interests, on the one hand, and either peripheral or military-colonial interests, on the other hand. In this case, the two sides should settle on a two-track strategy that treats peripheral states and great powers differently. Toward the great powers, the coalition should support an internationalist strategy; toward peripheral states, it should favor either an interventionist or imperialist strategy, depending on cost and competitiveness.

Constraints

The foregoing hypotheses, which derive societal actors' positions on grand strategy from their sectoral economic interests, form the basis of the theory. Above that base, however, other factors inevitably come into play. These "intervening" variables should not cause any group to depart from its ideal strategy; rather, they should make it prefer a version of its ideal strategy that is more or less assertive than usual. That is, they should lead it to modulate its position on the continuum with isolationism (see figures 1.1 and 1.2). For the purpose of clarity, I separate these constraining factors into "international" and "domestic" types. Nevertheless, it should be emphasized that they are analytically equivalent in the construction of the theory. Each can influence individuals' evaluation of the marginal utility of committing additional resources to the pursuit of their strategic goals, but none is a fundamental determinant of grand strategy.

International Constraints

International constraints affect some societal actors in different ways than others. Of the four key interest groups that I have identified, domestic and military-colonial interests should be the least responsive to changes in their external environment. Domestic interests should prefer greater military spending when threats to the homeland increase, and less military spending when threats decrease, but nothing more than that. The level of conflict in the international system as a whole should mean little to them as long as it has no direct impact on their domestic security. For military-colonial interests, the logic is slightly different: they always benefit from high-spending, aggressive policies, so their preferences should not fluctuate radically when the level of threat in the international system varies. This is not to imply that they will be completely unaffected by international factors; of course, their demands will escalate if tensions with other countries increase. However, they should resist switching to a less aggressive strategy when tensions decrease.

Peripheral and core interests should be much more sensitive to international constraints. In some circumstances, an aggressive, high-spending version of their ideal strategy will provide them with the most "bang for the buck," whereas in other circumstances, an adverse international environment will make it impossible for them to achieve their goals at any price. Core interests should be particularly sensitive to the level of conflict between the great powers. As tensions increase, it will become more difficult to convince states to agree on common norms of behavior and to cooperate in multilateral institutions. Peripheral interests, in contrast, should be most concerned by geopolitical competition for control over distant territories and strategic chokepoints. With each additional entrant into the "great game" of imperialism, the higher the stakes become, making gains both more valuable and more costly to achieve.

Domestic Constraints

There are three main types of domestic constraints. First, sectoral groups' willingness to pay for an aggressive grand strategy depends in part on the availability of fiscal resources. When the national debt is extraordinarily high, as is usually the case after a lengthy war, its repayment consumes tax revenue that might otherwise be allocated to the military, foreign aid, or colonial administration. The cost of servicing the debt squeezes out, or at least competes with, other forms of government spending. Thus, it should make societal actors hesitate to take on new international commitments.

A second type of domestic constraint is monetary instability. If a state's current account deficit is high, a strategy that spends great sums on foreign aid or military operations abroad could cause a currency crisis.[20] Major war scares can have a similar effect. If investors lose confidence in the system, capital will flee the country, exchange rates will plummet, and financial markets will crash. In anticipation of such consequences, sectors that are vulnerable to monetary instability may be reluctant to take a hard line in international crises.

The third factor, recessions, can have mixed effects. On the one hand, they might serve as an impetus for a more aggressive grand strategy. Businesses in desperate need of customers may turn to their government for help in opening new markets for export. On the other hand, recessions drain state resources. When the economy shrinks, tax revenue falls and the value of the currency declines, giving rise to the aforementioned fiscal and monetary constraints. Consequently, I do not attempt to theorize the net impact of recessions. That question can only be answered empirically, on a case-by-case basis. The point is that all of these factors might affect the conduct of grand strategy, so they all deserve attention in the course of analysis.

---

[20] Stephen Blank, "Britain: The Politics of Economic Policy, the Domestic Economy, and the Problem of Pluralistic Stagnation," in *Between Power and Plenty: Foreign Economic Policies of Advanced Industrialized States*, ed. Peter J. Katzenstein (Madison: University of Wisconsin Press, 1978), 89–137; Erik A. Devereux, "Industrial Structure, Internationalism, and the Collapse of the Cold War Consensus: Business, the Media, and Vietnam," in *Business and the State in International Relations*, ed. Ronald W. Cox (Boulder: Westview, 1996), 9–40. In unusual cases, such as the United States after World War II, the rapid outflow of capital may actually benefit financiers; see Fordham, *Building the Cold War Consensus*.

INTEREST AGGREGATION

Thus far, I have argued that different sectoral groups should have different positions on grand strategy. If sectors with divergent interests separate into opposing political coalitions, the politicians who represent them will have an incentive to act on behalf of their parochial interests. Will that be enough, however, to lead executive decision makers to adopt partisan policies? Presidents and prime ministers might resist pressures to subordinate grand strategy to "pork barrel" politics; instead, they may feel responsible to act as the executor of the "national interest," however defined. This is a question of interest aggregation, and it deserves closer attention.

Agential Interest Aggregation

As discussed at the beginning of this chapter, the preponderance of scholarship in the subfield of international security assumes that states act autonomously of societal interests. Outside this consensus, however, are two standard approaches to interest aggregation. In pluralist theories, politicians respond to electoral pressures to favor the interests of certain domestic actors over others. In ideational theories, politicians are socialized into a worldview that biases them to pursue the preferences of particular societal groups. Despite their differences, these two "agential" perspectives on interest aggregation share a critical assumption: that the key to understanding the origins of foreign policy lies in the minds of the individuals who make it.

Vote-Seeking

In the pluralist approach, self-interested politicians are the primary agent of interest aggregation. They are instrumentally rational actors who care only about reelection (or, if there are term limits, the future success of their party) and have no personal preferences over outcomes. Consequently, they will adapt their policies to whatever position will help them win votes. In this highly mechanistic conception of interest aggregation, a state leader must navigate between two competing pressures. On the one hand, he must maintain the support of the electorate at large so as to win a majority of votes in the next election. This pushes him toward the preferences of the median voter.[21] On the other hand, the state leader must also cater to the interests of the core constituency of his partisan coalition. If he does not, he may find it

---

[21] Realists and other systemic theorists might argue that median voter's position constitutes the "national interest"; however, to do so would require the heroic assumption that the median voter knows best how to protect the country.

impossible to secure renomination (in a presidential system), avoid votes of no confidence (in a parliamentary system), attract campaign contributions, or foster the goodwill of legislators on whom he depends for the authorization of his agenda. These considerations push his policies away from the median voter, toward the preferences of parochial interest groups.

The problem with the standard pluralist perspective on interest aggregation is that the assumptions it makes about human nature are unrealistically oversimplified. Clearly, the idea that politicians are mere "conveyor belts" for the expression of societal interests is a far cry from reality, particularly in international relations. Even the most venal office-seekers seek to insulate themselves from domestic pressures in the making of foreign policy; hence the maxim that "politics ends at the water's edge." This is the traditional realist view of foreign policy, and with good reason: it is hard to imagine that politicians would be so cynically, coldly calculating as to let their electoral interests dictate their position on something of such vital importance as grand strategy.

There is a great deal of anecdotal evidence for this claim. Leaders who have a far-reaching impact on their nation's foreign policy are rarely party hacks. Theodore Roosevelt and Woodrow Wilson, for example, were both guided by strong political ideologies and moral precepts, often refusing to swallow their beliefs for the sake of petty electoral politicking. Few scholars would claim that decision makers are completely unconstrained by public opinion or party pressures, but neither would they assert that vote-seeking is so powerful a force in politicians' minds as to make it the basis for a microfoundational theory of state behavior in international relations.

Socialization

Whereas pluralist theories assume that politicians consciously choose policies that will maximize their chances of reelection, ideational theories assert that politicians make decisions based on internalized societal norms. State leaders, no different from ordinary citizens, are products of their national cultures. If they live in an environment in which policy debates are grounded in certain irreducible principles, they cannot help but to be influenced by the dominant discourse. According to this view, individual leaders come to office with a certain set of ingrained biases that shape their underlying goals, the means by which they are willing to pursue those goals, and their perceptions of the motivation and behavior of other states. Thus, they will accept or dismiss certain policy options because to do otherwise would simply be unthinkable under their received system of beliefs.

Critically, the concept of socialization does not depend on the existence of a unitary, "national" ideology or culture. Quite to the contrary, one should

[26]

expect to see ideational differentiation and competition within states. According to social psychology theory, individuals naturally seek consistency in their system of beliefs. If they hold strong views over domestic politics, where public opinion is normally divided, they will try to adapt those positions to generate a logically coherent position on international affairs. For example, if conservatives are convinced that the best way to reduce crime is through harsh punishment rather than rehabilitation, they may conclude that the best way to deal with international adversaries is through military confrontation rather than diplomatic engagement. Liberals, in contrast, will tend to take the opposite view on both issues.[22]

Though intuitively appealing, the socialization model is suspect as a universal account of interest aggregation. Executive decision makers may be biased toward a particular set of policies, but they nevertheless have to consider the consequences of those policies. For example, democratic leaders may believe firmly in the promotion of political freedom and human rights, but they will find it costly to demand regime change of their allies and trading partners. Thus, they have strong incentives to make certain that their assumptions are questioned.

Coalitional Interest Aggregation

In contrast to the two agential models described above, I argue that societal preferences are aggregated not only in the minds of state leaders but also in the process through which coalitions choose their leaders. From this perspective, interest aggregation begins long before governments come to power. When domestic groups with divergent preferences separate into opposing coalitions, debates over policy will become polarized along party lines. Each side will view "national interests" through the prism of its own economic, ideological, or cultural interests, believing that what is best for itself is best for the country as a whole. To ensure that its preferred policies are followed, it will select party leaders whose sincerely held positions correspond to its parochial biases. Such leaders, once elected to public office, will already be inclined to enact policies that benefit their coalition's material interests.

In this "coalitional" form of interest aggregation, much depends on the method by which the executive is chosen. In a hereditary monarchy, for example, it is not applicable at all: succession to the throne is determined by genetics, not politics. Of course, monarchs do engage in agential forms of interest aggregation, often directed at economic elites and military officers, to deter challenges to their rule. However, they do not normally have

---

[22] David H. Lumsdaine, "The Intertwining of Domestic Politics and International Relations," *Polity* 29, no. 2 (winter 1996): 299–306; Rathbun, *Contesting the National Interest*.

to compete with other "candidates" for succession to the throne. What this example reveals is that scholars cannot simply "pick and choose" plausible mechanisms of interest aggregation as if they were divorced from logical consistency and empirical reality. Thus, the coalitional dynamics of the two cases in this study, the United States and Great Britain, merit closer attention.[23]

In the United States, a presidential system, coalitional interests are aggregated first by state parties and then at national conventions. Candidates compete for their party's nomination by staking out positions that attract the support of activist voters, local officials, factional leaders, and campaign contributors. A politician whose stated views are significantly out of line with the preferences of his party's societal coalition is unlikely to win this contest. Consider, for example, the contemporary Republican Party, which has two main constituencies, businesses and social conservatives. In the primaries of 2000, John McCain took positions that directly antagonized these groups; thus, he became an easy target for George W. Bush. McCain was the more charismatic of the two candidates, and he likely would have performed better in the general election, but he was unable to mobilize enough party activists or attract sufficient financial support to prevail over Bush, whose own platform was right in line with the expectations of both the business community and social conservatives.

In Great Britain, a parliamentary system, coalitional interests are aggregated in party leadership elections. Candidates compete not for primary voters, but rather for the support of party elites. Nevertheless, the distribution of preferences within the party's electoral coalition is usually approximated in the distribution of preferences among its elite members. Consequently, the winning candidate is almost always an individual whose views are congruent with those of the party's main constituencies. Once in office, party leaders must continue to pay close attention to their supporters' interests. If the preferences of a prime minister and his cabinet or parliamentary coalition diverge, the prime minister may be forced to resign. For example, William E. Gladstone quit his post in 1894 when a revolt by Liberal Imperialists over naval spending left him in the minority of his government.

In sum, partisan coalitions tend to choose leaders whose policy positions correspond to their aggregated interests. The source of a politician's views, be it internalized cultural norms, careerist vote-seeking, or even psychological pathology, may not matter as long as it predictably produces desired outcomes. Consequently, coalitions will sometimes select leaders whose internal motives bear no apparent connection to their parochial

---

[23] For a detailed comparison, see Waltz, *Foreign Policy and Democratic Politics*.

interests, even though their parochial interests determine which leaders are selected. Through this selection process, parties usually ensure that politicians act as if they are mechanistic interest aggregators, even when they are not.

Interest aggregation is not always as simple as depicted thus far, in which stable, discretely defined coalitions select leaders who will represent their priorities in the making of policy. If the principal-agent relationship between societal groups and their political representatives breaks down, even the most logically persuasive preference-based theory will likely confront empirical anomalies. There are two main types of principal-agent problem to consider.

First, sometimes it is leaders who choose coalitions, the reverse of usual. Especially in times of economic and political turmoil, ruling parties may weaken or split apart, forcing the executive to try to assemble a new coalition while in office. Even in a stable two-party system, politicians sometimes make creative decisions about how to win elections. The executive is not a mindless "conveyor belt" for societal interests but rather an independent actor that can take advantage of the institutional powers of its office to build support for itself.

Second, political coalitions might not always be successful in selecting leaders who represent their interests. They might support a candidate without fully knowing his views, or they might choose to nominate a politician who has well-known positions but later has a change of heart. Even with full information, coalitions might not always choose leaders whose policy preferences mirror their own. If only a few individuals can mount a credible challenge for the leadership of their party, and if none of them perfectly represents his party's aggregated preferences over every relevant issue, then voters, campaign contributors, and political elites will have to support a candidate with whom they sometimes disagree. In such a situation, they might consider sacrificing their international interests to obtain their ideal position over high-salience domestic concerns. The less important that an issue is to voters, the less likely it is that theories based on the coalitional view of interest aggregation will accurately forecast politicians' approach toward it.

Theories that follow the coalitional logic must be pitched at a sufficiently high level of generality to reflect its actual dynamics. Candidates for political office have little incentive to explain their views so thoroughly as to make clear what they would do under every possible circumstance, particularly in a policy environment as unpredictable as the international system. Instead, they declare the principles by which they intend to conduct foreign

[29]

policy and state their specific positions on the issues that are most salient at the time of their election. Therefore, coalitional theories are most likely to make accurate predictions when they try to explain patterns of behavior rather than individual decisions. They should be able to reveal which societal groups' ideological biases and economic interests will have the greatest overall impact on policymaking, but they will be of limited value in trying to predict the outcomes of crisis diplomacy and other unanticipated events.

Though principal-agent problems can wreak havoc on preference-based theories, they are not entirely unpredictable. As explained above, most candidates for high office have to compete with other members of their party to secure its nomination. Whether this competition occurs in open primaries, closed caucuses, or party conferences, it subjects each candidate's views and political skills to close scrutiny. Those who advocate positions that do not closely fit the interests of the party's societal coalition are quickly knocked out of the race. Only those candidates whose views consistently represent the opinion of the party as a whole can succeed. When all of these elements of the nomination process are present, coalitional theories of interest aggregation are most likely to render accurate predictions.

Among democracies, serious disjunctures between coalitional interests and politicians' beliefs are most likely to be found in countries in which a president is elected directly by voters. In parliamentary systems, candidates for party leadership must pass the careful judgment and intense scrutiny of their colleagues. In presidential systems, in contrast, charismatic individuals such as war heroes or celebrities may be able to win public support without clearly stating their positions. Their parties will nominate them because the certainty of victory outweighs the potential that their leader will act as an imperfect agent in pursuing their preferences. This form of interest aggregation can also break down when presidential candidates choose their own vice president. Instead of picking an ideological carbon copy of themselves, nominees often select a vice president who will help them win over a key electoral constituency that has different interests from the rest of their coalition. If the president dies while in office, his successor may be inclined to embark on new policies on behalf of that minority group.

Unfortunately, most of these scenarios are too complex, or too dependent on human agency, to theorize adequately. Rather than try to predict every possible breakdown in interest aggregation, I assume that executives will represent their coalitions' interests in a straightforward manner, or that deviations from this norm will average out. When they do not, the theory will likely fail. The critical question, therefore, is not whether the theory will produce anomalies, but whether the anomalies that it does produce are serious or frequent enough to undermine its fundamental causal logic.

Hypothesis Testing

The dynamics of interest aggregation have important implications for hypothesis testing. The sine qua non of realist theories of grand strategy is direct evidence of policymakers' motives, as documented in government records and personal files. For this study, however, actions speak louder than words. If, as I have argued, coalitions tend to elect leaders whose personal beliefs will benefit their parochial economic interests, then those leaders will pursue distributively biased policies for ideologically principled reasons. Consider, for example, Woodrow Wilson's decision to champion the League of Nations. It makes no difference what archival research reveals about the role of his religious beliefs, life experiences, or political philosophy in the formulation of his strategic views; instead, it matters only that Wilson was selected to be the Democratic candidate for president by a societal coalition that, for reasons deduced from a theory of preferences, wanted a leader who believed that the international system should be governed by legal norms rather than realpolitik.

Even evidence of agential interest aggregation that favors the theory, such as close ties between State Department officials and corporate lobbyists, should be treated with caution. The presence of private actors in public policymaking demonstrates only a congruence of interest between the two sides, not actual influence.[24] Consider, for example, the case of an American president who consults the CEO of United Fruit on a decision to intervene in Central America. Does he take action because he is beholden to the sectoral interests of foreign direct investors, or because, back when he was running for his party's nomination, campaign contributors threw their support to a candidate (him) whose ideological belief in the government's duty to protect American property abroad would benefit their sectoral interest in foreign direct investment? Given that evidence either for or against the first claim does not rule out the second, there is little point in looking for "smoking gun" statements that lay bare the political-economic logic behind decision makers' choices.

For these reasons, my historical case studies necessarily depend more on analytic inference than primary sources. In some instances, the role of sectoral interests in debates over grand strategy will be direct and obvious; on other occasions, it will be deeply obscured by overlapping ideological cleavages or competing claims about the "national interest." The true measure of a coalitional theory of interest aggregation lies not in an exhaustive analysis of the myriad arguments that politicians use to justify their positions, but rather in a demonstration of the soundness and consistency of the deductive logic

---

[24] Joanne Gowa, "Subsidizing American Corporate Expansion Abroad: Pitfalls in the Analysis of Public and Private Power," *World Politics* 37, no. 2 (January 1985): 180–203.

that connects domestic preferences to executive behavior. If a strong, coherent relationship exists between the hypothesized goals of socioeconomic groups, their positions on foreign policy, and the actual grand strategy chosen by their political representatives, there will be good reason to believe that the theory is correct.

This claim runs counter to conventional wisdom on qualitative research in international relations.[25] Most scholars readily admit that analyses of decision makers' speeches, memos, correspondence, and diaries are not always reliable; however, they may find it difficult to accept that, for a broad spectrum of theories based on societal preferences, these forms of evidence are essentially superfluous. In the view presented here, it does not matter what motivates politicians' behavior as long as their positions correspond to those of the partisan coalition that selected them to lead. The most productive research strategy will not be to pore over primary sources in a few select cases, but rather to use secondary sources to establish correlation consistency between predictions and policies over long periods of time. Evidence of decision makers' motives may help to corroborate such theories, but it will not ultimately be able either to confirm or disconfirm them. Some scholars may find this ambiguity to be intellectually unsatisfying, but that in itself does not make the theory any less likely to be correct.

Case Studies

I test the theory on two cases, the United States in 1865–1941 and Great Britain in 1868–1939. They are similar in many ways: both have a democratic regime, capitalist economy, liberal ideology, Protestant religion, and Anglo-Saxon culture, and both are geographically sheltered from invasion by another great power. Their similarities invite the criticism that, no matter how well the theory may explain these cases, it is applicable only to them. I do not accept this charge. To be sure, every state has a unique set of economic interests and strategic constraints, and such variation will inevitably require extensions to or revisions of the theory. The critical point, however, is that (1) all states must make trade-offs in their security policy, (2) these trade-offs often have distributive implications, and (3) almost all state leaders are selected by, or rely on the support of, groups that are affected by these trade-offs. As long as these conditions hold, similar dynamics should be evident in nearly every country and time period.

I defend this claim at greater length in the conclusion of the book. For now, I focus on the positive reasons for choosing the two cases: variation and salience. First, the late nineteenth and early twentieth centuries were

---

[25] Colin Elman and Miriam F. Elman, eds., *Bridges and Boundaries: Historians, Political Scientists, and the Study of International Relations* (Cambridge, Mass.: MIT Press, 2001).

a period of great flux for the political economies of both the United States and Great Britain. The United States went through political realignments in 1865 and 1931, structural shifts in its position in the international economy in the 1890s and 1930s, and rapid growth in its relative economic power. Great Britain experienced political realignments in 1868 and 1924, structural shifts in its position in the international economy in the 1880s and 1930s, and rapid decline in its relative economic power. This variation, in addition to frequent turnover in executive leadership, makes the two countries excellent candidates for comparative analysis.[26]

Second, the two cases are highly salient for the study of international security. Through much of the nineteenth century, Great Britain was the most powerful country in the world. It had the most advanced economy, its capital was the center of global finance, its fleet held mastery over the high seas, and it controlled a massive empire outside of Europe. Its army was relatively small, but it was nearly invulnerable to invasion, and it could bring together coalitions to counter any rival that threatened to disrupt the international balance of power. If any state deserves the title of hegemon in this period, it is Great Britain.

In the twentieth century, this mantle passed to the United States. Like Britain, the United States never kept a large peacetime army, but neither did it require one. It was more populous, had a larger economy, and was far more secure than any other great power. It could mobilize enormous resources when pushed to war, yet still not drain the reserve of its strength. Indeed, in the aftermath of World War I, its economic output was greater than that of all of Europe. It spanned an entire continent, giving it influence in both the Atlantic and Pacific oceans, and its power was unrivaled throughout the Western Hemisphere.

Over the last two centuries, these two countries have done more to shape the international order than any other state. At least one of them has been on the winning side of every system-wide war, played a key role in the design of every postwar peace settlement, and been the decisive counterweight in every era's balance of power. If international relations theory is to be of any practical value, it should be able to explain their grand strategies. Yet, the dominant paradigm in the study of international security, realism, has trouble accounting for some of the most basic elements of their behavior. Time and again, the United States and Great Britain have defied the conventional wisdom about how states should act. These empirical puzzles can be grouped into two main categories: the rate of expansion and the pattern of partisanship. I discuss each in turn below.

---

[26] Gary King et al., *Designing Social Inquiry: Scientific Inference in Qualitative Research* (Princeton: Princeton University Press, 1994), 140–41, 219–23.

Rate of Expansion

A standard assumption of realism is that relative power is the most important determinant of state behavior.[27] The more powerful a state is, the better able it will be to advance its interests in the international system. Thus, states should develop their diplomatic and military power in proportion to the growth of their economy. As their wealth increases, they will spend more on the expansion of their might and influence.

This view is highly problematic for the United States between 1865 and 1941. Its relative economic power grew almost continuously, but its involvement in international politics was terribly erratic. At the end of the Civil War, it possessed an enormous army and navy as well as a newly unified polity. It easily could have acquired numerous colonies in Latin America, and it probably could have fought for Canada as well. Yet it did not build an empire; instead, it retreated to a state of near-inactivity in the 1870s. In the late 1880s and 1890s, it finally began to take some halting steps toward an interventionist grand strategy, but, in comparison to the other great powers, there remained a significant gap between its domestic wealth and international influence.

By the end of World War I, the United States had become more powerful than ever before. According to the British Foreign Office, the United States was "twenty-five times as large, five times as wealthy, three times as populous, twice as ambitious, almost invulnerable, and at least our equal in prosperity, vital energy, technical equipment and industrial science"—and, perhaps most importantly, was not "still staggering from the effects of the superhuman effort made during the war."[28] At this very moment, however, the United States suddenly reversed gears. Under Woodrow Wilson, the country was poised to take a position of leadership over the international system; then, Warren Harding became president and initiated a decade-long retreat from America's participation in international politics. Relative power cannot explain this change; indeed, it predicts the exact opposite result. The growing economy of the United States may have enabled it to expand to the point that it did, but it did not make that expansion inevitable, nor did it govern the pace of expansion.

Realism also has trouble explaining the rate at which Great Britain expanded. In the mid nineteenth century, Britain was far more economically and militarily powerful than the United States. Its navy ruled the waves, its banks dominated the international financial system, and its industries were unrivaled in technological advancement and productive capacity. Yet,

[27] Gilpin, *War and Change*; Fareed Zakaria, *From Wealth to Power: The Unusual Origins of America's World Role* (Princeton: Princeton University Press, 1998).
[28] Quoted in B. J. C. McKercher, *The Second Baldwin Government and the United States, 1924–1929* (Cambridge: Cambridge University Press, 1984), 174.

like the United States, it did not live up to its full strategic potential. Just as Britain's relative power was peaking, anti-imperialist sentiment within the country was at its strongest. Between 1868 and 1877, Britain annexed only a few minor territories to its empire, and it gave Australia, New Zealand, and Canada greater powers of self-government. Not even the Franco-Prussian War of 1870–71 stirred Britain to action. It pledged to protect Belgium's neutrality but remained passive on the sidelines as Bismarck overthrew the balance of power in Europe.

In the final two decades of the nineteenth century, all of this changed. Britain's economy entered into a long decline, and its navy was challenged by the battleship construction programs of the continental European powers. Despite this reversal of fortune, however, Britain became much more aggressively imperialist. It annexed enormous swaths of land in Africa, Asia, and Oceania while entering into several dangerous, high-stakes confrontations with the other great powers to protect its gains. Thus, the expansion of Britain's international commitments did not result from growth in its relative power; if anything, the two variables were negatively correlated.

Pattern of Partisanship

Realists often argue that "politics ends at the water's edge," particularly in reference to "high politics" issues of military intervention, territorial annexation, and diplomatic alignments.[29] When state leaders make strategic decisions, they do so to protect their entire country, not to benefit some domestic groups at the expense of others. Given the high stakes of international politics, it would be nearly unthinkable for decision makers to treat foreign policy as just another part of the political "pork barrel." Even if they were inclined to do so, it is not obvious how they could; after all, what makes one citizen more secure will generally make all citizens more secure. In a realist world, there should be little domestic debate over foreign policy. Executive decision makers have much better information about the international environment and their own state's capabilities than anyone else in society; thus, citizens should trust that their leaders will make the right decisions to further the national interest.

A corollary of this point is that there should be few partisan differences over international affairs. When control over the government shifts from one party to another, foreign policy should not change, even if the two parties disagree over every possible domestic issue. Under the realist paradigm, leaders act according to national interests, not parochial ones, so they should realize that there is little to gain from diverging from their predecessors'

---

[29] Joanne Gowa, "Politics at the Water's Edge: Parties, Voters, and the Use of Force," *International Organization* 52, no. 2 (spring 1998): 307–24.

policies (unless they are compelled to do so by external developments, like the rise of a new threat). Different leaders might vary in terms of style or tone, but the substance of their actions should be the same, driven by the same set of structural imperatives.

Once again, the reality of American and British foreign policy in the late nineteenth and early twentieth centuries directly contradicts the realist conventional wisdom. In both countries, politicians often fought over the direction of grand strategy in the periphery. In the United States in the 1880s and 1890s, Republicans led the movement to extend American power and influence with the annexation of Hawaii, the acquisition of far-flung naval bases, and the construction of a battleship navy. In contrast, Democrats were reluctant to engage with the periphery, even to the point of reversing Republicans' prior advances and acquisitions. A similar debate arose in Britain in the 1860s, 1870s, and 1880s. Conservatives were often eager to annex new territories to the empire, whereas Liberals sought to avoid new commitments and scaled back on existing ones.

Grand strategy toward the great powers was even more contentious. In the United States, Democrats undertook ambitious schemes for the advancement of international law, binding arbitration, collective security, and the defense of international order, including the creation of the League of Nations. In contrast, Republicans acceded only to internationalist agreements that lacked meaningful commitments or obligations. Britain, too, was divided. The Liberal and Labour parties championed internationalist initiatives, whereas the Conservatives adhered to realpolitik. This cleavage came to be of great significance in 1913–14 and 1938–39, when the governing and opposition parties had different views on the conditions for and timing of a declaration of war against Germany.

In short, both countries experienced sharp partisan differences over grand strategy. The assumption that states follow a unitary "national interest," which underlies nearly all theoretical analyses of great power politics, is clearly not tenable here. To explain British and American behavior in 1865–1941, as well as any other case in which state leaders are presented with competing visions of the "national interest," it is necessary to examine the linkage between societal preferences and strategic choice.

Stages of Analysis

To solve these puzzles, I analyze each case in several stages. The first step is to determine how sectoral groups were represented within political coalitions. To this end, I investigate how each country's political geography corresponded to its economic geography. If a party consistently drew on a particular region for the bulk of its electoral support, I expect it to have favored that region's parochial economic interests. To confirm that my geographic findings accurately represent the relative power and distribution of societal groups in the party system, I also examine the historical literature on each country's political economy.

The second step is to ascertain which politically empowered sectors fell into which interest-group categories. Using macroeconomic statistics and the work of economic historians, I analyze the composition of the core, peripheral, and domestic interest groups within each state. At times, I find a clear consensus in the historical literature that certain sectors had strong expectations about how their competitive position and opportunities for profit in the international economy would change in the future. If the same research also reveals that those beliefs were reasonable in light of the information available at the time, and that they were formed independently of preferences over grand strategy (rather than as a post hoc justification for those preferences), I take them into account, albeit not without close scrutiny. I also evaluate whether military and colonial institutions had sufficient power within society for their preferences to have been relevant to the making of grand strategy.

Following this analysis, I test each of my basic hypotheses about the strategic preferences of interest groups. I look for evidence of groups' preferences in a variety of sources, including the positions taken by local opinion leaders, the demographics of membership in advocacy organizations, and the votes of legislators who represented communities that were highly dependent on particular economic sectors. Of course, not all group members can be expected to hold the same views on any given issue, especially when uncertainty in the policy environment is high. I do not expect unanimity of opinion within interest groups; a consistent majority suffices. Dissensus is a concern only when minority factions are so numerous or politically powerful that they are able to sway the selection of party leaders and policy decisions to their own ends.

Once I confirm that societal actors actually preferred their hypothesized strategy, I predict how party leaders should have aggregated their constituencies' interests. To test these predictions, I survey every "high politics" decision made by each president of the United States in 1865–1941 and each government of Great Britain in 1868–1939. At appropriate intervals, I consider how international and domestic constraints should have made different grand strategies more or less cost-effective, and I adjust my predictions accordingly.

Unlike most students of grand strategy, I do not delve into individual leaders' motives for critical decisions. Given the scope of my case studies, the amount of research required for this task would have been overwhelming. More important, though, my view of interest aggregation explicitly rejects the need for such evidence. Instead, I attempt to accomplish two specific goals: first, to identify the grand strategy of each executive decision maker, so as to determine whether the theory's predictions are accurate, and second, to evaluate whether that strategy was responsive to the material interests of the executive's coalition—in expectation, if not in outcome—so as to judge whether the internal logic and assumptions of the theory are confirmed.

Using these analytic tools, I demonstrate that the theory accounts for much of the variance in American and British grand strategy in 1865–1941. It does not explain everything; the cases contain some anomalies, including the first two observations on which I test the theory. My goal, however, is not to generate a perfect predictive record. In any study of human behavior, there will always be outliers and oddities that cannot be accounted for with reasonable parsimony. The true value of the theory is that it predicts American and British grand strategy *better* than any comparable theory, including realism and ideational perspectives. To establish this point, I review competing interpretations in each of the case studies and in the final chapter of the book.

[2]

The Political Economy of the United States, 1865–1941

The end of the Civil War in 1865 provides a natural starting point for an inquiry into the political economy of the United States. The Union victory restored the country's territorial integrity, but it left the American political landscape more deeply divided than ever before. The Northeast became predominantly Republican, while the South remained unshakably Democratic.[1] Each of these regions had a distinct economic profile and, not coincidentally, divergent interests in the international economy. The differences between them would generate and sustain a clear pattern of partisanship over American grand strategy for the entire period spanning 1865–1941.

REPUBLICANS

The Republicans were the party of the industrial Northeast.[2] This region was not as politically monolithic as the Democratic South, but it formed a solid bloc whenever a Republican candidate was able to win the presidency. As long as the party maintained its hegemony over the wealthy and

[1] I define the Northeast as Wisconsin, Michigan, Illinois, Indiana, Ohio, Pennsylvania, Maryland, Delaware, New Jersey, New York, Connecticut, Rhode Island, Massachusetts, Vermont, New Hampshire, and Maine. See Peter Trubowitz, *Defining the National Interest: Conflict and Change in American Foreign Policy* (Chicago: University of Chicago Press, 1998).
[2] Wilfred E. Binkley, *American Political Parties: Their Natural History* (New York: Knopf, 1963), chaps. 12, 14; Arthur M. Schlesinger, ed., *History of U.S. Political Parties, 1860–1910: The Gilded Age of Politics*, vol. 2 (New York: Chelsea House, 1973); Arthur M. Schlesinger, ed., *History of U.S. Political Parties, 1910–1945: From Square Deal to New Deal*, vol. 3 (New York: Chelsea House, 1973); Paul Kleppner, *Continuity and Change in Electoral Politics, 1893–1928* (New York: Greenwood, 1987).

Figure 2.1. Electoral College Votes for William McKinley, 1896

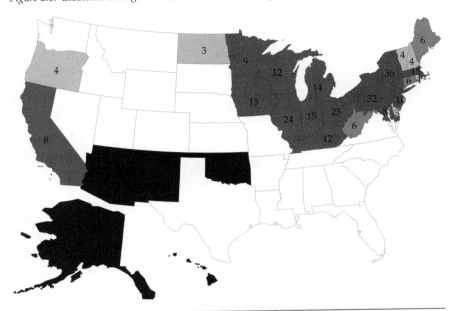

SOURCE: United States Bureau of the Census, *Historical Statistics of the United States: Colonial Times to 1970* (Washington, D.C.: Government Printing Office, 1972).
NOTE: Areas shaded black were not yet incorporated as states.

populous Northeast, it could control national elections with only a few more scattered states. William McKinley's sectional victory in 1896, which he won by an impressive margin of 271–176 in the Electoral College (see figure 2.1), illustrates starkly the political dominance of the Northeast.

Republicans also did well in the Great Plains states, but the interests of western farmers had little impact on the national party.[3] It was thoroughly dominated by northeastern businessmen, whose economic and organizational power brought a Republican candidate to the White House in twelve of the sixteen contests between the end of the Civil War and the beginning of the Great Depression. The party faltered in 1912, when it was divided by a struggle for power between William Taft's conservatives and Theodore Roosevelt's progressives, but the split was temporary, and it did not affect the regional basis of the coalition. Even the electoral realignment of the 1930s, in which Democrats made spectacular gains in the Northeast, did not

[3] James L. Sundquist, *Dynamics of the Party System: Alignment and Realignment of Political Parties in the United States*, rev. ed. (Washington, D.C.: Brookings, 1983), chaps. 6, 8.

break this continuity; it was not until the 1950s and 1960s that Republicans turned to the South.

The Northeast, as home to almost all of America's major cities, was far more industrialized than the rest of the country.[4] Its advanced economic development gave the Republican Party a natural source of political cohesion and a clearly identifiable sectoral constituency. Whether progressive or conservative, Republican politicians represented businesses, and particularly manufacturers. Manufacturing was the leading sector of the northeastern economy, serving as the engine of growth for retail, services, finance, transportation, and other sectors. Its interests, above all else, should have been the critical variable determining the grand strategy of the Republican Party.

Manufacturing

American manufacturing in the mid nineteenth century was funded in part by foreign capital, but it did not otherwise rely on the international economy. Instead, businesses looked to the undeveloped domestic market to fuel their growth.[5] In the first decade after the Civil War, one important source of demand was the reconstruction of the South. Southerners needed a massive amount of investment and capital goods to rebuild their war-ravaged economy, and the Northeast stood ready to gain from their misfortune. Even more lucrative, however, was the exploitation of the West. Western settlers borrowed money from northeastern financiers, sold foodstuffs cheaply back to northeastern workers, and used this income to purchase manufactured products from northeastern industries. The reciprocal, cross-country shipment of goods was made possible by extensive investment in intracontinental transportation networks, which further fed the growth of the northeastern iron, steel, and railroad sectors.[6] All of this economic activity created exceptional opportunities for profit. In 1880, the

[4] D. W. Meinig, *The Shaping of America: A Geographical Perspective on 500 Years of History: Continental America, 1867–1914*, vol. 3 (New Haven: Yale University Press, 1999), 241; Trubowitz, *Defining the National Interest*; Richard F. Bensel, *Sectionalism and American Political Development, 1880–1980* (Madison: University of Wisconsin Press, 1984); Chester W. Wright, *Economic History of the United States* (New York: McGraw-Hill, 1941), 711–12.

[5] Ann Markusen, *Regions: The Economics and Politics of Territory* (Totowa, N.J.: Rowman and Littlefield, 1987), 61–62, 71–72, 78–81; Harold G. Vatter, *The Drive to Industrial Maturity: The U.S. Economy, 1860–1914* (Westport, Conn.: Greenwood, 1975), chap. 5; Robert Higgs, *The Transformation of the American Economy, 1865–1914: An Essay in Interpretation* (New York: Wiley, 1971), 25–34, 56; Walter Licht, *Industrializing America: The Nineteenth Century* (Baltimore, M.D.: Johns Hopkins University Press, 1995), chap. 5; Wright, *Economic History*, 523–25; Victor S. Clark, *History of Manufactures in the United States, 1860–1893*, vol. 2 (New York: McGraw-Hill, 1929), chap. 16.

[6] Charles Hoffman, *The Depression of the Nineties: An Economic History* (Westport, Conn.: Greenwood, 1970), 273.

average rate of return on investments in the North Atlantic region was 8.4 percent, whereas in the Pacific and Mountain West it was 10.4 percent.[7]

Northeasterners received essentially the same benefits from the American West that Europeans sought from their empires in Africa and Asia. As Walter Burnham writes, "The United States was so vast that it had little need of economic colonies abroad; in fact it had two major colonial regions within its own borders, the postbellum South and the West."[8] So long as land and resources lay unexploited on the continental frontier, it would not be worth the trouble to try to establish a presence in foreign markets. American foreign trade statistics bear out this observation: throughout 1865–97, exports of finished manufactures consistently hovered around 1.0 percent of the national income (see figure 2.2) and rarely amounted to more than 16 percent of all merchandise exports. Thus, the overwhelming majority of American businesses must be categorized as domestic interests, even if they were competitive enough to have been capable of exporting.

In the mid 1880s, the United States' massive economic expansion began to slow dramatically. Between 1874 and 1884, per capita GNP growth averaged 3.8 percent; between 1884 and 1894, it was only 0.6 percent.[9] As a result, the potential for overproduction became a serious concern for businessmen. Even as far back as the late 1870s, "Excess capacity proved to be a problem in almost every branch of American manufacturing."[10] At the same time, the continental frontier that had long fed the growth of business was rapidly disappearing. The best land, natural resources, and investment opportunities had already been claimed and exploited in the two decades following the Civil War, and exceptional opportunities for profit were becoming scarce.[11] Furthermore, the national rate of growth in population had been dropping since the 1870s.[12] Clearly, businesses had good reason to be concerned about the ability of the home market to maintain economic prosperity. As Harold Vatter bluntly writes, "A frontier raises the rate of return on investment, and when it is gone, if this rate is to be sustained, it must be by other means."[13]

[7] Vatter, *Drive to Industrial Maturity*, 115.

[8] Walter D. Burnham, "The End of American Party Politics," *Transaction* 7, no. 2 (December 1969): 16.

[9] W. Elliot Brownlee, *Dynamics of Ascent: A History of the American Economy*, 2d ed. (New York: Knopf, 1979), 270.

[10] William H. Becker, "American Manufacturers and Foreign Markets, 1870–1900: Business Historians and the 'New Economic Determinists,'" *Business History Review* 47, no. 4 (winter 1973): 468–69.

[11] Brownlee, *Dynamics of Ascent*, 281; Vatter, *Drive to Industrial Maturity*, chap. 5.

[12] Brownlee, *Dynamics of Ascent*, 283; Licht, *Industrializing America*, 127–28.

[13] Vatter, *Drive to Industrial Maturity*, 113 (italics removed). See also Frederick J. Turner, "The Significance of the Frontier in American History," in *The Frontier in American History*, ed. Frederick J. Turner (New York: Holt, 1920), 1–38.

Figure 2.2. U.S. Merchandise Exports, as Share of National Income

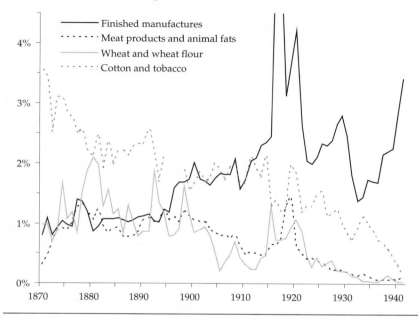

SOURCES: United States Bureau of the Census, *Historical Statistics*, 889–90, 898–99; Milton Friedman and Anna J. Schwartz, *Monetary Trends in the United States and the United Kingdom: Their Relation to Income, Prices, and Interest Rates* (Chicago: University of Chicago Press, 1982), 122–23.
NOTE: Exports of finished manufactures peaked at 6.0% in 1916.

What, then, might these "other means" have been? As Walter LaFeber, William A. Williams, and other revisionist historians have documented, manufacturers became increasingly interested in exporting. No longer could they rely on the continental frontier; instead, they would have to look for new markets and investment opportunities overseas. Although LaFeber and Williams have rightfully been criticized for exaggerating the extent to which both businesses and politicians were preoccupied with foreign trade in the 1860s and 1870s, one would nevertheless be hard-pressed to find any expert on the era who would deny that Americans' interest in exports did indeed increase in the 1880s, especially following the severe recession of 1884–86.[14]

[14] Walter LaFeber, *The New Empire: An Interpretation of American Expansion, 1860–1898* (Ithaca: Cornell University Press, 1963), 17–24; William A. Williams, *The Roots of the Modern American Empire: A Study of the Growth and Shaping of Social Consciousness in a Marketplace*

[43]

The problem of industrial overproduction intensified in the early 1890s, but it was not until the severe economic depression of 1893–97 that the impetus to find new markets become acute.[15] Foreign competition would not stand in the way; America's labor productivity surpassed that of Britain to become the highest in the world in the late 1890s.[16] Thus, when forced by depressed domestic demand to turn to foreign markets, American businesses responded impressively. Between 1893 and 1897, the portion of the national income earned through the export of finished manufactures jumped from 1.0 percent to 1.7 percent, an all-time high for the United States (see figure 2.2). Clearly, manufacturers' belief in the importance of exports proved to be correct. By the turn of the century, American industries' interest in the international economy had become consistent and entrenched, as their initial forays into foreign markets finally developed into a full-fledged "commercial invasion."[17]

Not all markets were equally open to invasion, however. Europe, the core of the international economy and great power politics, was almost completely closed off. Except for Britain, all of the major states on the continent raised tariffs on manufactured goods in the 1880s and 1890s (see figure 2.3).[18]

Economy (New York: Random House, 1969), 22, 50; Ray Ginger, *The Age of Excess: The United States from 1877 to 1914* (New York: Macmillan, 1965), 53–55, 158–59; Ernest R. May, *Imperial Democracy: The Emergence of America as a Great Power* (New York: Harcourt, Brace, and World, 1961), 8–9; David M. Pletcher, *The Diplomacy of Trade and Investment: American Economic Expansion in the Hemisphere, 1865–1900* (Columbia: University of Missouri Press, 1998), chap. 1; Edward P. Crapol, *America for Americans: Economic Nationalism and Anglophobia in the Late Nineteenth Century* (Westport, Conn.: Greenwood, 1973), chap. 3; Gerald T. White, *The United States and the Problem of Recovery after 1893* (University: University of Alabama Press, 1982), chap. 8; David E. Novack and Matthew Simon, "Commercial Responses to the American Export Invasion, 1871–1914: An Essay in Attitudinal History," *Explorations in Entrepreneurial History* 2, no. 3 (winter 1966): 124; Justus D. Doenecke, *The Presidencies of James A. Garfield and Chester A. Arthur* (Lawrence: Regents Press of Kansas, 1981), 165–67; Robert L. Beisner, *From the Old Diplomacy to the New, 1865–1900* (New York: Crowell, 1975), 71–72; David M. Pletcher, *The Awkward Years: American Foreign Relations under Garfield and Arthur* (Columbia: University of Missouri Press, 1962), chap. 1; Becker, "American Manufacturers and Foreign Markets."

[15] Brownlee, *Dynamics of Ascent*, 288.

[16] David A. Lake, *Power, Protection, and Free Trade: International Sources of U.S. Commercial Strategy, 1887–1939* (Ithaca: Cornell University Press, 1988), 120.

[17] Thomas J. McCormick, *China Market: America's Quest for Informal Empire* (Chicago: Quadrangle, 1967); Julius W. Pratt, *The Expansionists of 1898: The Acquisition of Hawaii and the Spanish Islands* (Chicago: Quadrangle, 1964), 252–53; LaFeber, *New Empire*, chap. 4; Emily S. Rosenberg, *Spreading the American Dream: American Economic and Cultural Expansion, 1890–1945* (New York: Hill and Wang, 1982), 14–28, 38–39; Herbert Ershkowitz, *The Attitude of Business toward American Foreign Policy, 1900–1916* (University Park: Pennsylvania State University, 1967), chap. 1; Charles S. Campbell, *Special Business Interests and the Open Door Policy* (New Haven: Yale University Press, 1951), chap. 1.

[18] Novack and Simon, "Commercial Responses to the American Export Invasion," 121–47; Pletcher, *Diplomacy of Trade and Investment*, 13–14. In the late 1880s, the United Kingdom absorbed approximately half of U.S. exports, but this number began to fall in the 1890s. See Lake, *Power, Protection, and Free Trade*, 93; United States Bureau of the Census, *Historical*

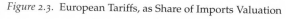

Figure 2.3. European Tariffs, as Share of Imports Valuation

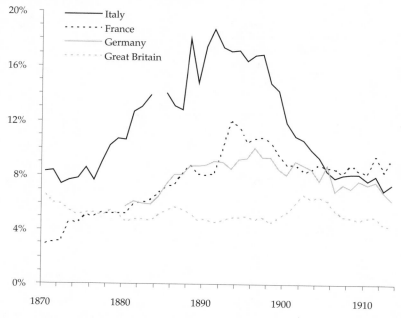

SOURCE: Forrest Capie, "Tariff Protection and Economic Performance in the Nineteenth Century," in *Policy and Performance in International Trade*, ed. John Black and L. Alan Winters (London: Macmillan, 1983), 20–21.

Their goal, in part, was to keep out their American rivals; thus, offers for reciprocity would be of no avail. Even the Payne-Aldrich Act of 1909, which was intended to force down European trade barriers, succeeded only in reducing the most blatant discrimination against American goods.[19] Faced with nearly insurmountable obstacles to trade with Europe, most American manufacturers who desired to export had little choice but to search for new markets in Latin America and East Asia.

At first, the actual volume of sales to the periphery was low, but, as early as the 1880s, a critical trend was developing: exports of finished manufactures to the periphery increased sporadically as a share of the national

Statistics of the United States: Colonial Times to 1970 (Washington, D.C.: Government Printing Office, 1972), 903–6.

[19] James Foreman-Peck, *A History of the World Economy: International Economic Relations since 1850* (Totowa, N.J.: Barnes and Noble, 1983), 118–23; Lake, *Power, Protection, and Free Trade*, 130–36.

Figure 2.4. U.S. Merchandise Exports to the Periphery, as Share of National Income

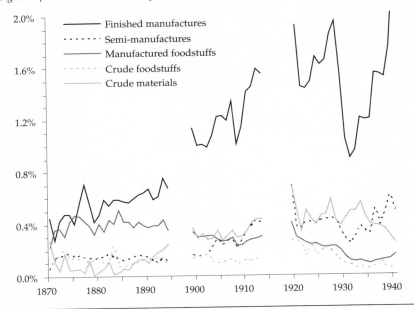

SOURCES: Matthew Simon and David Novack, "Some Dimensions of the American Commercial Invasion of Europe, 1871–1914: An Introductory Essay," *Journal of Economic History* 24, no. 4 (December 1964): 594–95; United States Bureau of the Census, *Historical Statistics*, 889–90; Friedman and Schwartz, *Monetary Trends*, 122–23.
NOTE: Exports of finished manufactures peaked at 2.8% in 1920 and 2.3% in 1941.

income (see figures 2.4 and 2.5), while exports of finished manufactures to Europe stagnated (see figures 2.6 and 2.7). This change had clear implications over the long run:

> Europe, by purchasing most of the surplus of agricultural products and raw materials, continued to lead in the foreign trade of the United States, but after 1890 the European proportion of the total exports of the United States slowly declined. . . . During the early years of the twentieth century it became clear that the commercial struggle between Europe and the United States centered not in the European market, but in the undeveloped markets throughout the remainder of the world.[20]

[20] Emory R. Johnson et al., *History of Domestic and Foreign Commerce of the United States* (Washington, D.C.: Carnegie Institute of Washington, 1915), 74, 90. See also Matthew Simon and David Novack, "Some Dimensions of the American Commercial Invasion of Europe, 1871–1914: An Introductory Essay," *Journal of Economic History* 24, no. 4 (December 1964): 591–605; Trubowitz, *Defining the National Interest*, 64–68; Pletcher, *Diplomacy of Trade and Investment*, 17–19.

Figure 2.5. U.S. Merchandise Exports, as Share Sent to the Periphery

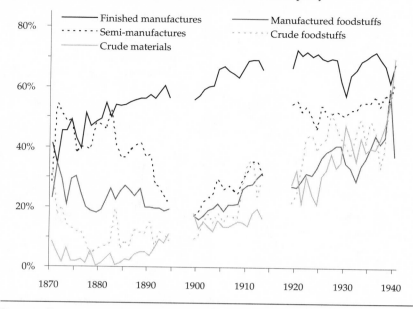

SOURCES: Simon and Novack, "Some Dimensions of the American Commercial Invasion," 594–95; United States Bureau of the Census, *Historical Statistics*, 889–90.

Thus, it was eminently rational for manufacturers and their dependent sectors in the northeastern business community to think that their future prosperity would be tied to peripheral export. In the mid 1880s, only a small proportion of businesses actually exported to the periphery, but many began to believe that they would be doing so in the near future. By the end of the decade, peripheral interests were growing rapidly among northeastern businesses.

The socioeconomic power of peripheral interests in the mid to late nineteenth century should not be overstated. These trends were slow to develop, and their impact on the national income was small at first. As Charles S. Campbell writes, "Most businessmen were apathetic about exporting until the mid-1890s."[21] By the turn of the century, however, much had changed. Between 1897 and 1914, exports to the periphery were continuously increasing relative to exports to Europe in every major category of goods, led by finished manufactures. Overall, more than two-thirds of finished manufactures exports were sold in the periphery in the decade

[21] Charles S. Campbell, *The Transformation of American Foreign Relations, 1865–1900* (New York: Harper and Row, 1976), 141.

Figure 2.6. U.S. Merchandise Exports to Europe, as Share of National Income

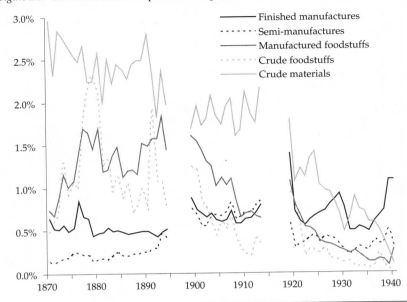

SOURCES: Simon and Novack, "Some Dimensions of the American Commercial Invasion," 594–95; United States Bureau of the Census, *Historical Statistics*, 889–90; Friedman and Schwartz, *Monetary Trends*, 122–25.

preceding World War I. As a percentage of the national income, exports of finished manufactures to the periphery more than doubled between 1895 and 1914, from 0.67 percent to 1.55 percent.

After World War I, the proportion of finished manufactures exports sent to the periphery leveled out at 70 percent. Yet, as a share of the national income, they continued to grow through much of the 1920s, to nearly 2.0 percent in 1929. This figure may not seem terribly impressive, but it represents only income generated directly from exports. To understand how important peripheral markets were to the American economy, one must also take into account all of the trade, transportation, and service industries whose welfare was dependent on the success of manufacturing exports. The positive externalities and multiplier effects of foreign commerce cannot be estimated here, but they surely were not trivial.

Another factor in the increasing dependence of American business on peripheral markets was overseas investment.[22] In the first three decades

[22] Cleona Lewis, *America's Stake in International Investments* (Washington, D.C.: Brookings Institution, 1938); Mira Wilkins, *The Emergence of Multinational Enterprise: American Business*

Figure 2.7. U.S. Merchandise Exports, as Share Sent to Europe

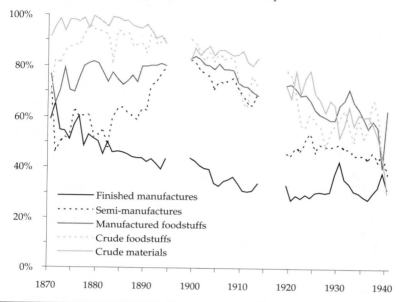

SOURCES: Simon and Novack, "Some Dimensions of the American Commercial Invasion," 594–95; United States Bureau of the Census, *Historical Statistics*, 889–90.

following the Civil War, its impact was marginal. Only in three countries other than Canada did Americans risk significant amounts of capital abroad: Mexico (railroads), Cuba (sugar and tobacco), and Hawaii (sugar).[23] The real shift came at the turn of the century. From 1897 to 1914, American investment in the periphery grew sevenfold in real dollars (1929), from $0.24 billion to $1.77 billion, nearly doubling in proportion to the national income. By 1929, it had risen to six times the 1914 total, to $10.65 billion (see table 2.1).

Abroad from the Colonial Era to 1914 (Cambridge, Mass.: Harvard University Press, 1970); Lance E. Davis and Robert J. Cull, *International Capital Markets and American Economic Growth, 1820–1914* (New York: Cambridge University Press, 1994), 92–107; Rosenberg, *Spreading the American Dream*, 23–28; Royal Institute of International Affairs, *The Problem of International Investment* (London: His Majesty's Government, 1937), 179–94.

[23] David M. Pletcher, "1861–1898: Economic Growth and Diplomatic Adjustment," in *Economics and World Power: An Assessment of American Diplomacy since 1789*, ed. William H. Becker and Samuel F. Wells (New York: Columbia University Press, 1984), 122; Davis and Cull, *International Capital Markets*, 79–91; Thomas K. O'Horo, "American Foreign Investments and Foreign Policy: The Railroad Experience, 1805–1898" (Ph.D. diss., Rutgers University, 1976), 1–57.

Table 2.1. U.S. Foreign Investment, in Millions of Real Dollars (1929=100)

	Years						
	1897	1908	1914	1919	1924	1929	1935
Europe	67	277	439	2,120	2,642	4,601	2,333
Canada	85	395	551	1,646	2,621	3,660	2,820
Central America	121	532	815	1,739	2,253	2,415	1,524
South America	17	74	232	828	1,406	3,014	1,985
Africa	0	3	8	33	59	119	97
Asia	10	133	156	330	669	1,040	706
Oceania	1	6	11	58	140	403	319
All foreign investments (incl. short-term credits) relative to nationalincome	5.4%	10.7%	11.4%	10.0%	14.3%	18.8%	23.5%

SOURCES: Cleona Lewis, *America's Stake in International Investments* (Washington, D.C.: Brookings Institution, 1938), 606; Milton Friedman and Anna J. Schwartz *Monetary Trends in the United States and the United Kingdom: Their Relation to Income, Prices, and Interest Rates* (Chicago: University of Chicago Press, 1982), 122–25.

When investment, exports, and the multiplier effects of export income are viewed together, it is evident that the basis on which America's national wealth was acquired had been fundamentally altered in the 1890s and early 1900s. As a result, the relative size of peripheral interests within the American economy—and especially among manufacturers—increased considerably. World War I briefly skewed the pattern of trade in favor of Europe, but once hostilities ended, all of the key indicators of business interest in peripheral markets either returned to their prewar levels or continued to rise.

In contrast, northeastern businesses were never able to gain much traction in core markets. The absolute value of finished manufactures exports to Europe increased throughout the late nineteenth century, but its share of the national income held fairly constant (see figure 2.6). Furthermore, the proportion of all finished manufactures exports that were sent to Europe steadily decreased after 1876 (see figure 2.7). There was little hope of reversing this trend; Europeans repeatedly raised their tariffs on manufactured goods after 1880. Consequently, the relative power of core interests among northeastern exporters was not increasing, and it may even have been declining. In the mid 1890s, the proportion of the national income composed of exports of finished manufactures to Europe hovered near 0.5 percent; for most of 1897–1929 (excluding the war years), it remained between 0.6 percent and 0.7 percent. Due to the sluggishness of this growth, the relative importance of European markets to American manufacturers continued to decline until World War I, then leveled off in the 1920s.

[50]

To the extent that individual firms in the Northeast had an interest in Europe, it probably derived more from investment than export. Faced with insurmountable tariff barriers, they began to amass large sums of capital to build production facilities on the continent.[24] The value of American foreign investment in Europe rose from $67 in 1897 to $439 million in 1914 (real dollars, 1929), then to $4.60 billion in 1929. Relative to other markets, though, Europe lagged behind. Even in the late interwar period, American manufacturers' exports to and investments in the periphery far outweighed their stake in the core. For the purposes of grand strategy, their priorities should have remained with the periphery.

In conclusion, the northeastern manufacturing sector that formed the basis of the Republican Party consistently had a strong contingent of domestic interests throughout 1865–1941. After 1880, however, it included a growing number of peripheral interests. Neither of the other two groups, core interests and military-colonial interests, should have had significant influence in the Republican coalition.[25]

Strategic Interests: Periphery

The foregoing analysis reveals that northeastern manufacturers were composed almost exclusively of domestic interests in 1865. The ideal grand strategy for domestic interests, as explained in chapter 1, is isolationism. This group should have opposed all forms of international engagement not needed for self-defense. Expansion into the periphery would have wasted government revenue on naval construction and overseas bases, created unwanted diplomatic commitments with unreliable governments, and risked military conflict with the great powers over spheres of influence.

There is a great deal of support for this prediction. In the first few decades after the Civil War, the vast majority of American businesses, as well as the public at large, was disdainful of foreign entanglements.[26] On occasion, Americans could be roused to anger over issues that hit close to home, such as Spain's brutal repression of Cuban revolutionaries in the

---

[24] Johnson et al., *History of Domestic and Foreign Commerce*, 90–91; Wilkins, *Emergence of Multinational Enterprise*, 70–73; Simon and Novack, "Some Dimensions."

[25] On the relative weakness of military-colonial interests in the United States prior to World War II, see Ben Baack and Edward Ray, "The Political Economy of the Origins of the Military-Industrial Complex in the United States," *Journal of Economic History* 45, no. 2 (June 1985): 369–75; Paul A. C. Koistinen, *Mobilizing for Modern War: The Political Economy of American Warfare, 1865–1919* (Lawrence: University Press of Kansas, 1997); Paul A. C. Koistinen, *Planning War, Pursuing Peace: The Political Economy of American Warfare, 1920–1939* (Lawrence: University Press of Kansas, 1998).

[26] Pletcher, *Awkward Years*, 351–54; Foster R. Dulles, *America's Rise to World Power* (New York: Harper, 1955), 17–20; Doenecke, *Presidencies of James A. Garfield and Chester A. Arthur*, 167; Donald M. Dozer, "Anti-Imperialism in the United States, 1865–1895: Opposition to Annexation of Overseas Territory" (Ph.D. diss., Harvard University, 1936).

1870s, but such sentiment did not translate into a sustained desire for the government to be consistently engaged in international politics. As Foster R. Dulles writes, "The America of post–Civil War years was launched on the great era of industrial development. National attention and national energy were primarily absorbed in the development of industry and the settlement of the West. . . . Popular interest in foreign affairs sank to the lowest ebb in all American history—in comparison with either pre–Civil War days or the twentieth century."[27]

The Northeast should have begun to change its strategic outlook in the 1880s and 1890s. By that time, businesses' concerns about the problem of overproduction had begun to generate a strong constituency of peripheral interests in the Republican Party. As explained in chapter 1, peripheral interests' hypothesized position on grand strategy depends on their ability to compete effectively with their foreign counterparts. Those experiencing serious difficulties should support imperialism, whereas those that are highly competitive should be satisfied with a less costly strategy of interventionism. By the end of the nineteenth century, American manufacturers were firmly in the latter category.[28] They had no need for their government to establish colonial monopolies for them; all they required was equal access in foreign markets. Thus, they should have favored a strategy of "open door" interventionism. This would have entailed building a global military infrastructure, interfering occasionally in the domestic politics of unstable peripheral governments, and preventing the other great powers from annexing markets in which American traders were active.

This prediction is confirmed by extensive historical research. Herbert Ershkowitz, quoting an American banker, explains the need for an interventionist strategy:

> Schiff said it had been a great comfort of European investors to know that if a foreign government failed to live up to its obligations an individual could expect his government to "back him up diplomatically and even otherwise in enforcing his just demands. The courts are not open to international financiers . . . and our ships must unfortunately take the place of receiverships and foreclosures. Until we can feel certain that our government will maintain the rights of American citizens, who have made legitimate investments in foreign countries, it is hopeless to try to create here a rich market for foreign securities."[29]

---

[27] Dulles, *America's Rise to World Power*, 18. See also Theodore C. Smith, "Expansion after the Civil War, 1865–71," *Political Science Quarterly* 16, no. 3 (September 1901): 412–36.

[28] Becker, "American Manufacturers and Foreign Markets," 474–79.

[29] Ershkowitz, *Attitude of Business*, 40.

Peripheral interests rejected imperialism, reasoning that their economic power and competitiveness would suffice for them to prosper in most peripheral markets; yet, at the same time, they expected their government to intervene with military force whenever American lives and property were threatened.[30] To this end, they advocated the acquisition of a global network of naval bases and a battleship fleet.[31] Finally, they strongly supported measures that were designed specifically to give them direct commercial benefits, such as the construction of an isthmian canal, the revival of the merchant marine, and the Open Door policy in China.[32] In short, peripheral interests favored the kind of strategic initiatives that the theory predicts.

Strategic Interests: Core

In 1865–80, American manufacturers focused on the domestic market, not foreign trade. Consequently, they had no reason to advocate either cooperation or confrontation with the great powers. In that period, their ideal strategy toward the core should have been isolationism. Then, from the 1880s onward, manufacturers began to take an interest in export; however, they focused primarily on peripheral markets, not the core. Thus, engagement with Europe should have remained low on their list of priorities. Internationalist initiatives would waste their diplomatic capital, draw them into conflicts in which they had nothing at stake, and hinder the unilateral use of American military and economic power. Instead, they should have supported a strategy of realpolitik, in which the United States could threaten the use of force against great powers that hindered the expansion of its influence in the periphery.

The first part of this prediction was confirmed above: from the end of the Civil War to the 1880s, northeasterners were uninterested in international engagement, whether in the core or the periphery. Public attention followed the occasional diplomatic flare-up with Britain; Americans took satisfaction in "twisting the lion's tail" from time to time. Otherwise, however, the Northeast demonstrated little desire for sustained engagement with the European great powers, whether for cooperative or coercive purposes.

---

[30] Joan H. Wilson, *American Business and Foreign Policy, 1920–1933* (Lexington: University Press of Kentucky, 1971), 157–65; Ershkowitz, *Attitude of Business*, chap. 4; William H. Becker, "1899–1920: America Adjusts to World Power," in *Economics and World Power: An Assessment of American Diplomacy since 1789*, ed. William H. Becker and Samuel F. Wells (New York: Columbia University Press, 1984), 182–84, 193; Rosenberg, *Spreading the American Dream*, 47–48.

[31] Trubowitz, *Defining the National Interest*, 31–75; Becker, "1899–1920," 186–87; Bensel, *Sectionalism*, 88–101; Pratt, *Expansionists of 1898*, 266–78; LaFeber, *New Empire*, 326–417; Campbell, *Special Business Interests*, 15–17; Rosenberg, *Spreading the American Dream*, 43, 49–51.

[32] Ershkowitz, *Attitude of Business*, 5–20; Trubowitz, *Defining the National Interest*, 53–54; Becker, "1899–1920," 179–80, 192–93; Campbell, *Special Business Interests*; McCormick, *China Market*.

Also as expected, there was a shift in popular attitudes at the end of the nineteenth century. Northeasterners took more of an interest in relations with the great powers, and their policy preferences tended toward realpolitik over internationalism. I will present the evidentiary bases for this claim below, when I discuss the strategic preferences of southerners. In the meantime, it suffices to note that northeasterners were demonstrably less internationalist than either southerners or westerners. The same applies to their representatives in Congress, who tended to oppose internationalist initiatives, such as the League of Nations, and support realpolitik measures, such as the construction of battleships.

After World War I, the situation became less clear-cut. As increasing numbers of manufacturers invested in and traded with Europe, some northeastern constituencies reversed their traditional opposition to free trade and diplomatic engagement.[33] Consequently, they should also have become more open to an internationalist grand strategy. The Northeast's overall stake in Europe was still relatively low, so I do not expect core interests to have played a major role in the design of Republican grand strategy; however, it would not be surprising to find evidence that their influence was growing in the years leading up to World War II.

Hypotheses

Republicans were backed primarily by domestic interests (i.e., most northeastern businesses), whose hypothesized grand strategy was isolationism. From the 1880s onward, however, the party had a growing secondary constituency of peripheral interests (i.e., some northeastern businesses). Thus, Republican presidents should have been isolationist until about 1880, then increasingly interested in a periphery-oriented grand strategy through the turn of the century. At that time, American manufacturing was becoming highly competitive internationally, so Republican presidents should not have started down the path to imperialism. Rather, they should have made cautious moves to advance the more moderate, threat-based strategy of interventionism.

Specifically, Republicans should first have sought to exercise influence in Latin America and Hawaii, where American businesses had already

---

[33] Trubowitz, *Defining the National Interest*, 107–8; Thomas Ferguson, "From Normalcy to New Deal: Industrial Structure, Party Competition, and American Public Policy in the Great Depression," *International Organization* 38, no. 1 (winter 1984): 41–94; Jeffry A. Frieden, "Sectoral Conflict and Foreign Economic Policy, 1914–1940," *International Organization* 42, no. 1 (winter 1988): 59–90; Douglas A. Irwin and Randall S. Kroszner, "Interests, Institutions, and Ideology in Securing Policy Change: The Republican Conversion to Trade Liberalization after Smoot-Hawley," *Journal of Law and Economics* 42, no. 2 (October 1999): 643–73.

begun to establish a commercial foothold.[34] East Asia was also promising—particularly China, due to the sheer size of its market. However, the expansion of American power into the Far East would confront greater obstacles than in Latin America. The Chinese government was not easily bullied, and other European countries were already competing for exclusive influence across Asia. Distance was also a factor; the navy would need coaling stations and military bases in the Pacific Ocean to refuel its ships and station marines in the region. To that end, the construction of a Central American canal should have been a priority. It would reduce the transportation cost of shipping goods from the northeastern United States to Asian consumers, making American exports more competitive, while improving the navy's ability to transfer forces from the Atlantic to the Pacific. Africa, on the other hand, should have held little appeal: its markets were poorly developed and its natural resources had been the target of European empire-builders since the mid 1880s.

As northeastern manufacturers became increasingly dependent on peripheral export and investment, they should have become increasingly willing to risk blood and treasure on an interventionist grand strategy. By the 1890s, therefore, Republican presidents should have been active on a number of fronts, including the protection of American property, the annexation of overseas bases, and the assertion of American rights against the claims of other great powers. In the interwar period, they might have felt some pressure to deviate from this strategy on behalf of businesses with interests in Europe, but it should not have been strong. Far more manufactures and investment were sent to the periphery than the core, so the preferences of interventionists should have dominated those of internationalists within the Republican coalition. Resources committed to grand strategy would be spent more productively on the protection of peripheral commerce than in fostering cooperation with the great powers.

DEMOCRATS

If regional identification had been the only factor determining partisan affiliations, the Democrats would have been destined for permanent minority status.[35] Their electoral base, the South, was far less populous than

[34] John M. Dobson, *Reticent Expansionism: The Foreign Policy of William McKinley* (Pittsburgh: Duquesne University Press, 1988), 11.

[35] Binkley, *American Political Parties*, chaps. 13, 15; Schlesinger, ed., *History of U.S. Political Parties, 1860–1910*; Schlesinger, ed., *History of U.S. Political Parties, 1910–1945*; John B. Wiseman, *The Dilemmas of a Party out of Power: The Democrats, 1904–1912* (New York: Garland, 1988); Kleppner, *Continuity and Change in Electoral Politics*.

the Northeast, putting them at a serious disadvantage in national elections. Fortunately for them, American politics in the "Gilded Age" was based as much on patronage as sectionalism. As long as Democratic leaders tailored their positions to benefit wealthy businessmen, they could compete successfully in parts of the Northeast, particularly in urban centers with strong party machines. Only one Democrat was elected president in the first four decades after the Civil War (Cleveland, twice), but the races were often quite close, and Democrats at times controlled the House of Representatives by large margins.

The Democrats' reliance on the Northeast is clearly evident in the election of 1884, which Cleveland won by a tally of 219–182 in the Electoral College (see figure 2.8). Had Cleveland not carried New York, he would have lost to James Blaine. Conversely, if Blaine had taken the entire Northeast, he would have won without the support of a single additional state, either southern or western. Since the Northeast had far more voters than the South, no Democrat could ever become president without winning some states in the Northeast. The Democratic Party was firmly grounded in the interests of southern farmers, but it also had to cater to the interests of northeastern

Figure 2.8. Electoral College Votes for Grover Cleveland, 1884

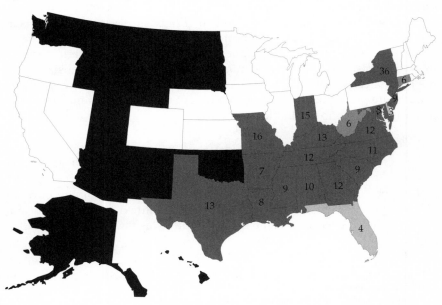

SOURCE: United States Bureau of the Census, *Historical Statistics*, 1075–76.
NOTE: Territories shaded black had not yet been incorporated as states.

[56]

businessmen. Thus, the socioeconomic coalition of Democratic presidents comprised both southern farmers and northeastern businesses.

Left out of this picture are western voters, who were mostly farmers. They were well represented in Congress, but, before 1897, they were unable to shake the eastern establishment's stranglehold over the major parties. They pushed for a platform of railroad regulation, antitrust laws, and conversion to a bimetallic monetary standard, but to no avail. Neither Democratic nor Republican presidential candidates were willing to make any significant concessions on these issues, because the most populous swing states—New York, New Jersey, Ohio, and Illinois—were also the most heavily industrialized. As James L. Sundquist writes,

> At the national level the domination of the Democratic party by men close to monopolies and the "money power" was even more pronounced. . . . Six of its [seven] candidates [between 1868 and 1892] came from New York, the citadel of the new capitalism, where the Democratic party had consistently vied with the Republican in demonstrating economic "soundness" to the bankers, industrialists, and political contributors of downtown Manhattan.[36]

Western farmers simply lacked the economic, electoral, and institutional power to affect policymaking at the national level. Both parties needed to maintain the support of businesses, so presidential candidates had a dominant electoral strategy of favoring the Northeast over the West.

The Depression of 1893–97 briefly pushed the Democratic Party off this equilibrium. Westerners were hit hard by the economic crisis. During this period, the wholesale price index for food fell by nearly 20 percent, and the real earnings of farm laborers declined by nearly 5 percent.[37] In response, western states demanded a shift to bimetallism, which would have caused inflation and therefore redistributed wealth from eastern bankers to western debtors. When it became clear that neither the Republicans nor the Democratic president, Grover Cleveland, would unilaterally abandon the gold standard, the West revolted against the political establishment. The most radical farmers defected to the Populist (People's) Party, while moderates worked to reform the major parties from within. Democrats were more successful in transforming their party than were Republicans. At the 1896 Democratic National Convention, reformers secured the nomination of William Jennings Bryan, a Nebraskan agrarian populist, as their candidate for

---

[36] Sundquist, *Dynamics of the Party System*, 131.

[37] United States Bureau of the Census, *Statistical Abstract of the United States* (Washington, D.C.: Government Printing Office, 1960), 117; Paul H. Douglas, *Real Wages in the United States, 1890–1926* (Boston: Houghton Mifflin, 1930), 187. See also Hoffman, *Depression of the Nineties*, 280.

president. Politics polarized around the gold question in 1896, and a true realignment of interests occurred.

The flow of desertion and recruitment between the parties was not equal, however: the Democrats lost in relative power as they gained in socioeconomic homogeneity. Businessmen and professionals, who regarded Bryan as a dangerous, rabble-rousing revolutionary, defected en masse to the Republican Party, taking with them the gilt that had helped Democrats to past victories in the Gilded Age. McKinley's campaign spent at least $3.5 million in the election of 1896; Bryan was able to raise only $650,000.[38] This shift in business loyalty greatly strengthened the Republican Party in the Northeast, allowing it to dominate the American political scene until the Great Depression.

The Democrats' coalitional status remained in flux for sixteen years after 1896. The "reorganizers," who represented the progold, northeastern wing of the party, fought mightily to regain control from the populists. It was a seesaw battle: Bryan won the presidential nomination in 1900, lost in 1904 to a reorganizer, then won again in 1908. The struggle finally came to an end in 1912, when the two sides settled on a compromise candidate, New Jersey governor Woodrow Wilson. Wilson's urban progressivism, which stressed tax reform and opposition to monopolies, met with the approval of both farmers and small businesses. After sixteen years of division and defeat, the Democrats reconciled themselves to the iron law of American electoral politics: no party could win national elections without appealing to northeastern interests. This was clearly evident in the election of 1916 (see figure 2.9), in which Wilson carried almost every western and southern state but still would have lost had he not taken either Ohio or Maryland and Vermont. In short, all of the upheaval of 1896–1912 had little long-term impact on the political economy of the Democratic Party. By 1912, it had become less conservative than in the Cleveland era, but it retained the same essential coalition: southern farmers and northeastern businesses.

In the Great Depression of the 1930s, the Democrats once again abandoned northeastern businessmen and professionals in favor of a new constituency. This time, their target was not western farmers but rather northeastern workers. In 1896, Bryan had failed to win the support of the industrial lower class; in 1932, Roosevelt succeeded. The result was a major realignment of the American party system. Critically, however, the sectoral basis of the Democratic coalition was not affected by the change. Both factory owners and factory workers had the same stake in export markets, so they should have held similar views over grand strategy.[39] Thus, the politi-

[38] Sundquist, *Dynamics of the Party System*, 156–57.
[39] An exception to this rule is rearmament policy. See Kevin Narizny, "Both Guns and Butter, or Neither: Class Interests in the Political Economy of Rearmament," *American Political Science Review* 97, no. 2 (May 2003): 203–20.

[58]

Figure 2.9. Electoral College Votes for Woodrow Wilson, 1916

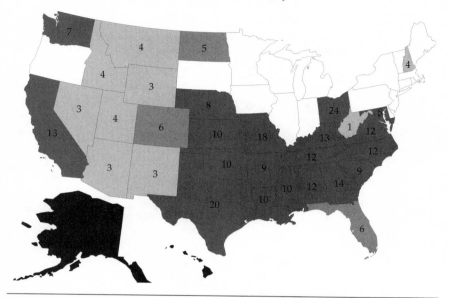

Source: United States Bureau of the Census, *Historical Statistics*, 1075–76.
Note: Territories shaded black had not yet been incorporated as states.

cal economy of the Democratic Party remained divided between southern agriculture and northeastern manufacturing throughout 1865–1941. Since I discussed the optimal strategy of northeastern manufacturers in the previous section, I cover only southern farmers below.

Southern Farmers

The economic interests of southerners are easy to analyze because the region was heavily dependent on the production of just two commodities, cotton and tobacco. There was an enormous market for both of these products in Europe. In 1905–14, approximately two-thirds of the entire American cotton crop was exported (see figure 2.10), and in every one of those years more than 93 percent of cotton exports were sent to Europe (see figure 2.11).[40] After World War I, both these indicators fell somewhat, but not by nearly enough to alter cotton farmers' fundamental dependence on

[40] United States Bureau of the Census, *Statistical Abstract of the United States, 1954*, 302, 546–47; John A. Todd, *The World's Cotton Crops* (London: Black, 1915), 416–17; United States Bureau of the Census, *Statistical Abstract of the United States* (Washington, D.C.: Government Printing Office, 1924), 650; United States Bureau of the Census, *Statistical Abstract of the United States* (Washington, D.C.: Government Printing Office, 1930), 716.

Figure 2.10. U.S. Agricultural Exports, as Share of Domestic Production

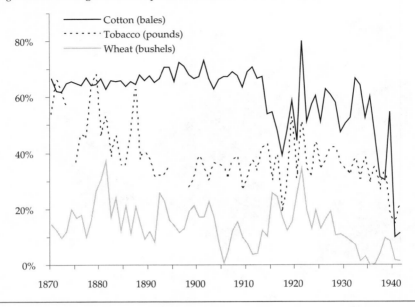

SOURCE: United States Bureau of the Census, *Statistical Abstract*.

the great powers. From the late 1920s through the mid 1930s, the portion of the crop that was exported was 50–60 percent, and Europe's share of those exports was 60–80 percent. Tobacco followed a similar pattern: approximately one-third of the crop was exported, and, in most years, 60–80 percent of unmanufactured tobacco exports were sent to only six European markets (the United Kingdom, Germany, France, Italy, Belgium, and the Netherlands).[41] In short, southern farmers had strong core interests.

Conversely, southerners had weak peripheral interests. First, the share of their exports that was sent to peripheral markets, particularly for cotton, was low, so its contribution to their income was negligible. Second, the prices of agricultural commodities, even those that were exported in quantity to peripheral markets, were set in Europe.[42] Profits on raw cotton and tobacco were a function of global supply, not the entrepreneurial efforts of

[41] United States Bureau of the Census, *Statistical Abstract of the United States, 1954*, 302–3, 546–47; United States Department of Agriculture, *Yearbook of the United States Department of Agriculture* (Washington, D.C.: Government Printing Office, various years).

[42] Wright, *Economic History*, 615, 620–24; Jules Backman and M. R. Gainsbrugh, *Economics of the Cotton Textile Industry* (New York: National Industrial Conference Board, 1946), 102; McCormick, *China Market*, 49. See also Pletcher, *Diplomacy of Trade and Investment*, 15–16.

Figure 2.11. U.S. Agricultural Exports, as Share Sent to Europe

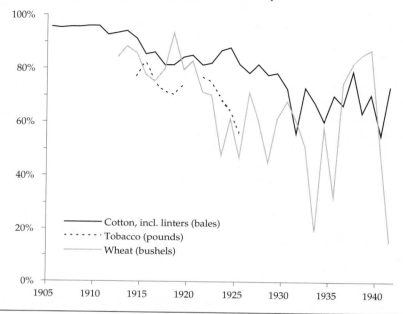

SOURCES: Cotton in 1905–14 from John A. Todd, *The World's Cotton Crops* (London: Black, 1915), 416–17; all other figures from United States Bureau of the Census, *Statistical Abstract of the United States* (Washington, D.C.: Government Printing Office, various years); United States Department of Agriculture, *Yearbook of Agriculture* (Washington, D.C.: Government Printing Office, various years).
NOTE: Tobacco exports to Europe include only Belgium, Netherlands, Italy, France, Germany, and the United Kingdom.

individual producers. Traders would benefit from finding new markets for these goods, but rural farmers would not. Thus, most Southerners had little to gain from the periphery.

Strategic Interests: Core

As explained in chapter 1, the hypothesized strategy of core interests is internationalism, which promotes adherence to international law and seeks to institutionalize mechanisms for peaceful dispute resolution. For core interests in the United States in 1865–1941, the main target of this strategy should have been Great Britain. It was by far the South's largest export market, its navy controlled the all-important North Atlantic trade route, and it was the only power that had territorial disputes with the United States. If core interests were to try to co-opt any great power into internationalist agreements, they should have started with Britain. Their attentions should

[61]

not, however, have been limited to Britain; other goals should have included the advancement of norm-based cooperation, the creation of multilateral organizations, and the defense of international order.

In the first three decades following the end of the Civil War, no American president undertook any costly internationalist initiatives, so systematic evidence of support for the strategy is lacking. The first opportunity for a national debate came with the Olney-Pauncefote Treaty of 1897, in which the United States and Great Britain agreed to binding arbitration for their bilateral disputes. This observation is problematic, however, for reasons unique to the mid 1890s. At the time, American farmers were hit hard by deflation, debt, and depression, and they blamed their leaders' adherence to Britain's gold standard for their woes. Thus, they became unusually sensitive to a measure designed to bring them closer to the hated British "money barons." Only 19 percent of southern and midwestern Senators supported the unamended treaty, whereas 28 percent of northeastern Senators did.[43]

In most other situations, southerners were overwhelmingly internationalist. They supported the creation of the League of Nations, and the vast majority of senators who voted to ratify its covenant without reservations were from the South. Throughout the interwar period, in fact, southern Democrats were more likely to vote for the semi-internationalist proposals of Republican presidents than were their Republicans colleagues in the Senate.[44] In general, the point that southerners strongly favored internationalist policies is well established in the historical literature.[45] Southern senators' voting record in 1897 contradicts the theory, but it does not outweigh the considerable evidence in favor of the hypothesis that southerners were consistently more interested in a cooperative grand strategy than northeasterners.

[43] Nelson M. Blake, "The Olney-Pauncefote Treaty of 1897," *American Historical Review* 50, no. 2 (January 1945): 242. Other short-term considerations had an adverse effect on southern senators' support for arbitration in 1911; see E. James Hindman, "The General Arbitration Treaties of William Howard Taft," *Historian* 36, no. 1 (November 1973): 64; Robert Fischer, "Henry Cabot Lodge and the Taft Arbitration Treaties," *South Atlantic Quarterly* 78, no. 2 (spring 1979): 244–58.
[44] George L. Grassmuck, "Sectional Biases in Congress on Foreign Policy," *Johns Hopkins University Studies in Historical and Political Science* 68, no. 3 (1951): 73, 82.
[45] George B. Tindall, *The Emergence of the New South, 1913–1945* (Baton Rouge: Louisiana State University Press, 1967), 33–69; Trubowitz, *Defining the National Interest*, 126; Paul Seabury, *The Waning of Southern "Internationalism"* (Princeton: Center for International Studies, 1957), 4; Grassmuck, "Sectional Biases in Congress," 73, 82. Alexander DeConde argues that southern senators' support for the league was motivated by their partisan affiliation with Wilson, not a preference for internationalism; however, he bases this claim on scant evidence. See Alexander DeConde, "The South and Isolationism," *Journal of Southern History* 24, no. 3 (August 1958): 332–46. George C. Herring and Gary R. Hess assert that southerners did not consistently support an active foreign policy, but they make no distinction between

Strategic Interests: Periphery

Unlike northeastern manufacturers, southern farmers should have whole-heartedly opposed interventionism.[46] It would have required increased taxation, but it would not have provided any offsetting benefits for their exports to the core. Indeed, expanded trade with the periphery threatened to increase imports of subtropical agricultural goods, like tobacco and sugar, that southern farmers produced themselves. Finally, the use of coercive force in the periphery would lead to diplomatic tension with the same European countries that were purchasing southerners' exports. For all of these reasons, southern farmers' ideal strategy toward the periphery was noninvolvement—that is, isolationism.

Ample evidence exists that southerners were reluctant to pursue an active grand strategy in the periphery. Throughout 1865–1941, the South was far less likely than the Northeast to support treaties extending American influence in the periphery, including an 1884 agreement to give the United States exclusive rights to build a canal in Nicaragua (in contravention of the Anglo-American Clayton-Bulwer Treaty of 1850), the annexation of Hawaii, the annexation of the Philippines, the establishment of a de facto protectorate over Cuba via the Platt Amendment, and intervention in the Dominican Republic via the Roosevelt Corollary to the Monroe Doctrine.[47] In short, southerners' support for diplomatic engagement with the great powers did not also translate into support for an active peripheral strategy.

Hypotheses

The Democratic Party had a diverse set of interests to aggregate: first, core interests (i.e., southern farmers), who should have been internationalist; second, domestic interests (i.e., most northeastern businesses), who should have been isolationist; and third, after 1880, a growing number of peripheral interests (i.e., some northeastern businesses), who should have been

---

interventionist and internationalist policies. For example, they note that southerners supported the League of Nations and World Court, both of which were designed to promote international norms, but rejected the Four-Power Treaty of 1922, which was essentially a sphere-of-influence arrangement. See George C. Herring and Gary R. Hess, "Regionalism and Foreign Policy: The Dying Myth of Southern Internationalism," *Southern Studies* 20, no. 3 (fall 1981): 247–77. On the internationalist basis of southerners' opposition to the Four-Power Treaty, see Thomas N. Guinsburg, "Victory in Defeat: The Senatorial Isolationists and the Four-Power Treaty," *Capital Studies* 2 (spring 1973): 32–33.

[46] Trubowitz, *Defining the National Interest*, 68–75.

[47] Edward W. Chester, *Sectionalism, Politics, and American Diplomacy* (Metuchen, N.J.: Scarecrow, 1975), 110–11, 128, 133, 146, 158–59; Edwina C. Smith, "Southerners on Empire: Southern Senators and Imperialism, 1898–99," *Mississippi Quarterly* 31 (winter 1977–78): 89–107; Trubowitz, *Defining the National Interest*, 68–75; Joseph A. Fry, *Dixie Looks Abroad: The South and U.S. Foreign Relations, 1789–1973* (Baton Rouge: Louisiana State University Press,

interventionist. To try to please all elements of their coalition, the Democrats should have adopted a two-track grand strategy. In their relations with the great powers, they should have been consistently international-ist, though only modestly so before 1917. Until then, the United States had only marginal influence over European affairs, so it could have done little to make the international system more cooperative, peaceful, and law-bound. However, Democratic presidents certainly could have promoted the use of binding arbitration, conciliation, and other internationalist instruments on a limited bilateral basis.

Meanwhile, the Democrats' stance toward the periphery initially should have been isolationist, then increasingly interventionist after 1880. In that sense, changes in their position should have mirrored changes in the Republicans' grand strategy, because both parties needed to seek the support of the same group, northeastern businessmen. However, there should have been one important difference in their approach. Republicans counted on northeastern businesses as their primary constituency, so their strategy should have directly represented the interests of this group. Democrats, on the other hand, relied on northeastern businesses only as a secondary constituency. The party was above all responsive to the interests of southern farmers, who were generally opposed to interventionism. Thus, Democrats' support for interventionism in the 1880s and beyond should have lagged behind that of Republicans.

AN ASIDE: MIDWESTERN FARMERS

Though midwestern farmers were not the core constituency of either major party, the relationship between their economic interests and strategic preferences merits attention.[48] Not only does it present an additional test of the logic of the theory, but it also addresses a long-standing point of confusion in the historical literature. Like southern farmers, midwesterners produced far more than could be consumed domestically

---

2002), 109, 112–19, 128–31, 136–37. The South was not monolithically anti-expansionist; its nascent textile and steel industries had an interest in interventionism that was similar to that of northeastern manufacturing. See Tennant S. McWilliams, "The Lure of Empire: Southern Interest in the Caribbean, 1877–1900," *Mississippi Quarterly* 29 (winter 1975–76): 43–63; O. Lawrence Burnette, "John Tyler Morgan and Expansionist Sentiment in the New South," *Alabama Review* 18 (July 1965): 163–82; Patrick J. Hearden, *Independence and Empire: The New South's Cotton Mill Campaign, 1865–1901* (DeKalb: Northern Illinois University Press, 1982), chap. 4; Fry, *Dixie Looks Abroad*, 109–12, 131–35.

[48] I define the Midwest as a subset of the West, inclusive of the ten states of the Missouri River basin: Missouri, Iowa, Minnesota, Kansas, Nebraska, South Dakota, North Dakota, Colorado, Wyoming, and Montana.

and were particularly dependent on European markets. For example, 10–20 percent of unmilled wheat was exported in most years before 1929 (see figure 2.10), and more than 80 percent of those exports were sent to Europe (see figure 2.11).[49] If the crop surplus could not be sold abroad, it would have to be dumped on the American market, causing domestic prices to plummet.[50]

In contrast, farmers' economic interest in peripheral trade remained low. It increased gradually over time, but in 1914, the proportion of foodstuff exports sent to Europe was still approximately 70 percent (see figure 2.5). For the most important midwestern agricultural sector, unmilled wheat, the share of exports purchased by Europeans in 1914 was even higher, 86 percent. In the three largest categories of exported animal products—lard, bacon, and ham—between 70 and 90 percent of all foreign purchases in 1914–29 went to Europe.[51] Furthermore, the price of farm goods was set in European commodity markets, not in the periphery. Thus, agricultural exports to the periphery would benefit primarily traders, not farmers themselves.

In the mid to late 1920s, American foodstuff exports, both crude and manufactured, began to decline rapidly. Their combined value averaged $884 million (18–21 percent of total exports) in 1923–27, $534 million (14–16 percent of total exports) in 1928–32, and $226 million (8–12 percent of total exports) in 1933–37. Wheat farmers were hit particularly hard. Their market bottomed out in 1935, when exports of unmilled wheat and wheat flour fell to 3 percent of total production, compared to more than 30 percent for much of the 1920s.[52] By the early 1930s, the Midwest's connection to core markets had been almost completely severed.

Given these facts, the theory renders a clear prediction about the strategic preferences of midwestern farmers. Until at least the mid 1920s, their dependence on European markets should have made them strongly internationalist, just like southern farmers. Not until the foodstuff export market collapsed and they were no longer economically linked to Europe should they have become truly isolationist. These predictions clearly contradict the conventional wisdom that midwesterners were isolationist throughout the entire interwar period, so they present a critical test for the theory.

---

[49] This statistic significantly understates wheat farmers' sensitivity to foreign demand because it does not take flour exports into account. See United States Bureau of the Census, *Statistical Abstract of the United States, 1954*, 297, 546–47; United States Department of Agriculture, *Yearbook*.

[50] Pletcher, *Diplomacy of Trade and Investment*, 15; Morton Rothstein, "America in the International Rivalry for the British Wheat Market, 1860–1901," *Mississippi Valley Historical Review* 47, no. 3 (December 1960): 410–18.

[51] United States Department of Agriculture, *Yearbook*.

[52] United States Bureau of the Census, *Historical Statistics*, 511, 889, 898.

That the agrarian Midwest was isolationist in the 1930s has been established conclusively in numerous studies.[53] Less well known is the fact that the most prominent representatives of farmers' interests in the first three decades of the twentieth century were among the most ardent supporters of internationalism.[54] Nebraskan William Jennings Bryan, the leader of the agrarian revolt in the Democratic Party, strongly favored an active foreign policy based on the promotion of international law. Even though he protested Woodrow Wilson's entry into World War I, he advocated that the Senate ratify the League of Nations Covenant without amendments.[55] Of the three Senators from the agrarian Midwest who irreconcilably opposed the Versailles Treaty, two of them—North Dakotan Asle J. Gronna and Nebraskan George W. Norris—advocated key internationalist policies such as the abolition of secret diplomacy, the promotion of interdependence, and the establishment of an international court of arbitration.[56] These "peace progressives" were by no means isolationist; rather, they were more stridently devoted to internationalist principles than Wilson himself. According to Ralph Stone, they "protested most loudly against the Treaty's violations of the Fourteen Points. . . . The League, they thought, would be controlled by the great powers who wanted to freeze the status quo and preserve the spoils of war."[57]

In most instances in which historians make well-supported claims about midwestern isolationism, their evidence does not conflict with my predictions. There are two reasons for this. First, many of them focus on the 1930s and later years, when farmers' exports—and therefore their expected interest in an active grand strategy—plummeted to a fraction of prior levels.[58] The theory is confirmed, not contradicted, by studies of midwestern isolationism in the 1930s. Second, authors who discuss isolationism in earlier

[53] Ralph H. Smuckler, "The Region of Isolationism," *American Political Science Review* 47, no. 2 (June 1953): 386–401; Leroy N. Rieselbach, "The Basis of Isolationist Behavior," *Public Opinion Quarterly* 24, no. 4 (winter 1960): 645–57; Trubowitz, *Defining the National Interest*, 145–64.

[54] Kendrick A. Clements, *William Jennings Bryan: Missionary Isolationist* (Knoxville: University of Tennessee Press, 1982), 136; Ralph Stone, *The Irreconcilables: The Fight against the League of Nations* (New York: Norton, 1970), 6–10, 41, 179–80; John M. Cooper, *The Vanity of Power: American Isolationism and the First World War, 1914–1917* (Westport, Conn.: Greenwood, 1969), 104, 151, 184–85, 198; Fred Greenbaum, "The Foreign Policy of Progressive Irreconcilables," in *Toward a New View of America: Essays in Honor of Arthur C. Cole*, ed. Hans L. Trefousse (New York: Franklin, 1977), 209–30.

[55] Clements, *William Jennings Bryan*, 136.

[56] The third was James A. Reed of Missouri. Under a broader definition of the Midwest, three other senators would be included. One of these, Robert M. La Follette of Wisconsin, was an internationalist in the mold of Asle and Gronna. Two other irreconcilables, from industrial Illinois, aligned with their anti-internationalist colleagues from the Northeast.

[57] Stone, *Irreconcilables*, 179.

[58] For example, see Smuckler, "Region of Isolationism"; Rieselbach, "Basis of Isolationist Behavior."

years typically define the term as opposition to defense spending and military alliances. As a result, they misleadingly group together individuals who favored an antimilitaristic strategy of institutionalized, norm-based cooperation with those who rejected the making of any sort of international commitments at all.[59]

The few historians who do make a distinction between isolationism and uncompromising internationalism draw the same conclusions that I have about midwestern farmers. For example, Warren F. Kuehl contrasts isolationists with internationalist "polity thinkers," who "seek to advance their goal of amity through the building of institutions, primarily political and legal."[60] He surveys the editorials of thirty midwestern newspapers between 1918 and 1935, finding that "far more than a majority [of editors] could be described as polity thinkers willing to commit their government to international political and legal institutions."[61] The implications of this research are striking:

> Legends and myths die slowly, but it seems time at last to put to rest some of the hoary stereotypes regarding Middle West isolationism in the interwar years. If that mood ever dominated, it did so in the middle to late 1930s, certainly not before. More significantly, this region, if editorial views are representative of thought, endorsed internationalist policies more regularly than the opposite pole. Perhaps it is time to start talking about the internationalist Middle West.[62]

Kuehl does not inquire as to why midwesterners, like southerners, should have been more internationalist than northeasterners, but the political economy perspective provides a clear-cut answer. Lacking a common ethnicity, culture, or sectarian denomination, the only factor that both tied southerners and midwesterners together and distinguished them from northeasterners was their dependence on exports to Europe.

---

[59] For example, see Selig Adler, *The Isolationist Impulse: Its Twentieth-Century Reaction* (New York: Abelard-Schuman, 1957), 28–29, 43–45; Cooper, *Vanity of Power*, 2, 184–85, 198. On the problem of concept stretching in the term *isolationism*, see Albert K. Weinberg, "The Historical Meaning of the American Doctrine of Isolation," *American Political Science Review* 34, no. 3 (June 1940): 539–47; Harvey Starr, "Alliances: Tradition and Change in American Views of Foreign Military Entanglements," in *American Thinking about Peace and War: New Essays on American Thought and Attitudes*, ed. Ken Booth and Moorhead Wright (New York: Barnes and Noble, 1978), 44–48.

[60] Warren F. Kuehl, "Midwestern Newspapers and Isolationist Sentiment," *Diplomatic History* 3, no. 3 (summer 1979): 286. See also William G. Carleton, "Isolationism and the Middle West," *Mississippi Valley Historical Review* 33, no. 3 (December 1946): 381–82; Grassmuck, "Sectional Biases in Congress," 82, 162.

[61] Kuehl, "Midwestern Newspapers," 302.

[62] Ibid., 306.

CONCLUSION

The political economy of the United States in 1865–1941 was riven by a major sectoral cleavage between northeastern manufacturers and southern farmers (see table 2.2). In the first few decades following the Civil War, manufacturers had little stake in the international economy. They already had profitable opportunities for expansion within the United States due to the reconstruction of the South, the development of the frontier West, and a population boom. They did not take an interest in foreign markets until the 1880s and 1890s, when all of these trends began to decelerate and domestic profits declined. Europe, which had high tariffs and well-established competition, held little promise for them. In contrast, Latin America and East Asia offered great opportunity for expansion. By the turn of the century, American manufacturing exports and investment in the periphery were growing rapidly. Hence, the party that represented the manufacturing sector, the Republicans, should have adopted a grand strategy that gradually transitioned from isolationism to interventionism in the 1880s and 1890s.

On the other side of the political-economic divide were southern farmers, who were highly dependent on export to European markets but had almost no stake in the periphery. They should have opposed efforts to involve the United States in Latin America and East Asia, especially when doing so would be costly, create conflict with other great powers, or open the home market to imports of competing subtropical agricultural goods. In response, the party that represented southern farmers, the Democrats, should have been reluctant to take aggressive action in the periphery. However, Democrats needed the support of some northeastern manufacturing states to win the presidency, so they could not have ignored peripheral interests entirely. Instead, they should have adopted a modest, less adventurous compromise between isolationism and whatever level of interventionism Republicans were pursuing at the time.

The two parties should have divided more sharply over grand strategy toward the great powers. Until the 1880s and 1890s, northeastern manufacturers had little interest in the international economy, so the Republican Party should have avoided any engagement in European affairs. Not until the end of the century did their growing ambitions in the periphery begin to bring them into conflict with other great powers. At that point, they should have adopted a strategy of realpolitik to ensure that American trade and investment in Latin America and East Asia would not suffer from the imperial depredations of other great powers. They had no interest in international law or collective security; an internationalist strategy would only hamper the ability of the United States to extend its power and assert its diplomatic prerogatives.

[68]

Table 2.2. U.S. Predicted Strategic Interests (Absent Constraints)

Republicans

Northeastern manufacturing and dependent sectors	Domestic interests → isolationism declining c. 1880–1914	1865–c. 1880: isolationism
	Peripheral interests → interventionism + realpolitik none 1865–c. 1880, increasing c. 1880–1914	c. 1880–1914: increasing interventionism + increasing realpolitik 1914–1941: interventionism + realpolitik

Democrats

Southern farmers (primary)	Core interests → internationalism	1865–c. 1880: isolationism + internationalism
Northeastern manufacturing and dependent sectors (secondary)	Domestic interests → isolationism declining c. 1880–1914	c. 1880–1914: increasing interventionism (less than Republicans) + internationalism
	Peripheral interests → interventionism + realpolitik none 1865–c. 1880, increasing c. 1880–1914	1914–1941: interventionism (less than Republicans) + internationalism

Southern farmers, in contrast, were enormously dependent on European markets, particularly Britain. To protect this vital interest, Democratic leaders should have pursued an internationalist strategy toward the great powers. Before 1917, they would have been highly constrained by the adverse international environment and the United States' lack of influence over European politics, but they nevertheless should have been able to propose bilateral initiatives for the peaceful resolution of international disputes. After World War I, when the United States played a larger role in international diplomacy, they should have taken advantage of the opportunity to press even further. In short, there should have been clear differences in how the two parties engaged with both the periphery and the great powers, proving the point that American grand strategy was governed not by objective "national interests" but rather by the parochial interests of its ruling coalitions.

Before testing these hypotheses, it is worth asking to what extent Democratic and Republican executives were actually capable of conducting grand strategy on their coalition members' behalf. Compared to the leaders of other great powers, American presidents' ability to engage in diplomatic maneuvering was quite constrained.[63] Under the U.S. Constitution, the ratification of treaties required the "advice and consent" of two-thirds of the Senate, and the approval process was by no means a rubber stamp. Even when treaties were approved by the Senate, their implementation was not assured because the House of Representatives could refuse to fund any attendant expenses. American presidents also lacked military instruments on par with the other great powers. In 1880, the United States had fewer than half the military personnel of the next-closest state, Japan, and less than one-tenth that of the British armed forces.[64] Simply put, the United States was ill-equipped to fight any wars other than for defense or minor peripheral interventions.

In the next chapter, I discuss a theory, state-centered realism, that seeks to explain outcomes in American foreign policy as a function of these constraints. I find serious flaws in this view, but in some ways the issue is moot: the dependent variable of this study, grand strategy, does not refer to outcomes per se but rather the general principles by which the executive pursues its goals in the international system. In other words, I seek to explain presidential initiatives. In so doing, I disregard a question that state-centered realism treats as critical: whether or not the executive's strategy is carried past domestic institutional obstacles to fruition.

For the purposes of this study, institutional constraints on the executive could be relevant in two ways. First, the individuals who had the most control over the day-to-day details of foreign policy were not presidents but rather their secretaries of state, who had considerable freedom of action in the nineteenth century. On rare occasions, secretaries of state were able to use their institutional power (i.e., the threat of resignation and control over the flow of information) to influence their presidents' decision-making calculus. In the following chapters, I make note of such instances whenever they occurred. However, agency problems were the exception rather than the norm. Cabinet officers are appointed by presidents, and can be fired by them, so a harmony of purpose generally obtains. Even when a secretary of state has a more coherently elucidated conception of grand strategy than his president, or when a secretary of state is able to persuade a president of

---

[63] Stephen Cooney, "Political Demand Channels in the Processes of American and British Imperial Expansion, 1870–1913," *World Politics* 27, no. 2 (January 1975): 236–39; Fareed Zakaria, *From Wealth to Power: The Unusual Origins of America's World Role* (Princeton: Princeton University Press, 1998); W. Stull Holt, *Treaties Defeated by the Senate* (Baltimore: Johns Hopkins Press, 1933), chaps. 6–7.

[64] Paul Kennedy, *The Rise and Fall of the Great Powers: Economic Change and Military Conflict from 1500 to 2000* (New York: Random House, 1987), 203.

the value of a particular policy, ultimate decision-making responsibility still lies with the president.

Another concern is that presidents could have been dissuaded from adopting aggressive policies because they anticipated congressional obstructionism. From this perspective, the United States was condemned to isolationism until the institutional powers of the executive were expanded in the late nineteenth century. I argue, in contrast, that a dominant Congress did not force the president into strategic inaction; rather, societal interests constrained both the president and Congress. I develop this argument in greater detail in the next chapter. For now, I assume that institutional factors did not place any systematic constraints on the conduct of grand strategy that would dictate a revision of the predictions in table 2.2.

[3]

American Grand Strategy
toward the Periphery

American grand strategy toward the periphery changed course dramatically several times in 1865–1941. At first, it was weakly imperialist. In the late 1860s and early 1870s, the United States attempted to annex such diverse territories as Iceland, Greenland, Alaska, Hawaii, Cuba, and the Dominican Republic; however, it was unwilling to use aggressive means to obtain them. Instead, it tried to build an empire through purchases and voluntary accession. With the exception of Alaska, all of its efforts failed or were defeated by internal opposition, and it soon gave up the game. The navy, relegated to the role of coastal defense, was allowed to rot, while the army, used only for suppressing Native Americans, was beset with cronyism.

Not until the late 1880s, after more than a decade of isolationism, did the United States reassert itself in the periphery. It took an active interest in Hawaiian politics, intervened with increasing regularity in Latin America, maneuvered for control over a prospective isthmian canal, and forcefully revived the long-neglected Monroe Doctrine. The climactic moment of this "outward thrust" was the Spanish-American War of 1898, in which the United States seized colonies in the Philippines, Guam, and Puerto Rico. Then, having established itself as a major player in East Asia, it sought to pressure the other great powers to maintain an "open door" to trade in China. It did not continue to acquire territory, but it did remain highly engaged in the defense of its newfound political influence and economic interests.

After World War I, the United States began to draw back from its involvement in the periphery. It held firmly to the Monroe Doctrine, but it intervened less frequently in Central America and withdrew some of its forces there. In 1933, it finally renounced its "right" to interfere in the domestic politics of Latin American countries. Even in the face of serious violations of U.S. citizens' property rights, it chose to resolve disputes through peaceful negotiation rather than intervention. By 1941, its power in the periphery had declined considerably from its peak prior to World War I.

This brief overview of American grand strategy in the periphery makes little sense under standard realist assumptions. If, as offensive realists assert, states expand their influence whenever capable of doing so, the United States should have acted much more aggressively than it did. In 1865, the American economy was large enough that it could have sustained an imperialist grand strategy, and the Union's enormous military could easily have been used to obtain territorial concessions in Canada and Mexico. The United States might have been only a borderline great power, but it was sufficiently autarchic and geographically isolated that it could have fought even Britain without fear of military disaster. After all, the power differential between the two countries had been narrowing rapidly since the War of 1812, which had been initiated by the United States.

Only when the United States went to war with Spain, more than thirty years after the end of the Civil War, did it come anywhere near to taking full advantage of its vast domestic resources. However, even that case presents some serious anomalies. President McKinley tried long and hard to avoid war, and once it was won, he refused to annex the Spanish colony over which it was fought, Cuba. Even more surprisingly, subsequent presidents made no further attempt at territorial expansion. They intervened frequently in Latin America but did not establish permanent structures of authority there. After World War I, the relative power of the United States was greater than ever before, yet the country chose at that time to withdraw its deployments in Central America. If states expand their international power in proportion to their domestic capacity, then the United States should have built a global empire in the interwar period, not retreated to its borders.

To resuscitate the offensive realist interpretation of American grand strategy, Fareed Zakaria argues that domestic institutions severely constrained executive power after the Civil War.[1] Even though the *nation* was growing in power, the governing apparatus of the *state* was not able to marshal enough resources from society to conduct an effective foreign policy. From 1865 to 1889, Congress repeatedly blocked diplomatic treaties, cut military appropriations, and denied funding for territorial purchases. Not until successive presidents established greater authority over the legislature could the United States expand its power in the international system in proportion to its economic might. This change came gradually over 1877–96: the civil service, foreign service, and military were professionalized and

---

[1] Fareed Zakaria, *From Wealth to Power: The Unusual Origins of America's World Role* (Princeton: Princeton University Press, 1998).

strengthened; Grover Cleveland asserted the "emergency" power of the president to break strikes without the consent of local authorities; Rutherford B. Hayes set a precedent for the aggressive use of the veto; congressional influence over executive appointments and dismissals was weakened; and patronage was eliminated. By the 1890s, the executive had finally become sufficiently powerful vis-à-vis the legislative branch that it could carry out an expansionist grand strategy.

Though Zakaria's "state-centered" realism seems tailor-made to explain American foreign policy in the late nineteenth century, its interpretation of the case is nevertheless problematic. In particular, the causal link between "the transformation of state structure" and declining congressional opposition to expansionism is weak. The two most important constraints on the executive's conduct of foreign policy, the ratification of treaties in the Senate and the "power of the purse" in both houses of Congress, have remained intact since the founding of the Republic. The institutional developments cited by Zakaria, while important, hardly suffice to explain why legislators decided not to exercise their formal authority against the expansionist initiatives of the 1890s. Were they intimidated by the fearsome new powers of the executive branch, coerced into compliance by presidents' threats to withhold domestic goods from them? Zakaria does not say. In response, Sean Lynn-Jones points to a clear alternative: "If congressional opposition to plans for expansion reflected political and policy disagreement more than state structure, then Zakaria's attempt to explain U.S. policy as a consequence of state strength or weakness becomes less persuasive."[2] Perhaps, then, a change in domestic preferences, not the loosening of institutional constraints, accounts for the outstretch of American power in the 1890s.

State-centered realism encounters even greater interpretive difficulties in other time periods. It cannot account for the vast territorial expansion of the United States in the early nineteenth century, nor can it explain why the country should not have pursued an aggressively expansionist strategy in the interwar period, after the institutional shackles on executive power had already been lifted.[3] Once state-centered realists conclude that the state developed sufficient competence vis-à-vis the nation to pursue its preferred policies, the theory becomes indistinguishable from offensive realism and hence suffers from all of its interpretive defects.

Defensive realism, which asserts that states normally expand only in response to foreign threats, provides a more reasonable interpretation of events. The United States faced few threats after the Civil War, so naturally it tended toward isolationism. By this logic, its shift to interventionism in

---

[2] Sean M. Lynn-Jones, "Realism and America's Rise: A Review Essay," *International Security* 23, no. 2 (fall 1998): 179.

[3] David C. Hendrickson, "Review," *Foreign Affairs* 77, no. 4 (July/August 1998): 120.

the 1890s must have been a response to international pressures—specifically, heightened competition for colonies among the European great powers. After World War I, the threat vanished, so the United States once again adopted a relatively passive grand strategy.

Though perfunctorily plausible, this account has several flaws. First, the timing is off. The United States did not take decisive action to expand until 1898, by which time Europeans had already claimed most of Africa and Asia. If Americans had felt threatened by the New Imperialism of the late nineteenth century, they should have begun to build an empire in the mid 1880s, not the late 1890s. Second, the country's greatest act of expansion, the annexation of the Philippines, could not have been motivated by security concerns. The United States did not need the Philippines to protect Hawaii, much less its western coastline or the Panama Canal. Third, defensive realism cannot explain why the United States should have been imperialist in the late 1860s and early 1870s but not in the late 1870s and early 1880s, since it faced no more of a threat in the former period than the latter.

Finally, neither offensive nor defensive realism is capable of explaining partisanship. The expansion of American influence in the periphery was not governed by a clear-cut "national interest"; instead, it proceeded in fitful starts and stops corresponding to shifts in party control over the presidency. In the 1880s and 1890s, Republicans led the movement to extend American power and influence with the annexation of Hawaii, the acquisition of far-flung naval bases, and the construction of a battleship navy. Democrats, in contrast, were reluctant to abandon isolationism. Whenever a Democrat replaced a Republican in office, the new president would retreat from parts of his predecessor's expansionist program. For example, in 1893, Grover Cleveland withdrew Benjamin Harrison's treaty to annex Hawaii, and in 1913, Woodrow Wilson ended William Taft's support for investors' consortia in China. Democratic presidents did pursue an interventionist strategy, but at a substantially lesser degree of aggressiveness than their Republican counterparts.

IDEAS AND CULTURE

In contrast to the realist arguments outlined above, several scholars have proposed that culture and ideas, not power, account for the shift after the Civil War from isolationism to interventionism. Frederick Merk argues that expansionist ideologies, popularized as "Manifest Destiny" in the early nineteenth century and "Insular Imperialism" in the late nineteenth century, were "traps" that temporarily perverted the country's democratic idealism. Julius Pratt, in turn, focuses on the introduction of social Darwinist ideas into the foreign policy discourse, while Ernest May asserts that political elites in the United States based their strategic views on ideas they encountered in their travels to Europe.[4]

Each of these theories raises more questions than it answers. Merk clearly demonstrates that expansionist ideologies have waxed and waned at different points in American history, but he fails to explain why. May claims to resolve this lacuna, but his account of the diffusion of ideas from Europe to the United States has a serious timing problem. In the face of a long lag between the revival of popular imperialism in Britain, which dates to Benjamin Disraeli's Crystal Palace speech of 1872, and the flowering of American expansionism more than two decades later, May resorts to hand waving: "By 1898, when Hawaiian annexation came up again and the Philippine issue presented itself, much more had been heard and seen across the Atlantic."[5] Finally, Pratt's discussion of social Darwinism is badly one-sided. Theories of racial hierarchy did become increasingly popular toward the end of the century, but they were used as much to oppose expansionism as to support it. Some argued that it was needed to bestow the benefits of civilization on lesser races; others asserted that dark-skinned natives were unfit for democratic rule.[6]

Another ideational perspective focuses specifically on the Spanish-American War of 1898, the single most important episode in American grand strategy toward the periphery. Richard Hofstadter characterizes public support for the war as a displaced emotional reaction to the "civic frustrations" of immigration, industrialization, depression, and class conflict.[7] The nation was experiencing a "psychic crisis," so it lashed out at the easiest target outside its borders. This account has two serious problems. First, it is weak on the timing of the crisis. In the spring of 1898, the American economy had already begun to recover from the Depression of 1893–97, and, in a reversal

---

[4] Frederick Merk, *Manifest Destiny and Mission in American History: A Reinterpretation* (New York: Knopf, 1963), chaps. 11–12; Julius W. Pratt, *The Expansionists of 1898: The Acquisition of Hawaii and the Spanish Islands* (Chicago: Quadrangle, 1964), 3–22; Ernest R. May, *American Imperialism: A Speculative Essay* (New York: Atheneum, 1968).

[5] May, *American Imperialism*, 176.

[6] Christopher Lasch, "The Anti-Imperialists, the Philippines, and the Inequality of Man," *Journal of Southern History* 24, no. 3 (August 1958): 319–31; Eric T. L. Love, *Race over Empire: Racism and U.S. Imperialism* (Chapel Hill: University of North Carolina Press, 2004).

[7] Richard Hofstadter, *The Paranoid Style in American Politics and Other Essays* (New York: Knopf, 1965), chap. 5. See also Frank A. Ninkovich, *The United States and Imperialism* (Malden, Mass.: Blackwell, 2001), chap. 1; Edward Rhodes, "Constructing Power: Cultural Transformation and Strategic Adjustment in the 1890s," in *The Politics of Strategic Adjustment: Ideas, Institutions, and Interests*, ed. Peter Trubowitz, Emily O. Goldman, and Edward Rhodes (New York: Columbia University Press, 1999), 29–78; Kevin Narizny, "The New Debate: International Relations Theory and American Strategic Adjustment in the 1890s," *Security Studies* 11, no. 1 (autumn 2001): 151–70.

of a decades-long trend, the dollar began to inflate in value.[8] Social tensions should have been falling, not cresting, in 1898.

Second, support for the escalation of the crisis took the form of demands for an end to Spanish brutality, not war per se. If Spain had backed down and renounced its *reconcentrado* policies, Americans' humanitarian interests would have been satisfied, and there never would have been a war. Nothing particular to this point in history made Americans responsive to graphic, high-profile media reports of suffering and repression abroad. At the end of the twentieth century, calls for armed intervention in Haiti, Somalia, Bosnia, and Kosovo were not characterized as "emotional and often insubstantial binges"; why, then, should modern scholars take such a condescending attitude toward public opinion at the end of the nineteenth century?[9] The existence of humanitarian interventions shows that materialist assumptions about human nature are incomplete, but nothing about the Spanish-American War indicates that American foreign policy at the turn of the century was uniquely biased by nonrational factors, as a "psychic crisis" explanation implies.

POLITICAL ECONOMY

In this chapter, I present a very different account of the origins of American grand strategy in the periphery. This interpretation depends heavily on the work of other scholars. In the 1930s, Charles A. Beard published a number of books on the domestic sources of American foreign policy, including a section in *The Rise of American Civilization* in which he linked "Collective Internationalism" to agriculture and "Imperial Isolationism" to the manufacturing sector.[10] Then, in the 1960s, there was a veritable explosion of interest among historians regarding the nature and causes of late-nineteenth-century American foreign policy. At the center of this movement were Walter LaFeber's *The New Empire* and William A. Williams's *The Roots of the Modern American Empire*.[11] In these books, LaFeber and Williams argued in the strongest possible terms that American expansionism was driven by domestic groups'

---

[8] Milton Friedman and Anna J. Schwartz, *Monetary Trends in the United States and the United Kingdom: Their Relation to Income, Prices, and Interest Rates* (Chicago: University of Chicago Press, 1982), 122–25.

[9] Quotation from Gerald G. Eggert, *Richard Olney: Evolution of a Statesman* (University Park: Pennsylvania State University Press, 1974), 176.

[10] Charles A. Beard and Mary R. Beard, *The Rise of American Civilization: America in Midpassage*, vol. 3 (New York: Macmillan, 1939), 442–58. See also Charles A. Beard, *The Idea of National Interest: An Analytical Study in American Foreign Policy* (Westport, Conn.: Greenwood, 1934).

[11] Walter LaFeber, *The New Empire: An Interpretation of American Expansion, 1860–1898* (Ithaca: Cornell University Press, 1963); William A. Williams, *The Roots of the Modern American Empire: A Study of the Growth and Shaping of Social Consciousness in a Marketplace Economy* (New York: Random House, 1969).

desire to find new markets to relieve the problem of surplus production. Several historians subsequently challenged the polemic elements of this thesis, providing much-needed qualification to the two works. However, most accept the essential argument that economic interests are a necessary, and perhaps dominant, causal factor in explaining changes in American grand strategy in the latter half of the nineteenth century.

It was not until recently that political scientists began to pick up on this revolution in American diplomatic history. Richard F. Bensel's *Sectionalism and American Political Development* demonstrates how the geographic diversity of the United States created political-economic cleavages in Congress over tariffs and territorial expansion, while Peter Trubowitz's *Defining the National Interest* explains societal divisions over American foreign policy in three critical decades of strategic change.[12] These two studies, which use quantitative methods to analyze legislative behavior, provide great insight into the relationship between societal preferences and grand strategy in 1865–1941. However, they do not focus directly on executive decision making. As a result, they remain open to the charge that their theoretical claims apply only to Congress. In this view, the executive, who is elected by the entire country, attempts to carry out policies that he believes are in the unitary national interest (per realist assumptions), while legislators, who are elected by local districts, attempt to adjust those policies to suit their constituencies' parochial interests (per Bensel and Trubowitz). If the political economy perspective is to be considered more than a subordinate qualifier to realism, it must show how executive behavior can be deduced from societal preferences.

Drawing on the hypotheses developed in the previous chapter, I attempt to explain American grand strategy in the late nineteenth and early twentieth centuries in precisely these terms. Throughout this period, the dominant economic constituency of the Republican Party was northeastern manufacturers. In the 1860s and 1870s, they focused on expanding into the western United States, not overseas markets. It was not until the 1880s, as the frontier economy matured, that they began to develop an interest in export to the periphery. From that point, Republican presidents adopted an increasingly interventionist strategy toward Latin America and East Asia.

Democratic leaders had a more complicated coalitional calculus. Their primary economic constituency was southern farmers, who had little interest in peripheral markets. However, the party could not win national elections without the support of some northeastern states. Consequently, it had to compromise between manufacturers' growing demands for an

---

[12] Richard F. Bensel, *Sectionalism and American Political Development, 1880–1980* (Madison: University of Wisconsin Press, 1984); Peter Trubowitz, *Defining the National Interest: Conflict and Change in American Foreign Policy* (Chicago: University of Chicago Press, 1998).

[78]

interventionist strategy and farmers' opposition thereto. Every Democrat who reached the White House initially stepped back from some of the most aggressive elements of his Republican predecessor's interventionist strategy, but none withdrew from it entirely.

Societal preferences determined decision makers' choice of strategy, but other factors influenced the degree of assertiveness with which that strategy was pursued. In the seventy-six years between 1865 and 1941, there was considerable variation in the constraints on foreign policymaking. On the international side, imperial rivalries between the great powers at the turn of the century complicated efforts to extend American influence into East Asia, while the Allied powers' victory in World War I relieved those tensions. On the domestic side, the United States experienced severe economic depressions in 1893–97 and 1929–39, and its budget was burdened with overwhelming debt after the Civil War and World War I. To show how these factors affected the conduct of American grand strategy, I divide the case into five subsections: 1865–81, 1881–97, 1897–1917, 1918–29, and 1929–41. At each juncture, changing international and domestic constraints provide new opportunities to test the theory's predictions under different environmental conditions.

1865–81: THE CONTINENTAL ECONOMY

The United States emerged from the Civil War with enormous residual military power. The four years of conflict had been exhausting, but the reunified country easily could have adopted any strategy it pleased. It could have built an empire in Central America and the South Pacific, or it could have withdrawn into total isolation. Indeed, if the United States had been willing to endure a blockade by the British Royal Navy, it could have conquered Canada without risk of defeat. Britain may have been a maritime hegemon, but it could not have overcome the battle-hardened Union army in North America.

American grand strategy was constrained more by domestic conditions than the international environment. The Civil War debt imposed great burdens on the country's public finances (see figure 3.1). In 1860, the federal debt was $65 million; by 1866, it had reached nearly $2.8 billion. The annual payments on this sum were enormous, consuming nearly 40 percent of government spending in the 1870s. Even though revenue consistently exceeded expenditures, budgetary resources remained scarce. Thus, regardless of which strategies they chose to pursue, both parties had a strong incentive to avoid overreaching. Foreign ventures would not have bankrupted the Treasury, but they would have had to offer substantial returns to pass muster with the American taxpayer.

Figure 3.1. Government Spending, as Share of National Income

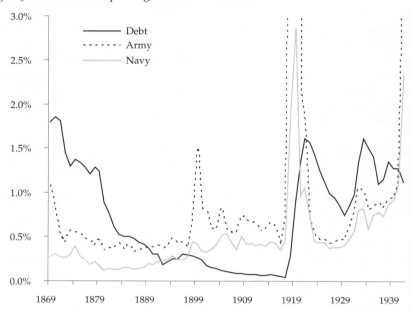

SOURCES: United States Bureau of the Census, *Historical Statistics of the United States: Colonial Times to 1970* (Washington, D.C.: Government Printing Office, 1972), 1114; Milton Friedman and Anna J. Schwartz, *Monetary Trends in the United States and the United Kingdom: Their Relation to Income, Prices, and Interest Rates* (Chicago: University of Chicago Press, 1982), 122–25.
NOTES: Spending on the army peaked at 12.9% in 1919 and 4.0% in 1941; spending on the navy peaked at 2.9% in 1919 and 2.3% in 1941.

Democrats

The first decade and a half after the Civil War was a turbulent time for the Democratic Party. Its overriding concern was the military occupation and economic reconstruction of the South. Democrats struggled to regain control of their electoral base from the coalition of carpetbaggers, scalawags, and freed slaves that initially governed southern states after the war. In 1872, party leaders did not even attempt to nominate their own candidate for president; instead, for purely tactical reasons, they chose to endorse a Liberal Republican, Horace Greeley, who shared their position on the Reconstruction but little else. The Democrats were not competitive in national elections until the mid 1870s, when the last of the federal troops were withdrawn from the South. Even then, they were unable to win the presidency until 1885, two decades after the end of the Civil War.

Throughout this period, Democrats had no sectoral interest in an aggressive grand strategy. Their primary constituency, southern farmers, was deeply reliant on export to core markets but had almost no stake in the periphery. An aggressive peripheral strategy would not only have wasted budgetary resources, but it also might have created diplomatic tensions between the United States and other great powers, endangering farmers' trade with the core. Furthermore, it might have opened the door to greater trade between the United States and subtropical countries whose agricultural exports competed with southern farmers' crops. These considerations, combined with the domestic constraint of an enormous national debt, should have made Democrats favor an isolationist strategy toward the periphery. Before the Civil War, the party had sought to expand into Latin America to create more slave states; after 1865, it had no such incentive.

No Democrat was elected president between 1865 and 1881; however, one Democrat did serve in the White House. In the wartime election of 1864, Abraham Lincoln selected an antislavery Democrat from Tennessee, Andrew Johnson, to be his running mate. This symbolic gesture of national reconciliation produced one of the greatest ironies in the history of American politics: with the assassination of Lincoln, just four days after the end of the Civil War, a southern Democrat became the leader of the Union. Johnson initially retained the cabinet members appointed by Lincoln, including a Republican, William Seward, as secretary of state, but he was by no means a caretaker president. To the contrary, Johnson caused such consternation among Republican legislators that he was impeached, and nearly convicted, in May 1868. Thus, I treat the Johnson administration as Democratic and predict that its grand strategy in the periphery should have been isolationist.

In fact, whether the administration is treated as Democratic or Republican, it constitutes a disconfirming observation for the theory.[13] With Johnson's assent, Seward continuously undertook to extend American influence in the periphery. Some of his policies were interventionist, like his attempts to acquire naval bases in the Caribbean and secure legal rights to a future isthmian canal; others were imperialist, like his efforts to annex Alaska, Greenland, and Cuba.

---

[13] See Glyndon G. Van Deusen, *William Henry Seward* (New York: Oxford University Press, 1967), chaps. 33–37; Charles S. Campbell, *The Transformation of American Foreign Relations, 1865–1900* (New York: Harper and Row, 1976), 12–24. Also useful are Walter LaFeber, *The New Empire*, 24–32; Robert L. Beisner, *From the Old Diplomacy to the New, 1865–1900* (New York: Crowell, 1975), 44–48; David M. Pletcher, *The Diplomacy of Trade and Investment: American Economic Expansion in the Hemisphere, 1865–1900* (Columbia: University of Missouri Press, 1998), 123–24, 159–60; Henry W. Temple, "William H. Seward," in *The American Secretaries of State and Their Diplomacy*, vol. 7, ed. Samuel F. Bemis (New York: Knopf, 1928), 105–14; Hans L. Trefousse, *Andrew Johnson: A Biography* (New York: Norton, 1989), 261, 270, 345, 348–49.

Andrew Johnson (April 1865–March 1869)

Interventionism

Coercive diplomacy

- Sent fifty thousand troops to the border to demand the withdrawal of French forces that were supporting Emperor Maximilian's claim to the throne in Mexico.

Overseas bases

- Attempted to purchase the islands of St. Thomas and St. John from Denmark; Culebra and Puerto Rico from Spain; St. Bartholomew from Sweden; and Martinique from France.
- Claimed the uninhabited Midway Islands.
- Negotiated a treaty with Nicaragua for the right of transit over a prospective canal route.
- Negotiated a treaty with Colombia for exclusive rights to build and control a canal in the province of Panama.

Commercial expansion

- Negotiated a treaty with Hawaii for trade reciprocity.

Imperialism

Landmass annexation

- Purchased Alaska from Russia.
- Attempted to purchase Greenland and Iceland from Denmark and Cuba from Spain.

Clearly, this was not isolationism. However, it is equally clear that the administration's views on grand strategy were not representative of popular opinion among southern Democrats. As discussed in the previous chapter, the party's electoral base consistently opposed the expansion of American power in the periphery after the end of the Civil War.[14] Of the four national platforms the party produced in 1865–81, only one (1872) contains any reference to grand strategy: "It is the duty of the Government, in its intercourse with foreign nations, to cultivate the friendships of peace by treating with all on fair and equal terms."[15] This declaration explicitly rejects the underlying premise of both interventionism and imperialism, the idea that weak states should be coerced on unequal terms.

[14] Southerners generally supported the annexation of Alaska, but this is an unsurprising exception. It helped improve relations with Russia and did not create major problems with other great powers; furthermore, Alaskan goods did not compete with southern farm exports. See Edward W. Chester, *Sectionalism, Politics, and American Diplomacy* (Metuchen, N.J.: Scarecrow, 1975), 118–19.

[15] The Democratic Party, "Democratic Party Platform of 1872," The American Presidency Project, http://www.presidency.ucsb.edu/showplatforms.php?platindex=D1872 (last accessed April 2006).

Andrew Johnson came to office through an accident of history, a tortuous sequence of events that completely short-circuited the normal process of interest aggregation within the Democratic Party. Johnson did not represent his fellow southern Democrats; indeed, Lincoln chose him to be vice president precisely because he took a maverick position against slavery. Thus, it is not surprising that he was also an outlier among Democrats on foreign policy. Though Johnson did not behave as predicted, it seems safe to conclude that the problems with this observation reflect extraordinary circumstances rather than a serious flaw in the logic of the theory.

Republicans

Like the Democrats, Republicans had little reason to pursue an active peripheral strategy in the first fifteen years following the Civil War. The party's socioeconomic coalition, which was composed primarily of northeastern manufacturing and dependent sectors, was almost completely disconnected from the international economy. Businesses were expanding rapidly into the vast, undeveloped western frontier, so they did not need to concern themselves with international markets. Furthermore, much of the government's revenue was devoted to servicing the Civil War debt, leaving little room in the budget for a costly grand strategy. Without incentives to expand, and with strong disincentives to do so, Republican presidents in 1865–81 should have been isolationist.

The actual grand strategy of the first Republican leader to serve in this period, Ulysses S. Grant, contradicts this prediction.[16] Grant followed a similar strategy as Johnson, though he focused more on acquiring naval bases and an isthmian canal than large landmasses. His most imperialist initiative, which was also one of his first acts in office, was the negotiation of an annexation treaty with the Dominican Republic.

Ulysses S. Grant (March 1869–March 1877)

Interventionism

Coercive diplomacy
- Threatened Spain over harm caused to Americans in Cuba, where Spain was fighting a native rebellion.
- Threatened Germany against intervening in a revolution in Venezuela.

---

[16] See Allan Nevins, *Hamilton Fish: The Inner History of the Grant Administration*, rev. ed. (New York: Ungar, 1957); Campbell, *Transformation of American Foreign Relations*, 25–75. Also useful are LaFeber, *New Empire*, 32–39; Beisner, *From the Old Diplomacy to the New*, 48–54; Pletcher, *Diplomacy of Trade and Investment*, 125–28, 152–56; Joseph V. Fuller, "Hamilton Fish," in *The American Secretaries of State and Their Diplomacy*, vol. 7, ed. Samuel F. Bemis (New York: Knopf, 1928), 125–214; William S. McFeely, *Grant: A Biography* (New York: Norton, 1981), chap. 21.

Overseas bases
- Negotiated a treaty with Samoa for exclusive access to its harbor in Pago Pago.
- Negotiated a treaty with Colombia for the exclusive right to build and control a canal in the province of Panama.

Commercial expansion
- Negotiated a treaty with Hawaii for trade reciprocity.

Imperialism

Landmass annexation
- Negotiated a treaty to annex the Dominican Republic.

Neither Grant nor Johnson was an isolationist. Both presidents followed a weakly imperialist grand strategy, an outcome that directly disconfirms the theory's predictions. How, then, can we account for their behavior? Interestingly, realist theories fare no better with these observations. Defensive realism asserts that states should expand only when threatened; yet, Johnson's and Grant's territorial ambitions could not have been motivated by insecurity. The late 1860s and early 1870s were the nadir of imperialist sentiment in Europe, and the United States faced only two violations of the Monroe Doctrine in this period, both of which were easily countered.

Offensive realism, which claims that all states try to expand their power to the maximum extent possible, seems more plausible here. In this view, it was only natural for Johnson and Grant to have tried to add new territory to the United States. By the same logic, however, they did not try nearly hard enough. The Civil War left the military far better equipped for war than at any other time in American history, but neither president used it aggressively. Why, for example, did Johnson not occupy and annex northern Mexico in response to the presence of French troops in the country? Why did he not back up negotiations with Britain over the *Alabama* claims (see chapter 4) with the invasion of Canada? Why did Grant not seize Cuba from Spain in retaliation for abuses against American lives and property in the colony? These two presidents were clearly willing to add to their nation's massive debt and incur the costs of colonial administration and defense, but they had little desire to purchase an empire with American blood.

As noted above, Fareed Zakaria tries to close this explanatory gap with a variant of offensive realism, "state-centered" realism. He asserts that Johnson and Grant would have acted more aggressively had they not been constrained by domestic institutions. To a certain extent, this point is undeniably true, since the Senate refused to ratify a number of their territorial annexation treaties. However, legislators could not have prevented the executive from provoking military conflict in diplomatic disputes with Mexico, Britain, and Spain. Thus, state-centered realism, like offensive realism, predicts greater aggressiveness than is actually observed. Even a weak executive can incite a crisis that leads to conquest, as did President James K. Polk in the Mexican-American War of 1846–48.

To illustrate the state-centered realist view, Fareed Zakaria proposes a counterfactual: "Had the United States had . . . a stronger central government and a parliament with the executive and legislative branches fused— it is almost certain that many of the executive's plans would have become national policy."[17] This conclusion is flawed. Few Americans had an economic interest in an expansionist grand strategy, so few members of Congress were willing to support expansionist policies. Had legislators been able to choose their leaders, as in a parliamentary system, they would have favored individuals whose strategic preferences mirrored their own. Only in rare circumstances, like that which brought Winston Churchill to power in World War II, do political outsiders and policy contrarians become prime minister. Yet Johnson became president because Lincoln was assassinated, and Grant was elected as a war hero. Neither man had to face the kind of selection pressures that would have weeded him out of the running for his party's leadership in a parliamentary system. Thus, each was able to pursue his own aberrant foreign policy preferences as president.

Following Grant's retirement, the election of the Republican Rutherford B. Hayes marked a return to normality in American grand strategy.[18] The international system was relatively calm during Hayes's tenure in office, and he did nothing to stir things up. Unlike his predecessors, he made no effort to annex peripheral territories. Indeed, his four years as president were among the quietest ever in the history of American foreign relations. This can be attributed in part to a lack of exogenous disturbances, but it is also the consequence of Hayes's own inactivity. Though he made a minor advance in U.S. influence over Samoa and tried to establish naval bases on American-owed land in Nicaragua, his grand strategy was almost entirely one of isolationism. As such, it counts as a confirmation of the theory.

Rutherford B. Hayes (March 1877–March 1881)

Interventionism
> Overseas bases
> - Accepted an informal agreement with Britain and Germany to share influence over Samoa.

---

[17] Zakaria, *From Wealth to Power*, 87.
[18] See Ari Hoogenboom, *The Presidency of Rutherford B. Hayes* (Lawrence: University Press of Kansas, 1988), 184–92. Also useful are LaFeber, *New Empire*, 39–46; Claude G. Bowers and Helen D. Reid, "William M. Evarts," in *The American Secretaries of State and Their Diplomacy*, vol. 7, ed. Samuel F. Bemis (New York: Knopf, 1928), 228–57; Pletcher, *Diplomacy of Trade and Investment*, 85–87, 130–31, 135–36; Joseph Smith, *Illusions of Conflict: Anglo-American Diplomacy toward Latin America, 1865–1896* (Pittsburgh: University of Pittsburgh Press, 1979), 101–6.

- Attempted to establish naval bases on American-owned grant land on both coasts of Nicaragua.

1881–97: SHIFTING FRONTIERS

American grand strategy in the periphery was no more constrained by international pressures in the 1880s and 1890s than it had been in the previous two decades. The other great powers began to compete for control over parts of Africa and Asia, but they made little effort to expand their empires into Latin America. They occasionally intervened in the region to protect their commercial interests, but they respected the Monroe Doctrine's injunction against asserting control over territory. European statesmen had nothing to gain from antagonizing the United States, so they generally avoided meddling in the Western Hemisphere. Once again, the United States was free to follow any strategy it pleased without compromising its physical security.

This freedom of action was reinforced by the decline of a major domestic constraint. By 1884, the government had paid off more than one-third of the debt from 1866, and the portion of the annual budget allocated to interest had fallen from 40 percent to a manageable 22 percent. Furthermore, consistent budget surpluses, through both boom and recession, convinced many voters that tariffs should be cut. In response, protectionist businessmen and their political representatives began to look for ways to increase spending so as to justify maintaining the high rates that protected industry.[19] Thus, the budgetary constraint on grand strategy was not only diminishing but perhaps even providing a positive opportunity for expansion. The critical question, therefore, would be whether either party had a sectoral interest in adopting an active grand strategy.

Republicans

In the 1880s, Republicans' strategic calculus did indeed begin to change. Their main constituency, northeastern businessmen, increasingly began to believe that the economy was afflicted with the problem of overproduction.

---

[19] Justus D. Doenecke, *The Presidencies of James A. Garfield and Chester A. Arthur* (Lawrence: Regents Press of Kansas, 1981), 11, 168; Catherine Ruggles Gerrish, "Public Finance and Fiscal Policy, 1866–1918," in *The Growth of the American Economy,* ed. Harold F. Williamson (Englewood Cliffs, N.J.: Prentice-Hall, 1951), 632–33; Ben Baack and Edward Ray, "The Political Economy of the Origins of the Military-Industrial Complex in the United States," *Journal of Economic History* 45, no. 2 (June 1985): 372–73.

In the first fifteen years following the Civil War, they had expanded rapidly into the undeveloped western part of the country. As that frontier matured, they realized that they would soon need to look elsewhere for unexploited markets. Over the course of the 1880s, they gradually turned their attention to the periphery. In response to their changing interests, Republican leaders should have taken slow, incremental steps toward implementing a strategy aimed at the coercion of peripheral states—that is, interventionism. (Imperialism would have been too costly, especially in this early stage of expansionism, and many American industries were becoming competitive enough not to have needed the added advantages it would have provided them.) Specifically, they should have focused on the parts of the world that promised manufacturers the greatest benefits for the least effort. The Caribbean, Central America, and Hawaii fit this description for three reasons: first, they were the only peripheral territories in which American business already had a significant amount of investment or trade; second, they were not firmly in the sphere of influence of any European powers; and third, they were relatively proximate to the United States, so their defense did not require the creation of a connecting chain of naval outposts.

The first Republican president in this period was James A. Garfield.[20] Together with Secretary of State James G. Blaine, Garfield worked assiduously to try to ensure that the United States would control the construction of any future isthmian canal. Moreover, and somewhat surprisingly, he significantly extended the reach of American foreign policy by signing trade treaties with Madagascar and Korea. Only six months after Garfield was inaugurated, however, he was incapacitated by an assassination attempt. With such a brief observation, it is impossible to assert with confidence whether his behavior confirms the theory.

At the end of September 1881, Garfield died and was replaced by Chester A. Arthur.[21] The new president carried forward much of his prede-

---

[20] See David M. Pletcher, *The Awkward Years: American Foreign Relations under Garfield and Arthur* (Columbia: University of Missouri Press, 1962). Also useful are Campbell, *Transformation of American Foreign Relations*, 91–96; John M. Dobson, *America's Ascent: The United States Becomes a Great Power, 1880–1914* (DeKalb: Northern Illinois University Press, 1978), 27–36; LaFeber, *New Empire*, 46–48; Doenecke, *Presidencies of James A. Garfield and Chester A. Arthur*, 55–74; Joseph B. Lockey, "James Gillespie Blaine," in *The American Secretaries of State and Their Diplomacy*, vol. 8, ed. Samuel F. Bemis (New York: Knopf, 1928), 261–97; Smith, *Illusions of Conflict*, 39–40, 65–72, 117–20.

[21] See Pletcher, *Awkward Years*. Also useful are Campbell, *Transformation of American Foreign Relations*, 96–106; Dobson, *America's Ascent*, 36–39; LaFeber, *New Empire*, 47–53; Doenecke, *Presidencies of James A. Garfield and Chester A. Arthur*, 127–79; Philip M. Brown, "Frederick T. Frelinghuysen," in *The American Secretaries of State and Their Diplomacy*, vol. 8, ed. Samuel F. Bemis (New York: Knopf, 1928), 9–43.

cessor's work, negotiating a new canal treaty with Nicaragua and signing several reciprocity treaties with Latin American countries. He also sent a representative to a European conference on the colonial status of the Congo, hoping to secure equal access for American exports to Africa. With these small steps, the germ of a global strategy was slowly beginning to take shape. Both Garfield and Arthur acted cautiously; the difference between them and Hayes was not great. As such, however, their actions correspond closely to what the theory predicts: the beginnings of a gradual transition from isolationism to interventionism.

James A. Garfield (March 1881–September 1881)

Interventionism
Overseas bases
- Quashed Colombia's attempt to convince European powers to guarantee its sovereignty over the province of Panama.

Commercial expansion
- Negotiated treaties for trade reciprocity with Madagascar and Korea.

Chester A. Arthur (September 1881–March 1885)

Interventionism
Overseas bases
- Threatened abrogation of the Clayton-Bulwer Treaty of 1850, which forbade either Britain or the United States from sole possession of an isthmian canal.
- Negotiated a treaty with Nicaragua for control over a prospective canal route.

Commercial expansion
- Negotiated treaties for trade reciprocity with Hawaii, Mexico, the Dominican Republic, Colombia, El Salvador, and the Spanish colonies of Cuba and Puerto Rico.
- Participated in the Congo Conference and signed its treaty.

The Republicans lost the election of 1884, then returned to the White House in 1889. Over that time, northeastern businessmen's concerns about overproduction continued to mount. They sought relief in peripheral markets, and, to that end, demanded that their government pursue an interventionist grand strategy. Consequently, Republican leaders should have undertaken more systematic efforts to open the periphery to American business, with a concomitant increase in spending on the requisite military infrastructure. This should not have constituted a qualitative departure from Garfield and Arthur's mild interventionism; rather, it should have

[88]

resulted in a quantitative increase in the breadth and depth of the same policies.

Benjamin Harrison's actual strategy corresponds well to these predictions.[22] Most notably, he ordered the navy to intervene directly in revolutions in Haiti and Chile, a clear step forward for the interventionist paradigm. He also negotiated an annexation treaty with Hawaii, a vital requisite for the expansion of American power into the Pacific. The Hawaiian islands themselves were of little commercial importance; instead, their acquisition was intended to give the United States a naval stepping-stone to the vast markets of East Asia. Harrison left office before the Senate could take up the treaty, but his actions clearly maintained the steady advance of the Republican agenda of interventionism.

Benjamin Harrison (March 1889–March 1893)

Interventionism

Overseas bases

- Negotiated a treaty of annexation with Hawaii.
- Negotiated with Britain and Germany to partition Samoa, giving the United States predominant influence over Pago Pago.
- Negotiated unsuccessfully to obtain a naval base in the Dominican Republic.

Political intervention

- Demanded that Haiti cede naval bases and control over its foreign policy to the United States. When refused, directed the U.S. Navy to break Haiti's blockade of insurgents' supply lines, causing the overthrow of the government.
- Supported the Chilean government by interdicting arms shipments to insurgents, but failed to prevent its overthrow. Subsequently, threatened war against the new regime over the death of two U.S. Navy sailors in a riot in Valparaiso.

Commercial expansion

- Negotiated for treaties of trade reciprocity with most countries in Latin America.

---

[22] See Homer E. Socolofsky and Allan B. Spetter, *The Presidency of Benjamin Harrison* (Lawrence: University Press of Kansas, 1987), 95–156; Campbell, *Transformation of American Foreign Relations*, 82–83, 161–86. Also useful are LaFeber, *New Empire*, chap. 3; John A. S. Grenville and George Berkeley Young, *Politics, Strategy, and American Diplomacy: Studies in Foreign Policy, 1873–1917* (New Haven: Yale University Press, 1966), 74–101; Dobson, *America's Ascent*, 46–50, 61–62; Pletcher, *Diplomacy of Trade and Investment*, 240–79, 299–310; Smith, *Illusions of Conflict*, 114, 135–69, 185–201; Beisner, *From the Old Diplomacy to the New*, 86–95; Lockey, "James Gillespie Blaine," 115–84; William R. Castle, "John Watson Foster," in *The American Secretaries of State and Their Diplomacy*, vol. 8, ed. Samuel F. Bemis (New York: Knopf, 1928), 193–219.

Democrats

Democrats faced a far more difficult task of interest aggregation than Republicans.[23] An indispensable element of the party's coalition, northeastern manufacturers, would have benefited from the sort of policy pursued by Arthur and Harrison—that of cautious, low-cost, market-opening interventionism. Yet, the Democrats' primary constituency, southern farmers, had no interest in a strategy designed to promote trade with the periphery. Their exports to it were negligible, and some of them, such as sugar growers, competed directly with Latin American producers. Interventionism would not only waste southerners' tax dollars but also might cause them direct economic harm. Furthermore, it implied the aggressive enforcement of the Monroe Doctrine, which risked offending their customers in Europe.

Faced with the problem of satisfying two groups with opposing interests in foreign policy, Democratic leaders' optimal course of action was to attempt a compromise. On the one hand, they should have supported business interests with some degree of interventionism; on the other hand, they should have been less aggressive than Republicans, since they had to take into account the preferences of anti-interventionist southern farmers. Democrats could not ignore the periphery entirely without losing votes in the Northeast, but neither could they be as active as Republicans without offending their southern base. They should have pulled back from Republican presidents' most aggressive initiatives in the periphery, but only for the sake of finding a more moderate synthesis, not to leave exporters without at least a modicum of support from their government.

The actual grand strategy pursued by Democratic president Grover Cleveland in his first term in office confirms this prediction.[24] On nearly every international issue, Cleveland defended preestablished American commercial interests but rejected opportunities to create new ones. For example, he advocated the ratification of a treaty to maintain the status quo on trade reciprocity with Hawaii; however, he withdrew from the Senate several other agreements negotiated by Arthur that established new commitments. Cleveland was identifiably interventionist, but he was significantly less so than Arthur, his Republican predecessor.

---

[23] On Cleveland's coalition, see Grenville and Young, *Politics, Strategy, and American Diplomacy*, 43–46.

[24] See Richard E. Welch, *The Presidencies of Grover Cleveland* (Lawrence: University Press of Kansas, 1988), 157–69, 177–79; Campbell, *Transformation of American Foreign Relations*, 65–66, 71, 77–82. Also useful are Dobson, *America's Ascent*, 37–46; Smith, *Illusions of Conflict*, 114, 130–33; Lester B. Shippee, "Thomas Francis Bayard," in *The American Secretaries of State and Their Diplomacy*, vol. 8, ed. Samuel F. Bemis (New York: Knopf, 1928), 71–106.

Grover Cleveland (March 1885–March 1889)

Isolationism
  Full retreats
  • Withdrew Arthur's treaties on the Congo Conference, trade with Cuba and Puerto Rico, and a canal route in Nicaragua.

Interventionism
  Coercive diplomacy
  • Sent warships to Samoa to threaten Germany against establishing a de facto protectorate over the islands.
  Commercial expansion
  • Advocated the ratification of Arthur's treaty for trade reciprocity with Hawaii, but opposed an amendment to establish a naval base at Pearl Harbor.

Cleveland faced a complicated set of constraints in his discontinuous second term. Following the financial panic of 1893, businesses became more desperate than ever for the assistance of their government. The main cause of the crisis was the outflow of gold. By encouraging exports, Cleveland could help reverse the trend. This would meliorate the problem of deflation and restore international investors' confidence in the dollar, which in turn would help stem the flight of capital and further promote recovery. Exports would also help businesses survive the crash in demand, allowing them to sell their surplus goods in markets that were in better economic health than the United States. At the start of his second term, Cleveland should have been reluctant to expand American influence overseas, just as he had been in his first term. However, as the Depression of 1893–97 deepened, he should have adopted an increasingly aggressive interventionist strategy.

The actual strategy pursued by Cleveland conforms fairly well to these predictions.[25] Just like in 1885, he began his term in 1893 by pulling back from the most ambitious of his predecessors' interventionist policies. Whereas Harrison wanted to annex Hawaii regardless of native sentiment, Cleveland was far more cautious. To investigate the situation, he sent a commissioner to the islands, who reported that the natives opposed

---

[25] See LaFeber, *New Empire*, 197–325; Campbell, *Transformation of American Foreign Relations*, 194–246; Welch, *Presidencies of Grover Cleveland*, 169–75, 179–99. Also useful are Montgomery Schuyler, "Walter Quintin Gresham," in *The American Secretaries of State and Their Diplomacy*, vol. 8, ed. Samuel F. Bemis (New York: Knopf, 1928), 242–69; Montgomery Schuyler, "Richard Olney," in *The American Secretaries of State and Their Diplomacy*, vol. 8, ed. Samuel F. Bemis (New York: Knopf, 1928), 277–319; Eggert, *Richard Olney*, 174–281; Pratt, *Expansionists of 1898*, 110–212; Beisner, *From the Old Diplomacy to the New*, 95–106; Ernest R. May, *Imperial Democracy: The Emergence of America as a Great Power* (New York: Harcourt, Brace, and World, 1961), 13–111;

annexation. Thus, the president withdrew the treaty, a major setback for the interventionist agenda.

With the subsequent collapse of the economy, Cleveland began to take firmer action to advance U.S. commercial interests. Beginning in late 1893, he used the military to defend American trade and political influence in Brazil and Nicaragua. This turn toward interventionism climaxed in 1895–96, when he decided to weigh in on a long-festering dispute over the border between Venezuela and British Guiana. At the time, there was little public demand for action, and the situation on the ground had not changed significantly in a decade.[26] Yet, Cleveland was not free from political pressures, as many voters blamed the depression on his tight-money policy. As a result, he had strong incentives to use the Venezuelan boundary dispute for both diversionary and economic purposes.

Cleveland's interest in the affair may also have been piqued by the recent discovery in the disputed area of "the largest gold nugget ever found anywhere."[27] If Venezuela were to have gained control over this territory, then American, rather than British, companies would have mined the ore. In a time of painful deflation, anything Cleveland could have done to bring gold into the United States, either through gold imports or merchandise exports, would have boosted his popularity.[28] His missive to Britain, a vociferous demand that it agree to arbitration with Venezuela, met with enthusiastic approval from the American public. Eventually Britain conceded to his terms, and in so doing implicitly recognized U.S. predominance over Latin America. It was not enough to save Cleveland's presidency from the economic crisis, but, in combination with his initial retreat from interventionism, it does support the theory.

Grover Cleveland (March 1893–March 1897)

Isolationism
Full retreats
- Withdrew Harrison's treaty for the annexation of Hawaii and demanded that the illegitimate, pro-American government relinquish power.

Dobson, *America's Ascent*, 62–99; Smith, *Illusions of Conflict*, 169–84, 201–9; Pletcher, *Diplomacy of Trade and Investment*, 292–95, 311–32.

[26] Pletcher, *Diplomacy of Trade and Investment*, 315; Nelson M. Blake, "Background of Cleveland's Venezuelan Policy," *American Historical Review* 47, no. 2 (January 1942): 262.

[27] Campbell, *Transformation of American Foreign Relations*, 204.

[28] Grenville and Young, *Politics, Strategy, and American Diplomacy*, 165, 167–68, 182; Walter LaFeber, "The American Business Community and Cleveland's Venezuela Message," *Business History Review* 34 (winter 1960): 393–402; Campbell, *Transformation of American Foreign Relations*, 203–5; Blake, "Background of Cleveland's Venezuelan Policy," 259–77; Pletcher, *Diplomacy of Trade and Investment*, 316–17.

- Requested that Congress consider withdrawal from Samoa.

Interventionism
  Coercive diplomacy
- Sent warships to Nicaragua to pressure Britain to withdraw its forces from the Mosquito Reservation, part of a prospective canal route.
- Threatened Britain to accept the arbitration of a boundary dispute between British Guiana and Venezuela.
- Threatened Spain to make concessions to rebel forces in Cuba.

  Political intervention
- Directed warships to escort American merchant vessels to Brazilian ports, breaking a naval blockade by rebel forces and ensuring that the pro-American government would continue to receive customs revenue.

1897–1917: A New Equilibrium

By the turn of the century, the United States was more secure than ever before, invulnerable to invasion and essentially unchallenged in the Western Hemisphere. During World War I, there were some concerns that the belligerent powers might try to violate the Monroe Doctrine, but little came of it. The country's grand strategy was limited only by the extent of its leaders' ambitions: the further they pushed outside their established sphere of influence, the more resistance they would encounter.

Republicans

At the turn of the century, northeastern manufacturers were rapidly becoming more dependent on export to and investment in Latin America and East Asia. They had turned to foreign markets to survive the Depression of 1893–97, and they continued to search for new customers after the economy recovered. To satisfy this growing constituency of peripheral interests, Republicans presidents in 1897–1917 had an unambiguous strategic imperative: interventionism. Specifically, they should have strengthened their political, military, and commercial dominance over Latin America while seeking to exert greater influence over the far-off markets of China, Southeast Asia, and perhaps even Africa.

The first Republican to serve in this period, William McKinley, did pursue a moderately aggressive interventionist strategy, but his actions had unexpectedly imperialist consequences.[29] On taking the presidency, he faced a major diplomatic crisis with Spain. The native population of Cuba had once again risen in revolt against their colonial masters, and Spain was determined to defeat them by any means possible, no matter how brutal and inhumane. Outraged by Spanish atrocities, many Americans and their representatives in Congress called for war. Yet, McKinley patiently negotiated with Spain for ten long months. Critics accused him of being weak and vacillating; some even insisted that his "pacifism" was due to his being beholden to the interests of businesses and bankers who held $500 million in Spanish bonds.[30] Although there may be some merit to the latter charge, the former could not be further from the truth. The president's cautious diplomacy and dismissal of what he called "jingo nonsense" reflected a strong sense of purpose and will in the face of public pressure.[31]

Why, then, did McKinley persist so long with negotiations before declaring war? As Charles S. Campbell explains, "McKinley was confirmed in his peaceful disposition by the attitude of the business community, on whose favors he depended politically. . . . The country was climbing out of depression following the panic of 1893; the last thing businessmen wanted was the uncertainty of warfare."[32] Trade journals filled with dire predictions about the consequences of war: maritime commerce would be disrupted, demand would be distorted, and businesses would defer investment decisions until international stability was reestablished.[33] Businessmen also feared that war would break the budget, create inflation, and induce a panic among foreigners with investment in the United States, thereby causing a currency crisis that would depress the economy and renew public interest in silver coinage.

As negotiations dragged on and public outrage mounted, however, businesses came to the conclusion that war would be far less damaging to the economy than the uncertainty of a never-ending diplomatic crisis. Three factors caused business opinion to tilt in favor of a quick resolution to the impasse. First, a war seemed increasingly to be inevitable. No other action

---

[29] See Lewis L. Gould, *The Presidency of William McKinley* (Lawrence: Regents Press of Kansas, 1980); John Dobson, *Reticent Expansionism: The Foreign Policy of William McKinley* (Pittsburgh: Duquesne University Press, 1988). Also useful are Campbell, *Transformation of American Foreign Relations*, chaps. 13–17; LaFeber, *New Empire*, 326–417; Thomas J. McCormick, *China Market: America's Quest for Informal Empire* (Chicago: Quadrangle, 1967); Philip S. Foner, "Why the United States Went to War with Spain in 1898," in *American Interventionism: Critical Issues*, ed. Marilyn Blatt Young (Boston: Little, Brown, 1973), 2–20; May, *Imperial Democracy*, chaps. 10–18; Pratt, *Expansionists of 1898*; H. Wayne Morgan, *America's Road to Empire: The War with Spain and Overseas Expansion* (New York: McGraw-Hill, 1993).
[30] Gould, *Presidency of William McKinley*, 87.
[31] Quoted in Dobson, *Reticent Expansionism*, 33.
[32] Campbell, *Transformation of American Foreign Relations*, 247–48.
[33] Pratt, *Expansionists of 1898*, 240.

offered any hope of ending the stalemate, and delay would accomplish nothing but to make the stock market chronically skittish. Second, concern for a balance of payments crisis declined with a surge of American exports and the discovery of new deposits of gold in Alaska. By 1898, the economy was ready for the shock of war.[34] Third, prospects for an easy victory improved. Fears that Spain would be able to rally a coalition behind it evaporated as European governments made clear that they had little to gain from joining a war against the United States. McKinley, therefore, took the most rational course of action for the leader of the Republican Party: he waited for business and public opinion to converge, and then he struck.[35]

The foregoing account of McKinley's decision for war is not completely consistent with the assumptions of political economy theory. It was economically rational for the business community to turn in favor of war as the crisis developed, but the cause of that crisis lay elsewhere. Newspaper reports, particularly those originating in William Randolph Hearst's inflammatory "yellow press," exposed (and exaggerated) the extent of Spanish atrocities against the Cuban rebels, and empathetic Americans came to the conclusion that the existing state of affairs was intolerable. Their immediate motives were humanitarian, not economic. Had the public not been agitated by McKinley's inability to improve conditions in Cuba with patient, low-cost diplomacy, business opinion might never have come to support a decisive resolution to the problem, and the president might never have declared war.

Once at war with Spain, McKinley commanded the U.S. Navy to attack the Spanish Pacific fleet and land an army at Manila. He also ordered the navy to take Guam, a way-station between Hawaii and the Philippines. These decisions, which broadened the war from the Caribbean to East Asia, are consistent with the prediction that McKinley should have been interventionist, since the seizure of bases at Manila and Guam gave the United States two critical stepping-stones on the way to the promising

---

[34] LaFeber, *New Empire*, 404.
[35] Morgan, *America's Road to Empire*, 15, 55. Interestingly, Democrats and farmers were more eager to escalate the crisis than many big businesses. There are two likely reasons for this. First, opposition legislators, who have no real control over events, sometimes have greater incentives to try to embarrass the executive politically than to advocate policies that conform strictly to the economic preferences of their coalition members. See Kenneth A. Schultz, *Democracy and Coercive Diplomacy* (Cambridge: Cambridge University Press, 2001). Second, if one assumes that every American obtained an equal amount of positive utility from humanitarian intervention, variance in support for the war must have been caused by the unequal distribution of the costs of the war. Southern and western farmers had less of a stake than northeasterners in fiscal orthodoxy (as was evident in the debate over bimetallism), so they should have been less deterred by the fear that war would have resulted in speculative crises. On agrarian support for war, see Williams, *Roots of the Modern American Empire*, chaps. 14–15. On Democratic support for the war, see Gould, *Presidency of William McKinley*, 63, 70; Joseph A. Fry, *Dixie Looks Abroad: The South and U.S. Foreign Relations, 1789–1973* (Baton Rouge: Louisiana State University Press, 2002), 120–26.

Chinese market. However, the president did not stop at Manila; he annexed the entire Philippine island chain. To understand what motivated this imperialist outcome, it is necessary to examine McKinley's decision-making process.

At first, McKinley intended only to seize the harbor at Manila.[36] This position was criticized by his military staff, who argued that the harbor could not adequately be defended unless the entire island of Luzon were occupied. McKinley therefore instructed his representatives at the Paris peace conference to demand control of Luzon from Spain. Yet, this was also problematic. As the diplomats pointed out, the Philippines were economically and politically interdependent. To separate Luzon from the rest might lead to turmoil in the entire group. Furthermore, to declaim control over the other islands would be to invite other imperial great powers, particularly Germany, to fill the vacuum. After much deliberation, McKinley decided to accept his advisers' recommendation to claim the entire island chain.

Clearly, international constraints influenced the president's final choice. Concern over German meddling was a factor, as may have been the intensification of European competition over China. Nevertheless, McKinley's behavior could not have been motivated by any notion of "national security." The Philippines served no purpose in the defense of the American homeland; its only value was as a forward outpost to the Chinese market. Thomas McCormick takes this interpretation a step further, asserting that business opinion "chiefly shaped and supported McKinley's decisions" to take the Philippines and "played a significant, though not paramount part in the outlook of the military advisors who exercised a more limited but still crucial influence upon the President's policies."[37] Whether or not one accepts this view, it is difficult to find any viable alternative to the conclusion, supported by extensive historical research, that business opinion was more important than any other factor in shaping McKinley's definition of the "national interest."[38] To that end, the president inaugurated the "Open Door" policy, in which he tried to persuade the great powers not to close off their commercial spheres of influence in China.

McKinley did not intend for American control over the Philippines to be permanent.[39] The natives would be put under the "tutelage" of a military governor, who would work to strengthen the country's economy and

[36] Dobson, *Reticent Expansionism*, 109–13; Pratt, *Expansionists of 1898*, 332–38.
[37] McCormick, *China Market*, 117.
[38] Charles S. Campbell, *Special Business Interests and the Open Door Policy* (New Haven: Yale University Press, 1951); Herbert Ershkowitz, *The Attitude of Business toward American Foreign Policy, 1900–1916* (University Park: Pennsylvania State University, 1967); LaFeber, *New Empire*, chap. 8; McCormick, *China Market*.
[39] Dobson, *Reticent Expansionism*, 104–6; Gould, *Presidency of William McKinley*, 115.

political institutions to the point at which there would be no danger of revolution or fiscal irresponsibility, hence no pretext for other great powers to intervene. Once it granted independence to the Philippines, the United States would keep its naval base, commercial position, and political influence over the islands, but it would not have to pay the costs of a permanent occupation. This policy simply followed in the pattern established by the Monroe Doctrine in Latin America, and as such does not resemble European-style imperialism.

The other territories that McKinley annexed each served specific purposes in an interventionist strategy. Hawaii was the military and economic lynchpin of Americans' commercial penetration of Asia; Guam and Wake Island were similarly useful as naval stepping-stones; and Puerto Rico held a militarily important spot on the eastern entryway to the Caribbean. Critically, McKinley chose not to annex the crown jewel of the Spanish Empire, Cuba. Instead, he worked with Senator Orville Platt to enact a law that required the Cuban government to recognize the right of the United States "to intervene for the preservation of Cuban independence" and "the maintenance of a government adequate for the protection of life, property, and individual liberty."[40] The Platt Amendment also mandated that Cuba cede a naval base to the United States. In return, McKinley sought to facilitate the quick removal of American forces. The U.S. Army occupied and ruled Cuba for only three years, which it spent building physical infrastructure and political institutions.

The terms of the Platt Amendment may seem harsh, but, as John M. Dobson notes, the administration's policy must be judged in historical perspective: "Perhaps the most remarkable aspect of the whole affair is not that the United States restricted Cuban independence before it removed its occupation force, but that it did actually withdraw. At a time when every other major power was working to expand its colonial empire, the United States went against the international trend."[41] McKinley also rejected a proposal that would have given two other Spanish possessions, the Caroline and Marianas island chains, to the United States: "Seeking only individual cable and coaling stations for limited purposes, they were in no way disposed to exercise indiscriminate sovereignty over numerous, widely dispersed islands."[42] In short, whenever McKinley could achieve interventionist ends without resorting to annexation, he did. Cuba illustrated the rule of his grand strategy, whereas the Philippines was an exception. At first glance, this observation raises some warning flags, but closer inspection reveals that it is broadly consistent with the theory.

[40] Quoted in Dobson, *Reticent Expansionism*, 134.
[41] Ibid., 136.
[42] McCormick, *China Market*, 123.

William McKinley (March 1897–September 1901)

Interventionism

Coercive diplomacy
- Threatened war against Spain in response to humanitarian abuses in Cuba; attacked its colonial garrisons in Latin America and East Asia.

Overseas bases
- Annexed Puerto Rico, Guam, and Wake Island from Spain.
- Assumed control of Guantánamo Bay in Cuba.
- Annexed Hawaii and eastern Samoa.
- Persuaded Britain to overturn the Clayton-Bulwer Treaty.

Political intervention
- Occupied Cuba and prepared it for self-government.
- Participated in a joint force to put down the Boxer Rebellion in China.

Commercial expansion
- Pressured Britain, France, Germany, Russia, and Japan not to discriminate against other countries' exports in their respective spheres of influence in China (the Open Door policy).

Imperialism

Landmass annexation
- Annexed the Philippines from Spain; fought a three-year war against native insurgents.

In September 1901, the newly reelected McKinley was shot dead by an anarchist, leaving the presidency in the hands of Theodore Roosevelt. Roosevelt was more progressive than McKinley, but the two Republicans nevertheless shared the same northeastern electoral base, which was becoming increasingly dependent on income from peripheral trade and investment. Consequently, Roosevelt should have continued to advance the interventionist program of his Republican predecessors—that is, to build an isthmian canal, to protect American commercial rights overseas, to enforce the Monroe Doctrine, and to acquire strategically located islands across the globe. Roosevelt should have had little interest in imperialism, since northeastern manufacturers were sufficiently competitive that they had no need for protected markets in the periphery.

These predictions fit Roosevelt's actual grand strategy well.[43] He expanded the Monroe Doctrine, intervened in Cuba and the Dominican

---

[43] See Frederick W. Marks III, *Velvet Iron: The Diplomacy of Theodore Roosevelt* (Lincoln: University of Nebraska Press, 1982); Howard K. Beale, *Theodore Roosevelt and the Rise of America*

Republic, aided the secession of Panama from Colombia, and broke ground on the Panama Canal. In East Asia, he not only engaged actively in diplomatic wrangling to maintain the Open Door policy but also threatened the Chinese government with military intervention to force it to end a popular boycott of American exports. For all of his martial rhetoric, however, Roosevelt was not a traditional imperialist. As he wrote of the Dominican Republic in 1904, "I want to do nothing but what a policemen has to do in Santo Domingo. . . . I have about the same desire to annex it as a gorged boa constrictor might have to swallow a porcupine wrong-end-to."[44] His policy on the Philippines, as he instructed his secretary of war, was that "if they handle themselves wisely in their legislative assembly we shall at the earliest possible moment give them a nearly complete independence."[45] In short, Roosevelt followed closely, and incrementally extended, the interventionist principles of his Republican predecessors.

Theodore Roosevelt (September 1901–March 1909)

Interventionism

Coercive diplomacy
- Sent warships to the Caribbean to threaten Germany against intervening in Venezuela to collect on government debt.
- Declared the "Roosevelt Corollary" to the Monroe Doctrine, which asserted that the United States would exercise "police power" in Latin America to enforce contracts, restore stability, and preempt European intervention.

Overseas bases
- Attempted to purchase the western Virgin Islands from Denmark.
- Negotiated a treaty with Colombia for control over a six-mile-wide canal zone. After its legislature rejected the agreement, helped the province of Panama to secede from Colombia, then secured de facto sovereignty over a ten-mile canal zone.

Political intervention
- Sent American forces back to Cuba to suppress an armed insurgency and temporarily take control over the government.

---

to World Power (Baltimore: Johns Hopkins University Press, 1956); Lewis L. Gould, *The Presidency of Theodore Roosevelt* (Lawrence: University Press of Kansas, 1991), chaps. 3–4, 8, 11. Also useful are Dobson, *America's Ascent*, chaps. 5–7; John Morton Blum, *The Republican Roosevelt*, 2d ed. (Cambridge, Mass.: Harvard University Press, 1977), chap. 8; Richard H. Collin, *Theodore Roosevelt's Caribbean: The Panama Canal, the Monroe Doctrine, and the Latin American Context* (Baton Rouge: Louisiana State University Press, 1990).

[44] Quoted in Gould, *Presidency of Theodore Roosevelt*, 176.

[45] Quoted in Dobson, *America's Ascent*, 130. See also ibid., 146; Marks, *Velvet Iron*, 162 (fn. 34); Beale, *Theodore Roosevelt*, 73.

- Coerced the Dominican Republic to cede control over its customs to the United States to ensure the repayment of foreign creditors.
- Prepared to send an expeditionary force of twenty thousand men to China to force the government to suppress a boycott of American exports.

Commercial expansion

- Maintained diplomatic pressure for the Open Door in China.

The next president, the Republican William H. Taft, adhered closely to the same agenda.[46] In China, he tried to ensure nondiscriminatory access for American exporters and arranged for American investors to participate in a railroad consortium with French, German, and British bankers. Closer to home, Taft took his cues from Roosevelt's "dollar diplomacy" with the Dominican Republic. Fearing that unstable governments in Nicaragua, Honduras, Liberia and again the Dominican Republic, would default on their debts, he offered loans in return for control over their customs houses. The overall result was a moderately expansive and straightforwardly interventionist grand strategy in the periphery.

William H. Taft (March 1909–March 1913)

Interventionism

Overseas bases

- Negotiated for exclusive rights to build a canal and naval base in Nicaragua.

Political intervention

- Offered loans in return for control over customs in Honduras, Nicaragua, Liberia, and the Dominican Republic; sent warships to force the Dominican Republic to accept.

Commercial expansion

- Maintained diplomatic pressure for the Open Door in China.
- Arranged for Americans to participate in a consortium with French, German, and British bankers to fund a major railroad project in China.

[46] See Paolo E. Coletta, *The Presidency of William Howard Taft* (Lawrence: University Press of Kansas, 1973), chaps. 9–11; Walter V. Scholes and Marie V. Scholes, *The Foreign Policies of the Taft Administration* (Columbia: University of Missouri Press, 1970); Herbert F. Wright, "Philander Chase Knox," in *The American Secretaries of State and Their Diplomacy*, vol. 9, ed. Samuel F. Bemis (New York: Knopf, 1929), 320–49; David H. Burton, *William Howard Taft: In the Public Service* (Malabar, Fla.: Krieger, 1986), chap. 6; Dobson, *America's Ascent*, 203–19.

Democrats

From 1896 to 1912, the national Democratic Party was in a state of flux, pulled back and forth between the extremes of William Jennings Bryan's agrarian radicalism and Cleveland's conservative, probusiness "reorganizers." Not until the rise of Woodrow Wilson did the party find a leader who could reconcile its two wings. By the logic of the theory, the revival of the Democratic coalition dictated a return to the kind of compromise Cleveland followed in 1885–89 and 1893–97. For northeastern manufacturers, Wilson should have made a show of support for interventionism; for southern farmers, he should have retreated from some of the most costly or aggressive elements of his Republican predecessors' policies.

These predictions correspond reasonably well to the president's actual grand strategy.[47] Sometimes he sought to cooperate peacefully with peripheral countries; at other times, he used coercion to advance American economic interests. In China, Wilson withdrew support for the consortium that Taft had arranged to win concessions for American investors. He did not want to lose the Chinese market, but he refused to make costly commitments for it. In the same vein, he granted partial independence to the Philippines in 1916. The islands were allowed to govern themselves with their own bicameral legislature, the laws of which would be subject to veto by an American governor-general. Wilson was even more accommodating— indeed, internationalist—in South America. He proposed the Pan-American Pact, a quasi-collective security agreement between the United States and South American nations, and he signed strong conciliation treaties with China, Brazil, and Ecuador (see chapter 4).

Wilson's approach toward Central America was more typical of the interventionist grand strategy of his Republican predecessors. In a policy reminiscent of Taft's "dollar diplomacy," Wilson tried to negotiate for control of Haiti's customs houses. This effort was unsuccessful, so, after a series of revolutions in the country, the president directed the U.S. Navy to take it by force in 1915. A similar scenario played out in the Dominican Republic in 1916. Wilson also intervened repeatedly in the Mexican civil

---

[47] See Kendrick A. Clements, *The Presidency of Woodrow Wilson* (Lawrence: University Press of Kansas, 1992), chaps. 6–10; Frederick S. Calhoun, *Uses of Force and Wilsonian Foreign Policy* (Kent: Kent State University Press, 1993); Arthur S. Link, *Wilson: The New Freedom* (Princeton: Princeton University Press, 1956), chaps. 9–12; Arthur S. Link, *Wilson: Confusions and Crises, 1915–1916* (Princeton: Princeton University Press, 1964), chaps. 2, 11; Sidney Bell, *Righteous Conquest: Woodrow Wilson and the Evolution of the New Diplomacy* (Port Washington, N.Y.: Kennikat, 1972). Also useful are N. Gordon Levin, *Woodrow Wilson and World Politics: America's Response to War and Revolution* (New York: Oxford University Press, 1968); Mark T. Gilderhus, *Pan American Visions: Woodrow Wilson in the Western Hemisphere, 1913–1921* (Tucson: University of Arizona Press, 1986).

war, and he sought to maintain order in Nicaragua by signing a treaty that would have made it a de facto American protectorate.

Woodrow Wilson (March 1913–April 1917)

Isolationism
Full retreats
- Withdrew support for the railroad consortium that Taft had arranged to gain concessions and political influence for American investors in China.

Interventionism
Partial retreats
- Granted partial independence to the Philippines; promised full independence in the near future.

Overseas bases
- Accepted an offer from Nicaragua to make it a de facto protectorate.
- Purchased the western Virgin Islands from Denmark.

Political intervention
- Sent troops to Haiti and the Dominican Republic in response to revolutionary disorder; took control of their governments.
- Sent troops to Mexico to protect American investment, promote democratization, and capture rebel general Pancho Villa.
- Offered loans to Haiti and the Dominican Republic in return for control over their customs.

Internationalism
Multilateralism
- Proposed the Pan-American Pact, a treaty with South American countries that would have forbidden the use of force among signatories, prevented them from taking sides against each other in disputes with third parties, and established "a common and mutual guaranty of territorial integrity and of political independence under republican forms of government."
- Signed strong conciliation treaties with China, Brazil, and Ecuador.

When examining the motives behind Wilson's diplomacy, historians often emphasize his Christian morality, humanitarian concerns, and desire to promote democracy.[48] Yet in no case were these values necessary for him

[48] Clements, *Presidency of Woodrow Wilson*, 106; Arthur S. Link, *Wilson the Diplomatist: A Look at His Major Foreign Policies* (New York: New Viewpoints, 1957), 13–15, 20–21.

to make the decisions he did in the periphery. He did not go out of his way to attack stable, nondemocratic governments; rather, he intervened only when American commerce (or American naval power, which protected commerce) was under direct threat. Indeed, he was a vocal proponent of the idea, popularized by Frederick Jackson Turner, that the closing of the western frontier impelled Americans to search for foreign markets. Wilson viewed commercial expansion as both an economic necessity and a moral imperative, contrasting "exploitative" European investment with "emancipating" American investment.[49] Whether Wilson was a canny office-seeker or a righteous Christian, however, does not much matter: either view is compatible with the coalitional theory of interest aggregation presented in chapter 1. Regardless of what Wilson believed, his actions confirm the prediction that he would make the sort of compromises required of the leader of a united Democratic coalition.

1918–29: The New World Order

The successful prosecution of World War I left the United States in a very different strategic environment than only a few years prior. On the one hand, it faced few external constraints. Germany was stripped of its colonies and navy, the Bolshevik revolution forestalled Russia's designs on China, France focused nearly all of its attention on Germany, and Britain was willing to appease the United States. The only great power likely to cause trouble was Japan, which sought to expand its sphere of influence in China. With little geopolitical competition, American presidents could have conducted a more effective interventionist strategy for the same cost, or they could have maintained the same level of effectiveness at a lower cost.

At the same time, the United States was burdened with a massive increase in the federal debt. In 1916, payments on the debt had fallen to a mere 0.05 percent of the national income; in 1921, they shot up to 1.62 percent, a level not seen since 1871 (see figure 3.1). Since welfare programs were nearly nonexistent in the early twentieth century, cuts in spending would have to come mostly from military appropriations, which consumed approximately 45 percent of the federal budget each year between 1898 and 1916. This internal constraint should have made domestic interest groups

---

[49] Bell, *Righteous Conquest*, 73. See also ibid., 35–36, 40, 48, 73, 128–29; William A. Williams, *The Tragedy of American Diplomacy* (New York: Norton, 1972), 70–72; Levin, *Woodrow Wilson and World Politics*, 14–19; Martin J. Sklar, *The United States as a Developing Country: Studies in U.S. History in the Progressive Era and the 1920s* (New York: Cambridge University Press, 1992), 114–16.

more reluctant to undertake costly strategic initiatives than they had been before the war.

Democrats

The end of World War I brought a return to the sectoral trends that had shaped American grand strategy at the turn of the century. Northeastern manufacturers continued to focus predominantly on peripheral markets, while Southern farmers remained tied to Europe. The former group had an interest in interventionism; the latter did not. Hence, Democratic president Woodrow Wilson should have continued to pursue a compromise strategy: maintain American commercial interests in the periphery, but not as aggressively as Republicans.

In 1918–21, Wilson was preoccupied with the negotiation and attempted ratification of the Versailles Treaty. This brief period provides little direct evidence that could be used either to confirm or disconfirm the theory. However, it is possible to draw some conclusions based on the president's position on colonial issues at the Paris Peace Conference. He wanted the German and Ottoman empires to be mandated to the League of Nations and prepared for independence, but he had to settle for British, French, and Japanese "tutelage," or "administrative advice and assistance," of those territories under the league's auspices. It was not an ideal solution, but rather a step in his preferred direction.

At the same time, Wilson secured British and French concessions over distinctly American interests. Lest any interventionists in his coalition fear that the internationalist league might limit the United States' freedom of action in its own sphere of influence, he included in its charter an unambiguous caveat: "Nothing in this Covenant shall be deemed to affect the validity of international engagements, such as treaties of arbitration or regional understandings like the Monroe doctrine, for securing the maintenance of peace." Although Wilson's attention was focused elsewhere in 1918–21, his behavior regarding the periphery is consistent with the theory.

Woodrow Wilson (November 1918–March 1921)

Interventionism
    Commercial expansion
        • Attempted to revive the American railroad consortium in China in response to Japan's seizure of Shantung.
    Other
        • Incorporated the Monroe Doctrine in the Covenant of the League of Nations.
        • Negotiated to have the former colonies of the German and Ottoman Empires be supervised by the League of Nations.

Republicans

As noted above, World War I did not vitiate prior trends in the political economy of the United States. In 1918–29, the Republicans' main constituency, northeastern businesses, continued to expand into peripheral markets while making little headway in the European core. The proportion of exports of finished manufactures sent to the periphery leveled out at 70 percent, while investments in the periphery continued to increase. Investments to Europe also grew, but exports to the continent stagnated in the face of high tariff barriers. American manufacturers continued to focus primarily on the periphery, so their representatives in the Republican Party should have continued to favor a straightforwardly interventionist grand strategy.

Despite these continuities in sectoral interests, the constraints on grand strategy changed significantly after the war. First, the massive increase in the national debt made it difficult for politicians to sustain high levels of military spending. Second, international tensions declined, allowing policymakers to provide the same level of support to American exporters and foreign investors with a less aggressive grand strategy. These two constraints, taken together, suggest an important modification to the foregoing prediction: Republican leaders, while remaining interventionist, should have taken advantage of the favorable international environment by avoiding major new commitments and trying to economize on military expenses wherever possible.

The actual peripheral strategy of the first Republican president in this period, Warren G. Harding, conforms closely to this expectation. Harding actively pursued policies that would make the exercise of American influence abroad more economical, but he did not brook any substantive retreat from the interventionist agenda of his Republican predecessors.[50] At first,

---

[50] See Eugene P. Trani and David L. Wilson, *The Presidency of Warren G. Harding* (Lawrence: Regents Press of Kansas, 1977), chaps. 5–6; Warren I. Cohen, *Empire without Tears: America's Foreign Relations, 1921–1933* (Philadelphia: Temple University Press, 1987); L. Ethan Ellis, *Republican Foreign Policy, 1921–1933* (New Brunswick: Rutgers University Press, 1968). Also useful are Robert F. Smith, "American Foreign Relations, 1920–1942," in *The Twenties: The Critical Issues*, ed. Joan H. Wilson (Boston: Little, Brown, 1972), 60–71; John Braeman, "Power and Diplomacy: The 1920's Reappraised," *Review of Politics* 44, no. 3 (July 1982): 342–69; John Braeman, "The New Left and American Foreign Policy during the Age of Normalcy: A Re-examination," *Business History Review* 57, no. 1 (spring 1983): 73–104; Kathleen Burk, "The Lineaments of Foreign Policy: The United States and a 'New World Order,' 1913–39," *Journal of American Studies* 26, no. 3 (December 1992): 377–91; Emily S. Rosenberg, *Spreading the American Dream: American Economic and Cultural Expansion, 1890–1945* (New York: Hill and Wang, 1982), chaps. 7–8; Joan H. Wilson, *American Business and Foreign Policy, 1920–1933* (Lexington: University Press of Kentucky, 1971); Melvyn P. Leffler, "1921–1932: Interventionist Impulses and Domestic Constraints," in *Economics and World Power: An Assessment of American Diplomacy since 1789*, ed. William H. Becker and Samuel F. Wells (New York: Columbia University Press, 1984), 225–75; Samuel F. Bemis, *The Latin American Policy of the United States: A Historical Interpretation* (New York: Harcourt, Brace, 1943), chap. 12.

he removed the marines that Wilson had sent to Cuba and began preparations to pull out from Nicaragua, the Dominican Republic, and Haiti. There was no real risk that this policy would lead to the weakening of the United States' sphere of influence in Latin America; after all, troops could be sent right back into these countries in the event of further instability. Following a coup in Honduras, Harding landed marines, helped select a provisional government, and arranged for debt forgiveness to put the new regime on a firmer footing. Throughout his presidency, he refused to renounce the right of intervention, even when pressured to do so at the Inter-American Conference of 1923. Most tellingly, he disavowed any intent to expedite the transfer of full sovereignty to the Philippines.

Warren G. Harding (March 1921–August 1923)

Isolationism
Full retreats
- Removed troops from Cuba.
- Prepared for the removal of troops from Haiti, Nicaragua, and the Dominican Republic.

Interventionism
Political intervention
- Sent troops to Honduras to protect American lives and property from revolutionary disorder; worked to stabilize the regime.
- Repudiated Wilson's promise to grant independence to the Philippines.

Harding died in August 1923, leaving the presidency to Calvin Coolidge.[51] Coolidge essentially maintained the precedent set by Harding. He completed the scheduled withdrawal of troops from the Dominican Republic and Nicaragua, but he left marines in Haiti and steadfastly refused to declaim interventionism. The withdrawal of American troops from Nicaragua led to civil war, so Coolidge sent more than five thousand marines back to reestablish order and oversee new elections. Like Harding, Coolidge was willing to experiment with cost-saving measures, but not at the expense of giving

---

[51] See Robert H. Ferrell, *The Presidency of Calvin Coolidge* (Lawrence: University Press of Kansas, 1998), chaps. 7–8; Cohen, *Empire without Tears*; Ellis, *Republican Foreign Policy*. Also useful are Smith, "American Foreign Relations"; Braeman, "Power and Diplomacy"; Braeman, "New Left and American Foreign Policy"; Burk, "Lineaments of Foreign Policy"; Robert Sobel, *Coolidge: An American Enigma* (Washington, D.C.: Regnery, 1998), chap. 12; Rosenberg, *Spreading the American Dream*, chaps. 7–8; Wilson, *American Business and Foreign Policy*; Leffler, "1921–1932."

up control over established spheres of influence. Thus, both presidencies confirm the theory's predictions.

Calvin Coolidge (August 1923–March 1929)

Isolationism
Full retreats
- Carried out Harding's plan to remove troops from Nicaragua and the Dominican Republic.

Interventionism
Political intervention
- Returned American forces to Nicaragua to end civil conflict and hold elections.

1929–41: DEPRESSION AND WITHDRAWAL

The external constraints on American grand strategy in the periphery intensified throughout the 1930s. Japan occupied Manchuria in 1931, then entered into a full-scale war with China in 1937; Italy invaded Abyssinia in 1935; and Nazi Germany sought to expand its economic influence in Latin America. By the end of the decade, the world was at war once again. These developments did not directly threaten the United States, but they should have raised concerns about the security of its overseas possessions and foreign commerce.

The Great Depression provided a more immediate problem for policymakers. When the economy collapsed, so did government revenue, falling from $3.5 billion in 1931 to only $1.4 billion in 1933 (real dollars, 1929).[52] This fiscal catastrophe made an aggressive grand strategy even less politically palatable than in 1918–29, when debt repayment had been a serious concern. The United States still had sufficient military capability to intervene in the periphery, but the scarcity of budget resources should have made its leaders less willing to do so.

Republicans

The Great Depression had a devastating effect on the Republican Party's economic constituency, northeastern businesses. The export of finished manufactures to the periphery declined from 1.9 percent of the national income in 1929 to only 0.9 percent in 1932, while long-term investment in

---

[52] Price deflator from Friedman and Schwartz, *Monetary Trends in the United States and the United Kingdom*, 122–25.

the periphery dropped from $11.0 billion in 1929 to $7.6 billion in 1935 (real dollars, 1929). In the hard times of 1893–97, manufacturers had survived through exporting; in the 1930s, this was not an option. Peripheral markets, particularly in Latin America, were hit hard by the Great Depression. The combination of capital flight and the collapse of their own exports meant that they could no longer generate sufficient hard currency to absorb surplus output from the United States.

In these circumstances, a more aggressive grand strategy would have had limited benefits. Instead, American manufacturers needed a worldwide recovery that would give peripheral consumers greater purchasing power. The instrument of their revival would have to be economic policy, not grand strategy. Forced to choose between domestic relief, a balanced budget, and peripheral adventures, northeastern businessmen and their representatives in the Republican Party should have ranked peripheral adventures a distant third. President Herbert Hoover's grand strategy should have been recognizably interventionist, but he should have moved even closer on the continuum to isolationism than either Coolidge or Harding.

Hoover's actual strategy in the periphery confirms this prediction.[53] On the one hand, he did not undertake any military interventions, even as Latin American governments defaulted on debts totaling over $1 billion. He withdrew American troops from Nicaragua by January 1933 and planned the same for Haiti in 1934. On the other hand, he maintained control over both of these countries' national finances. Furthermore, just like Harding and Coolidge, he opposed any change in status of the United States' only colonial possession, the Philippines. Hoover's strategy was based on unilateral self-denial, not the recognition of a new norm against intervention.[54]

[53] See Robert H. Ferrell, *American Diplomacy in the Great Depression: Hoover-Stimson Foreign Policy, 1929–1933* (New Haven: Yale University Press, 1957). Also useful are Martin L. Fausold, *The Presidency of Herbert C. Hoover* (Lawrence: University Press of Kansas, 1985); Margot Louria, *Triumph and Downfall: America's Pursuit of Peace and Prosperity, 1921–1933* (Westport, Conn.: Greenwood, 2001); Alexander DeConde, *Herbert Hoover's Latin-American Policy* (Stanford: Stanford University Press, 1951); Irwin F. Gellman, *Good Neighbor Diplomacy: United States Policies in Latin America, 1933–1945* (Baltimore: Johns Hopkins University Press, 1979); Robert H. Ferrell, "Repudiation of a Repudiation," *Journal of American History* 51, no. 4 (March 1965): 669–73; Bemis, *Latin American Policy of the United States*, 268–70; Michael J. J. Smith, "Henry L. Stimson and the Philippines: American Withdrawal from Empire, 1931–1935," *Michigan Academician* 5, no. 3 (winter 1973): 335–48.
[54] Some historians speculate that Hoover may have been moving toward a repudiation of the "right" of intervention at the end of his term, but the fact remains that he did not. See Bemis, *Latin American Policy of the United States*, 268–70; DeConde, *Herbert Hoover's Latin-American Policy*, 60.

Herbert Hoover (March 1929–March 1933)

Interventionism
Partial retreat

- Removed troops from Nicaragua and planned the removal of troops from Haiti; however, retained control over both countries' finances.

Overseas bases

- Vetoed a bill granting independence to the Philippines.

Democrats

Since the end of the Civil War, Democratic leaders had been consistently less interventionist than Republicans. They could not win national elections without demonstrating some concern for the peripheral interests of northeastern manufacturers, but they also had a large constituency in the South that had little stake in the markets of less-developed parts of the world. Every time a Democratic president had come to power, he took a step back from the most adventurous elements of his Republican predecessor's peripheral strategy. Franklin D. Roosevelt, who came to the White House after Hoover in 1933, should have been no different.

In fact, Roosevelt confirms this prediction, even as the economy improved and the budget constraint declined.[55] Whereas Hoover had chosen not to intervene as a matter of course, Roosevelt enshrined nonintervention as a general principle of American grand strategy in the Western Hemisphere. His approach toward the periphery, the "good neighbor policy," was more than just high-minded rhetoric. He agreed to the revision or abrogation of several treaties, including the Platt Amendment, that gave the United States unequal rights over Latin American countries. He also granted independence to the Philippines, a measure that Hoover had vetoed. Roosevelt did not abstain from all forms of intervention; he seized several islands in the South Pacific to establish airbases from Hawaii to Australia. However, as predicted, he was demonstrably less interventionist than Hoover and the Republicans, nearly even to the point of isolationism.

---

[55] See Robert Dallek, *Franklin D. Roosevelt and American Foreign Policy, 1932–1945* (New York: Oxford University Press, 1979). Also useful are Gellman, *Good Neighbor Diplomacy*; David G. Haglund, *Latin America and the Transformation of U.S. Strategic Thought, 1936–1940* (Albuquerque: University of New Mexico Press, 1984); E. David Cronon, "Interpreting the Good Neighbor Policy: The Cuban Crisis of 1933," *Hispanic American Historical Review* 39, no. 4 (November 1959): 538–67; Smith, "Henry L. Stimson and the Philippines"; Lowell T. Young, "Franklin D. Roosevelt and America's Islets: Acquisition of Territory in the Caribbean and in the Pacific," *Historian* 35, no. 2 (summer 1975): 205–20.

Franklin D. Roosevelt (March 1933–December 1941)

Isolationism

Full retreats

- Signed a treaty from the Inter-American Conference of 1933 that renounced intervention as an instrument of American foreign policy in Latin America.
- Carried out Hoover's plan to remove troops from Haiti.

Interventionism

Partial retreats

- Signed a bill granting near-total independence (commonwealth status) to the Philippines.

Overseas bases

- Asserted control over several islets in the South Pacific to establish an air route between Hawaii and Australia. Two of the islets were already claimed by Britain, causing a dispute that was resolved by a joint-control agreement.

Internationalism

Multilateralism

- Agreed to the creation of the Inter-American Court of Justice and signed strong multilateral conciliation and arbitration agreements from the Inter-American Conference of 1933.

CONCLUSION

American grand strategy toward the periphery went through several distinct phases between the end of the Civil War and the beginning of World War II. In 1865–77, Andrew Johnson and Ulysses S. Grant sought to acquire numerous territories throughout the Western Hemisphere. Their behavior contradicts the theory, since their sectoral constituencies had little interest in the periphery at the time. Even northeastern manufacturers were not yet interested in foreign markets; instead, they focused on expanding into the western frontier of the United States. Not surprisingly, Republicans in Congress defeated nearly all of Johnson's and Grant's imperialist initiatives.

It was not until the 1880s, when the frontier was beginning to reach a mature stage of development, that manufacturers began to take an interest in export and overseas investment. They worried that industrial overproduction could have disastrous consequences for the economy if they did not find an outlet for their surplus goods and capital. American businesses were rapidly becoming among the most productive and efficient in the world, so they did not need an empire to compete effectively in peripheral markets. For their tax dollars, the most effective strategy would be one that opened new markets, protected their overseas investments, and prevented discrimination against their goods. Consequently, each successive Republican president in 1881–1901, from James Garfield to William McKinley, adopted an increasingly aggressive strategy of interventionism, climaxing in the Spanish-American War of 1898. McKinley did not start the war exclusively to benefit manufacturers' economic interests, but he did not hesitate to seize the opportunity to leverage it to that end.

By the turn of the century, Republican presidents had succeeded in fulfilling the requisites of an interventionist strategy. They had begun to build a powerful battleship navy, acquired military bases in the Caribbean and East Asia, established the United States' predominant position in Latin America, and were rapidly approaching the point of breaking ground on an isthmian canal. Theodore Roosevelt and William Taft did not make as great a leap forward as had McKinley, but both men clearly continued to advance the interventionist program.

Democrats had a different coalitional calculus. Their primary constituency, southern farmers, would not benefit from interventionism, much less the acquisition of a peripheral empire. Southerners produced unmanufactured agricultural goods like cotton, tobacco, lumber, rice, and sugar, and they exported much of it to Europe. Subtropical countries in Latin America and East Asia were their competitors, not their customers. Yet, the South was not the Democrats' only important constituency. The population of the United States was heavily concentrated in the Northeast, so a Democrat would never be able to win the presidency without carrying a few manufacturing states. As a result, candidates had to adopt a compromise strategy. On the one hand, they had to be less interventionist than Republicans to satisfy their constituents in the agrarian South; on the other hand, they had to be interventionist enough to make inroads into the industrial North. Thus, in each of Grover Cleveland's two discontinuous terms, he started out by backing off of his Republican predecessors' most aggressive policies, then he began moving forward again by the end of his term.

The Democrats continued to adopt a compromise position in the early twentieth century. When Woodrow Wilson first took office, he drew back from American involvement in China, established a timetable for the independence of the Philippines, and sought to promote cooperation between the United States and South American republics. After the outbreak of World War I, however, he became increasingly concerned that one of the belligerents might try to establish naval bases in Central America. Furthermore, revolution and disorder in the region threatened his northeastern constituents' economic interests. In response, he adopted a more aggressively interventionist position, including fighting with Mexico and agreeing to make a protectorate of Nicaragua.

The end of World War I brought about major changes in the constraints on the conduct of American grand strategy. The massive war debt made Americans reluctant to pay for costly interventions, and the Great Depression only made matters worse. At the same time, the defeat of Germany, combined with the exhaustion of Britain and France, allowed the United States to maintain its influence in the periphery at a lower cost than ever before. In response, Republican presidents Warren Harding, Calvin Coolidge, and Herbert Hoover were more economical than their predecessors in the use of force overseas, even withdrawing troops from some countries. However, they did not abandon their party's fundamental strategic principles. They refused to declaim the United States' right to intervene in Latin America, and they backed out of Wilson's commitment to grant independence to the Philippines.

When the Democrats returned to the White House in 1933, they took the Republicans' strategic retrenchment a step further. Roosevelt renounced the right of intervention in Latin America and made numerous concessions over the United States' unequal treaties in the region. He continued to withdraw American troops from the Caribbean, and he granted independence to the Philippines. By the time the United States entered World War II, he had abandoned interventionism almost entirely. This was an extraordinary turnaround: American grand strategy toward the periphery in the mid 1930s is hardly distinguishable from that in the late 1870s. The United States accumulated a number of overseas bases in the interim, but Franklin D. Roosevelt did little more with them than had Rutherford B. Hayes without them.

As emphasized at the beginning of this chapter, theories that view state behavior in terms of the "national interest" are unable to account for the enormous amount of variation in American foreign policy. The relative economic power of the United States grew almost continuously throughout 1865–1941, but its involvement in the periphery did not. Instead, its behavior tracked changes in the sectoral interests of economic actors and their political coalitions' control over the presidency. Whether this also holds true for American grand strategy toward the great powers is the subject of the next chapter.

[4]

American Grand Strategy toward the Great Powers

The United States was involved only sporadically with the great powers between 1865 and 1941. It negotiated general arbitration treaties with Britain in 1897, 1911, and 1928, but it did not ratify any of them; it entered both world wars, but only after an extended period of neutrality; and it created the League of Nations and laid the groundwork for the Permanent Court of International Justice in 1918–19, but it did not join either organization. Its lack of sustained engagement in great power politics makes its grand strategy difficult to characterize, much less explain. Nevertheless, there were two common themes in its behavior. First, the United States was not wholly indifferent to events in Europe. It came into World War I of its own initiative, not because it was forced to do so, and it sided with Britain against Nazi Germany long before the bombing of Pearl Harbor made it an official participant in World War II. Second, many of its forays into great power politics were highly internationalist. It did more than any other country to advance the cause of international law and multilateral cooperation, even if it did not do so consistently.

The apparent incoherence of American grand strategy toward the great powers poses a formidable interpretive challenge to international relations theories. The dominant paradigm in the study of international security, realism, focuses on the position of the United States in the geopolitical balance of power. In this view, policymakers had little incentive to risk blood and treasure in the game of great power politics in the late nineteenth century. As long as no single state threatened to dominate the international system, their only strategic imperative was to consolidate their influence over the Western Hemisphere. Not until 1917, when the war in Europe began to turn in Germany's favor, was the United States compelled to respond. According to this logic, its entry into the conflict was perfectly timed. By rescuing its exhausted allies from the verge of defeat, the United States was assured not only of preventing German hegemony but also of maximizing its influence over the peace settlement. With only a few changes, the same story can be told for the American entry into World War II.[1]

Though the outline facts of the case correspond fairly well to realist expectations, three critical details are highly problematic. First, realism cannot account for why the United States should have made commitments to arbitration or collective security. International law constrains states' ability to expand their influence in the international system, so it benefits weak and declining powers at the expense of strong and rising powers. Since the United States was in the latter camp, it should have opposed internationalism, not promoted it. Second, realism fails to explain why the United States should have withdrawn from great power politics in the interwar period. As a potential hegemon, it should not have been so reluctant to participate in European affairs. Its response to World War II is particularly troubling from this perspective. In a realist world, the United States would have declared war on Germany and sent troops to Europe and North Africa immediately following the collapse of France. Instead, it waited for another year and a half, until Germany forced its hand by declaring war on it first.

A final problem for realism is that the conduct of American grand strategy toward the great powers was divided along partisan lines. Democratic presidents were internationalist, seeking to engage directly with Europe, whereas Republicans transitioned from isolationism to realpolitik. In 1918–21, Democratic president Woodrow Wilson spent an enormous amount of diplomatic capital on the creation of the League of Nations; yet, his Republican successors not only refused to join the organization but also opposed establishing any official diplomatic presence in it. Under the realist assumption that foreign policy is determined by objective "national interests," it is not possible to explain why partisan turnover in the executive office produced such monumental shifts in state behavior. Only by examining domestic preferences can one account for the discontinuities in American grand strategy toward the great powers between 1865 and 1941.

IDEAS AND CULTURE

Ideational and cultural theorists offer a very different interpretation of the case. Frank Ninkovich, for example, argues that American foreign policy periodically alternates between two guiding principles, each of which

---

[1] John J. Mearsheimer, *The Tragedy of Great Power Politics* (New York: Norton, 2001), 250–61.

is rooted in liberal ideology.[2] "Normal internationalism," a cautious, incrementalist strategy, derives from the optimistic belief that the international system naturally will become more peaceful and cooperative over time. "Wilsonian internationalism," in contrast, arises in times of crisis. It is based on the fear that progress will collapse and therefore demands radical measures to set the world aright. According to Ninkovich, the shock of World War I swayed many Americans to the latter strategy. With peace reestablished, however, the United States soon rediscovered its aversion to foreign entanglements. In this view, individual decision makers may have some influence on outcomes, but liberal ideology is fundamental.

A simple counterfactual provides a devastating rebuttal to this interpretation. Suppose that Woodrow Wilson had not been elected president in 1916. Unless the theory depends entirely on Wilson's personality—in which case it can hardly be considered an overarching theory of American foreign policy—it predicts that a Republican president in the same situation would also have proposed a radical, "Wilsonian internationalist" initiative during World War I. This proposition is quite implausible in light of Republican leaders' ambivalence over the League of Nations.[3] Charles Evans Hughes, the Republican presidential nominee in 1916, showed little interest in early proposals for the league; Senator Henry Cabot Lodge opposed any organization that would impose legal obligations on the United States; Theodore Roosevelt was adamantly against collective security; and Warren Harding, on becoming president, ruled out American membership in the league. Ex-president Taft did campaign for it, but his influence in the Republican Party was limited after his crushing defeat in the election of 1912. In contrast, the concept of a "League to Enforce the Peace"—which did not originate with Wilson, but rather gained public prominence in both the United States and Great Britain only a few months after the outbreak of war—had many supporters in the Democratic Party, including three-time presidential nominee William Jennings Bryan.

The problem with Ninkovich and other ideational theorists, therefore, is that they fail to recognize the analytic significance of partisanship. What causes the triumph of one strategic idea over its many possible alternatives is not a collective rethinking of the dominant orthodoxy, which rarely exists anyway, but rather the rise to power of a societal coalition that favored the

[2] Frank A. Ninkovich, *The Wilsonian Century: U.S. Foreign Policy since 1900* (Chicago: University of Chicago Press, 1999). See also Jeffrey W. Legro, *Rethinking the World: Great Power Strategies and International Order* (Ithaca: Cornell University Press, 2005), chap. 3; Colin Dueck, *Reluctant Crusaders: Power, Culture, and Change in American Grand Strategy* (Princeton: Princeton University Press, 2006), chaps. 2–3.

[3] Thomas J. Knock, *To End All Wars: Woodrow Wilson and the Quest for a New World Order* (Princeton: Princeton University Press, 1992), 48–69, 99–101.

idea all along and that is able, given international constraints, to implement it. In short, politics decides policy.

To account for partisanship, a theory of strategic ideas would have to demonstrate a logical connection between parties' domestic ideologies and their grand strategies. Both liberalism and internationalism, for example, are based on the assumption that social actors have the capacity for rational action and moral improvement and that progress can be achieved through the creation of well-engineered institutions. Thus, supporters of liberal causes in the domestic sphere should be inclined to favor internationalist policies in foreign affairs. By the same reasoning, traditional conservatives, who are pessimistic about human nature and skeptical of change, should prefer realpolitik. If these hypotheses were confirmed, it would raise the possibility that ideology, not economic interest, serves as the basis of American grand strategy toward the great powers.

A brief scan of the relevant evidence shows that this is not, in fact, the case. The most internationalist presidents, Woodrow Wilson and Franklin Delano Roosevelt, did push for liberal reform domestically. However, so did Theodore Roosevelt, who was one of the League of Nations' most vociferous critics. Furthermore, support for internationalist policies was strongest in the South, which was the least liberal, least progressive part of the country. Southern culture in 1865–1941 stood for institutionalized inequality, not democratization; social tradition, not reform; and racial superiority, not moral perfectibility.[4] By comparison, the Northeast was far more liberal but far less internationalist. In view of these lacunae, it is necessary to look elsewhere for the source of domestic cleavages over grand strategy.

POLITICAL ECONOMY

The political economy perspective is well equipped to explain American grand strategy toward the great powers. As noted in the previous chapter, there is a rich tradition of research on the subject. In 1939, Charles Beard argued that "collective internationalism" served the interests of societal actors involved in the production and export of commodities, particularly cotton, while "imperial isolationism" benefited manufacturers and overseas

[4] Peter Trubowitz, *Defining the National Interest: Conflict and Change in American Foreign Policy* (Chicago: University of Chicago Press, 1998), 126–27. Anne-Marie Burley argues that American internationalism in the 1930s was an external projection of the Democrats' New Deal reforms, but she does not attempt to explain partisan cleavages in earlier years. See Anne-Marie Burley, "Regulating the World: Multilateralism, International Law, and the Projection of the New Deal Regulatory State," in *Multilateralism Matters: The Theory and Praxis of an Institutional Form*, ed. John G. Ruggie (New York: Columbia University Press, 1993), 125–56.

investors.[5] In recent years, several political scientists have expanded greatly on these insights. Important advances on the 1865–1941 period include Richard Bensel's examination of congressional voting on military preparedness prior to World War I, Thomas Ferguson's study of the international objectives of the New Deal coalition, and Peter Trubowitz's analysis of the sectional basis of congressional voting on trade and neutrality legislation in the 1930s.[6]

Building on this literature, I use the political economy perspective to provide a comprehensive account of American grand strategy toward the great powers from the end of the Civil War to the country's entry into World War II. The Democrats' primary economic constituency, southern cotton and tobacco growers, was deeply dependent on European markets. Consequently, Democratic leaders sought to promote cooperative relations between the great powers, using international law and collective security to resolve interstate disputes. They were particularly eager to build a strong relationship with Great Britain, which not only was their largest export market but also supported free trade, unlike all of the other great powers.

In contrast, Republicans had little reason to support an internationalist agenda. After the Civil War, their primary constituency, northeastern manufacturers, was almost completely detached from the international economy. In the 1880s and 1890s, when manufacturers finally began to take an interest in export and overseas investment, they focused on Latin America and East Asia rather than Europe. Republicans leaders' strategic imperative was to use the U.S. Navy to defend peripheral markets from the encroachment of other great powers, not to take on the burden of fostering peace and cooperation in the international system.

The external environment and internal conditions of the United States shifted several times in 1865–1941, at each point creating new opportunities and constraints on the conduct of grand strategy. Some of these developments were gradual, like the escalating crisis with Japan in the 1930s; others were sudden, like the onset of the Great Depression and the Allied victory at the end of World War I. To take them into account, I divide the case into five subsections: 1865–81, 1881–97, 1897–1917, 1918–29, and 1929–41.

---

[5] Charles A. Beard and Mary R. Beard, *The Rise of American Civilization: America in Midpassage*, vol. 3 (New York: Macmillan, 1939), 456.
[6] Thomas Ferguson, "From Normalcy to New Deal: Industrial Structure, Party Competition, and American Public Policy in the Great Depression," *International Organization* 38, no. 1 (winter 1984): 41–94; Richard F. Bensel, *Sectionalism and American Political Development, 1880–1980* (Madison: University of Wisconsin Press, 1984), 105–28; Trubowitz, *Defining the National Interest*, chap. 3.

1865–81: At Home Alone

The United States in 1865 faced no international threats, had almost no commitments outside of the Western Hemisphere, and rarely interacted with any of the great powers other than Britain. After four years of civil war, with minimal interference from outside powers, its grand strategy was virtually a blank slate. Though the United States was not yet highly populated or economically developed enough to be considered in the same class as the most important European states, it was completely unconstrained by the international system. The only serious limitation on its conduct of grand strategy was the Civil War debt, which consumed 30–40 percent of the national budget in nearly every year between 1865 and 1881. Otherwise, American presidents could promote internationalist causes, form realpolitik alignments, or remain disconnected from great power politics as they pleased.

Democrats

The primary constituency of the Democratic Party, southern farmers, had a strong interest in cultivating close relations with the great powers. Since the founding of the original thirteen colonies in North America, the economy of the South had been based on the export of cotton and tobacco to Europe. During the Civil War, the Confederate states invested considerable effort in trying to secure aid and diplomatic recognition from their best customers, Britain and France. Though unsuccessful, they faced the same structural trade situation after their defeat. To recover from the devastation of war, southern farmers would once again need to send their goods to Europe. Thus, the Democrats' strategy toward the great powers in 1865–81 should have been demonstrably internationalist.

The evidence does not support this prediction. The only Democrat to have served as president in the period, Andrew Johnson, showed no interest in sustained interaction with the great powers. Apart from negotiations for territorial purchases and conflict with France over Mexico (see chapter 3), the administration's only major "high politics" diplomacy was the *Alabama* claims dispute with Britain.[7] During the Civil War, private British shipyards had sold three commerce-destroying ships to the Confederacy, in violation of Britain's own neutrality laws. These ships did serious harm to the Union war effort, leading many Americans to demand compensation. To sort out the matter, Johnson called on Britain to submit to binding arbitration. Under most circumstances, such a demand would constitute clear

---

[7] Glyndon G. Van Deusen, *William Henry Seward* (New York: Oxford University Press, 1967), chap. 34.

evidence of internationalism, but the *Alabama* dispute was a special case. It was not about contested territory, in which both sides had something to lose; instead, the United States was simply asking for a massive cash payment without putting anything comparable at stake in return. Thus, Johnson's behavior provides little indication of his strategic principles.

Even outside of presidential policymaking, it is difficult to find definitive evidence of the Democrats' position on grand strategy in 1865–81. As explained in the previous chapter, the party's overwhelming priority was the economic reconstruction and political rehabilitation of the war-ravaged South. Until that task was complete, foreign policy would be a distant concern. If southern farmers had perceived a threat to their agricultural exports to Europe, they might have devoted more attention to international affairs; however, no such threat existed. Given the paucity of evidence for internationalist sentiment in the party, I count this observation as a disconfirmation of the theory. Not until the next period, 1881–97, would the revived Democratic Party produce a clearly internationalist president.

Republicans

Republicans had few incentives to seek active engagement with the other great powers in the first few decades following the Civil War. Their primary economic constituency, the northeastern manufacturing sector, had not yet taken an interest in foreign markets. Manufacturers were expanding rapidly into the vast, undeveloped American West and consequently had no cause to concern themselves with Europe. Thus, Republicans' approach toward the great powers should have been largely isolationist.

The grand strategy of the two Republicans who served as president between 1865 and 1881, Grant and Hayes, confirms this prediction. One of the few issues on Grant's diplomatic agenda was the ongoing *Alabama* claims dispute. It was finally resolved in 1871 by the Treaty of Washington, which created an arbitration court to determine British liability for damages caused by ships sold to the Confederacy. As explained above, the use of international law to settle this particular conflict was essentially costless for the United States; it provides no more evidence of internationalism for Grant than it did for Johnson.[8] In his eight years in office, Grant had only

---

[8] As part of the settlement, the United States did agree to the arbitration of counterclaims made by Britain about wartime property damage and fishing rights. However, the sums at stake in these cases were much lower than in the *Alabama* claims. In the end, Britain was awarded $7,429,819, while the United States received $15,500,000. The Washington Treaty also included a provision for the arbitration of a disputed water boundary in the Pacific Northwest, but this issue was of no strategic significance. See A. M. Stuyt, *Survey of International Arbitrations, 1794–1970* (Dobbs Ferry, N.Y.: Oceana, 1972), 96–100; Allan Nevins, *Hamilton Fish: The Inner History of the Grant Administration*, rev. ed. (New York: Ungar, 1957), 410–46, 470–93, 511–66.

one other strategically important encounter with a European state, and that pertained to a peripheral territory, Spanish Cuba (see chapter 3). Overall, his grand strategy toward the great powers was isolationist, consistent with the theory's prediction.

After resolving the *Alabama* claims, Republicans had no reason to engage in high-politics diplomacy with any of the great powers. The last president to serve in 1865–81, Rutherford B. Hayes, did not embark on any strategic initiatives directed toward the great powers, much less attempt to advance internationalist ideals. Thus, his behavior clearly confirms the theory. Not until the 1880s, when northeastern manufacturers began to develop an interest in peripheral markets, would the Republican Party begin to emerge from its diplomatic isolation.

1881–97: New Encounters

The European "scramble for colonies" in the late nineteenth century transformed the international politics of Africa and Asia, but it left the Western Hemisphere largely untouched. As long as the great powers respected the Monroe Doctrine, the United States would be free from serious concerns about encroachment on its established sphere of influence. The only challenge it faced was commercial, as other industrializing states sought to expand their trade in Latin America. Thus, neither threats nor a shifting balance of power dictated that the United States end its isolation and begin to engage in great power politics. Instead, the path that it followed would depend on the economic interests of its leaders' electoral coalitions.

Republicans

Beginning in the 1880s, the Republican Party's economic and strategic interests began to change. Its constituents were not becoming more interdependent with Europe, however. Tariff barriers on the continent were rising, not falling, dashing hopes that exports of manufactures might penetrate any core market other than Britain. Instead, Republican businessmen's interest in the great powers was indirect, originating in their newfound interest in the periphery. As northeastern manufacturers turned their attention from the western frontier of the United States to Latin America and East Asia, they found that their ambition for new markets increasingly put them into conflict with the other great powers. To support their interests, Republican presidents had to begin to maneuver the dangerous shoals of European geopolitics. Specifically, they needed to adopt a realpolitik grand strategy toward the core to support their interventionist grand strategy toward the periphery.

The change in Republican strategy in 1881–97 was most evident in naval policy. The navy was the most basic building block in a realpolitik strategy; without it, the United States would have little capacity to coerce other great powers. In 1869–81, successive Republican presidents had badly neglected the fleet, leaving it incapable of anything but river and littoral operations. Thus, Presidents James Garfield and Chester Arthur initiated many important reforms to professionalize the service and revamp the aging fleet. Their secretary of the navy, William E. Chandler, secured funding for a total of five cruisers, four monitors, two gunboats, and one clipper. These ships were not on par with European battleships; however, they would still be useful for supporting American commercial interests in disputes in the periphery.[9] Their construction did not require a major budgetary commitment, but they did represent the beginning of a new era for the U.S. Navy. Since the end of the Civil War, it had focused exclusively on coastal defense; now, with the addition of cruisers, it was developing the capability to project American power overseas.

Whereas Garfield and Arthur had simply wanted to modernize the navy, the next Republican president, Benjamin Harrison, went a step further. He aspired to transform the navy into a world-class instrument of war that would be powerful enough to challenge rival great powers on the high seas. To accomplish this, the president and his secretary of the navy, Benjamin F. Tracy, embarked on an intense effort to convince Congress and the American public that full-sized battleships, which had never before been used by the U.S. Navy, were of critical importance to the nation's security and prosperity. There was little chance that the Congresses of the early 1890s would have endorsed Tracy's long-term goal—to build a fleet that would be second only to Britain's—but legislators did fund four battleships and three large cruisers before Harrison left office. Even more notably, the Naval Department budget averaged $24.7 million between 1889 and 1892, up from $15.5 million between 1885 and 1888.[10] Tracy, like many Republicans, believed that the cost was well justified by the potential returns: "It is the premium paid by the United States for the insurance of its acquired wealth and its growing industries."[11]

Some scholars attribute this transformation in naval strategy to the rise of new ideas, particularly those of Alfred T. Mahan in his popular treatise, *The*

---

[9] Justus D. Doenecke, *The Presidencies of James A. Garfield and Chester A. Arthur* (Lawrence: Regents Press of Kansas, 1981), 166–67.

[10] United States Bureau of the Census, *Statistical Abstract of the United States* (Washington, D.C.: Government Printing Office, 1960), 718.

[11] Quoted in Walter LaFeber, *The New Empire: An Interpretation of American Expansion, 1860–1898* (Ithaca: Cornell University Press, 1963), 124.

Influence of Sea Power upon History (1890).[12] Yet, it is unlikely that Harrison's naval policy would have been significantly different had Mahan never existed.[13] The logic of the situation was both simple and compelling; it took no feat of genius to realize that America's biggest ships, which in 1886 displaced only forty-five hundred tons, could not defeat European ships that displaced fifteen thousand tons.[14] If the government intended to promote and protect its manufacturers' commercial expansion in the periphery, then conflict with the other great powers would become increasingly frequent, and it would be necessary for the United States to have a fleet that was strong enough to coerce its rivals. It was equally obvious that, if the new navy were to be an effective instrument of power projection, it would require a network of bases and coaling stations in the far corners of the globe. Mahan filled in certain details in this logic, but his apparent influence was more an artifact of fortuitous timing than anything else. If his work had been published a decade earlier, before economic conditions had advanced to the point at which businesses began to see interventionism as benefiting their material interests, it surely would have fallen on deaf ears.

Harrison did not have the opportunity to deploy his new navy against a European power, but it would not be long before it was put to use. In the Spanish-American War of 1898, William McKinley sent the fleet to Cuba and the Philippines, where it handily defeated the decrepit Spanish navy. Then, in the Venezuelan Crisis of 1903, Theodore Roosevelt sent warships to demonstrate resolve against the expansion of German influence in the Western Hemisphere. Without battleships, it would have been much more difficult to extend American influence in the periphery, where many other great powers were already jockeying for the spoils of empire. Aggressive posturing and skillful diplomacy could win some battles, but in the long run American ambition would have to be backed up with American power. Not surprisingly, every Republican president in the period spanning 1889 to 1917 supported naval expansion.

---

[12] Edward Rhodes, "Constructing Power: Cultural Transformation and Strategic Adjustment in the 1890s," in *The Politics of Strategic Adjustment: Ideas, Institutions, and Interests*, ed. Peter Trubowitz, Emily O. Goldman, and Edward Rhodes (New York: Columbia University Press, 1999), 67–69; Mark R. Shulman, "Institutionalizing a Political Idea: Navalism and the Emergence of American Sea Power," in *The Politics of Strategic Adjustment: Ideas, Institutions, and Interests*, ed. Peter Trubowitz, Emily O. Goldman, and Edward Rhodes (New York: Columbia University, 1999), 81–87.
[13] Robert Seager II, "Ten Years before Mahan: The Unofficial Case for the New Navy, 1880–1890," *Mississippi Valley Historical Review* 40, no. 3 (December 1953): 491–512; John A. S. Grenville and George Berkeley Young, *Politics, Strategy, and American Diplomacy: Studies in Foreign Policy, 1873–1917* (New Haven: Yale University Press, 1966), 1–11.
[14] Walter R. Herrick, *The American Naval Revolution* (Baton Rouge: Louisiana State University, 1966), 36.

Also as expected, Republican presidents were uninterested in making high-politics commitments to international law. Neither Garfield nor Arthur initiated any internationalist policies. Harrison did agree to a multilateral arbitration agreement at the Inter-American Conference of 1889–90, but its terms were too weak to impose any substantive constraints on the United States.[15] Republican grand strategy in 1881–97 was not particularly aggressive, moving only gradually away from isolationism, but its path was clearly one of realpolitik, not internationalism.

Democrats

Democratic presidents should have had a very different perspective on international politics. Their primary economic constituency, southern cotton and tobacco growers, was enormously dependent on European markets. At minimum, they should have aspired to maintain friendly relations with the great powers, ensuring that their transatlantic trade would not be endangered by diplomatic or military conflict. When the opportunity arose, they also should have sought to create legalistic and multilateral mechanisms of conflict resolution. Prospects for the latter were not good; the tension-laden international environment and geopolitical insularity of the Western Hemisphere limited what they could hope to accomplish. Nevertheless, the United States was a sufficiently important player in international diplomacy that its leaders should have been able to follow a recognizably internationalist strategy.

The only Democratic president to have served between 1881 and 1897, Grover Cleveland, provides mixed evidence for this prediction. In his first term in office, he scuttled several of Arthur's trade agreements that could have hurt the interests of southern farmers, but he made no attempt to initiate policies that would have benefited core interests. His only significant interaction with the great powers in 1885–89 came in the Samoan Crisis of 1889, in which he sent American warships to deter Germany from taking control over the Samoan Islands.

It was not until his second term in the White House, in 1893–97, that Cleveland revealed an internationalist bent. In early 1895, he started negotiations with British prime minister Lord Salisbury to make international arbitration compulsory for all Anglo-American disputes that could not be resolved through normal diplomacy. Talks were suspended after the death of Secretary of State Richard Olney, but they were renewed on the heels of

---

[15] James B. Scott, ed., *The International Conferences of American States, 1889–1928* (New York: Oxford University Press, 1931); Kevin Narizny, "Rational Idealism: The Political Economy of Internationalism in the United States and Great Britain, 1870–1945," *Security Studies* 12, no. 3 (spring 2003): 17.

the Venezuelan Crisis of 1897 (see chapter 3). The resulting treaty was impressively comprehensive, and it would have been stronger still had Salisbury not insisted on the inclusion of a clause that allowed the two states to avoid an unfavorable judgment over territorial claims. Otherwise, the treaty made no exceptions for questions involving the "national honor" or "vital interests."[16] On its completion, Cleveland proclaimed that "the example set and the lesson furnished by the successful operation of this treaty are sure to be felt and taken to heart sooner or later by other nations, and will thus mark the beginning of a new epoch in civilization."[17] This unprecedented advance in internationalist principles did not last long, however. Henry Cabot Lodge led the Senate to defeat the treaty with a barrage of eviscerating amendments, just as he would do twenty-five years later with the League of Nations Covenant.

Meanwhile, Cleveland's position on naval reform mirrored the development of his peripheral strategy. In his first term as president, he rejected his naval secretary's plea for battleships on the grounds that the country could not afford it at the time.[18] When he returned to the White House for a second term, he initially took a similar stance, arguing that the projected deficit was too high to consider a naval buildup.[19] Yet, just a year later, when the nation's finances were still in the red, Cleveland changed his mind, asserting in his annual address that "if we are to have a navy for warlike operations, offensive and defensive, we certainly ought to increase both the number of battle ships and torpedo boats."[20]

Extraordinary circumstances account for the shift: the country was in the midst of a severe economic depression, and northeastern businesses were more desperate than ever to find new markets abroad, as well as to secure federal funds for military spending in their region. Cleveland derived most of his electoral support from the South, so he had good reason to take a less pronaval position than most Republicans. However, any Democrat who completely ignored the interests of business would have found it impossible to raise enough money and win enough Electoral College votes to prevail in a national election. Thus, Cleveland came to office with a moderate position

---

[16] Nelson M. Blake, "The Olney-Pauncefote Treaty of 1897," *American Historical Review* 50, no. 2 (January 1945); Richard E. Welch, *The Presidencies of Grover Cleveland* (Lawrence: University Press of Kansas, 1988), 192–94; Montgomery Schuyler, "Richard Olney," in *The American Secretaries of State and Their Diplomacy*, vol. 8, ed. Samuel F. Bemis (New York: Knopf, 1928), 317–19; Gerald G. Eggert, *Richard Olney: Evolution of a Statesman* (University Park: Pennsylvania State University Press, 1974), 250–53; J. A. S. Grenville, *Lord Salisbury and Foreign Policy: The Close of the Nineteenth Century* (London: Athlone, 1964), 70–73.

[17] Quoted in Welch, *Presidencies of Grover Cleveland*, 194.

[18] Herrick, *American Naval Revolution*, 160.

[19] Kenneth J. Hagan, *This People's Navy: The Making of American Sea Power* (New York: Free Press, 1991), 203.

[20] Quoted in LaFeber, *New Empire*, 231.

between the interests of northerners and southerners, and he subsequently adjusted it according to the political currents of the moment. In 1885 and 1893, he refused to break the budget for battleships but did not declaim them per se; then, in 1895, when businesses became much more strident in demanding a grand strategy that actively supported their interest in export, he embraced naval reform.[21] By building battleships and pursuing an arbitration treaty with Britain at the same time, he compromised between the interests of northeastern manufacturers and southern farmers, very much in line with the logic of the theory.

1897–1917: Onto the World Stage

The United States dramatically reshaped its external environment at the turn of the century. In the Spanish-American War of 1898, it acquired several island territories in the Pacific Ocean and East Asia, opening a new world of strategic opportunity for itself. The combination of far-flung naval bases and a rapidly expanding battleship fleet suddenly made the United States a credible player in the game of great power politics. It could try to transform the international system through internationalist initiatives, use realpolitik as a means to extend its influence in the periphery, or reverse course and withdraw into isolationism. How it used its newfound power, therefore, would be entirely a function of its political economy.

Republicans

Northeastern manufacturers, the sectoral constituency at the heart of the Republican Party, reached an economic turning point at the close of the century. By the early 1890s, most had come to recognize the importance of overseas markets, but few had actually taken up the challenge of exporting. It was not until the devastating Depression of 1893–97 that necessity pushed them to act. Exports of finished manufactures increased from 1.0 percent of the national income in 1893 to 1.7 percent in 1897, then continued to rise to 2.3 percent in 1914. Overseas investment also grew at an impressive rate, more than doubling relative to the national income from 1897 to 1914. The American "commercial invasion" of the world, long feared by Europeans, had finally arrived.

Yet, the vast majority of this commercial activity was directed at peripheral markets, not the core. The absolute value of manufactured exports and investment to Europe was slowly increasing, but opportunities for profit

---

[21] Herrick, *American Naval Revolution*, 174.

were much greater in Latin America and East Asia. As a result, Republican leaders should have continued to see little advantage in internationalism. Their constituents would not benefit from measures designed to promote cooperation with Europe; rather, a realpolitik strategy would be needed to protect their markets from the encroachments of other great powers in the periphery.

East Asia

The grand strategy of the three Republicans to serve as president in 1897–1917 mostly confirms this prediction. William McKinley came to office in 1897 in hopes of convincing Spain to end its repression of Cuba, but negotiations failed, and he chose at last to sunder the Spanish Empire. Soon after the war, he sought to parlay his military gains into concrete economic benefits in East Asia, particularly in China. He faced an uphill struggle, though, having entered late into a competition in which the other players had already staked their claims. Russia was set on annexing northern China, France controlled southern China, Japan wanted to create its own dependency in Manchuria, and Britain sought to maintain its lucrative position along the Yangtze Valley. Secretary of State John Hay's response to these constraints was the Open Door policy, which demanded that each of the great powers pledge not to discriminate against other countries in its sphere of influence in China. The initiative met with mixed success: Russia had little interest in cooperation, and it could not be isolated because it had the support of France. Nevertheless, McKinley and Hay pursued the Open Door policy vigorously, using realpolitik maneuvering with the great powers to advance American commercial expansion in the periphery.[22]

The next Republican president, Theodore Roosevelt, continued this strategy. His diplomacy helped to end the Russo-Japanese War of 1904–5, thereby preventing either side from gaining full control over Manchuria, an outcome that would have led to greater discrimination against American commercial interests. Roosevelt also signed the Taft-Katsura Agreement of 1905, in which the United States and Japan pledged mutual noninterference in each other's Asian sphere of interest (the Philippines and Korea, respectively). He then sought to enlist Japan's help to prevent Russia from sabotaging the Open Door policy. Finally, Roosevelt's successor, William H. Taft, also struggled to uphold freedom of trade in China. In the face of a

---

[22] Historians disagree over the full extent of McKinley's commitment to the Open Door. For contrasting views, see Thomas J. McCormick, *China Market: America's Quest for Informal Empire* (Chicago: Quadrangle Books, 1967), 168–69; John Dobson, *Reticent Expansionism: The Foreign Policy of William McKinley* (Pittsburgh: Duquesne University Press, 1988), 192. Note that the Open Door policy was not internationalist, as it made no reference to international law and was not conducted through an international organization.

deteriorating international environment, however, he could do little more than encourage American investors' participation in railroad consortia.

Armaments

Republicans remained at the forefront of efforts to strengthen the U.S. armed forces in 1897–1917. Intent on establishing the most powerful fleet in the world after Britain, McKinley, Roosevelt, and Taft all sought to increase spending on the navy.[23] Since Harrison set out to build the first American battleships in 1889–90, Republicans had followed the same strategic logic: trade, or expectations thereof, required the expansion of political influence over foreign markets, which in turn led to conflict with the other great powers, who would not back down unless opposed with superior force. In short, interventionism implied realpolitik, and realpolitik required instruments of coercion.

The partisan cleavage over military appropriations sharpened in 1914–17, under the cloud of war in Europe. For the reasons stated above, Republicans entered the debate with a preexisting preference for higher levels of spending than Democrats. Furthermore, most armaments industries and naval yards were located in the Republican Northeast. Thus, prominent Republicans, like Theodore Roosevelt and Henry Cabot Lodge, led the fight for military preparedness, whereas many Democrats were reluctant to accept what amounted to a massive transfer of wealth from the South and Midwest to the Northeast.[24]

Though Republicans clamored for rearmament, few advocated a hasty entry into the war. Among their leaders, only Roosevelt advocated belligerence against Germany. Notably, he failed in a bid to become his party's presidential nominee in 1916, and the Republican national convention made clear its position with a call for "strict and honest neutrality" in the party platform. Both candidates in the election of 1916, Democrat Woodrow Wilson and Republican Charles Evans Hughes, promised to keep the United States out of the conflict.[25] As explained below (in the section on Wilson), the two parties' sectoral coalitions' stakes in the outcome of World War I dictated similar strategies, albeit for different reasons.

---

[23] George T. Davis, *A Navy Second to None: The Development of Modern American Naval Policy* (New York: Harcourt, Brace, 1940), 107, 168–173.

[24] Bensel, *Sectionalism*, 105–128.

[25] The Republican Party, "Republican Party Platform of 1916," The American Presidency Project, http://www.presidency.ucsb.edu/showplatforms.php?platindex=R1916 (last accessed April 2006); S. D. Lovell, *The Presidential Election of 1916* (Carbondale: Southern Illinois University Press, 1980), 64–69; Patrick Devlin, *Too Proud to Fight: Woodrow Wilson's Neutrality* (Oxford: Oxford University Press, 1974), 335–37.

International Law

Republican presidents signed several internationalist treaties in 1897–1917, but, with only one partial exception, none of these agreements created a meaningful, binding commitment to international law. As a rule, Republicans were willing to accept internationalist treaties only when they could do so without putting any serious constraints on the pursuit of other interests. Only twice did McKinley dabble in internationalism, and in neither case did he make any substantive commitments. First, he indicated that he supported the idea of an Anglo-American arbitration treaty, but he did not push for the ratification of the one that his Democratic predecessor, Grover Cleveland, had just negotiated.[26] Second, he advocated the creation of the Permanent Court of Arbitration at the First Hague Peace Conference of 1899, but his delegation to the conference demanded that disputes involving territory, the political independence of states, and "interoceanic canals"—that is, nearly everything in the domain of high politics and American grand strategy—be excluded from obligatory arbitration.[27] The treaty that the conference finally produced was even weaker, in that it did not require a state to submit to arbitration under any circumstances. In short, McKinley's realpolitik was little tempered by internationalism.

The same applied to Roosevelt. He signed a number of bilateral arbitration agreements, but he insisted that all of them include the provision that disputes pertaining to "the vital interests, the independence, or the honor of the two Contracting States" would be exempt from mandatory arbitration.[28] He also supported the negotiation of an international arbitration treaty in the Second Hague Peace Conference of 1907, but this agreement was far too weak to constrain the conduct of grand strategy. The only treaty Roosevelt signed that involved a binding, high-politics commitment to international law was the International Prize Court Convention of 1907. This agreement created a permanent court for the arbitration of civil damages pursuant to violations of maritime law.[29] It had important implications for the conduct of British grand strategy (see chapter 7), but it was not particularly costly for the United States. American military planners had no intention of ever conducting a major war of blockade, but they had serious concerns about

---

[26] Ernest R. May, *Imperial Democracy: The Emergence of America as a Great Power* (New York: Harcourt, Brace, and World, 1961), 122.

[27] Francis A. Boyle, *Foundations of World Order: The Legalist Approach to International Relations, 1898–1922* (Durham: Duke University Press, 1999), 27–28.

[28] Quoted in James Brown Scott, "Elihu Root," in *The American Secretaries of State and Their Diplomacy*, vol. 9, ed. Samuel F. Bemis (New York: Knopf, 1929), 225–26. See also Boyle, *Foundations of World Order*, 31–33.

[29] Calvin D. Davis, *The United States and the Second Hague Peace Conference: American Diplomacy and International Organization, 1899–1914* (Durham: Duke University Press, 1975), 220–27.

being adversely affected by one in a conflict between the European great powers. Consequently, the Prize Court was a proposition from which they could only benefit. Like the *Alabama* claims arbitration with Johnson and Grant, it cannot be considered as evidence that Roosevelt was actually pursuing an internationalist grand strategy.

Roosevelt's attitude toward legal mechanisms of dispute resolution and norm-based cooperation was exemplified by his diplomatic maneuvering in a long-running dispute over the Alaska-Canada boundary. He rejected arbitration on the grounds that it might lead to an unfavorable partition of the territory in question. Instead, he convinced Britain to let a six-member panel of "impartial jurists" resolve the matter. The three men he appointed—Henry Cabot Lodge, Elihu Root, and George Turner—were neither impartial nor jurists, so there was no chance that Roosevelt could do worse than a deadlock. As one historian writes, he "had accepted arbitration, but only on condition that the award was favourable to him."[30]

The only Republican president to come close to breaking with his party's opposition to costly commitments to internationalism was Taft. Though his strategy toward the periphery confirms the theory's predictions, his approach toward the great powers is ambiguous. In 1910–11, Taft negotiated general, compulsory arbitration treaties with Great Britain and France that, unlike Roosevelt's, would not have excepted questions of "vital interests" or "national honor."[31] (Taft made the same offer to Germany, but it declined.) Instead, they featured two new safeguards. First, they required that disputes be "justicable"—that is, that they be covered by the existing body of international law. If there was any doubt, either country could easily force a deadlock. Second, the treaties mandated the creation of a *compromis* agreement to prespecify the terms of each arbitration. This would be negotiated by the president and subject to the "advice and consent" of the Senate, giving both actors a veto over the process. Nevertheless, Taft's treaties were criticized harshly by many Republicans, including Roosevelt and Lodge.[32]

Does this mean that Taft should be classified as an internationalist? The answer to that question might not have been clear even to Taft himself:

[30] Lord Newton, *Lord Lansdowne: A Biography* (London: Macmillan, 1929), 264. See also Davis, *United States and the Second Hague Peace Conference*, chap. 4.

[31] Davis, *United States and the Second Hague Peace Conference*, 321–26; E. James Hindman, "The General Arbitration Treaties of William Howard Taft," *Historian* 36, no. 1 (November 1973): 52–65; "Anglo-American Treaty of Arbitration," *Advocate of Peace* 73, no. 9 (September 1911): 196–98.

[32] John P. Campbell, "Taft, Roosevelt, and the Arbitration Treaties of 1911," *Journal of American History* 53, no. 2 (September 1966): 279–98; Robert Fischer, "Henry Cabot Lodge and the Taft Arbitration Treaties," *South Atlantic Quarterly* 78, no. 2 (spring 1979): 244–58.

It is strange how one happens on this sort of thing. When I made that speech in New York advocating the arbitration of questions, even those affecting the honor of a nation, I had no definite policy in view. I was inclined, if I remember rightly, merely to offset the antagonism to the four battleships for which I was then fighting, and I threw that suggestion out merely to draw the sting of old Carnegie and other peace cranks, and now the suggestion threatens to become the main fact of my four years as president.[33]

The details of an Anglo-American dispute over the Panama Canal cast further doubt on Taft's commitment to legalism. To the great consternation of the British government, he signed a bill that exempted American intercoastal shipping from having to pay canal tolls. A 1901 treaty between the two countries required that "all nations" be treated "on terms of equality"; Taft interpreted this as meaning "all *other* nations."[34] When Britain suggested arbitration under Roosevelt's 1908 arbitration treaty (Taft's own agreement was gutted by Senate amendments and then withdrawn by him), he quickly demurred. Similarly, at the Fourth Pan-American Conference of 1910, Secretary of State Philander Knox refused to admit the applicability of arbitration over Colombia's complaints against the United States. Although Taft did pursue arbitration with Britain over "low politics" issues—fishing rights and pelagic sealing—the only remotely strategic issue he agreed to arbitrate was a minor dispute over the naval border between Maine and New Brunswick.

Though the depth of his commitment to arbitration is questionable, the fact remains that Taft produced an arbitration treaty that was strong enough to provoke serious criticism from fellow Republicans. Thus, I count his presidency as a borderline disconfirmation. How, then, to account for this anomaly? Taft eventually became a Supreme Court justice, so he may have been unusually interested in the use of courts to address political problems. Or, as the foregoing quote suggests, perhaps his decision was simply a capricious blunder. After all, he had never held political office before reaching the presidency, and historians universally judge him to have been utterly incompetent at the game of politics. Although Taft came to office in a landslide, his administration alienated so many voters—including his former mentor, Theodore Roosevelt—that, in his reelection bid of 1912, he managed to win a plurality of votes only in Utah and Vermont.

Though the theory is weak in this case, it does offer insight into why Taft was an outlier. He secured the Republican nomination in 1908 not because he ran a successful campaign, but rather because the enormously popular

---

[33] Quoted in Paolo E. Coletta, *The Presidency of William Howard Taft* (Lawrence: University Press of Kansas, 1973), 170–71.

[34] Ibid., 174; Campbell, "Taft, Roosevelt, and the Arbitration Treaties," 294.

Roosevelt handpicked him to be his successor. Like Andrew Johnson, who took office on the assassination of Lincoln, and Ulysses S. Grant, who was elected as a war hero, Taft may have been able to reach the presidency only because he was not subject to the close scrutiny and tests of judgment normally required of presidential nominees. In other words, critical processes of coalitional interest aggregation were circumvented. To make definite claims about this case would be premature; however, the similarities between Taft and both Johnson and Grant are suggestive.

Democrats

For the Democratic Party, whose constituents earned their livelihood from exports to Europe, internationalism should have been far less controversial. Democratic leaders should have sought to maintain a stable international system, promote legalistic means of dispute resolution, and work to end imperialist competition. In the years leading up to World War I, diplomatic tensions between the great powers posed a serious constraint on the pursuit of this strategy. Nevertheless, the only Democratic president to serve in 1897–1917, Woodrow Wilson, should have evinced a clear internationalist bent, just as Cleveland had in the preceding period.

Prewar Diplomacy

Wilson's actual grand strategy confirms this prediction, both prior to and after the outbreak of war in Europe. In the administration's first year and a half in office, while the world was still at peace, the president and Secretary of State William Jennings Bryan launched several internationalist initiatives. First, they had to deal with British objections to a law, originally signed by Taft, that exempted American intercoastal shipping from having to pay tolls on the Panama Canal. As noted above, this measure clearly violated the United States' treaty obligations to Britain. Taking the view that American foreign policy should be governed by the rule of law rather than short-term gains-seeking, Wilson persuaded the Democratic majority in Congress to repeal it.

A second internationalist project of the administration was the negotiation of conciliation treaties with twenty-nine states. In the event of a crisis, the signatories would be obliged to refrain from the use of force against each other for a six-month "cooling off" period while a commission met to investigate the matter. Most of the agreements assumed that the disputants would cooperate to initiate the conciliation process, so neither state was compelled to act against its interests. However, six of the treaties (with France, Russia, Spain, China, Brazil, and Ecuador) specifically provided that one side could activate the commission and the six-month cooling-off

[131]

requirement without the direct consent of the other, so these provided a meaningful commitment to restraint.[35]

Finally, Wilson sent his close adviser, Edward House, to meet with the foreign ministers of Germany, Britain, and France to explore the possibility of creating an informal entente and arms-reduction treaty between them. War broke out soon thereafter, so it is difficult to determine exactly what kind of commitments, if any, Wilson would have been willing to make for the sake of peace in Europe. Nevertheless, he clearly demonstrated his commitment to the promulgation of international law and multilateral cooperation in the short period of time before war broke out.

Neutrality

The theory also serves well to explain Wilson's position on World War I. The onset of the conflict had a disastrous effect on American exporters, especially core interests. The source of the problem was Britain's naval blockade of Germany and Austria-Hungary. At first, Britain seized only munitions and manufactured goods with potential military uses. By the end of October 1914, however, it added cotton, food, oil, and most other raw materials to the list of prohibited goods. As a result, American exports to the blockaded powers fell from $169.3 million in 1914 to $1.8 million in 1915.[36]

This collapse was catastrophic for the Democrats' primary constituency, southern cotton farmers. They had high yields in the summer of 1914 and were counting on sales to Central Europe, as Germany alone had purchased 18 percent of the crop in 1913.[37] Though the British navy allowed some cotton through the blockade, prices slid from 12.4 cents per pound in August 1914 to 6.3 in November 1914.[38] As a result, the normally Anglophile South, facing economic ruin, erupted in hostility toward Britain, ending any chance that the British might have had to win over the largest constituency of American internationalists in the initial phase of the war.[39] Faced with two serious violations of international law against

[35] Norman L. Hill, "International Commissions of Inquiry and Conciliation," *International Conciliation* 278 (March 1932): 96, 127–29; Committee on Foreign Relations, United States Senate, *Treaties, Conventions, International Acts, Protocols, and Agreements between the United States of America and Other Powers, 1910–1923*, vol. 3 (Washington, D.C.: Government Printing Office, 1923).

[36] Sidney Bell, *Righteous Conquest: Woodrow Wilson and the Evolution of the New Diplomacy* (Port Washington, N.Y.: Kennikat, 1972), 166.

[37] Ibid., 92.

[38] Richard L. Watson, *The Development of National Power: The United States, 1900–1919* (Boston: Houghton Mifflin, 1976), 198. Western farmers were not nearly as hard-hit; wheat prices actually rose from 1913 to 1914.

[39] Arthur S. Link, "The Cotton Crisis, the South, and Anglo-American Diplomacy, 1914–1915," in *Studies in Southern History*, ed. J. Carlyle Sitterton (Chapel Hill: University of North Carolina Press, 1957), 122–38; Bensel, *Sectionalism*, 120–21.

the rights of neutrals—Britain's seizure of noncontraband trade and Germany's occupation of Belgium—southerners naturally focused on the one that constituted an immediate threat to their livelihoods.

Northeastern manufacturers, also an important Democratic constituency, were less reliant on European markets. Nevertheless, the war had indirect effects on their exports to the periphery: "Non-European markets for American goods had been financed in the past by European capital, and once the flow of credit was cut off those areas could no longer purchase American products."[40] Consequently, U.S. exports to Latin America fell from $348 million in 1913 to $309 million in 1914 and $275 million in 1915.

Wilson's short-term imperative was clear: restore American trade to Europe. Yet, this was not his only material consideration; he also had to take into account how his short-term policies would impact the long-term issue of the postwar world order. To form hypotheses about how Wilson should have reacted to the upheavals of 1914, it is necessary to consider how different long-term scenarios would have affected the economic interests of his electoral coalition. First, the best outcome for every major domestic interest group would have been that the war end quickly through diplomatic negotiation. If the Triple Entente (Britain, France, and Russia) and the Central Powers (Germany, Austria-Hungary, and Turkey) could agree to a settlement that approximated the prewar status quo, trade would resume and the United States could return to its peaceful "commercial invasion" of the world's markets.

The second-best outcome for most Americans would have been a quick victory by the Triple Entente. The advantages to this scenario were similar to the first. Britain would retain its benign primacy over international politics—weakened by war, to be sure, but strengthened by the defeat of its strongest European naval rival—so both core and peripheral interests in the United States would continue to benefit from a relatively liberal world trading system. Unfortunately, the Triple Entente's prospects for achieving a quick victory without the help of the United States were dim; after all, the main battlegrounds were in northeastern France and western Russia, not Germany. A German surrender, if it ever occurred, would be a long time coming. In the meantime, American trade would still be limited by the British blockade.

Third, the Triple Entente might have won with the direct military participation of the United States. This outcome should have been anathema to domestic interests, who had no reason to sacrifice their blood and treasure in the trenches of northern France unless their homeland was under direct threat. Among both core and peripheral interests as well, armed

---

[40] Bell, *Righteous Conquest*, 93.

intervention should have been an unappealing option. Still, it did offer some benefit for them, in that it would have given the United States great influence over the postwar settlement. Peripheral interests could demand that the defeated powers' colonies and spheres of influence in China, Africa, and the Middle East be governed under Open Door principles, rather than simply be folded into the British, French, and Japanese empires, while core interests could ask that American influence over its victorious allies be parlayed into new initiatives to promote norm-based cooperation.

Finally, the Central Powers could have achieved an unconditional victory. This outcome should have been deeply problematic for Americans with a stake in the international economy. Germany did not support free trade, nor did it ever prove itself to be particularly interested in norm-based cooperation, so the defeat of the Triple Entente would likely have been detrimental to core interests. Peripheral interests also had good reason to fear a powerful Germany, because it had been very aggressive in trying to capture peripheral markets for its own businesses and had shown little respect for the Open Door policy.[41]

In short, both core and peripheral interests should have had a similar ranking of preferences over outcomes: first, a quick negotiated settlement; second, a Triple Entente victory without the United States; third, a Triple Entente victory with the United States; and last, a Central Powers victory. Since Wilson counted on core interests as his primary coalition members and also needed the electoral support of peripheral interests, he clearly should have adapted his grand strategy to reflect these two groups' common priorities.[42] He could also maintain the approval of domestic interests as long as he did not enter the war, and there was little reason to consider such an unpleasant scenario in 1914. Even if Wilson had been inclined to intervene, the tiny American army could not have been mobilized and shipped out soon enough to make a difference at the most critical juncture of the war, the German march to the Marne in August 1914. After that point, the danger that Germany would win a quick decision faded, and Wilson had good reason to expect that the Triple Entente would do no worse than a stalemate, and probably would win.[43]

Thus, Wilson initially reacted to the war by pursuing core and peripheral interests' first-best hypothesized preference, a negotiated settlement—or, as he called it, "peace without victory." He instituted a ban on private loans to

[41] Ibid., 94–96.
[42] In all likelihood, this ranking represented Wilson's own preferences. See Arthur S. Link, *Wilson: The Struggle for Neutrality, 1914–1915* (Princeton: Princeton University Press, 1960), 53.
[43] Edward H. Buehrig, "Wilson's Neutrality Re-Examined," *World Politics* 3, no. 1 (October 1950): 3.

the belligerent powers, thinking that "the war did not affect American interests and that the United States could shorten it by starving it financially," then he sent Edward House to try to broker a diplomatic settlement.[44] At the same time, Wilson sought to bring an end to the British blockade. For the first few months of the war, he strongly protested British violations of American neutrality rights, particularly regarding the maritime seizure of cotton exports. He also advocated a bill to subsidize the construction of a merchant marine, since only nine American-flagged ships worked transatlantic routes at the outbreak of the war, and most of Britain's huge commercial fleet had been put into the service of its war effort. Without more ships, Americans would not be physically capable of sending their products to the Central Powers or even neutral states, regardless of what Britain did with the blockade. This decision constituted a sharp reversal from Democrats' decades-old opposition to government spending on a merchant marine; however, it was unsurprising in 1914 because its intent was to benefit cotton farmers.

By October 1914, it had become evident that Wilson's policy of strict neutrality was failing. First, there was nothing he could do, short of making threats, to end violations of Americans' maritime rights. The British government did try to soften the impact of its blockade by buying extra cotton and being generous in the settlement of the claims of American traders whose goods it seized, but it would not be swayed to change its policy by mere protests. Second, the military situation in Europe dictated that the war would not be ending any time soon—or that if it did end soon, it would not be with an Allied victory. Therefore, Wilson had to reconsider how he could reconcile his short-term goal, increasing exports to Europe, with his long-term goal, obtaining the best possible outcome to the war.

The president had two remaining options to boost exports: threaten to embargo trade with Britain unless it ceased its seizures, or accept a pro-British stance on neutrality. The first policy promised Americans an enormous increase in wartime trade with both the Allies and the Central Powers, but it had serious potential costs. Wilson did not know whether Britain would accede to his threats, so he would have had to risk losing the rest of America's trade with Europe (or at least a major part of it, if he embargoed only munitions) at a time when it was needed most. Furthermore, Britain, unlike Germany, was unprepared for the war, so its own factories were insufficient to supply its troops. Meanwhile, France had lost its industrial heartland behind German lines. If the British government decided not to back down in the face of an American embargo, the Triple Entente's war effort would suffer terribly, and the worst-case scenario of a Central Powers

---

[44] Kendrick A. Clements, *The Presidency of Woodrow Wilson* (Lawrence: University Press of Kansas, 1992), 118.

victory would become more likely. Even if Britain did acquiesce and remove the blockade, Germany would gain from access to American goods.

In contrast, a pro-British form of neutrality became increasingly attractive with each passing day, as heightened British demand for American supplies began to compensate for the loss of the German market. Britain soon began to run out of cash to pay for its imports, so Wilson partially lifted the ban on loans in October 1914, and he fully withdrew it a year later. In short time, Britain was importing more from the United States than it and Germany had in combination before the war. Consequently, American exports surged far past normal levels. Even the price of cotton recovered to 11.2 cents per pound in 1915. Then, in 1916, it soared to 35.3 cents per pound.[45] Of course, Americans could have done even better had they been able to sell their goods to both the Central Powers and the Triple Entente, but they were faring well enough under the status quo, and the dangers of an embargo to both Wilson's long-term and short-term goals were not insignificant. The president's final decision, to accept the convergence of Anglo-American economic interests, comports well with the theory.

Entry into War

As the war dragged on, the German navy began using submarines to sink merchant ships, resulting in the deaths of American sailors. Wilson responded by demanding that American vessels not be targeted, and Germany, which was loathe to push American sympathies closer to Britain, complied. Tensions increased further, however, when German submarines attacked several passenger ships suspected of carrying munitions. After 128 Americans died on board the *Lusitania*, Wilson persuaded the German government not to target passenger ships. Even then, it continued to sink foreign merchant vessels with American crewmen, so Wilson demanded that it give warning before torpedoing unarmed ships, allowing sailors time to escape safely. Throughout this diplomatic wrangling, trade with Britain continued to increase by leaps and bounds: "By November 1916 fully 40 per cent of British war expenditure was devoted to North American supplies."[46]

The variables in the equation that led Wilson to seek "peace without victory" began to change in early 1917. In January, the German government decided that a quick victory could be won—before the United States had time to mobilize—if its submarines were not restricted in their targets. On the last day of the month, the German ambassador announced to the State Department that American ships would no longer be protected. In response,

[45] United States Bureau of the Census, *Statistical Abstract of the United States, 1954,* 301.
[46] Kathleen Burk, *Britain, America, and the Sinews of War, 1914–1918* (Boston: Allen and Unwin, 1985), 5.

Wilson broke off diplomatic relations but did not yet ask for a declaration of war. Instead, he decided to hold out, at least until Germany actually began to sink American ships, for the possibility that it would back down from its new policy.[47] Nevertheless, he did ask Congress to allow the arming of merchant ships, an outcome that surely would have led to battles between American sailors and German submarines, and, consequently, war.[48] Nothing came of it, however, because the bill was filibustered by antiwar senators.

The next blow came on February 28, when the British government passed to the State Department an intercepted telegram in which German foreign secretary Arthur Zimmerman promised Mexican president Venustiano Carranza "generous financial support" and aid to recapture "the lost territory in Texas, New Mexico and Arizona" in return for bases for German submarines.[49] Again, Wilson declined to declare war. Instead, he made an executive order to allow the arming of American merchant ships, summarily overriding Senate opposition. Then, on March 18 came the first serious incident since Germany's announcement to engage in unrestricted submarine warfare: U-boats sank three American ships without warning, killing fifteen crewmembers. Two days later, the president convened his cabinet to ask for advice, and by the following day he had made up his mind.[50] On April 2, the earliest day that Congress could be brought into session, Wilson called for a declaration of war.

There is significant disagreement among historians over the motive behind this decision.[51] Some have argued that Wilson was concerned foremost for the rights of neutral states; therefore, he entered the war only because the German U-boat campaign had violated his sense of morality and international law.[52] Britain had also breached neutrals' maritime rights, and therefore also drawn Wilson's ire, but the questionable legality of the blockade paled before Germany's taking of American lives. Other historians agree that the unrestricted submarine warfare was the sole cause of

[47] Charles Seymour, "American Neutrality: The Experience of 1914–1917," *Foreign Affairs* 14 (October 1935): 34–36; Devlin, *Too Proud to Fight*, 658.
[48] Arthur S. Link, *Wilson: Campaigns for Progressivism and Peace, 1916–1917* (Princeton: Princeton University Press, 1965), 413; Ernest R. May, *The World War and American Isolation* (Cambridge, Mass.: Harvard University Press, 1959), 426–34.
[49] Quoted in Devlin, *Too Proud to Fight*, 648.
[50] Ibid., 666; Lloyd E. Ambrosius, *Wilsonian Statecraft: Theory and Practice of Liberal Internationalism during World War I* (Wilmington: Scholarly Resources, 1984), 85–86.
[51] Daniel M. Smith, "National Interest and American Intervention, 1917: An Historiographical Appraisal," *Journal of American History* 52, no. 1 (June 1965): 5–24; Edith James, "Wilsonian Wartime Diplomacy: The Sense of the Seventies," in *American Foreign Relations: A Historiographical Review*, ed. Gerald K. Haines and J. Samuel Walker (Westport, Conn.: Greenwood, 1981), 115–31.
[52] Seymour, "American Neutrality"; Frederick S. Calhoun, *Uses of Force and Wilsonian Foreign Policy* (Kent: Kent State University Press, 1993), 47–51. Arthur S. Link considers this

the president's intervention but note that Americans had been dying inter-mittently throughout the war, including on the *Lusitania*. Wilson had not declared war then, so the immediate cause of his intervention must have been the increased threat to trade. Even though most of the ships being destroyed were British, their cargo was mostly American made, and the losses—"a quarter of all ships that left port between January and April" of 1917—were severe.[53]

Another school of thought states that Wilson gradually came to under-stand that a German victory would be contrary to American commercial and political interests; therefore, he purposefully chose a form of neutral-ity intended to benefit Britain.[54] In this view, he was well aware that his policies would force Germany to retaliate. One last interpretation argues that Wilson's primary objective was to force the other great powers to ac-cept his internationalist vision of world order on the war's conclusion.[55] In May 1916, while the United States was still neutral, he proposed to create a "universal association of the nations . . . to prevent any war begun either contrary to treaty covenants or without full warning and full submission of the causes to the opinion of the world."[56] At the time, he believed that he could achieve this goal by mediating the negotiation of a peace settlement among the stalemated belligerents. By the end of March 1917, however, the increasing likelihood of a German victory led Wilson to realize that he would need to join the Triple Entente to ensure that his ideas would be accepted.[57]

None of these perspectives is necessarily exclusive of the others; it is quite possible that Wilson considered all such factors and that none alone would have been sufficient to make him ask for a declaration of war. In-deed, they all make sense, at least indirectly, under the assumption that Wilson was concerned above all with the material prosperity of his do-mestic coalition. To satisfy core and peripheral interests' preferences, the president had to balance the present and future of trade with Europe. In the short term, which corresponds to the first two interpretations above, Wilson could not abide by either severe violations to neutral shipping

reason to be necessary but not sufficient; see Arthur S. Link, *Wilson the Diplomatist: A Look at His Major Foreign Policies* (New York: New Viewpoints, 1957), 82, 86–88.
[53] Clements, *Presidency of Woodrow Wilson*, 138.
[54] Edward H. Buehrig, *Woodrow Wilson and the Balance of Power* (Bloomington: Indiana University Press, 1955), chaps. 4–5.
[55] Devlin, *Too Proud to Fight*, 673–88; Knock, *To End All Wars*, 118; Link, *Wilson: Campaigns for Progressivism and Peace*, 414.
[56] Quoted in Knock, *To End All Wars*, 77.
[57] Whether Wilson actually believed that Germany would win is not clear; see Smith, "National Interest and American Intervention." This uncertainty undermines the realist argument, cited at the beginning of this chapter, that the United States intervened to prevent the rise of a hegemon in Europe.

rights or the destruction of the British merchant marine. In the long term, which corresponds to the latter two interpretations, he could not tolerate a victory by an illiberal commercial competitor and he sought to ensure that the peace settlement would prevent future disruptions in transatlantic trade. All of these imperatives converged on a single response, war, at the same time. It makes little sense to try to determine which of the various historians' explanations provide necessary or sufficient causes of Wilson's decision for war, because they are all different facets of the same underlying cause.[58]

1918–29: New World Order versus Normalcy

As Wilson intended, the declaration of war gave the United States enormous influence over the design and implementation of the postwar world order. More than ever before, American grand strategy was unconstrained by its external environment. The greatest barrier to internationalism, insecurity among the great powers, was significantly reduced by the defeat of the Central Powers. Important barriers to cooperation remained, but the end of the war provided a unique window of opportunity for the advancement of international law. It also facilitated realpolitik, in that the wartime expansion of the military, particularly the navy, gave the United States tremendous leverage against the other great powers. Finally, of course, the country could retreat into isolationism if it so desired. Its grand strategy was limited only by the war debt, on which interest payments peaked at 1.6 percent of the national income in 1921.

Democrats

The new peace created an exceptional strategic opening for Democrats. Given their sectoral interest in internationalism, they should have seized the moment to reconstruct the world order according to their principles. Without having to know anything about Woodrow Wilson's personal preferences, the theory clearly predicts that he would have undertaken an ambitious new effort in 1918 to promote norm-based cooperation between the great powers.

The president first laid out his vision in the "Fourteen Points" speech of January 1918. Several of his "points" either derived from or were compatible with internationalism: disarmament, freedom of the seas, Open Door trade, the abolition of secret diplomacy, and collective security. The most

---

[58] For a similar argument, see Bell, *Righteous Conquest*, 182–83, 186–87, 190–93.

important was the last, which called for the creation of a "League of Nations." At the Paris Peace Conference, Wilson pursued this goal above all
else, intending the league to be the crowning achievement of, and justification for, American involvement in the war.[59] It was conceived not simply
as the organizational codification of the other thirteen points; rather, it was
intended to serve as the mechanism by which a norm-based international
system would be constructed and maintained.

Wilson's proposal for the league underwent many revisions between the
summer of 1918, when he decided on a first draft, and the spring of 1919,
when the allied leaders signed the covenant. However, its basic design
remained the same.[60] At its essence, the league was a collective security
organization:

> The Members of the League undertake to respect and preserve as against ex-
> ternal aggression the territorial integrity and existing political independence
> of all Members of the League. In case of any such aggression or in case of any
> threat or danger of such aggression the Council shall advise upon the means
> by which this obligation shall be fulfilled. . . . Should any Member of the
> League resort to war in disregard of its covenants under Articles 12, 13 or 15,
> it shall *ipso facto* be deemed to have committed an act of war against all other
> Members of the League, which hereby undertake immediately to subject it
> to the severance of all trade or financial relations, the prohibition of all in-
> tercourse between their nationals and the nationals of the covenant-breaking
> State, and the prevention of all financial, commercial or personal intercourse
> between the nationals of the covenant-breaking State and the nationals of any
> other State, whether a Member of the League or not.[61]

To carry out this mandate, the league had two governing bodies. In the
Assembly, each of the member-states would have one vote; in the smaller
Council, only the wartime allies (excluding Russia) would have a permanent seat and a veto, and four rotating seats would be set aside for lesser
powers. The Council would deal with the most important issue before the
league, interstate conflict, and coordinate collective military action.

In a world governed by international law, diplomatic disputes would
have to be resolved by courts, not through coercion. Thus, the covenant
included provisions for arbitration:

> The Members of the League agree that whenever any dispute shall arise be-
> tween them which they recognize to be suitable for submission to arbitration

---

[59] Knock, *To End All Wars*, 200–1; Devlin, *Too Proud to Fight*, 673–88.
[60] Ambrosius, *Wilsonian Statecraft*, 133; Knock, *To End All Wars*, 224–25.
[61] League of Nations, "The Covenant of the League of Nations," The Avalon Project,
Yale Law School, www.yale.edu/lawweb/avalon/leagcov.htm (last accessed May 2006),
arts. 10, 16.

or judicial settlement and which cannot be satisfactorily settled by diplomacy, they will submit the whole subject-matter to arbitration or judicial settlement. . . . The Members of the League agree that they will carry out in full good faith any award or decision that may be rendered, and that they will not resort to war against a Member of the League which complies therewith. In the event of any failure to carry out such an award or decision, the Council shall propose what steps should be taken to give effect thereto.[62]

Though this passage implies that member states were legally bound to accept the arbitration of their disputes, the league was not required to enforce arbitral decisions. Wilson knew the Senate would never consent to such a provision, so he chose "to finesse the issue rather than face it squarely."[63] The exact nature of states' obligation to arbitration was to be determined in the charter of the Permanent Court of International Justice. In negotiations over the PCIJ, Britain secured an "opt-out" clause for any state that wanted to avoid making a commitment to binding, compulsory arbitration. Thus, the promise of juridical dispute resolution went largely unfulfilled.

Wilson made a number of grudging compromises at the Paris Peace Conference. He agreed to the allied occupation of the Rhineland, an American guarantee of France's border with Germany, a crushingly large indemnity on Germany, and border rectifications that benefited Poland at the expense of German self-determination. These policies might have been somewhat appealing to peripheral interests, who had a clear stake in ensuring that Germany would never again recover the ability to make trouble outside of Europe. However, they were unambiguously harmful to core interests, since they would create lasting diplomatic conflicts and damage the prospects for political and economic cooperation in Europe. Wilson accepted these provisions not because they fit his vision of world order, but because they were necessary to appease France. If he had stood his ground on every issue, he would have risked the breakup of the conference and the stillbirth of his all-important league.[64]

In conclusion, the theory fares well at predicting Wilson's grand strategy toward the great powers. Even though his league was like nothing else in the history of international politics, it is easily explained as the product of the interests of the Democratic electoral coalition. This argument undermines much of the extant literature's interpretation of Wilson's grand strategy, in which scholars attribute the supposed uniqueness of his approach to the eccentricities of his personality. In contrast, the theory advanced here asserts that, if a different Democratic politician had managed to unite his

---

[62] Ibid., art. 13.
[63] Knock, *To End All Wars*, 220–21.
[64] Ibid., 246–51; Clements, *Presidency of Woodrow Wilson*, 180–81.

party and win the presidency in 1916, he likely would have adopted a strategy similar to that of Wilson. Any such executive would have been reluctant to enter World War I, but eventually would have been drawn into the Triple Entente, then would have seized on the window of opportunity after the war to propose a bold new internationalist initiative. Of course, this is not to say that contingency did not play any role, or that the specifics of Wilson's foreign policy were perfectly foreseeable. However, the configuration of coalitional preferences and strategic constraints on the United States in 1918–21 does generate a clear prediction, and that prediction is confirmed by actual events.

Republicans

By the time Woodrow Wilson left office, the political economy of the United States had essentially returned to its prewar condition. The Republican Party's main constituency, northeastern businesses, continued to expand into peripheral markets. The share of finished manufactures exports sent to the periphery leveled out at 70 percent, while investments in the periphery rapidly increased relative to the national income. Investment to Europe also grew, but exports to the continent stagnated. Thus, American manufacturers remained focused primarily on the periphery, not the core. To support their interventionist interests in the periphery, they should have continued to favor a realpolitik grand strategy toward the great powers. The only limiting factor was the enormous new war debt, which consumed 20–30 percent of the budget throughout the 1920s. The two Republican presidents who served in the 1920s, Warren G. Harding and Calvin Coolidge, should have adhered to the principle of realpolitik, but they also should have sought to conserve fiscal resources whenever possible.

Both men's policies confirm this prediction. Harding's most important diplomatic initiative was the Washington Conference of 1921–22, at which the victors of World War I met to negotiate naval arms reductions and resolve contentious issues between them. It produced several agreements. First, the Five-Power Treaty established a 5 : 5 : 3 : 1.75 : 1.75 ratio of tonnage for capital ships between the United States, Britain, Japan, France, and Italy. Second, the Four-Power Treaty between Britain, France, Japan, and the United States affirmed the territorial status quo in East Asia. It also created a mechanism for joint consultation in the event that a dispute should arise between any of the powers. Third, the Nine-Power Treaty committed its signatories (the five major naval powers plus Belgium, the Netherlands, Portugal, and China) to respect China's territorial rights and adhere to the Open Door policy. Finally, Japan agreed to withdraw its forces from Siberia and the Shantung province of China. All of these treaties amounted to "a procession of gigantic horse trades in which each power sought to buy maximum security at minimum expense."[65] As such, the Washington Conference was pure realpolitik. American negotiators made no serious attempt to promote international law, and supporters of the League of Nations condemned the Four-Power Treaty for its exclusivity.[66]

In general, Harding opposed any internationalist proposal that might have limited the United States' freedom of action. He negotiated a treaty of accession to the PCIJ but refused to commit to compulsory arbitration, a position that was essentially costless.[67] Harding adamantly opposed joining the new League of Nations or even establishing diplomatic relations with it: "A world super-government is contrary to everything we cherish and can have no sanction by our Republic."[68] He took a similar stance toward engagement with Europe: "We do not mean to be entangled. We will accept no responsibility except as our own conscience and judgment, in each instance, may determine." Since the Senate had rejected the Versailles Treaty, he signed bilateral peace treaties with Germany, Austria, and Hungary, and he withdrew the remaining fifteen thousand American troops from Germany. Harding did agree to reschedule wartime loans to Britain and France, but only to facilitate repayment; he ruled out debt forgiveness.[69] He also refused to grant diplomatic recognition to the Soviet Union.[70]

Calvin Coolidge, who took office after Harding's death in August 1923, pursued a very similar grand strategy. His only major diplomatic initiative was an attempt to extend the naval arms limitations of the Washington Conference to categories of vessels other than capital ships. At the Geneva Naval Conference of 1927, the British and American delegations staked out irreconcilable positions over how to deal with cruisers, and the negotiations ended acrimoniously.[71]

[65] L. Ethan Ellis, *Republican Foreign Policy, 1921–1933* (New Brunswick: Rutgers University Press, 1968), 107. See also Davis, *Navy Second to None*, chap. 12; Richard W. Fanning, *Peace and Disarmament: Navy Rivalry and Arms Control, 1922–1933* (Lexington: University Press of Kentucky, 1995), 1–16; Thomas H. Buckley, *The United States and the Washington Conference, 1921–1922* (Knoxville: University of Tennessee Press, 1970).

[66] Joan H. Wilson, *American Business and Foreign Policy, 1920–1933* (Lexington: University Press of Kentucky, 1971), 46–47; Thomas N. Guinsburg, "Victory in Defeat: The Senatorial Isolationists and the Four-Power Treaty," *Capital Studies* 2 (spring 1973): 27–28, 32–34.

[67] Michael Dunne, *The United States and the World Court, 1920–1935* (London: Pinter, 1988), 78–79.

[68] Quoted in Eugene P. Trani and David L. Wilson, *The Presidency of Warren G. Harding* (Lawrence: Regents Press of Kansas, 1977), 141–142. On business opinion of the league, see Wilson, *American Business and Foreign Policy*, 23–25.

[69] Melvyn Leffler, "The Origins of Republican War Debt Policy, 1921–1923: A Case Study in the Applicability of the Open Door Interpretation," *Journal of American History* 59, no. 3 (December 1972): 589–90, 596.

[70] Trani and Wilson, *Presidency of Warren G. Harding*, 121; Melvyn P. Leffler, "1921–1932: Interventionist Impulses and Domestic Constraints," in *Economics and World Power: An Assessment of American Diplomacy since 1789*, ed. William H. Becker and Samuel F. Wells (New York: Columbia University Press, 1984), 242.

[71] Davis, *Navy Second to None*, 305–33; Fanning, *Peace and Disarmament*, 16–96.

The rest of Coolidge's diplomacy with the great powers was uneventful and aloof. He consented to the Dawes Plan, which provided loans for German reparations, but would not countenance the cancellation of wartime debts. He maintained the policy of nonrecognition toward the Soviet Union, and he rejected any possibility of joining the League of Nations. Coolidge was even unenthusiastic about Harding's treaty of accession to the PCIJ, which was pending consideration by the Senate when he came to office. He supported an amendment which stated that "the court shall not . . . without the consent of the United States, entertain any request for an advisory opinion touching any dispute or question in which the United States has or claims an interest."[72] This reservation was disallowed by the members of the court, so the treaty died.

In 1928, Coolidge did agree to the infamous Kellogg-Briand Pact, in which states agreed to "renounce . . . [war] as an instrument of national policy." In doing so, however, he did not stray one whit from a realpolitik grand strategy. Secretary of State Frank B. Kellogg proposed the multilateral treaty as a means to deflect a popular French proposal to disclaim war bilaterally, the effect of which would have been to discourage American retaliation for French restrictions on neutral shipping in the event of another Franco-German war.[73] Lacking any costs or commitments, Kellogg's diplomacy amounted to little more than a clever bit of public relations work. It did not signify the transformation of the administration into a group of true believers in internationalism, nor did it represent a meaningful advance in international law.[74]

Secretary Kellogg also proposed general arbitration treaties with Britain, France, Germany, and several other countries. Like Taft, he did not exempt "vital interests" from their purview. However, he did make an exception for "any dispute the subject matter of which . . . depends upon or involves the maintenance of the traditional attitude of the United States concerning American questions, commonly described as the Monroe Doctrine."[75] As British foreign minister Austen Chamberlain noted, "[Kellogg] excepts every question which the United States were ever likely to have covered by the old formula [in Theodore Roosevelt's arbitration treaties] of 'vital in-

[72] Quoted in Robert H. Ferrell, *The Presidency of Calvin Coolidge* (Lawrence: University Press of Kansas, 1998), 158.

[73] Warren I. Cohen, *Empire without Tears: America's Foreign Relations, 1921–1933* (Philadelphia: Temple University Press, 1987), 60; Ferrell, *Presidency of Calvin Coolidge*, 159–60; Stephen J. Kneeshaw, *In Pursuit of Peace: The American Reaction to the Kellogg-Briand Pact, 1928–1929* (New York: Garland, 1991), 12.

[74] Kneeshaw, *In Pursuit of Peace*, 25; Selig Adler, *The Uncertain Giant, 1921–1941: American Foreign Policy between the Wars* (New York: Macmillan, 1965), 90.

[75] Committee on Foreign Relations, United States Senate, *Treaties, Conventions, International Acts, Protocols, and Agreements between the United States of America and Other Powers, 1923–1937*, vol. 4 (Washington, D.C.: Government Printing Office, 1938).

terests, honour and integrity.'"[76] The treaty further required that the terms of each arbitration be determined by a "special agreement," repeating the wording that Taft had used in 1911 to ensure that negotiators could stalemate the legal process before it had begun.

In sum, the theory fares reasonably well with the Harding and Coolidge administrations. It accurately predicts their desire to conserve costs, as evidenced by their attempts at naval disarmament, and it is not disconfirmed by their weak attempts at internationalism. Coolidge's arbitration treaties were highly qualified, and other aspects of his strategy, such as his disregard for Europe and the League of Nations, were clearly anti-internationalist. Republican grand strategy toward the great powers in the 1920s, through both Harding and Coolidge, was essentially realpolitik.

1929–41: DEPRESSION DIPLOMACY

The rise of aggressively expansionist regimes in Germany, Italy, and Japan in the 1930s did not pose a direct threat to the continental United States or its sphere of influence in the Western Hemisphere. It did, however, have important consequences elsewhere. Japan's invasion of Manchuria and subsequent war with China endangered American interests in East Asia, while German and Italian antagonism toward the Versailles settlement threatened to draw the United States into another conflagration in Europe.

The international environment was not the only problem. The Great Depression led to both a precipitous decline in tax revenue and a sharp increase in demands for welfare assistance, making it difficult to avoid cuts in military spending. The combination of internal and external constraints forced a difficult choice on American leaders: they could keep the other great powers at arm's length, refusing to respond to interstate aggression so long as their homeland borders were not threatened; they could focus on the defense of their peripheral interests; or they could hazard the political unpopularity, budgetary cost, and strategic risk of trying to enforce international law and collective security.

Republicans

The Great Depression imposed severe constraints on grand strategy, but it did not alter Republican constituents' interest in the international economy. In the 1918–29, northeastern businesses developed closer financial ties to

---

[76] Quoted in Lorna Lloyd, *Peace through Law: Britain and the International Court in the 1920s* (Suffolk: Boydell, 1997), 131.

Europe, but the distribution of manufacturing exports and overseas investment still favored the periphery. After 1929, the collapse of international trade and the global rise of protectionism should have reinforced businesses' long-standing disinterest in engagement with the great powers. As a result, the Republican Party should have continued to oppose meaningful, binding commitments to international law and collective security. Only when American trade with the periphery was directly threatened by events in the core should Republican presidents have considered intervention in European affairs. Their main concern should not have been international pressures but rather domestic constraints. As noted above, the Depression caused a collapse in revenue for the federal government, creating strong incentives for politicians to economize on armaments.

The grand strategy of Republican president Herbert Hoover corresponds well to these predictions. His priorities were most clearly evident in his response to the developing crisis in China. In 1931–32, Japanese forces invaded Manchuria, mounted a punitive expedition against Shanghai, and began advancing into the province of Jehol. These actions violated two treaties from the Washington Conference of 1921–22: the Four-Power Treaty, which guaranteed the territorial status quo in East Asia, and the Nine-Power Treaty, which upheld the Open Door policy. It also made a mockery of the Kellogg-Briand Pact, which promised to end war as an instrument of national policy. For internationalist Democrats, the sanctity of international law and the principle of collective security demanded a forceful response. However, the United States had almost no commercial interests in Manchuria, and its commerce in Shanghai was only temporarily disrupted by the Japanese raid. For realpolitik Republicans, a simple protest of Japan's breach of its diplomatic commitments sufficed.

Hoover had been an ardent internationalist in the early 1920s, but he abandoned this position after becoming a leading candidate for the Republican presidential nomination.[77] As Japanese violations of international law became more egregious, Secretary of State Henry L. Stimson advocated taking a harder line, perhaps even to impose economic sanctions, but Hoover refused.[78] He sent an American envoy to the League of Nations to observe its response to the crisis, but he opposed any form of diplomatic coordination

---

[77] Alexander DeConde, "Herbert Hoover and Foreign Policy: A Retrospective Assessment," in *Herbert Hoover and the Historians*, ed. Mark M. Dodge (West Branch, Iowa: Hoover Presidential Library Association, 1989), 91–94.

[78] Historians are divided on the question of Stimson's willingness to consider an embargo. For contrasting views, see Margot Louria, *Triumph and Downfall: America's Pursuit of Peace and Prosperity, 1921–1933* (Westport, Conn.: Greenwood, 2001), 184, 195–96; Gary B. Ostrower, "Secretary of State Stimson and the League," *Historian* 41, no. 3 (May 1979): 467–82.

with the league.[79] Instead, he opted for the weakest substantive response possible: nonrecognition. This policy—dubbed the Stimson Doctrine, but authored by Hoover—stated that the United States would not accept the validity of any treaties or concessions stemming from the annexation of Manchuria.[80] The Japanese were unmoved, but Hoover would go no further. In his final months in office, he took Stimson's advice to ask Congress for the power to impose an arms embargo on aggressor states, but it is unlikely that he actually would have used that power.[81]

Hoover's only major strategic initiative was arms reduction. The navy opposed compromise on the issues that had doomed the Geneva Naval Conference of 1927, but Hoover was determined to obtain an agreement that would allow the United States to reduce its budget for naval construction. At the London Conference of 1930, American, British, and Japanese negotiators set tonnage limitations on all categories of ships, not just the capital ships covered by the Washington Conference of 1921–22. Following the conference, Hoover announced major cuts in naval construction, leaving the fleet well below its treaty limits.[82] He proposed further reductions at the Geneva Disarmament Conference of 1934, but the international environment had deteriorated so far as to make a multilateral agreement impossible. In sum, his strategy was a limited form of realpolitik, designed to maintain a margin of security for American interests abroad without having to make fiscal sacrifices for their defense.

After Hoover lost the election of 1932, Democrats dominated the national political scene for the remainder of the decade, controlling both the executive and legislature throughout. Republicans remained out of the White House until 1953, by which time the domestic political economy of the United States and its strategic constraints had changed dramatically. The late interwar period, one of the most politically contentious and strategically portentous times in American history, is therefore analytically problematic. It leaves open a critical question: Would Republicans have responded to the international crises of the 1930s with a different strategy than the Democrats?

The American transition from neutrality to belligerence back in 1914–17 did not create sharp partisan cleavages, but the road to war in 1933–41

---

[79] Louria, *Triumph and Downfall*, 188, 193, 217; Ostrower, "Secretary of State Stimson"; Robert H. Ferrell, *American Diplomacy in the Great Depression: Hoover-Stimson Foreign Policy, 1929–1933* (New Haven: Yale University Press, 1957), 132–34, 139–140, 142–43, 147–48, 161–62, 165.

[80] Ferrell, *American Diplomacy in the Great Depression*, 157.

[81] Robert A. Divine, "Franklin D. Roosevelt and Collective Security, 1933," *Mississippi Valley Historical Review* 48, no. 1 (June 1961): 45–48.

[82] DeConde, "Herbert Hoover and Foreign Policy," 104–5.

was dissimilar in several ways. First, Democratic core interests had more reason to worry about Adolf Hitler than Kaiser Wilhelm II. Wilhelmine Germany was protectionist, imperialist, and militarist, and it committed a serious breach of international law in its violation of Belgian neutrality, but it was not generally perceived to be an "outlaw state," intent on the destruction and overthrow of international order.[83] Indeed, it was not even the first state to mobilize for war in 1914. Nazi Germany, on all accounts, was far worse, even before its full intentions were revealed in 1939. Moreover, the most salient issue for Americans in the early stages of World War I was Britain's naval blockade of trade to the Central Powers. It led to a collapse in cotton prices and, consequently, outrage among southern internationalists over British abuses of American maritime rights. In the 1930s, in contrast, Hitler sought to wean Germany from its reliance on American cotton long before Britain had a chance to cut off its supply.

Second, peripheral interests in the Republican Party should have seen Hitler as less of a threat than the Kaiser. In the earlier period, Germany had a world-class battleship fleet, a growing empire, and a recent history of military intervention in Latin America. Nazi Germany, in contrast, confined its ambitions to Europe. Hitler saw little value to distant colonies and did not waste scarce resources on naval arms races; thus, the American sphere of influence in the Western Hemisphere was more secure in 1939 than 1914. Only if Britain and France were defeated, a remote possibility until June 1940, would it come under threat.

None of this means that Democrats should have been eager to fight or that Republicans should have been indifferent to events overseas. Rather, the point is that the various external and internal constraints that influenced the domestic politics of American intervention in Europe in 1914–17 had shifted considerably by 1933–41, and that their effect was to push the two parties in the opposite direction. Thus, the theory yields an unambiguous prediction: Democrats should consistently have been more forceful than Republicans in their response to German, Italian, and Japanese challenges to international order in the 1930s.

This claim can easily be tested against the voting record of Republican legislators and the rhetoric of Republican presidential nominees. First, in congressional debates, Republicans consistently voted against measures that would give the executive the ability to enforce international law, participate in collective security, or prepare for war in Europe. For example, over numerous roll call votes on the Neutrality Acts in 1935–41, 75 percent of House Democrats voted to loosen restrictions, whereas only 13 percent of

---

[83] Ido Oren, *Our Enemies and US: America's Rivalries and the Making of Political Science* (Ithaca: Cornell University Press, 2003), chap. 1.

House Republicans did.[84] On the issue of rearmament, 86 percent of House Democrats voted for the Selective Service Act of 1940, whereas only 35 percent of House Republicans did.[85] Many Republican legislators turned to isolationism in the hard times of the Great Depression, while others maintained their adherence to realpolitik. Few, however, were internationalist, and few supported intervention in the war.

The same is true for the Republican nominee for president in 1936, Alf Landon. Had he won the election, he would have led the country in the critical period of January 1937 through January 1941—or, with a second term, to 1945. Landon was a "Theodore Roosevelt nationalist," an advocate of a strong military and the robust defense of the Western Hemisphere.[86] He opposed the Neutrality Acts, favored rearmament, supported the draft, and believed in diplomatic engagement with the great powers. These views were on the more assertive side of the Republican strategic spectrum; however, they did not break the mold. Like all of his Republican predecessors, he offered rhetorical support for international cooperation, but only "where it is distinctly understood [that] no political commitments are involved."[87] The outbreak of war in Europe only hardened his views. He would countenance economic aid to Britain, but no more. Even the Lend-Lease Act was unacceptable: "The American people should insistently demand that Congress put a stop to the step-by-step projection of the United States into undeclared war."[88] As president, he almost certainly would not have provoked the Axis to the extent that Franklin D. Roosevelt did, and, as a result, the United States might never had entered the war.

By June 1940, the international situation had created sharp divisions within the Republican Party. Its isolationist wing, led by Robert A. Taft, continued to demand strict neutrality. For those with a stake in trade or investment in the periphery, however, the defeat of France was cause for concern. An Axis victory, now a strong possibility, would impose serious constraints

---

[84] George L. Grassmuck, "Sectional Biases in Congress on Foreign Policy," *Johns Hopkins University Studies in Historical and Political Science* 68, no. 3 (1951): 120. On northeastern isolationism, which was concentrated in rural areas that lacked economic ties to Europe, see also Trubowitz, *Defining the National Interest*, chap. 3; Ralph H. Smuckler, "The Region of Isolationism," *American Political Science Review* 47, no. 2 (June 1953): 386–401.

[85] John O'Sullivan, *From Voluntarism to Conscription: Congress and Selective Service, 1940–1945* (New York: Garland, 1982), 259. Class as well as sectoral interests had an critical impact on this debate; see Kevin Narizny, "Both Guns and Butter, or Neither: Class Interests in the Political Economy of Rearmament," *American Political Science Review* 97, no. 2 (May 2003): 214–15.

[86] George H. Mayer, "Alf M. Landon, as Leader of the Republican Opposition, 1937–1940," *Kansas Historical Quarterly* 32, no. 3 (Autumn 1966): 332. See also Donald R. McCoy, *Landon of Kansas* (Lincoln: University of Nebraska Press, 1966), chaps. 17–19.

[87] Quoted in McCoy, *Landon of Kansas*, 325.

[88] Ibid., 472.

on their interests. In East Asia, American bases would be surrounded by, and vulnerable to, the Japanese Empire, and the United States would lose access to China. In Latin America, U.S. influence would be challenged both in commercial terms, through German efforts to establish a closed barter system, and in political terms, through attempts by ethnic German settlers to create client states. Thus, as the Allied armies in France crumbled, so too did Republican support for isolationism. Just as France surrendered, the party's national convention met to nominate a candidate for president. On the sixth ballot, it abandoned its isolationist frontrunner, Thomas E. Dewey, in favor of Wendell L. Willkie, a man whose views on intervention in World War II closely resembled those of Franklin Roosevelt.[89] Notably, Willkie was not part of the Republican establishment; he had never held elected office and had been a committed Democrat until 1939.

While some might argue that the nomination of Willkie confirms the idea of a "national interest," it is important to keep in mind that Dewey likely would have come out ahead had the Republican convention been held only a few weeks earlier. The late convergence of the two parties does not redeem the substantial differences between them in the late 1930s. These differences had major policy implications: "While Roosevelt did not go so far as he might have, the opposition party attacked vociferously even those measures he did propose . . . Had the leadership of the Republican Party controlled the Government or even the Congress, the state of the national defense would have been worse."[90] Landon himself said it best in October 1940: "Let us have done with the nonsense about there being no difference between the foreign policies of the White House and the Republican party. There is a difference, and that difference may be written in the blood of our youth."[91]

Democrats

The Great Depression had a devastating effect on transatlantic trade. Not only was there a widespread decline in consumer demand, but most countries raised tariff barriers to protect their domestic industries. Even Britain,

[89] Donald B. Johnson, *The Republican Party and Wendell Willkie* (Urbana: University of Illinois Press, 1960), chaps. 3–4; James H. Madison, ed., *Wendell Willkie: Hoosier Internationalist* (Bloomington: Indiana University Press, 1992).
[90] Robert C. Ehrhart, "The Politics of Military Rearmament, 1935–1940: The President, the Congress, and the United States Army" (Ph.D. diss., University of Texas at Austin, 1975), 375. See also H. Bradford Westerfield, *Foreign Policy and Party Politics: Pearl Harbor to Korea* (New Haven: Yale University Press, 1955), 130–35.
[91] Quoted in McCoy, *Landon of Kansas*, 451.

which for nearly a century had stood for free trade, instituted a preferential tariff for its empire in 1932. It was not until 1934, when Congress passed the Reciprocal Trade Agreements Act, that the situation began to improve. The RTAA enabled the president to negotiate bilateral tariff reductions with many of the United States' major trading partners, including Belgium (May 1935), the Netherlands (February 1936), France (June 1936), and Britain (January 1939). A most-favored-nation agreement was also concluded with the Soviet Union (July 1935). These treaties provided an important measure of relief for export-dependent sectors, as trade with RTAA signatories recovered at nearly double the rate of non-RTAA states between 1934–35 and 1938–39.[92]

Not all European countries were willing to cooperate, though. None of the future Axis powers agreed to open its markets; on the contrary, all of them pursued autarchy from the other great powers. The most egregious offender was Nazi Germany, which shifted its trade to countries that agreed to offer their goods for barter rather than hard currency. One of its greatest victims was American cotton farmers, the Democratic Party's most important sectoral constituency. In 1933, Germany imported 75 percent of its cotton from the United States; by 1935, that figure had fallen to 25 percent.[93] In October 1934, Germany gave notice to cancel its most-favored-nation treaty with the United States, to take effect after a required one-year waiting period. As a result, Germany's share of American exports plummeted from 8.4 percent in 1933 to 3.8 percent in 1937.[94] President Roosevelt refused to enter into the barter system; to do so would not only strike a blow to the principles of a liberal trading system but also wreck his efforts to open markets through the RTAA.

Germany's pernicious economic practices, combined with its increasingly egregious violations of international law, gave the internationalist Democrats a clear strategic imperative: align with Britain and France as early as possible to resist Hitler's assault on international order. The party also should have supported the League of Nations' efforts to enforce collective security, even though the United States was not a member of the organization. Democrats' willingness to pursue these goals should have been limited by the collapse of international trade and the concomitant growth of isolationist sentiment throughout the country; however, their strategy should nevertheless have been clearly identifiable as internationalist.

---

[92] David A. Lake, *Power, Protection, and Free Trade: International Sources of U.S. Commercial Strategy, 1887–1939* (Ithaca: Cornell University Press, 1988), 204–9.
[93] Patrick J. Hearden, *Roosevelt Confronts Hitler: America's Entry into World War II* (DeKalb: Northern Illinois University Press, 1987), 60–61.
[94] Ibid., 68.

Europe

From 1933 to 1941, the leader of the Democratic Party was President Franklin Delano Roosevelt. He acted as an internationalist, but not with the same degree of assertiveness as Woodrow Wilson. Instead, as expected, his strategic initiatives were tempered by the rising tide of isolationism.[95] In 1933, Roosevelt proclaimed his support for the League of Nations and insisted that the United States would cooperate with its efforts to enforce world peace, but he did not advocate membership.[96] He called for the United States to join the PCIJ, but he waited to put it on the agenda until 1935, after the Democrats had won more than two-thirds of the seats in the Senate.[97] He reluctantly conceded to amendments that limited the American commitment to the organization, yet the accession treaty was still defeated.

The limits of Roosevelt's internationalism in the mid 1930s are most clearly evident in the history of the Neutrality Acts. Shortly after coming to office, Roosevelt called on Congress to enact a law that would allow him to embargo the export of arms to states that he designated as aggressors.[98] With this power, he would be able to join the League of Nations in the enforcement of collective security. The House of Representatives granted his request in April 1934; however, the Senate was not so obliging. The best Roosevelt could obtain from that body was an impartial embargo law, one that would not grant him the power to discriminate between aggressors and victims. He reluctantly decided to sign the bill, the Neutrality Act of 1935, under the provision that it would be subject to renewal in six months, permitting him another opportunity to ask for discretionary powers.

In the short term, the Neutrality Act served Roosevelt's purposes well. He used it to place an embargo on Italy, which was deemed an aggressor state by the League of Nations following its invasion of Abyssinia. By the principle of impartiality, he also had to apply the law to Abyssinia, but

---

[95] This interpretation follows most of the historical literature on Roosevelt. A few scholars argue instead that he was an isolationist; see David G. Haglund, *Latin America and the Transformation of U.S. Strategic Thought, 1936–1940* (Albuquerque: University of New Mexico Press, 1984), 26–34; Victor L. Albjerg, "Isolationism and the Early New Deal, 1932–1937," *Current History* 35 (October 1958): 204–10; Elliot A. Rosen, "Intranationalism vs. Internationalism: The Interregnum Struggle for the Sanctity of the New Deal," *Political Science Quarterly* 81, no. 2 (June 1966): 274–97.

[96] Robert Dallek, *Franklin D. Roosevelt and American Foreign Policy, 1932–1945* (New York: Oxford University Press, 1979), 69–70.

[97] Ibid., 71, 95–96; Robert D. Accinelli, "The Roosevelt Administration and the World Court Defeat, 1935," *Historian* 40, no. 3 (May 1978): 463–78; Gilbert N. Kahn, "Presidential Passivity on a Nonsalient Issue: President Franklin D. Roosevelt and the 1935 World Court Fight," *Diplomatic History* 4, no. 2 (spring 1980): 137–59; Benjamin D. Rhodes, *United States Foreign Policy in the Interwar Period, 1918–1941* (Westport, Conn.: Praeger, 2001), 135–39.

[98] Stuart L. Weiss, "American Foreign Policy and Presidential Power: The Neutrality Act of 1935," *Journal of Politics* 30, no. 3 (August 1968): 672–95; Dallek, *Franklin D. Roosevelt*, 106–121.

American businesses would not have been able to supply arms to the land-locked country even without the embargo. As the crisis deepened, Roosevelt went a step further than the League of Nations. Though he had no formal power to restrict the sale of anything other than arms, he called on exporters to undertake a "moral embargo" of raw materials to Italy, used bureaucratic means to prevent American oil tankers from embarking for Italy, and submitted a revised version of the soon-to-expire Neutrality Act that would allow him to restrict raw materials exports to belligerents to prewar levels. Unfortunately, the Senate refused to make any changes to the bill, so he had little choice but to accept its renewal on the same terms as before. Roosevelt lifted the embargo on Italy and Abyssinia in June 1936, in step with Britain (see chapter 7). However, in accordance with the Stimson Doctrine, he refused to grant diplomatic recognition of Italy's gains.

Roosevelt also followed Britain's lead over the Spanish Civil War.[99] He disliked Franco, but he feared that intervention could lead to broader conflict between the European great powers. Since the Neutrality Act applied only to wars between states, Roosevelt asked for a new law that would give him the power to impose an arms embargo specifically on Spain. Congress obliged, and the president implemented it. Then, as the situation worsened, he considered stronger measures. In June 1937, he told Secretary of State Cordell Hull that he was prepared to extend the embargo to Germany and Italy, both of which had been intervening directly in the Spanish Civil War. Hull floated the idea to the British, who responded that such a measure not only might provoke a war but also would have to be extended to France and Russia, which were aiding Franco's opponents. Roosevelt deferred, but his willingness to adopt a hard line against the fascist powers is an important indicator of his internationalist bent.

Following the Munich Conference of September 1938, Roosevelt began to push more vigorously for an openly anti-German foreign policy.[100] He initiated a major aircraft rearmament program, partly to improve American military readiness but also to provide an additional source of supply for Britain and France. The U.S. Army, which had been severely underfunded and underequipped since the early 1920s, protested the sale of any of its limited supply of new planes. However, the president insisted that Britain and France would be less likely to appease Hitler if they could build up their air forces rapidly to challenge the *Wehrmacht*. Roosevelt also called for the revision of the Neutrality Act, but he was unable to overcome isolationist

---

[99] Dallek, *Franklin D. Roosevelt*, 131, 135–36, 142–43; Rhodes, *United States Foreign Policy*, 141–42.

[100] Dallek, *Franklin D. Roosevelt*, 172–75, 179–92, 199–205; David Reynolds, *The Creation of the Anglo-American Alliance, 1937–41: A Study in Competitive Co-operation* (London: Europa, 1981), 41–43, 54–58, 65–66; Rhodes, *United States Foreign Policy*, 156–57, 159–61, 165–67.

opposition in Congress. It was not until the outbreak of war in Europe that the tide turned. In October 1939, Congress approved a "cash and carry" law that allowed the sale of arms to belligerents who would pay upfront and transport the weapons themselves. Since Britain and France had imposed a naval blockade on Germany, the measure benefited only the Allies.

After the fall of France, Roosevelt continued to press against the boundaries of neutrality.[101] In June 1940, he began selling surplus military equipment to Britain; then, in August, he agreed to provide fifty older destroyers in exchange for naval bases in the Western Hemisphere. By December, Britain was running out of currency to pay for its "cash and carry" arms purchases, so Roosevelt persuaded Congress to pass a new law, the Lend-Lease Act, that would permit him to give arms to Britain in return for an empty promise that they would be replaced at the end of the war. Then, in 1941, he began to prepare for active combat. He negotiated a treaty to build bases in Greenland in March, sent marines to occupy Iceland in June, signed a joint Anglo-American declaration of principles for the construction of a postwar world order in August, and directed the navy to shoot German submarines on sight in September. He also demanded the full repeal of the Neutrality Acts, which Congress granted in November. By May 1941, he had reached the conclusion that the United States would eventually have to enter the war; by the fall of 1941, he was doing everything in his power to provoke Germany into attacking.

Russia

Like the Liberal and Labour Parties in Great Britain (see chapter 7), one of the Democrats' early priorities was the normalization of relations with Soviet Russia.[102] Not only was Russia a vast potential market for American exports, particularly raw cotton, but closer ties with it might deter Japanese expansionism in northeast Asia. In November 1933, Roosevelt granted diplomatic recognition of the Soviet Union in exchange for the curtailment of communist propaganda, respect for the religious freedom of Americans living in the USSR, and the partial repayment of debts incurred by Tsarist Russia. The Soviets reneged on the debt deal and maintained a low level of propaganda, but Roosevelt tolerated their misbehavior and signed a most-favored-nation trade agreement with them in July 1935.

---

[101] Dallek, *Franklin D. Roosevelt*, 227–28, 245–47, 254–68, 276, 281–92; Rhodes, *United States Foreign Policy*, 169–80; Waldo Heinrichs, *Threshold of War: Franklin D. Roosevelt and American Entry into World War II* (Oxford: Oxford University Press, 1988), 38–49, 85–90, 110–12, 116–17, 151–52, 155–60, 164–69.

[102] Thomas R. Maddux, *Years of Estrangement: American Relations with the Soviet Union, 1933–1941* (Tallahassee: University Presses of Florida, 1980), chaps. 1–3, 7–9, 11; Joan H. Wilson, "American Business and the Recognition of the Soviet Union," *Social Science Quarterly* 52, no. 2 (June 1971): 349–68; Dallek, *Franklin D. Roosevelt*, 78–81, 206–12, 278–81, 292–99.

Relations between the two countries remained lukewarm until autumn 1939, when the Soviets signed a nonaggression pact with Germany, invaded eastern Poland, took control over the Baltic states, and attacked Finland. These unwelcome developments saddled Roosevelt with two contradictory imperatives: uphold the principles of international order by siding with the victims of Soviet aggression, or align with the Soviets to counter an even greater threat to international order, Nazi Germany. Roosevelt's response to this conundrum was to split the difference.[103] Fearing that hostile measures might push the Soviet Union further into the German camp, he raised little protest against its occupation of Poland and the Baltic states. However, he could not ignore its bombing of civilian populations in Finland. He called for a moral embargo on the sale of airplanes, aluminum, and molybdenum to the Soviet Union, froze its assets, and approved a $20 million loan for Finland.

The German invasion of the Soviet Union in June 1941 quickly changed Roosevelt's position. He unfroze Soviet assets, received its requests for supplies, and began pressing his bureaucratic planners to allocate scarce resources to meet its needs. Given the enormous demands of the already underequipped American and British militaries, not much was available at first, but the export of both raw materials and armaments expanded rapidly. In September, the administration granted the Soviet Union a $1 billion aid package, then, in October, it began to extend credit to it under the Lend-Lease program. By December, the American "arsenal of democracy" had become a critical component of the Soviet war effort.

East Asia

Roosevelt's foremost strategic priority was the containment and defeat of Nazi Germany, not Imperial Japan. He was not unconcerned by conflict in East Asia, but it was not until late in events that he stood firm against Japan.[104] On the outbreak of the Sino-Japanese War in July 1937, he responded with only token measures to signal American neutrality. As long as the Neutrality Acts prevented him from discriminating between belligerents, he could not embargo Japan without also cutting off China, which needed desperately to import arms. The administration did not begin to take a harder line until November 1938, when Japan repudiated the Open Door policy in China. This action not only threatened American commercial

---

[103] Maddux, *Years of Estrangement*, chaps. 8–9; Dallek, *Franklin D. Roosevelt*, 206–12.

[104] Jonathan G. Utley, *Going to War with Japan, 1937–1941* (Knoxville: University of Tennessee Press, 1985), 8–37, 43–63, 72–81; Dallek, *Franklin D. Roosevelt*, 146–55, 193–95; Rhodes, *United States Foreign Policy*, 147–49, 185–88; Frederick C. Adams, "The Road to Pearl Harbor: A Reexamination of American Far Eastern Policy, July 1937–December 1938," *Journal of American History* 58, no. 1 (June 1971): 73–92.

interests but also openly violated treaties that Japan had signed with the
United States at the Washington Conference of 1921–22. Hull feared that
any kind of interference in the Sino-Japanese conflict would cause it to escalate, but Roosevelt insisted on action. He granted the Chinese government
a loan of $25 million in December, plus another $20 million in the following
spring, and directed the State Department to discourage American businesses from extending loans or credit sales to the Japanese. Then, in July
1939, he abrogated Japan's trade agreement with the United States.

From that point, it was only a matter of time before Roosevelt implemented a full embargo. Economic sanctions served not only as an instrument of coercion but also as a convenient excuse to keep down prices on
goods needed for the United States' own rearmament program. In July 1940,
Japan escalated its demands against Britain and France to close off their colonial borders with China, so Roosevelt began to limit the export of arms,
aluminum, magnesium, oil, and scrap metal to Japan. In September, when
Japan forced France to cede military bases and transit rights in Indochina,
he cut off all exports of scrap iron and steel. A few months later, he added
nearly all metals, both scrap and unmanufactured, to the list, and extended
a new $100 million loan to China. The final blow came at the end of July
1941, when Japan tightened its hold over Indochina and began building up
forces in Manchuria for a potential attack on the Soviet Union. Roosevelt
revoked all licenses for the export of oil to Japan and froze its assets, then,
a month later, undertook a full embargo.[105] If the United States could deter
Japan from joining Germany against the beleaguered Russia, it would be
well worth the risk of conflict. For the president, the greatest risk of hostilities in the Pacific was that it would draw resources from his undeclared war
against Germany in the Atlantic.[106]

Nevertheless, the Japanese raid on Pearl Harbor on December 7, 1941,
came as a relief to Roosevelt. With American territory under attack, congressional isolationists conceded to demands for full mobilization, allowing the
president to bring the enormous resources of the United States to bear in his
struggle for an internationalist world order. The only remaining question
was how to rally public opinion for the initiation of war against Japan's
allies in Europe. Having intercepted Japanese messages indicating that the
Axis would do the favor for him, he decided to wait. The bet soon paid

[105] Heinrichs, *Threshold of War*, 132–36, 141–42, 177–78, 246–47. Some scholars have argued
that Roosevelt originally ordered a partial embargo and that his policy was converted into a
full embargo by insubordinate bureaucrats while he was away from Washington for a meeting with Churchill. See Utley, *Going to War*, 151–56; Irvine H. Anderson, "The 1941 De Facto
Embargo on Oil to Japan: A Bureaucratic Reflex," *Pacific Historical Review* 44, no. 2 (May
1975): 213–30.
[106] Dallek, *Franklin D. Roosevelt*, 275–76; Heinrichs, *Threshold of War*, 99, 193–99, 205–10.

off: on December 11, both Hitler and Mussolini declared formal hostilities against the United States. At last, Roosevelt had the war he wanted.

CONCLUSION

The inconsistencies and anomalies in American grand strategy toward the great powers in 1865–1941, as discussed at the start of this chapter, become comprehensible from the perspective of the domestic political economy of the United States. The most striking pattern in the period is the divide between internationalist Democrats and realpolitik Republicans. Three of the four Democrats who served as president sought to make strong, high-politics commitments to the advancement of international law or the defense of international order against aggressors. In contrast, only one of eleven Republicans did. That single Republican (Taft) did not consistently pursue an internationalist agenda, whereas two of the four Democrats (Wilson and Roosevelt) did.

Oddly, historians and political scientists who study American foreign policy prior to the Cold War often ignore the partisan divide. There are three likely reasons for this. First, many scholars focus on international outcomes rather than executive strategies. Viewed solely in terms of the former, American foreign policy toward the great powers in 1865–1941 was far more consistent than depicted here. The Senate failed to ratify the two strongest internationalist initiatives negotiated by Democrats, Cleveland's arbitration treaty with Britain and Wilson's League of Nations Covenant. As a result, the United States was not bound to abide by its quixotic forays into international law and collective security. Looking at this record, realists conclude that the United States consistently acted according to a straight-forward "national interest."

This conclusion is based on false assumptions. The United States appeared to follow a "national interest" not because its leaders were actually doing so, but because its domestic political institutions were biased in favor of the status quo. As long as the U.S. Constitution allowed only one-third of the Senate to veto foreign treaties, isolationists and realpolitikers could unite to impose a certain continuity of inaction over internationalism. Furthermore, treaties can have far-reaching consequences even when they are not ratified. Wilson's commitment to the League of Nations had a tremendous impact on international diplomacy in the interwar period (see chapter 7) even though the United States did not ultimately join the organization. Conflict between the executive and legislative branches of government over foreign policy does not resolve to the "national interest"; rather, it produces strategic incoherence.

A second potential reason why scholars tend to neglect the issue of partisanship in 1865–1941 is that many Republican presidents were willing to sign arbitration, conciliation, and antiwar treaties that did not create binding commitments. As a result, the period is littered with weak, low-politics agreements that are too easily lumped together with more substantive, high-politics proposals. In this jumble it is difficult to see any real patterns in American internationalism. Only when the strong, costly initiatives are separated from the rest does one observe a definite partisan effect.

Finally, Woodrow Wilson and Franklin Roosevelt happened to have been in office during the two world wars, so it is only natural to conclude that their internationalism should be attributed to historical circumstance rather than their party identification. According to this view, a Republican president in the same situation would have made similar proposals. Yet, as explained at the beginning of the chapter, this counterfactual is implausible. Throughout the interwar period, most Republican Party leaders were either ambivalent or outright hostile to the League of Nations. In contrast, it is not difficult to imagine that another Democrat in the same position would have seized on the chance to advance the cause of international law and multilateral cooperation.

It should also be noted that the coding of Wilson and Roosevelt as internationalists does not depend on their wartime diplomacy. Before World War I, Wilson made a substantive advance in international law by negotiating six strong conciliation, or "cooling-off," treaties, which bound signatories to refrain from the use of force for a six-month period following the initiation of an international crisis. Before World War II, Roosevelt sought to keep the United States in step with, and even ahead of, the League of Nations in the imposition of economic sanctions on Italy. Thus, neither Wilson nor Roosevelt needed the advent of war to establish himself as an internationalist. Their strategic views were a function of their party affiliation, not their happenstance opportunity to negotiate a new world order.

[5]

The Political Economy of
Great Britain, 1868–1939

The Reform Act of 1867 marked a major transition in British politics. At one stroke, 938,000 names were added to the electoral rolls, almost doubling the franchise. To win the support of these new voters, political coalitions had to become more centralized and disciplined, with permanent organizational structures, coherent ideologies, and well-articulated national platforms.[1] As a result, cleavages between the two major parliamentary parties, the Liberals and the Conservatives, became more clearly defined than ever before. British politics began to settle into a predictable pattern of behavior dictated by the interests of stable electoral constituencies rather than the whims of charismatic figures like Lord Palmerston. These changes make 1868, the year in which the first government elected by the enlarged franchise came to power, a natural point of departure for a study of the political economy of British grand strategy.

CONSERVATIVES

Prior to the Reform Act of 1867, the Conservatives were the party of the social and economic elite, representing above all the interests of the gentry.[2] Even in 1868, nearly half of all Conservative members of Parliament derived

[1] Martin Pugh, *The Making of Modern British Politics, 1867–1939*, 2d ed. (Cambridge, Mass.: Blackwell, 1993), chaps. 1–4.
[2] Rohan McWilliam, *Popular Politics in Nineteenth-Century England* (London: Routledge, 1998), 49; David Cannadine, *The Decline and Fall of the British Aristocracy* (New Haven: Yale University Press, 1990), 65; Malcolm Pearce and Geoffrey Stewart, *British Political History, 1867–1990: Democracy and Decline* (London: Routledge, 1992), 69, 74–75; H. J. Hanham, *Elections and Party Management: Politics in the Time of Disraeli and Gladstone* (London: Longmans, 1959), 225.

Table 5.1. Parliament Members' Economic Interests, as Share within Parties

	1868		1892		1910	
	Liberal	Conserv.	Liberal	Conserv.	Liberal	Conserv.
Landowning	26.1	45.9	9.0	24.1	7.2	21.6
Military	6.9	13.6	1.8	8.6	2.6	9.5
Finance, commerce	16.4	10.3	16.5	22.5	16.9	20.9
Manufacturing	12.0	4.4	24.8	12.1	27.3	20.1

SOURCE: P. J. Cain and A. G. Hopkins, *British Imperialism: Innovation and Expansion, 1688–1914,* vol. 1 (London: Longman, 1993), 139.

income from landowning, compared to only a quarter of Liberals (see table 5.1). This political elitism had definite advantages when the franchise was small, but it posed a serious problem for the Conservatives after the expansion of the electorate in 1867. At that point, the party had to find some way to win votes in the now-critical middle class without compromising its basic values.

The key to success, Conservative leaders found, lay in the political assimilation of segments of society whose interests were congruent with those of the gentry. While voters were drawn to the party for a number of reasons exogenous to this study, including allegiance to the Anglican Church and opposition to Irish home rule, Conservatives focused on co-opting a group with strong preferences toward the international economy: the London-based trade and financial services sector. The resulting alliance between the gentry and the financial elite was so close-knit that many historians refer to its members collectively as the "gentlemanly capitalists."[3]

The concept of gentlemanly capitalism is critical to understanding the evolution of the Conservative Party because it bridges the gap between the pre-1867 period, in which the franchise was small and the party was dominated by the landed elite, and the 1890s, in which the franchise had broadened significantly and the party's primary economic constituency had become the investing bourgeoisie.[4] Table 5.1 illustrates this shift. In 1868, the Liberals were represented by more parliamentarians with "commercial and financial" interests, but by 1892 the ratio between the parties had flipped in favor of the Conservatives. This partisan cleavage is also evident in the electoral geography of Britain. Conservatives dominated

[3] P. J. Cain and A. G. Hopkins, *British Imperialism: Innovation and Expansion, 1688–1914,* vol. 1 (London: Longman, 1993), 33; Marvin Swartz, *The Politics of British Foreign Policy in the Era of Disraeli and Gladstone* (New York: St. Martin's, 1985), 6–7; C. H. Lee, "The Service Sector, Regional Specialization, and Economic Growth in the Victorian Economy," *Journal of Historical Geography* 10, no. 2 (April 1984): 152.

[4] Richard Shannon, *The Age of Disraeli, 1868–1881: The Rise of Tory Democracy* (London: Longman, 1992), 169, 180–81.

Table 5.2. Conservative Seats in Parliament, as Share of Total Seats

	1874–80	1892–1910	Interwar
Above 60%	79 East Anglia 72 S.E. England 67 Wessex	78 Wessex 78 West Midlands 74 S. E. England	79 Wessex 68 Central region 66 West Midlands 63 S.E. England 62 East Anglia

Below 40%	33 Yorkshire
	31 Northern England
	28 Wales and
	    Monmouthshire
	22 Scotland
		40 East Midlands
		39 Devon and
		    Cornwall
		36 Yorkshire region
		32 Peak-Don
		31 Scotland
		26 Northern England
		12 Wales and
		    Monmouthshire
			33 Scotland
			32 Northern England
			19 Peak-Don
			13 Wales and
			    Monmouthshire

SOURCE: J. P. D. Dunbabin, "British Elections in the Nineteenth and Twentieth Centuries: A Regional Approach," *English Historical Review* 95, no. 375 (April 1980): 259.
NOTE: The distribution of seats is normalized to give Conservatives 50% of each Parliament.

elections in southeast England (see table 5.2), where the service sector and its gentlemanly capitalists were highly concentrated.[5]

By the end of World War I, the transformation of the Conservative Party was essentially complete. Mass suffrage, the declining profitability of land-holding, and the rise of a wealthy bourgeoisie greatly diminished the inde-pendent sociopolitical power of the gentry.[6] The war itself was particularly devastating to the landed class: of all the peers who served in the conflict, one in five died, compared to one in eight of all Britons.[7] As a result, the gentry lost both their cohesiveness and their electorally disproportionate influence over British politics. The Conservatives became the party of fi-nance, whose power and wealth originated not in aristocratic estates but rather in the City, London's financial district. Even with a wide social base in the interwar period, the Conservative Central Office received up to three-quarters of its elections funding from the City.[8]

[5] E. Spencer Wellhofer, *Democracy, Capitalism, and Empire in Late Victorian Britain, 1885–1910* (New York: St. Martin's, 1996), 142–43; Cain and Hopkins, *British Imperialism*, 1:113–16; Lee, "Service Sector"; C. H. Lee, "Regional Growth and Structural Change in Victorian Britain," *Economic History Review* 34, no. 3 (August 1981): 438–52; Ranald Michie, "The City of Lon-don and International Trade, 1850–1914," in *Decline and Recovery in Britain's Overseas Trade, 1873–1914*, ed. D. C. M. Platt (London: Macmillan, 1993), 21–63; Roy Church, *The History of the British Coal Industry, 1830–1913* (Oxford: Clarendon, 1986), xxi, 3; J. A. Hobson, "The Gen-eral Election: A Sociological Interpretation," *Sociological Review* 3, no. 2 (April 1910): 112–14.
[6] Cannadine, *Decline and Fall*, chaps. 2–8; W. L. Guttsman, *The British Political Elite* (Lon-don: MacGibbon and Kee, 1963), chap. 5.
[7] Cannadine, *Decline and Fall*, 83.
[8] Robert W. D. Boyce, *British Capitalism at the Crossroads, 1919–1932* (Cambridge: Cam-bridge University Press, 1987), 21, 380.

In sum, the Conservative Party shifted from the control of the landed gentry to the financial service sector in the late nineteenth century. In the following pages, I examine the economic interests of these two groups, form hypotheses about their strategic preferences, and briefly test these hypotheses. At the end of this section, I make predictions about how Conservative governments should have aggregated their constituents' interests.

Landed Gentry

In 1868, when the gentry were still the dominant force behind the Conservative Party, their primary source of income was rent from landholdings. This position did not give them a particular stake in the international economy, much less grand strategy. However, the gentry also had strong military-colonial interests. The law of primogeniture dictated that the first-born son of an estate owner would inherit his father's entire fortune, leaving most younger sons with no choice but to seek employment elsewhere.[9] Some entered the business world, but many others sought positions in prestigious organizations that recruited men of high social status. For a price, wealthy families could secure for their younger sons offices that would provide them with a steady income and social respectability. Through favoritism and purchase, the gentry came to dominate the highest ranks of the judiciary, the Anglican Church, and, more to the point, the civil service and armed forces.

The army was of particular appeal for the younger sons of the landed elite.[10] While some peers obtained appointments so as to lavish their personal fortunes on horses, heraldry, and leisure in the Home Army, gentlemen of lesser means could earn a satisfactory income by serving in India or other imperial outposts. Even after purchase was abolished in 1871, the military remained a haven of social privilege. In 1899, 38 percent of colonels and 51 percent of generals in the British army were members of the gentry, a fantastic share for such a small subset of the general population.[11] Indeed, a study from 1883 found that "one in four peers and one in three of the greater gentry had served in the army."[12] The navy was less popular, since

---

[9] F. M. L. Thompson, *English Landed Society in the Nineteenth Century* (London: Routledge and Kegan Paul, 1963), 70–75; G. E. Mingay, *The Gentry: The Rise and Fall of a Ruling Class* (London: Longman, 1973), 116–17; Edward M. Spiers, *The Army and Society, 1815–1914* (London: Longman, 1980), 8–10; Cannadine, *Decline and Fall*, 236–39.

[10] Spiers, *Army and Society*, 24–25, 194; Thompson, *English Landed Society*, 74–75; Cannadine, *Decline and Fall*, 264–80; Gwyn Harries-Jenkins, *The Army in Victorian Society* (London: Routledge and Kegan Paul, 1977), chap. 2; Anthony Bruce, *The Purchase System in the British Army, 1660–1871* (London: Royal Historical Society, 1980), 156–66.

[11] Edward M. Spiers, *The Late Victorian Army, 1868–1902* (Manchester: Manchester University Press, 1992), 94.

[12] Harries-Jenkins, *Army in Victorian Society*, 33.

it required skills more specific than a gentlemanly bearing, but many of the gentry nevertheless made careers there as well.

The gentry also permeated the upper echelons of Britain's civil service.[13] In particular, the Foreign Office and Diplomatic Service (merged as the Foreign Service in 1919) were considered bastions of gentlemanly elitism deep into the twentieth century. To a lesser extent, the same applied to the Colonial Office. John Bright's famously acerbic comment that British foreign policy constituted "neither more nor less than a gigantic system of outdoor relief for the aristocracy of Great Britain" was an overstatement, but it was not entirely baseless.[14] The business of governing the empire was not in itself profitable enough to sustain the conspicuous consumption of British high society, but it provided substantial subsidies.

Strategic Interests: Periphery

The gentry's ties to Britain's military and colonial institutions gave them an enormous special interest in the empire. Any retreat from imperialism would constitute an attack on their privileges, and any expansion of British colonial rule would provide them with greater opportunities for employment. To maintain their socioeconomic position, the gentry had a clear strategic imperative. Like any societal group with military-colonial interests, they should have favored whatever peripheral strategy would require the state to devote the most budgetary resources to the instruments of foreign policy. In the international environment of 1868–1939, that strategy was imperialism. It required spending on civil servants to administer the colonies, military officers to protect them, and diplomats to maintain relations with bordering states. Neither of the other options, isolationism, interventionism, or internationalism, could compare.

Although the historical literature on the domestic sources of British foreign policy in the late nineteenth and early twentieth centuries focuses primarily on the preferences of manufacturers and investors, numerous studies show that the aristocracy did play a decisive role in supporting the expansion of the empire in earlier years.[15] Furthermore, institutions dominated by the gentry

[13] Cannadine, *Decline and Fall*, 239–50, 280–95; Cain and Hopkins, *British Imperialism*, 1:123–25; Zara S. Steiner, *The Foreign Office and Foreign Policy, 1898–1914* (London: Cambridge University Press, 1969), 16; R. T. Nightingale, "The Personnel of the British Foreign Office and Diplomatic Service, 1851–1929," *American Political Science Review* 24, no. 2 (May 1930): 310–31. The Anglican Church, which was dominated by the upper class, also had an interest in imperialism, as the annexation of colonies created opportunities to make converts.

[14] Quoted in Raymond A. Jones, *The British Diplomatic Service, 1815–1914* (Waterloo, Ont.: Wilfred Laurier University Press, 1983), 8. See also ibid., 144.

[15] On the late nineteenth century, see A. P. Thornton, *The Imperial Idea and Its Enemies* (London: Macmillan, 1959), 88–99. On the early twentieth century, see Gregory D. Phillips, *The Diehards: Aristocratic Society and Politics in Edwardian England* (Cambridge, Mass.: Harvard University Press, 1979), 82–83, 89–93. On prior periods, see the works summarized in Cain and Hopkins, *British Imperialism*, 1:84–104.

tended to be strongly imperialist. Military officers consistently sided with hawkish politicians in domestic debates over foreign policy, while the Colonial Office repeatedly drew Britain into imperial intrigues, even when the government opposed taking on additional commitments.[16] In short, British military and colonial institutions supported imperialism, and so did the social class that was economically and politically reliant on these institutions.

Strategic Interests: Core

The gentry should not have been so eager to acquire territory in the core of the international system. Any attempt to prey on the weak states of Europe could quickly have led to war with one or more of the continental great powers. As an island nation with a middling population and a weak army, Britain was in no position to enter such conflicts on its own. Even if it were, however, the expected costs of this strategy would overwhelm its potential benefits. Expansion into the periphery, in contrast, would provide professional opportunities for military-colonial interests at an acceptable level of risk.

Without a definite interest in the conquest of, or cooperation with, the great powers, the gentry might have been tempted to turn away from the core entirely. Given their interest in the British Empire, however, this would have been possible only if the great powers had been willing to give Britain a free hand in the periphery. Clearly, they were not; thus, Britain could not avoid dealing with its peers. In short, isolation from the core was incompatible with imperialism toward the periphery. Instead, the gentry should have subordinated their core strategy to their peripheral strategy. When the empire was not affected by events in the core, they should have sought to stay aloof from great power politics; when the empire was at risk, they should have engaged in realpolitik maneuvering against states that threatened it.

In practice, it is difficult to find direct evidence of mass, or even elite, support for realpolitik. Unlike internationalism, supremacism, or isolationism, this strategy is not principled; rather, it is an injunction against commitments to principle. That is, it treats interactions with other great powers as a matter of expediency, limited from case to case and for narrow, instrumental purposes—in this case, to protect the empire. As a result, support for realpolitik is not always well articulated, at least not as a coherent program independent of the particular interests it serves. Instead, the best

---

[16] Stephen Cooney, "Political Demand Channels in the Processes of American and British Imperial Expansion, 1870–1913," *World Politics* 27, no. 2 (January 1975): 249, 251–52; Hew Strachan, *The Politics of the British Army* (Oxford: Clarendon Press, 1997), 40, 74–79, 95, 98–99; W. Murray Hogben, "British Civil-Military Relations on the North West Frontier of India," in *Swords and Covenants*, ed. Adrian Preston and Peter Dennis (London: Croom Helm, 1976), 140–42. On the representation of the military in the House of Commons, see Strachan, *Politics of the British Army*, 23–33; Spiers, *Late Victorian Army*, 163–68.

evidence for it is often indirect, based on the process of elimination: if opinion is neither isolationist nor supremacist nor internationalist, it is more than likely realpolitik.

This was indeed the case for the British gentry. They were certainly not isolationist; no significant constituency in Britain was. Some advocated "splendid isolation," but this referred to the avoidance of formal military alliances, not diplomatic disengagement. Neither were they supremacist: unlike French Bonapartists, for example, few harbored thoughts of conquest on the continent. Finally, and most important, they were not typically internationalist. In a historical analysis of international political philosophies in the nineteenth century, Carsten Holbraad identifies the British strain of realpolitik, "balance of power theory," with the dominant ideology of the landed gentry, Toryism.[17] Internationalism, in contrast, was associated with opposition to aristocrat privilege, Radicalism. A subset of the gentry, the Whigs, also leaned internationalist; however, these individuals were distinguished by their commercial entrepreneurialism and, as such, were less likely to depend on income from government employment than the rest of the gentry. Thus, Whigs are the exception that proves the rule.

Financial Services and Trade

Despite the inevitable decline of the gentry, the Conservative Party did not lose its connection to the empire. Instead, it co-opted a new constituency, the financial services and trade sector, that shared the strategic interests of the gentry. This sector, which was based in London, derived much of its income from investment in the periphery. Lance Davis and Robert Huttenback's research reveals its distinctive economic profile:

> London merchants, manufacturers, professionals, and managers all invested far less frequently in home and far more frequently in Empire activities. On average, London businesspeople were only one-fifth as likely to invest in domestic securities as those businesspeople who lived in places like Sheffield or Manchester, but they were half again as likely to put their resources to work in the Empire. Overall, Empire investors tended to be drawn from two groups: elites, wherever they lived, and businesspeople (particularly merchants) who resided in London. The attractiveness of the Empire seemed to decline almost exponentially the farther one traveled north from the city. In terms of the socioeconomic background of its participants, the British capital market was clearly two markets, and it is from those segments, elites

---

[17] Carsten Holbraad, *The Concert of Europe: A Study in German and British International Theory, 1815–1914* (Harlow: Longmans, 1970). See also Paul Laity, *The British Peace Movement, 1870–1914* (Oxford: Oxford University Press, 2001), 9–10.

and London businesspeople, that the most strident Empire support could have been expected to come.[18]

According to Davis and Huttenback's estimates, approximately two-thirds of all British capital called up for foreign investment between 1870 and 1912 was sent to peripheral countries.[19] This figure excludes Canada but includes Japan; if these two countries are recategorized, the periphery's share of British foreign investment is closer to 75 percent. Considering that the London-based gentlemanly capitalists had an even greater stake in the empire than the average British investor, the importance of peripheral markets to the economy of southeast England can hardly be overstated. From 1870 to 1905, the share of the national income derived from returns on foreign property grew from 4.0 percent to 7.6 percent, and it remained near this level through the 1920s (see figure 5.1).[20]

Another vital sector in southeast England was shipping. Historians have paid less attention to the geographical distribution of overseas shipping than investment, but the limited evidence that is available indicates that the two sectors followed a similar pattern. In 1936, 38.8 percent of earnings from shipping were generated by trade between Britain and the empire, 7.7 percent came from routes connecting different parts of the empire, and 13.6 percent derived from trade between the empire and foreign countries.[21] Unfortunately, the existing data are not sufficiently disaggregated to reveal how much of the remainder (25.2 percent between Britain and foreign countries and 14.7 percent between foreign countries) was connected to the periphery. However, London likely did proportionately less business with core markets than Britain's other major ports, since it did not handle any of the country's most important export to Europe, coal.[22] Even the trade that

[18] Lance E. Davis and Robert A. Huttenback, *Mammon and the Pursuit of Empire: The Political Economy of British Imperialism, 1860–1912* (New York: Cambridge University Press, 1986), 314. Unlike in other advanced industrialized countries, there was a clear separation between the economic interests of finance and industry in Great Britain. See Geoffrey Ingham, *Capitalism Divided? The City and Industry in British Social Development* (London: Macmillan, 1986), chap. 3.

[19] Davis and Huttenback, *Mammon*, 46.

[20] Finance was tied to the international economy in two other ways. First, both insurance and banking firms exported their services, as represented in figure 5.1. Second, insurance companies indemnified Britain's enormous overseas shipping industry. I have been unable to find data on the value and distribution of maritime insurance, but it stood as one of the most important pillars of the industry (along with fire and life) and must have contributed greatly to London's imperial orientation. See Harold E. Raynes, *A History of British Insurance* (London: Pitman, 1948).

[21] H. Leak, "The Carrying Trade of British Shipping," *Journal of the Royal Statistical Society* 102, no. 2 (1939): 254. Both before World War I and in the interwar period, British ships carried 95 percent of all trade between the home isles and the empire. See S. G. Sturmey, *British Shipping and World Competition* (London: Athlone, 1962), 89.

[22] Barry Supple, *The History of the British Coal Industry, 1913–1946* (Oxford: Clarendon, 1987), 181.

Figure 5.1. U.K. Invisible Exports, as Share of National Income

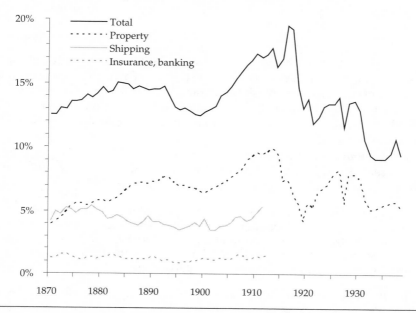

SOURCES: Shipping, insurance, and banking figures from C. K. Hobson, *The Export of Capital* (London: Constable, 1914), 197. Property and total figures from C. H. Feinstein, *Statistical Tables of National Income, Expenditure, and Output of the U.K., 1855–1965* (New York: Cambridge University Press, 1972), 37–38. National income figures from B. R. Mitchell and P. Deane, *Abstract of British Historical Statistics* (London: Cambridge University Press, 1962), 367–68.

it did carry to Europe would not have produced exceptional earnings, since rates on freight for a short hop to the continent were a small fraction of those charged for destinations like Bangkok and Santiago.[23]

In sum, the service sector that dominated southeast England's regional economy was deeply dependent on income from the empire and other peripheral markets, much more so than the rest of Britain.[24] The entire base of the Conservative Party, both masses and elites, shared this

[23] Douglass North, "Ocean Freight Rates and Economic Development, 1750–1913," *Journal of Economic History* 18, no. 4 (December 1958): 552.

[24] The new industries of the interwar period, including automobiles, airplanes, electrical equipment, and chemicals, tended to concentrate in the southeast; see C. H. Lee, *Regional Economic Growth in the United Kingdom since the 1880s* (London: McGraw Hill, 1971), 98–112. This sector was much less dependent on export than Britain's traditional manufactures, but what it did export was sent primarily to the dominions, not Europe or the United States. Thus, its strategic interests should have been consistent with those of the financial service sector. See H. W. Richardson, "The New Industries in Britain between the Wars," *Oxford*

interest: gentlemanly capitalists staked their fortunes on it, while those of modest means depended on it for their employment in finance and trade.

Strategic Interests: Periphery

In the mid 1880s, as investors began to displace the gentry as the primary socioeconomic constituency of the Conservative Party, they also began to find imperialism to be increasingly attractive. As Germany, France, and the United States industrialized, their financial sectors came into competition with London for new investment opportunities.[25] The British were left with only one major advantage: their foreign counterparts had little knowledge about economic conditions in distant parts of the periphery, whereas British businessmen had long-standing commercial relationships throughout the world. C. K. Hobson explains the competitive dynamic:

> Continental investors have to some extent followed in the footsteps of British investors, purchasing those kinds of securities which ignorance or caution had originally prevented them from buying. There has thus been a process of transference by which British capital has been able to continually advance into the more distant and less developed parts of the world.[26]

Since the investment of British capital in a particular market signaled to others that it was a safe bet, and therefore brought competition, the only way for British investors to stay ahead of the pack was to seek new, undeveloped frontiers. This required them to assume greater risks, which in turn increased their need for the support of the British military and Colonial Office. Thus, peripheral investors should have been at the forefront of demands for the extension of the empire in the late nineteenth century.

After 1914, the financial sector encountered further difficulties.[27] First, the Bolshevik Revolution led to the confiscation of all British investment in Russia, and the British government requisitioned and sold many properties in other parts of the world to generate foreign currency to pay for arms imports. Overall, Britain lost 10–15 percent of its overseas assets as a result

---

Economic Papers 13, no. 3 (October 1961): 362, 377–82; Alfred E. Kahn, *Great Britain in the World Economy* (New York: Columbia University Press, 1946), 65–70.

[25] C. K. Hobson, *The Export of Capital* (London: Constable, 1914), chaps. 5–6; P. L. Cottrell, *British Overseas Investment in the Nineteenth Century* (London: Macmillan, 1975), chaps. 2–3; Herbert Feis, *Europe, the World's Banker, 1870–1914* (New York: Norton, 1965), 17–26; Derek H. Aldcroft and Harry W. Richardson, *The British Economy, 1870–1939* (London: Macmillan, 1969), 86–87.

[26] Hobson, *Export of Capital*, 122. Before 1885, rates of return on investment in the British Empire were substantially higher than in the home isles. See Davis and Huttenback, *Mammon*, 104–10, 309.

[27] William Ashworth, *An Economic History of England, 1870–1939* (New York: Barnes and Noble, 1960), 344–48; John M. Atkin, *British Overseas Investment, 1918–1931* (New York: Arno,

of World War I.[28] Before the war, property income from abroad accounted for nearly 10 percent of the national income; in the 1920s, it dropped to the mid 7 percent range (see figure 5.1). New York banks, in contrast, reaped enormous profits from their lending to the Allies during the conflict. Second, the pound had to be taken off the gold standard in 1914–25. The dollar, meanwhile, was never compromised, making it a more attractive reserve currency. Finally, British bankers, unlike their American counterparts, were not taxed on bonds issued. Thus, borrowers could obtain lower rates in New York than London after the war.

The decline of the British financial service sector had political as well as economic causes.[29] The government was deeply indebted after the war, and it needed to borrow additional funds from the private capital market to service its short-term loans. At the same time, the manufacturing sector badly needed new infusions of capital to convert back to civilian production and modernize its aging infrastructure. If London bankers had returned to their prewar pattern of sending much of their investment abroad, neither the Treasury nor industry would have had much chance at recovery. Thus, the government imposed controls on the export of capital. Between 1918 and 1919, it explicitly forbade almost all foreign lending; then, for most of the next six years, it informally discouraged capital exports, particularly in the form of short and medium-term loans.

Once lending controls were lifted, British investors focused on the empire. Between 1918 and 1931, 75 percent of all overseas government issues and 52 percent of all overseas company issues went to the Dominions and dependent colonies.[30] In total, 66 percent of overseas issues were sent to the empire. The cumulative effects of World War I and its financial fallout are evident in table 5.3. In 1914, the distribution of British long-term overseas investment was 47 percent in the empire and 20 percent in the United States; in 1930, those figures stood at 59 percent and 5 percent.

In sum, the empire was a safe haven for British capital throughout the late nineteenth and early twentieth centuries. The financial services sector faced increased competition from the industrialization of the other great powers, was drained by World War I, and suffered badly in the Great Depression. To maintain its position, it needed an "inside track" on commercial opportunities in the periphery. As long as the empire did not become prohibitively

---

1977), 147–56; Royal Institute of International Affairs, *The Problem of International Investment* (London: His Majesty's Government, 1937), 135–38.

[28] Royal Institute of International Affairs, *Problem of International Investment*, 144; Ashworth, *Economic History of England*, 288; Derek H. Aldcroft, *From Versailles to Wall Street, 1919–1929* (London: Allen Lane, 1977), 240.

[29] Atkin, *British Overseas Investment*, 28–75; Royal Institute of International Affairs, *Problem of International Investment*, 134.

[30] Atkin, *British Overseas Investment*, 144, 161. See also Derek H. Aldcroft, *The Inter-War Economy: Britain, 1919–1939* (New York: Columbia University Press, 1970), 264–66.

Table 5.3. British Long-Term Overseas Investments

	1914		1930	
	Million pounds	Percentage of total	Million pounds	Percentage of total
British Empire	1,779	47.3	2,187	58.7
Canada and Newfoundland	515	13.7	525	14.1
Australia and New Zealand	416	11.1	617	16.6
India and Ceylon	379	10.1	540	14.5
South Africa	370	9.8	263	7.1
West Africa	37	1.0	46	1.2
Other	62	1.7	196	5.3
Latin America (excl. Br. Empire)	757	20.1	832	22.3
Argentina	320	8.5	450	12.1
Brazil	148	3.9	190	5.1
Chile	61	1.6	49	1.3
Other	228	6.1	143	3.9
Africa and Asia (excl. Br. Empire)	167	4.4	136	3.7
China	44	1.2	47	1.2
Other	123	3.3	89	2.4
Europe	243	6.4	295	7.9
Russia	110	2.9		
Turkey	24	0.6		
Other	109	2.9		
United States	755	20.1	201	5.4
Japan	63	1.7	74	2.0
Total periphery	2,703	71.8	3,155	84.7
Total core	1,061	28.2	570	15.3

SOURCES: Figures for 1914 adapted from George Paish, "Great Britain's Capital Investments in Individual Colonial and Foreign Countries," in *British Overseas Investments, 1907-1948*, ed. Mira Wilkins (New York: Arno, 1977), vi; adjustment to Russia from Herbert Feis, *Europe: The World's Banker* (New York: Norton, 1965), 23. Figures for 1930 adapted from Royal Institute of International Affairs, *Problem of International Investment* (London: His Majesty's Government, 1937), 142.

costly to maintain, the financial sector had every reason to want to protect and extend it with an imperialist grand strategy.

A substantial amount of evidence confirms that southeast England and the gentlemanly capitalists were, in fact, more imperialist than other regions and socioeconomic groups in Britain. Beginning with the seminal work of J. A. Hobson, there is a long tradition of historical research into investors' support for the empire.[31] Their attitude is captured perfectly in a speech made by the

[31] J. A. Hobson, *Imperialism: A Study*, 3d ed. (London: Allen and Unwin, 1938); N. Etherington, "Theories of Imperialism in Southern Africa Revisited," *African Affairs* 81, no. 324 (July 1982): 385–407; J. Forbes Munro, *Britain in Tropical Africa, 1880–1960: Economic Relationships and Impact*

chairman of the Stock Exchange before a cheering crowd in the City on the outbreak of the Boer War: "I do not believe that there is any body in England more patriotic and loyal than the Stock Exchange. . . . I think the Stock Exchange without shame may accept the name of jingo."[32] Also revealing is Lance E. Davis and Robert A. Huttenback's analysis of the foreign policy voting records of members of Parliament. They find not only that Conservatives were more imperialist than Liberals, but that Liberal MPs who represented London and the Home Counties were more imperialist than Liberals from other regions.[33] In short, there is ample reason to believe that public opinion in debates over grand strategy in the periphery was in line with the distribution of interests within Britain's domestic political economy.

Strategic Interests: Core

The fortunes of the financial services and trade sector were tied to the fate of the empire, not Europe. Of all of Britain's long-term publicly issued capital invested outside the home isles in 1914, only 6 percent was held in Europe (8 percent in 1930), while the United States had another 20 percent (5 percent in 1930).[34] With so little at stake in the markets of the continental great powers, the gentlemanly capitalists should have been unwilling to make diplomatic commitments to the core of the international system unless the security of the empire or the interests of finance were threatened. Otherwise, they should have prioritized the periphery.

In particular, the gentlemanly capitalists should not have trusted in internationalism. Any attempt to advance the cause of international law or multilateral decision making would not only squander Britain's diplomatic capital but also limit its ability to safeguard and extend the empire. An internationalist strategy would oblige the government to act according to the abstract principles of international law, making it difficult to adapt Britain's complex defense strategy to the changing exigencies of power politics and

---

(London: Macmillan, 1984), chap. 2; Phillip Darby, *Three Faces of Imperialism: British and American Approaches to Asia and Africa, 1870–1970* (New Haven: Yale University Press, 1987), 58–60; Cain and Hopkins, *British Imperialism*, vol. 1; P. J. Cain and A. G. Hopkins, *British Imperialism: Crisis and Deconstruction, 1914–1990*, vol. 2 (London: Longman, 1993); Anthony Webster, *Gentlemen Capitalists: British Imperialism in South East Asia, 1770–1890* (London: Tauris, 1998), 255–56; Raymond E. Dumett, ed., *Gentlemanly Capitalism and British Imperialism* (New York: Longman, 1999). On imperialist preferences in the shipping industry, see Andrew Porter, *Victorian Shipping, Business, and Imperial Policy: Donald Currie, the Castle Line, and Southern Africa* (New York: St. Martin's, 1986).

[32] Quoted in David Kynaston, *The City of London: Golden Years, 1890–1914*, vol. 2 (London: Chatto and Windus, 1995), 198. See also ibid., 79–86, 193–98.

[33] Davis and Huttenback, *Mammon*, 272.

[34] Davis and Huttenback's estimates for 1910–14, which include short-term lending but exclude direct investment, are 9–12 percent for Europe. See Davis and Huttenback, *Mammon*, 40–41, 46.

the rise of new threats. Since the empire was so far-flung and had so many points of vulnerability, the gentlemanly capitalists should have favored a more flexible strategy, realpolitik, for Britain's dealings with the great powers.

As noted earlier, it is difficult to determine the extent to which sectors prefer a strategy that eschews principle in favor of expediency. Support for realpolitik is evinced not in demands for a consistent set of behaviors, but rather in opposition to its alternatives, isolationism and internationalism. The former was notably absent from the foreign policy discourse in Britain; no broad-based socioeconomic group advocated principled detachment from great power politics. The latter, however, was consistently popular throughout 1868–1939. The critical question, then, is how support for internationalism was distributed.

In fact, the region of Britain in which the financial services and trade sectors were dominant, southeast England, was the least internationalist part of the country. Not only were northern England, Scotland, and Wales more enthusiastic about internationalism than southeast England, but many opinion leaders in the latter region were proactively hostile to specific initiatives for the advancement of international law and collective security. The evidence for these claims, which is detailed below in the section on the Liberal and Labour parties' sectoral interests, confirms that the heartland of gentlemanly capitalism was strongly disposed to realpolitik.

Hypotheses

Prior to the expansion of the electorate in 1867, the Conservative Party represented the gentry, a socioeconomic group with strong military-colonial interests. Due to the law of primogeniture, the "second sons" of aristocrats could not inherit their familial estates, so they turned to high-status careers in the army, navy, and civil service. Their control over the government and its instruments of coercion gave them a critical stake in the maintenance and extension of the empire. To this end, the Conservatives should have pursued an imperialist grand strategy.

After 1867, the financial services and trade sector gradually displaced the gentry as the primary constituency of the Conservative Party. This transition should not, however, have caused a shift in strategy. As Britain's economic hegemony declined, investors, insurers, and shippers faced increasing competition in the peripheral markets that they had once dominated. If they were to stay ahead of the Americans, French, Germans, and Japanese, they would need the support of their government to protect their interests in risky commercial and political environments. Thus, the Conservative Party should have remained imperialist throughout 1868–1939.

Neither the gentry nor the financial service sector had significant economic ties to any great power but the United States. As a result, Conservatives should have been unwilling to make commitments to internationalist initiatives, especially when doing so might have interfered with their freedom of action in the periphery. Yet, as long as the other great powers had imperial ambitions of their own, they could not risk isolation from the core. Instead, the Conservatives should have followed a strategy of realpolitik, using coercive diplomacy to curb the power of whatever states posed the greatest threat to the British Empire.

LIBERALS

Whereas the Conservatives represented the interests of the gentry and finance, the Liberals' main sectoral constituency was manufacturing.[35] Even as far back as 1832, when most politicians in both parties were wealthy landowners, the Liberals consistently beat the Conservatives in nearly every major manufacturing town.[36] Manufacturing was concentrated in northern England, Scotland, and Wales, while the economy of southeast England was dominated by financial services and trade (see figure 5.2). Consequently, Liberal candidates consistently did better in northern England, Scotland, and Wales than in southeast England (see table 5.2).

The Liberals had a number of peers in Parliament in 1868, but not for long: the influence of the landed gentry declined far more rapidly in the Liberal Party than the Conservative Party (see table 5.1). The degentrification of the Liberals accelerated after the election of 1886, in which a substantial portion of the most aristocratic, conservative wing of the party, the Whigs, split with Prime Minister William E. Gladstone over the issue of Irish home rule.[37] These "Liberal Unionists," as they came to be known, eventually merged with the Conservative Party. Thus, the Liberals after 1886 become more homogeneous. Manufacturing interests gained relatively within the party, as did middle-class professionals, while members of the gentry and military increasingly rejected it.

---

[35] Pearce and Stewart, *British Political History*, 69, 74–75; Hanham, *Elections and Party Management*, 74, 91–92, 225; McWilliam, *Popular Politics*, 49; Cannadine, *Decline and Fall*, 65.

[36] Robert Stewart, *The Foundation of the Conservative Party, 1830–1867* (London: Longman, 1978), appendix 8.

[37] Michael Pinto-Duschinsky, *British Political Finance, 1830–1980* (Washington, D.C.: American Enterprise Institute, 1981), 32. W. C. Lubenow dissents from the consensus on the class identity of the defectors, but his own research reveals that the proportion of landed gentleman politicians within the rump Liberal Party (37 percent) was appreciably less than that within the new Liberal Unionist Party (49 percent). See W. C. Lubenow, "Irish Home Rule and the Social Basis of the Great Separation in the Liberal Party in 1886," *Historical Journal* 28, no. 1 (March 1985): 125–42.

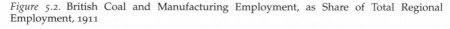

Figure 5.2. British Coal and Manufacturing Employment, as Share of Total Regional Employment, 1911

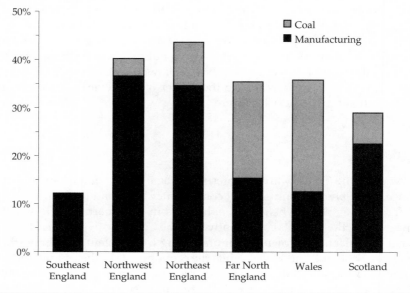

SOURCES: Coal employment figures from Roy Church, *The History of the British Coal Industry, 1830–1913* (Oxford: Clarendon, 1986), 304–5. Manufacturing and total regional employment figures from C. H. Lee, *British Regional Employment Statistics, 1841–1971* (Cambridge: Cambridge University press, 1979).

Although the Liberal Party was most closely identified with manufacturing, it also developed strong ties to the coal industry.[38] Britain's coal deposits fueled the growth of its metals manufacturing industry; the latter was built around the former. Indeed, coal played such an enormous role in the local economies of northern England, Scotland, and Wales that the Liberals could hardly have ignored it. By 1907, one out of every thirteen workers in these regions was employed as a coal miner, and the industry accounted for approximately 14 percent of Britain's net economic output.[39] Thus, the Liberals' socioeconomic coalition comprised both the manufacturing and coal sectors. To predict the party's choice of grand strategy in 1868–1939, it is necessary to examine these groups' interests in the international economy.

[38] Samuel H. Beer, *Modern British Politics: A Study of Parties and Pressure Groups*, 2d ed. (London: Faber, 1969), 168; C. H. Lee, *Scotland and the United Kingdom: The Economy and the Union in the Twentieth Century* (Manchester: Manchester University Press, 1995), 28; Pugh, *Making of Modern British Politics*, 151; Michael Kinnear, *The British Voter: An Atlas and Survey since 1885*, 2d ed. (London: Batsford, 1981), 82.
[39] Church, *History of the British Coal Industry*, 86, 758.

Figure 5.3. U.K. Merchandise Exports, as Share of National Income

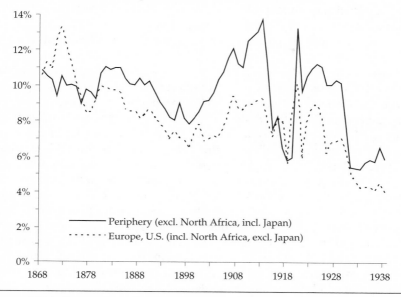

SOURCE: Mitchell and Deane, *Abstract of British Historical Statistics*, 283–84, 315–26, 367–68.

Manufacturing and Coal

Throughout 1868–1939, the British manufacturing sector was highly dependent on both core and peripheral markets. The extent of its penetration into the international economy can be seen in an analysis of British merchandise exports, which were composed almost entirely of manufactures and coal. In the late 1860s and early 1870s, at the peak of Britain's economic hegemony, exports to Europe and the United States generated 10–12 percent of the British national income, while exports to the rest of the world accounted for another 9–11 percent (see figure 5.3).

Over the next two decades, it became increasingly difficult for manufacturers to sell their products to the core. All of the other great powers were industrializing rapidly and sought to emulate successful ventures in Britain.[40] Even if Britain had retained its competitive lead, it would not have been able to maintain its market share in Europe and the United States once

---

[40] D. H. Aldcroft, "Introduction: British Industry and Foreign Competition," in *The Development of British Industry and Foreign Competition*, ed. D. H. Aldcroft (London: George Allen and Unwin, 1968), 17–26; R. C. O. Matthews et al., *British Economic Growth, 1856–1973* (Stanford: Stanford University Press, 1982), 451–53; R. S. Sayers, *The Vicissitudes of an Export Economy: Britain since 1880* (Sydney: Sydney University Press, 1965), 4–10.

its rivals raised tariffs to protect their own industries from imports.[41] Consequently, British manufacturers came to rely more and more on peripheral markets. By the turn of the century, the proportion of merchandise exports sent to Europe and the United States had fallen from 55 percent to 40–45 percent.

As serious as this decline in core markets was, it was not catastrophic. Around the turn of the century, the situation finally stabilized and even improved somewhat.[42] Between 1895 and 1904, exports to the core generated only 7 percent of the national income; then, between 1905 and 1914, this figure jumped to nearly 9 percent, and it remained more than 8 percent in the early 1920s. Partly responsible for this turnaround was coal. While manufacturing suffered, the coal industry was rising, and it was more reliant on core markets than manufacturers had ever been. In 1869, 9.8 percent of coal extracted in Britain was exported, then by 1887 it was 15.3 percent, and after 1900 it leveled off at 20–30 percent.[43] Throughout the entire period, the vast majority of coal exports—approximately 80 percent—were sent to continental Europe and the United States.[44] The displacement of manufacturing by coal meant that Liberal constituencies largely retained their core interests after 1880, even though manufacturing exports to Europe had contracted. Britain's older industries still struggled against foreign competition, and they faced increased tariffs after World War I, but merchandise exports to Europe and the United States held steady at about 42 percent of the total.[45]

In sum, the Liberal Party's sectoral constituency had a powerful stake in both core and peripheral markets. Over time, British manufacturing exports lost ground in Europe and the United States, but the fast-growing coal industry picked up the slack. As a result, an enormous share of Britain's national income, over 7 percent for most of 1868–1939, derived from merchandise exports to the core. Meanwhile, merchandise exporters also remained highly dependent on peripheral markets, from which they earned 9–13 percent of Britain's national income in most years.

---

[41] S. B. Saul, *Studies in British Overseas Trade, 1870–1914* (Liverpool: Liverpool University Press, 1960), 52–56; Paul Bairoch, "European Trade Policy, 1815–1914," in *The Cambridge Economic History of Europe: The Industrial Economies: The Development of Economic and Social Policies*, vol. 8, ed. Peter Mathias and Sidney Pollard (New York: Cambridge University Press, 1966), 51–83, 138–45.

[42] D. C. M. Platt, "Conclusion," in *Decline and Recovery in Britain's Overseas Trade, 1873–1914*, ed. D. C. M. Platt (London: Macmillan, 1993), 139–46.

[43] Church, *History of the British Coal Industry*, 19; Supple, *History of the British Coal Industry*, 174–75, 273.

[44] Church, *History of the British Coal Industry*, 35; Supple, *History of the British Coal Industry*, 292–93.

[45] Arthur Redford, *Manchester Merchants and Foreign Trade, 1850–1939*, vol. 2 (Manchester: Manchester University Press, 1956), 224–26. See also ibid., chaps. 17–18; Ashworth, *Economic History of England*, 308–17, 319–21, 342–44; Aldcroft, *Inter-War Economy*, 245–53.

Strategic Interests: Periphery

Under most circumstances, as explained in chapter 1, peripheral interests should favor an interventionist grand strategy, relying on coercion rather than conquest to secure their markets. They should tolerate pre-existing colonies if the cost of retaining them is low; however, if that cost increases, they should consider retrenchment and withdrawal. Only if peripheral interests are struggling to turn a profit, and therefore need an extra competitive advantage over foreign traders, should they support the annexation of new colonies. Thus, to form hypotheses about the strategic preferences of peripheral interests in the Liberal and Labour parties, it is necessary to answer two questions: first, was the existing empire costly, and second, how competitive were manufacturers?

Britain's most important colonies were in fact largely self-sufficient. Canada, Australia, New Zealand, and South Africa all had large populations of white settlers, so they were wealthy enough to provide for their own government, infrastructure, and social services. Even in impoverished India, local taxpayers were made responsible for sustaining the Raj. As a result, colonial administration and foreign consulates rarely took more than 1 percent of the national budget or more than one-tenth of 1 percent of the national income.[46] By 1868, most of the startup costs of pacifying the natives and establishing governance over Britain's largest colonies had long since been paid.

Defense was a different story. British leaders implored the colonials to take on a greater share of the burden, but to little avail: between 1860 and 1912, taxpayers in Britain paid approximately ten times as much per capita on defense as did their counterparts in Canada, Australia, New Zealand, and South Africa.[47] Nevertheless, the direct cost of the protection of these territories was not that great, particularly after the retrenchment of the 1860s. Britain increased its military presence in Canada for the American Civil War and the Fenian Raids, but after 1868 most of the troops were brought home, and in 1881 only 1,820 remained.[48] British forces were also withdrawn from New Zealand between 1865 and 1870, obliging the white settlers to negotiate an end to hostilities with the indigenous Maori people. Australia was pacific, requiring no troops whatsoever, while the colony with the biggest army of all, India, paid for 70 percent of its military expenses.[49] Other than

[46] Mitchell and Deane, *Abstract of British Historical Statistics*, 398–99.
[47] Davis and Huttenback, *Mammon*, 161. See also Patrick K. O'Brien, "The Costs and Benefits of British Imperialism, 1846–1914," *Past and Present* 120 (August 1988): 188–89, 192.
[48] A. N. Porter, ed., *Atlas of British Expansion* (London: Routledge, 1991), 120. See also Donald C. Gordon, *The Dominion Partnership and Imperial Defense, 1870–1914* (Baltimore: Johns Hopkins University Press, 1965), chap. 2; C. C. Eldridge, *Victorian Imperialism* (London: Hodder and Stoughton, 1978), 83–88.
[49] India sometimes even paid for the use of its army outside of the subcontinent, such as in the Second Afghan War of 1878; see Davis and Huttenback, *Mammon*, 154–55.

India, the only major British deployment outside of Europe was stationed in southern Africa.

The real cost of the empire was in the maintenance of its military infrastructure—that is, the navy and its numerous bases, coaling stations, and fortified garrisons. It kept shipping lanes safe, protected travelers, intervened in defense of business interests, and allowed for the projection of British military power throughout the world. Its duties, though extensive, were not exclusive to imperialism; an interventionist strategy would have had exactly the same requirements. Thus, the most expensive elements of Britain's foreign policy were equally necessary for both an imperialist and an interventionist strategy. If Britain had suddenly granted full self-government to its five largest colonies in 1868, its defense costs would not have changed radically because it still would have required a far-flung global military infrastructure to serve the interests of its peripheral exporters and investors.[50]

Estimates of the expense of Britain's various colonial wars and interventions, which typically occurred once every year or two, confirm that the empire was not a great drain on state resources.[51] For example, the Ashanti War of 1873–74 cost £900,000, which was less than 7 percent of the army's budget and only 1.2 percent of the government's income in 1874. Similarly, the Zulu War of 1879 cost British taxpayers £750,000, which constituted only 4.4 percent of the army's annual budget and less than 1 percent of the government's income. The Maori conflict cost approximately £3,000,000, but it spanned a period of more than twenty-five years. Not until 1899–1902, when Britain entered into a disastrous war with the Boers, did imperial policing entail a major drain on the Treasury. The empire did not offer something for nothing, but neither was it terribly burdensome for a great power whose army was already "ludicrously small" by continental standards.[52]

In the mid nineteenth century, however, peripheral interests should not have been eager for further acquisitions. Most prospective colonies would not be so stable or economically developed that they would be able to pay for their own government, much less their land defense, so extending the empire would have created significant new administrative costs. Until the 1880s, British manufacturers should have thought about grand strategy in similar terms as their American counterparts in the late nineteenth and early twentieth centuries: that is, concerned about the protection of their commerce and investments, but sufficiently economically competitive in

[50] O'Brien, "Costs and Benefits of British Imperialism," 186.

[51] Davis and Huttenback, *Mammon*, chap. 5. For a complete list of conflicts, see Brian Bond, ed., *Victorian Military Campaigns* (New York: Praeger, 1967), 310–11.

[52] Eldridge, *Victorian Imperialism*, 83. See also Paul Kennedy, *The Realities behind Diplomacy: Background Influences on British External Policy, 1865–1980* (Glasgow: Fontana, 1981), 32–33; C. A. Bodelson, *Studies in Mid-Victorian Imperialism* (Copenhagen: Gyldendals, 1924), 80–81.

international markets to see no need for costly annexations. In short, they should have been satisfied with the status quo on the empire.

This prediction is clearly confirmed by historical research on elite attitudes in the mid Victorian era. As Philip Darby writes, "Few economists showed any enthusiasm for colonialism in Africa and Asia, and in political circles opinion was even more firmly against it. Given British commercial and technological proficiency, merchants operating in an open market could conquer competition, while political rule was a drain on consolidated revenue which should be avoided."[53] Even scholars who argue that there was considerable continuity between the imperial stagnation of the mid nineteenth century and the aggressive New Imperialism of the late nineteenth century do not dispute the idea that there was little public support for the annexation of new territories before the 1880s.[54] In short, Britons showed little interest in extending the empire when their products were internationally competitive.

In the 1880s and 1890s, circumstances began to change in ways that dictated a shift in the preferred strategy of merchandise exporters. First, Britain's relative economic power declined rapidly after the 1860s. As France, Germany, and the United States industrialized, they began to produce more of the manufactured goods in which Britain had specialized, and British firms increasingly struggled to maintain their profits and market share.[55] Consequently, they began to turn to the periphery, where there was little competition from local businesses. British exporters were still far ahead of their closest industrial rivals in 1868; however, as their competitive advantages eroded in the final decades of the nineteenth century, they should have become more inclined to support an aggressive peripheral strategy.

Second, many of Britain's most important export markets were closing. Tariffs raised by Germany in 1879, France in 1882, the United States in 1883, and Italy in 1887 struck successive blows to British industry, particularly

[53] Darby, *Three Faces of Imperialism*, 61. See also Bodelson, *Studies in Mid-Victorian Imperialism*, chap. 1; Susan H. Farnsworth, *The Evolution of British Imperial Policy during the Mid-Nineteenth Century: A Study of the Peelite Contribution, 1846–1874* (New York: Garland, 1992); R. L. Schuyler, "The Climax of Anti-Imperialism in England," *Political Science Quarterly* 36, no. 4 (December 1921): 537–60.

[54] R. Robinson and J. Gallagher, *Africa and the Victorians: The Official Mind of Imperialism* (London: Macmillan, 1961), 15. They also argue, with meager evidence, that business was unenthusiastic about the expansion of the empire after the 1880s. This issue is addressed below.

[55] D. H. Aldcroft, "British Industry and Foreign Competition," in *The Development of British Industry and Foreign Competition*, ed. D. H. Aldcroft (London: Allen and Unwin, 1968), 17–26; D. A. Farnie, *The English Cotton Industry and the World Market, 1815–1896* (Oxford: Clarendon, 1979), chap. 5; Matthews et al., *British Economic Growth, 1856–1973*, 451–53; Sayers, *Vicissitudes of an Export Economy*, 4–10; R. H. Heindel, *The American Impact on Great Britain, 1898–1914* (Philadelphia: University of Pennsylvania Press, 1940), chap. 7.

the textile sector.[56] As the century drew to a close, the trend only worsened. French protectionism should have been of particular concern because France, the only power other than Britain to have had significant success at establishing an empire, began in 1877 to shut out foreign competitors from its colonial markets. At the same time, many countries in Latin America raised trade barriers on manufactured goods, and all of the colonies to which Britain had granted self-rule did the same in an attempt to promote their own industrialization.[57] In Australia, tariffs were raised in 1867, 1871, 1877, 1902, and 1906, with the result that import duties on manufactures averaged 16 percent by the eve of World War I. New Zealand got a later start down the path of protectionism, but, after tariff hikes in 1888, 1895, 1900, and 1907, its import duties on manufactures also averaged 16 percent in 1913. Canada, which substantially increased tariffs in 1879, was even worse: by 1913, its duties on manufactures averaged 26 percent. Even India's colonial government, which existed only to serve British interests, occasionally raised tariffs on cotton manufactures for revenue purposes.[58]

The tide of protectionism at the end of the nineteenth century left untouched, with few exceptions, only those parts of the world that lacked strong national governments—that is, Africa and Asia. It was in these regions, where the costs of conquest would be relatively low, that a strategy of imperialism would be most effective in aiding British exporters. The hoped-for trade did not always materialize; exports to Asia remained stagnant through the end of the nineteenth century. In sub-Saharan Africa, however, there was a fivefold increase in exports between 1868 and 1903. Given the decline of Britain's industrial competitiveness and the closure of its foreign markets, the theory renders a clear prediction: the preferred grand strategy of manufacturers with peripheral interests should have shifted from interventionism to imperialism toward the end of the nineteenth century.

This prediction is resoundingly confirmed by myriad studies of British political and economic history. C. A. Bodelson, who was one of the first scholars to document the connection between business interests and public opinion on imperialism, explains:

> As the feeling of commercial security and confidence of always being able to compete successfully with other countries were shaken, the old argument that the colonial markets presented advantages which no other market could offer . . . began to assume a new importance. This argument was at first only used to show that the colonial market offered special advantages which might be

---

[56] Saul, *Studies in British Overseas Trade*, 52–56; Bairoch, "European Trade Policy," 51–83, 138–45.
[57] Bairoch, "European Trade Policy," 145–60.
[58] William G. Hynes, *The Economics of Empire: Britain, Africa, and the New Imperialism, 1870–95* (London: Longman, 1979), 25, 27–28, 114.

lost with the severance of the political tie, and that the colonial trade might in [the] future assume a greater relative importance than at the present moment. . . . The cry that English industry was being threatened did not sound very loud during the first years of the Imperialism movement, but as more and more industries felt the pressure of foreign competition it swelled from year to year, until we get, about the turn of the century, that curious mixture of denunciations of British industrial decadence and lack of enterprise and glorification of British national qualities which characterized so much of the Imperialist propaganda at the time.[59]

In short, the foreign policy preferences of Britons changed with their economic circumstances, very much in the manner hypothesized in chapter 1. Though Bodelson wrote the above passage in 1924, his work has been confirmed by a continuous stream of research on the subject over the last seventy-five years.[60]

One of the most important of such studies is William G. Hynes's *The Economics of Empire*, which emphasizes the connection between manufacturers' beliefs about their economic interests and their strategic preferences. Hynes finds that

the general trend towards protectionism in Europe was a potent argument for opening new markets in parts of the world where there were no hostile tariffs. Moreover, the French tariff in Senegal suggested that French colonial activities in Africa and Asia would threaten British trade in regions where new markets might be found. . . . The recession of the late 1870s marked the beginnings of an important change in mercantile attitudes towards the "Dark Continent."[61]

This interest in markets heretofore considered marginal was strongest in the economic hard times of 1873–79, 1883–86, and 1890–95. These downturns, which were nested within the deflationary "Great Depression" of 1873–96,

---

[59] Bodelson, *Studies in Mid-Victorian Imperialism*, 82–83.

[60] Hynes, *Economics of Empire*, 26–27, 29; Darby, *Three Faces of Imperialism*, 55–58, 63–74; Cain and Hopkins, *British Imperialism*, vol. 1, chap. 11; C. W. Newbury, "The Tariff Factor in Anglo-French West African Partition," in *France and Britain in Africa: Imperial Rivalry and Colonial Rule*, ed. Prosser Gifford and William Roger Louis (New Haven: Yale University Press, 1971), 221–59; A. G. Hopkins, *An Economic History of West Africa* (London: Longman, 1973), 155, 161; Redford, *Manchester Merchants and Foreign Trade*, chaps. 6–7; W. L. Langer, *The Diplomacy of Imperialism, 1890–1902*, 2d ed. (New York: Knopf, 1951), 74–79, 95; B. M. Ratcliffe, "Commerce and Empire: Manchester Merchants and West Africa, 1873–95," *Journal of Imperial and Commonwealth History* 7, no. 3 (May 1979): 293–320; Bernard Porter, *Critics of Empire: British Radical Attitudes to Colonialism in Africa, 1895–1914* (London: Macmillan, 1968); Munro, *Britain in Tropical Africa*, chap. 2.

[61] Hynes, *Economics of Empire*, 26–27, 29. Britons had a number of economically rational reasons to oppose raising their own tariffs in response to foreign protectionism and relative decline; see Paul Kennedy, *The Rise of Anglo-German Antagonism, 1860–1914* (London: Allen and Unwin, 1980), 52–54.

led many British businessmen to believe that peripheral markets would
be needed to counter the effects of tariff hikes, increased industrial and
financial competition, and decreased competitiveness, as well as industrial
overproduction, the problem that so greatly concerned Americans in the
same period.[62]

Manufacturers' turn to imperialism in the late nineteenth century reflected
a long-term structural change in their position in the world economy. This
trend reached a plateau after 1900, when the distribution of British merchandise exports stabilized at a ratio of 42 percent to the core and 58 percent
to the periphery. Over the next four decades, many politicians spoke of promoting "home rule" in the dependent colonies, but their words had little
practical significance. As Phillip Darby explains,

> A substantial and revealing continuity in British thought in the inter-war pe-
> riod is the extent to which ideas about moral responsibility remained tied to
> political development rather than self-government. . . . Independence might
> be inevitable, but it was far in the future and there was little inclination to
> hurry it along. What held attention was how much remained to be accom-
> plished rather than such progress as had been made.[63]

Not even the rise of Labour broke the imperialist consensus; only the radical left wing of the party advocated anything more than an incremental
approach to limited self-government for the dependent empire.[64] Thus, the
theory is correct in its prediction that British manufacturers' preferences
over grand strategy in the periphery would transition from interventionism
to imperialism after the 1880s.

Strategic Interests: Core

British manufacturers' conversion to imperialism did not preclude them
from holding an entirely different set of interests and strategic preferences
regarding relations with the great powers. Even at the depths of Britain's
industrial decline in the 1890s, core markets remained an enormous source
of income for Liberal constituencies. Consequently, manufacturers should
have supported a strategy designed to foster trade, reduce the likelihood
of war, and encourage norm-based cooperation between the great powers.
As explained in chapter 1, that strategy is internationalism. Rather than
picking one single ally or alliance among their many commercial partners

---

[62] Darby, *Three Faces of Imperialism*, 56.
[63] Ibid., 109. See also Porter, *Critics of Empire*, 295–96, 327–29; Redford, *Manchester Merchants and Foreign Trade*, 228–32.
[64] Stephen Howe, *Anticolonialism in British Politics: The Left and the End of Empire, 1918–1964* (Oxford: Clarendon, 1993), 47–48; Darby, *Three Faces of Imperialism*, 109; Max Beloff, *Dream of Commonwealth, 1921–42* (London: Macmillan, 1989), 27.

in Europe, core interests should have sought to ensure that all states acted judiciously and justly in a stable international order. Only if a state posed a direct threat to the underlying principles of that order should they have aligned against it. To those ends, core interests in Britain should have supported the standard internationalist policy program: the promotion and development of international law, the creation of nonviolent mechanisms of dispute resolution, the institutionalization of multilateral diplomacy, and the use of collective security. After World War I, one further goal could be added to this list: the reintegration of the defeated powers into the international community.

There is strong evidence that core interests in Britain did, in fact, favor these policies. The political movement to which most advocates of international law belonged, the "Manchester School," was named after one of the country's most prominent industrial centers, and it drew much of its support from northern English textile manufacturers.[65] Not all members of the Manchester School had an economic interest in internationalism, but those that did, the industrial elites, "were unquestionably important in numbers, and they furnished the massive financial support the campaign needed."[66] Although the Manchester School is best known for its advocacy of free trade, its adherents did not stop there; they further concluded that, to prevent the rise of protectionism and reduce the threat of war, it would be necessary to promote deeper political ties between the great powers. To this end, they championed the principles of international law and concert diplomacy, and some even sought a retreat from the empire. In short, the political-economic coalition behind the ideology of the Manchester School was composed of individuals who had the most to gain from an internationalist strategy.

Though merchandise exports to the core declined at the end of the century, they remained high enough to sustain a strong sentiment for internationalism within Britain's coal and manufacturing communities.

---

[65] On the liberal, internationalist beliefs of northern English cotton manufacturers, as contrasted with the conservative, militaristic ideology of southern English elites, see Farnie, *English Cotton Industry*, 36–44. On Richard Cobden's strategic views, see Maureen M. Robson, "Liberals and 'Vital Interest': The Debate on International Arbitration, 1815–72," *Bulletin of the Institute of Historical Research* 32, no. 85 (May 1959): 44–48; Donald Read, *Cobden and Bright: A Victorian Political Partnership* (London: Arnold, 1967), 188. Not all of the members of the Manchester School were equally enthusiastic about all aspects of an internationalist strategy; for example, John Bright held internationalist ideals but at times supported isolationist policies. See A. J. P. Taylor, *The Trouble Makers: Dissent over Foreign Policy, 1792–1939* (London: Hamish, 1957), 54–57, 63–64; Read, *Cobden and Bright*, 103–4, 113, 119–37; William D. Grampp, *The Manchester School of Economics* (Stanford: Stanford University Press, 1960), 127. In contrast, Gladstone was critical of the pacifist elements of the Manchester School. See D. M. Schreuder, *Gladstone and Kruger* (London: Routledge and Kegan Paul, 1969), 44; Richard Shannon, *Gladstone: Heroic Minister, 1865–1898* (London: Allen Lane, 1999), 114–15.

[66] Grampp, *Manchester School*, chap. 1. See also John S. Galbraith, "Little Englanders," *Current History* 27, no. 160 (December 1954): 353–58; Bodelson, *Studies in Mid-Victorian Imperialism*, 82.

The best evidence for this point can be found in the "Peace Ballot" of 1935. That year, the League of Nations Union (LNU), a nonpartisan advocacy group led by Lord Robert Cecil, undertook a massive effort to poll the entire British public on their attitudes toward collective security. The survey was designed solely to promote the LNU's internationalist agenda, so it was worded so vaguely that it would elicit "yes" responses from pacifists, internationalists, and imperialists alike.[67] Thus the results of the poll are not particularly informative. Taken at face value, they indicate overwhelming support for the league throughout Britain but do not provide any clue as to the depth of this support—that is, what costs the public would have been willing to accept for the sake of collective security.

Far more revealing is the response rate to the poll. The LNU attempted to conduct the Peace Ballot as a sort of "national referendum," canvassing every voter in the country. Such a Herculean task required great numbers of enthusiastic volunteers and strong local organization, factors that were bound to be scarce in areas in which public support for the league was shallow.[68] Another potential obstacle was public resistance to the poll itself. The most powerful media magnate in the country, the Conservative Lord Beaverbrook, exhorted the readers of his newspapers to "tear up the ballot paper. Throw the pieces in the waste-paper basket."[69] If merchandise exporters with core interests favored internationalism, the LNU should have been most successful at securing responses in the parts of the country in which they were dominant: the manufacturing and coal mining communities of northern England, Wales, and Scotland.

Overall, the LNU received completed ballots from more than 38 percent of the eligible voting population. In 42 of Britain's 341 electoral constituencies, it managed a response rate of more than 60 percent.[70] Remarkably, every one of those 42 districts was located in either northern England or Wales. The figures for Scotland are less impressive, but efforts there were hindered by the refusal of the LNU's Glasgow and Dundee branches to cooperate

[67] The most relevant of the five questions was written as follows: "Do you consider that, if a nation insists on attacking another, the other nations should combine to compel it to stop by (a) economic and non-military measures? (b) if necessary, military measures?" On the design of the questions, see J. A. Thompson, "The Peace Ballot and the Public," *Albion* 13, no. 4 (winter 1981): 380–92; Michael Pugh, "Pacifism and Politics in Britain, 1931–1935," *Historical Journal* 23, no. 3 (September 1980): 641–56; Donald S. Birn, *The League of Nations Union, 1918–1945* (Oxford: Clarendon, 1981), 145–46; Martin Ceadel, "The First British Referendum: The Peace Ballot, 1934–35," *English Historical Review* 95, no. 377 (October 1980): 810–39.
[68] Dame Adelaide Livingstone, *The Peace Ballot: The Official History* (London: Gollancz, 1935), 51; Birn, *League of Nations Union*, 147.
[69] Quoted in Anne Chisholm and Michael Davie, *Beaverbrook: A Life* (London: Hutchinson, 1992), 326; A. J. P. Taylor, *Beaverbrook* (London: Hamilton, 1972), 350.
[70] Ceadel, "First British Referendum," 810, 829; Livingstone, *Peace Ballot*, 52–53. See also National Declaration Committee, *The National Declaration on the League of Nations and Armaments: Results in Each Constituency of the United Kingdom* (London: 1935).

with headquarters.[71] Otherwise, the data resoundingly confirm the hypothesis that core interests had internationalist preferences. The LNU's official dues-paying membership was concentrated in southeast England, but mass support for internationalism was much stronger in the rest of the country, where factory workers and coal miners were highly dependent on exports to Europe and the United States.

Hypotheses

Since the sectoral interests behind the Liberal coalition were narrowly divided between the core and periphery, the party should have bifurcated its grand strategy. In the periphery, it should initially have been interventionist. Manufacturers were sufficiently competitive in the 1860s and 1870s that they had no need for their government to take colonies for them. Thus, Liberal governments should have sought to cut costs in colonial administration and avoid territorial expansion. At the same time, however, they should have maintained their existing network of naval bases and intervened on behalf of British merchants when necessary.

After the early 1880s, Liberals should have become increasingly imperialist. Manufacturers were suffering from European and American competition, the economy was periodically afflicted by severe recession, tariffs were being raised throughout the world, and the rise of imperial rivalries meant that Britain would need to annex its markets to be certain of maintaining access to them. Of course, not all members of the Liberal coalition were equally vulnerable: a strong contingent of core interests, especially in the coal sector, had no interest in imperialism. To arbitrate between these factions, moderation was needed. Even after the hypothesized transition from interventionism to imperialism in the 1880s, Liberals should have acted less aggressively in the periphery than the Conservatives, whose constituency was composed almost exclusively of peripheral interests.

Toward the great powers, the Liberal Party had a clear strategic imperative throughout 1868–1939: support core interests by promoting norm-based cooperation and collective security. Though recurrent international tensions constrained this strategy, Liberals still should have been willing to try to advance the cause of international law and promote multilateral decision making. As part of this strategy, Liberal governments should have avoided aligning either with or against any one country or alliance. Instead, they should have maintained a judicious neutrality, a position that they could parlay into the role of mediator and peacemaker. Only if confronted with a threat to the future of the European trading system should they have openly

---

[71] Birn, *League of Nations Union*, 147.

aligned against a state, and in that case their response should have been to build a collective security coalition against the aggressor.

Around the turn of the century, Labour slowly began to build support in Liberal districts. On many issues the two parties were allied; some politicians even ran for election as "Lib-Lab" candidates, supported by both sides. However, the nucleus of the Labour movement was committed to the long-term goal of forming an independent majority in Parliament, and the only way this could be done was to usurp the Liberals.

Before World War I, the Labour Party never managed to win more than fifty-three seats in any given election.[72] Though it purported to represent the entire British proletariat, its ability to mobilize electoral support was largely limited to the coal mining industry.[73] Consequently, its prewar position on grand strategy very narrowly reflected the economic interests of this one sector. Approximately 80 percent of coal exports were sent to Europe and the United States, so Labour was composed almost exclusively of core interests, whose preferred strategy should have been internationalism. Thus, party members should have selected leaders who favored adherence to international law and sought to retreat from the periphery.

Labour was not able to mount a credible challenge to become the main party of the left until 1916. At that point, the Liberals split into rival factions led by David Lloyd George and Herbert Asquith. Their disunity, combined with the expansion of the electorate in 1918 and the postwar rise of trade unionism, allowed Labour to seize the initiative:

> What Labour achieved, broadly speaking, in the post-war years of 1918–24, was the displacement of the Liberals in working-class parliamentary constituencies throughout most of Britain. Having already secured large tracts of coalfields in 1918, the party proceeded to establish itself in almost all the other urban concentrations in the 1920s.[74]

In 1924, Labour politicians managed to win 191 seats in Parliament, compared to 159 for the Liberals and 258 for Conservatives.[75] With the tacit

[72] Duncan Watts, *Whigs, Radicals, and Liberals, 1815–1914* (London: Hodder and Stoughton, 1995), 169.

[73] Ross McKibbin, *The Evolution of the Labour Party, 1910–1924* (London: Oxford University Press, 1974), 24–28; Roy Gregory, *The Miners and British Politics, 1906–1914* (London: Oxford University Press, 1968); Kinnear, *British Voter*, 112–13, 116–17.

[74] Gordon Phillips, *The Rise of the Labour Party, 1893–1931* (London: Routledge, 1992), 35–36. See also McKibbin, *Evolution of the Labour Party*, 236–45; Chris Cook, *A Short History of the Liberal Party, 1900–1997*, 5th ed. (London: Macmillan, 1998), chaps. 6–8.

[75] Kinnear, *British Voter*, 43.

support of the dispirited Liberals, they finally formed a government of their own. It lasted only nine months, but it nevertheless signaled a permanent shift in power in the British electoral system.

For the purposes of this study, the critical question is whether the rise of Labour resulted in a realignment of Britain's political economy. Quite simply, the answer is no. Labour did not build a fundamentally new electoral coalition; instead, it took over the base constituency of the Liberal Party.[76] Of course, there were some important differences in the two parties' economic interests: Labour catered to the urban proletariat, while the Liberals appealed more to the middle class. However, by 1924, the two parties derived their support from precisely the same industries and geographic areas: manufacturing and coal, located mainly in northern England, Wales, and Scotland. Despite their differences over such domestic issues as the redistribution of wealth and the power of unions, they should have had the same interests over international trade.

As a result, Labour's strategic outlook should have converged with that of the Liberals. The manufacturing sector earned much of its income from core markets, but it was even more dependent on the periphery. Consequently, it had an interest in both internationalism and imperialism. If Labour wanted to retain the support of factory workers after the 1924 election, it would have to retreat from its strident opposition to the empire. It could not become a majority party by catering only to the interests of coal miners; it needed to co-opt the Liberals' entire coalition. Thus, the Labour Party faced a difficult conundrum: Should it maintain its pure anti-imperialist ideology, or should it sacrifice its principles to build electoral support? In the 1880s and 1890s, the Liberal Party confronted the same problem and took the latter option. Clearly, the theory predicts that the Labour governments of 1924 and 1929–31 would have done the same.

CONCLUSION

Different sectors of the British economy had very different optimal grand strategies (see table 5.4). Both the manufacturing and coal industries had a strong stake in core markets, while manufacturing also relied heavily on exports to the periphery. Consequently, the parties that represented these constituencies, Liberals and Labour, should have adopted a bifurcated grand strategy. They should have followed an internationalist approach toward the great powers, but they also should have been responsive to their constituents' peripheral interests. In the 1860s and 1870s, at the zenith of Britain's

[76] Phillips, *Rise of the Labour Party*, 35–36; McKibbin, *Evolution of the Labour Party*, chap. 3; Kinnear, *British Voter*, 82–85, 112–13.

Table 5.4. British Predicted Strategic Interests (Absent Constraints)

Conservatives

Gentry (until 1900s)	Military-colonial interests $\rightarrow$	imperialism + realpolitik	Imperialism + realpolitik
Financial services and trade (from 1880s)	Peripheral interests $\rightarrow$	imperialism + realpolitik	

Liberals / Labour after 1918

	Peripheral interests $\rightarrow$	1868–c. 1880: interventionism + realpolitik	1868–c. 1880: interventionism + internationalism
Manufacturing and coal		c. 1880–1939: imperialism + realpolitik	c. 1880–1939: imperialism (less than Conservatives) + internationalism
	Core interests $\rightarrow$ internationalism		

economic dominance, this meant a compromise between internationalism and interventionism. After that point, however, manufacturers faced increasing competition from Germany, France, and the United States. Thus, the Liberal Party, and eventually the Labour Party, should have transitioned to a synthesis of internationalism and imperialism.

The Conservative Party's strategic interests derived from the preferences of its "gentlemanly capitalist" constituency. Its base of power was southeast England, where the landed gentry and financial services sector were most concentrated. The former had long-standing military-colonial interests; the latter was deeply invested in the periphery, where it struggled to stay ahead of new competition. Consequently, the Conservative Party should have been imperialist throughout 1868–1939, and consistently more so than either the Liberals or Labour. Meanwhile, Conservative governments had little reason to support internationalist projects; doing so would only limit their ability to safeguard and extend the empire. To the extent that they formed lasting diplomatic relationships with the other great powers, it should have been for the realpolitik goal of protecting the empire, not promoting cooperation as a good in itself.

Before testing these hypotheses, a note on methodology is in order. For the United States, the primary object of analysis was individual presidents, since they are formally responsible for all of the executive's strategic initiatives. In

Britain, the situation is more complex. Unlike American presidents, British prime ministers do not always have full authority over policymaking. In some cases, they oversee every major decision, using the foreign minister as a glorified secretary of state; at other times, the foreign minister manages to gain the support of the cabinet to pursue policies that the prime minister opposes. The nature of governance in Britain makes it impossible to assume that grand strategy can always be attributed to a particular individual within the executive body.[77] Consequently, I do not attempt to test whether the theory explains the individual actions of either the prime minister or foreign minister. Instead, I seek to determine whether it predicts the cabinet's collective decisions.

Following in the convention of diplomatic historians, I often attribute a government's strategy to the minister who had the most control over it. I do so only for the sake of convenience; I do not intend to convey the impression that I am testing the theory for that minister alone. Thus, an assertion like "Prime Minister Gladstone's strategy corresponds to the theory's predictions" should be interpreted as shorthand for "Prime Minister Gladstone's Liberal government's strategy, which was formulated with Gladstone's direct approval, corresponds to the theory's predictions." Whenever the prime minister and foreign minister come into conflict, I discuss the situation at length so as to avoid any confusion.

[77] Cooney, "Political Demand Channels," 240–41; Kennedy, *Realities behind Diplomacy*, 62–63.

[6]

British Grand Strategy
toward the Periphery

In the mid nineteenth century, Great Britain was at the peak of its relative power. It possessed the strongest navy in the world, the most technologically advanced economy, and a vast empire in the periphery. Furthermore, its competitors were relatively weak. Russia had been defeated in the Crimean War of 1853–56, France had been falling behind Britain ever since the Napoleonic Wars, and Prussia had not yet unified Germany. Yet, like the United States, Britain did not live up to its full strategic potential. Other than the transfer of India from the British East India Company to the Crown in 1858, it acquired few colonies of significance in this period. Even as Bismarck's cunning diplomacy changed the map of Europe in the late 1860s and early 1870s, Britain did not seek compensation in the periphery. Instead, it declaimed alliances, kept its army small, and generally avoided conflict. Australia, New Zealand, and Canada were given greater powers of self-government, leading many contemporary observers to speculate that the dissolution of the British Empire would soon occur—if not from willful abandonment, then from neglect.

In the final two decades of the nineteenth century, all of this changed. Britain's economy began its long, steady decline, losing market share both abroad and at home to the newly industrializing powers of continental Europe and the United States. At the same time, Britain's military power was also eroding. Its ground forces, which had always been undersized, were dwarfed by the growing armies of Germany and Russia. Its fleet, though still unsurpassed, lost its aura of invulnerability as other great powers embarked on major new naval construction programs. Yet, in spite of these mounting weaknesses, Britain became much more aggressively imperialist. It may or may not have been responsible for initiating the "Scramble for Africa" in the 1880s and 1890s, but it was undoubtedly the most important player in the game. Britain took the plum targets of Egypt, Nigeria, and South Africa, while France was left with the "light soil" of the Sahara and Germany managed to gain only a few spare parcels of land in Africa and the South Pacific.

By 1900, nearly all of the periphery had been divided between the great powers. For the next decade and a half, Britain's leaders focused on consolidating and protecting their gains. However, their appetite for empire was not yet sated. After the defeat of Germany and the Ottoman Empire in World War I, Britain took the lion's share of the territorial spoils. It granted independence to a few of its new colonial mandates in the Middle East, but it continued to hold preponderant commercial, political, and military influence over them. In India, its largest and most economically valuable colony, it brutally repressed dissident movements and grudgingly granted only minor reforms. Through the onset of World War II, Britain remained the quintessential imperial power.

These changes in British grand strategy confound the conventional wisdom of realism, which asserts that states should expand their international power in proportion to their domestic economic capacity. When Britain was strongest, it was least active; when it weakened, it became much more aggressive. To resolve this conundrum, one might posit that states in relative decline expand to retain as much residual military and diplomatic power as possible. In other words, it may be that Britain sought to annex so much territory in the 1880s and 1890s exactly because it was losing ground to the other great powers. Of course, states do not always respond to threats by building empires, but in this situation Britain may not have had a choice. Nicholas Mansergh argues that the rise of Germany and Italy as national states, combined with the hardening of the alliance system in Europe, made traditional power balancing difficult.[1] This rigidity forced all of the great powers, including Britain, to turn to the periphery to gain strategic advantages over their opponents.

This modified realist interpretation, though somewhat theoretically ad hoc, is logically plausible and fits well with the outline facts of the case. However, there are several important aspects of British foreign policy that it cannot explain. One problem is that Britain's two major parties initially followed different strategies in the periphery. The Conservatives were consistently imperialist, whereas the Liberals transitioned from interventionism to imperialism in the 1880s and 1890s. It was not until the turn of the

---

[1] Nicholas Mansergh, *The Coming of the First World War: A Study in the European Balance, 1878–1914* (London: Longmans, Green, 1949), 15, chap. 3. See also A. J. P. Taylor, *The Struggle for Mastery in Europe* (Oxford: Clarendon, 1954), chap. 13; Phillip Darby, *Three Faces of Imperialism: British and American Approaches to Asia and Africa, 1870–1970* (New Haven: Yale University Press, 1987), 13–23, 26–30.

century, after the great powers had effectively completed the division of the periphery, that a consensus emerged within Britain over the value of the empire. Realism might purport to explain that convergence, but it cannot account for the prior disjuncture.

Second, the central claim of the realist interpretation, that the extension of the empire was intended to increase British security, is questionable. For the defense of the home isles, there was only one unshakable imperative: to maintain a fleet that would be powerful enough to repulse any invasion forces in the North Sea and English Channel, stopping them before they could reach the shore.[2] To accomplish this, Britain had no need for colonies; the empire was entirely superfluous. Even if one includes the white colonies of settlement as part of the vital homeland, it is hard to imagine how imperial expansion could have been intended for their defense. Australia and New Zealand faced no real threats, and Canada's long border with the United States could not have been made any more secure by the acquisition of territory in Africa and Asia. The Cape Colony might have benefited from the annexation of surrounding land to guard against future conflict with the Boers, but this hardly implies that Britain needed to take Nigeria, Egypt, Zanzibar, or nearly any other of its myriad additions to the empire. If British leaders had concluded that the sole object of "national security" was to protect British citizens and their permanent settlements, they could not have seen much need for further expansion.

Indeed, one might even argue that the empire was a serious liability for British security. First, it embroiled the country in disputes with nearly all of the other great powers, raising the possibility that Britain might someday face a hostile coalition intent on destroying its navy and invading the home isles. Though such a scenario may sound farfetched in retrospect, at times it was seriously considered by defense planners, so it cannot be discounted as a security cost of Britain's aggressive imperialism. More likely was the possibility that Britain's success in using its naval dominance to secure the "lion's share" of the periphery led the Germans, Russians, and French to counter with their own fleet-building programs. In other words, British imperialism may have been directly responsible for the naval arms races of the late nineteenth and early twentieth centuries, which clearly made the British Isles less secure. To make themselves safer, Britons should have abandoned their empire, not extended it.

---

[2] Not even Belgian neutrality was held sacred, contrary to popular misconception. In 1887, Prime Minister Lord Salisbury tried to open public debate on the subject by commissioning Alfred Austin to write a letter to the *Standard* that reflected Salisbury's personal views. The letter, anonymously signed "Diplomaticus," asserted that Britain should abandon its commitment in favor of allowing German armies to pass through Belgium on the march to France. See Andrew Roberts, *Salisbury: Victorian Titan* (London: Weidenfeld and Nicolson, 1999), 438–40.

A third anomaly for realism is the sheer parsimony of British grand strategy, even at the height of the scramble for Africa. Very rarely did Britain's leaders rush to annex territory that they considered to be economically or strategically important. They did not act as if they were engaged in a vital struggle for geopolitical power, in which ownership of particular tracts of land might someday provide critical advantages in a desperate game of survival. Rather, they behaved like penny-pinching shoppers at a market bazaar—always reluctant to buy, fretting over the quality of the goods and hoping that the price might eventually fall, then waiting until the last moment of availability before making a decision. If British governments considered the expansion of the empire to be necessary, or even useful, for the preservation of British military and diplomatic power, they ought to have pursued it much more aggressively.

Another interpretation of British imperialism, championed by Ronald Robinson and John Gallagher in *Africa and the Victorians*, begins with the political-economic assumption that policymakers were motivated by the desire to protect overseas trade and investment, particularly in India.[3] Contrary to political economy theories, however, Robinson and Gallagher assert that changes in Britain's domestic economy in the late nineteenth century had no effect on the making of foreign policy. Instead, the Foreign Office consistently used a single, simple heuristic to decide when to intervene: "Trade with informal control if possible; trade with rule when necessary." To explain the rapid growth of the empire in the 1880s and 1890s, Robinson and Gallagher focus on conditions in the periphery. Britain's leaders did not purposefully seek to acquire new colonies; instead, they were "pulled in"— in part by the ambitious aggressiveness of certain "men on the spot" (e.g., Cecil Rhodes), in part by the politics of native societies that were thrown into turmoil by European economic penetration, and in part by the need to protect India and the Suez trade route from rival great powers.

Like realist interpretations of British imperialism, this "excentric" thesis is question-begging. There was undoubtedly an increase in native resistance to European incursions in the late nineteenth century, which in turn led to greater efforts by Europeans to take direct control over territory and people. However, these developments did not arise ex nihilo. As P. J. Cain and A. G. Hopkins argue, "The fact that they occurred at all can be understood only in the context of the quickening beat of impulses transmitted from the metropole, which placed Britain in a position where circumstances

---

[3] R. Robinson and J. Gallagher, *Africa and the Victorians: The Official Mind of Imperialism* (London: Macmillan, 1961). See also John S. Galbraith, "The 'Turbulent Frontier' as a Factor in British Expansion," *Contemporary Studies in Society and History* 2, no. 2 (January 1960): 150–68; John Darwin, "Imperialism and the Victorians: The Dynamics of Territorial Expansion," *English Historical Review* 112, no. 545 (June 1997): 614–42.

'forcing' her to take action on the frontiers of empire were much more likely to arise."[4] In other words, the excentric interpretation must be nested within an understanding of changes in British economic interests.

Cain and Hopkins also argue that Robinson and Gallagher seriously overestimate the extent to which British imperialism in Africa was driven by a concern for the security of India.[5] On occasion, British leaders did conclude that it was desirable to annex distant lands to defend the Suez trade route, but there was no consensus within British society as to whether the security benefits of owning those territories merited the cost of acquiring them. In many cases, the expected gains were quite marginal, were based on dubious assumptions, or would become operative only in implausible worst-case scenarios. Furthermore, most additions to the empire, both inside Africa and without, lay far afield from the Suez passage to India (e.g., Nigeria, Transvaal, Malaysia, Fiji). In sum, there are serious flaws in every interpretation of British imperialism that privileges international pressures over domestic preferences.

IDEAS AND CULTURE

In contrast to the realist perspectives discussed above, some scholars argue that the expansion of the British empire at the end of the nineteenth century was motivated by nonmaterial factors. For example, Joseph Schumpeter asserts that, even though imperialism is inherently inimical to capitalist development, the British bourgeoisie embraced the empire because they desired to emulate the atavistic culture of the nobility.[6] Other authors point to beliefs that were said to have swayed the American public to interventionism, such as social Darwinism and the "missionary spirit."[7] These ideals surely had some influence on the minds of cabinet members and in the formation of public opinion, but they fare poorly as explanatory variables. The religious motive is easy to reject because, as a constant, it does not explain variance between the weak interventionism of the late 1860s and the aggressive imperialism of the late 1890s. The same

[4] P. J. Cain and A. G. Hopkins, *British Imperialism: Innovation and Expansion, 1688–1914*, vol. 1 (London: Longman, 1993), 361.

[5] Ibid., chap. 11.

[6] Joseph A. Schumpeter, *Imperialism and Social Classes*, trans. Heinz Norden (Fairfield, N. J.: Kelley, 1989).

[7] Wallace G. Mills, "Victorian Imperialism as Religion—Civil or Otherwise," in *The Man on the Spot: Essays on British Empire History*, ed. Roger D. Long (Westport, Conn.: Greenwood, 1995), 21–40; Darby, *Three Faces of Imperialism*, 23, 31–52; W. L. Langer, *The Diplomacy of Imperialism, 1890–1902*, 2nd ed. (New York: Knopf, 1951), 80–96; D. M. Schreuder, "The Cultural Factor in Victorian Imperialism: A Case-Study of the British 'Civilizing Mission,'" *Journal of Imperial and Commonwealth History* 4, no. 3 (May 1976): 283–317.

point applies to humanitarian impulses. Indeed, the slave trade had been reduced substantially by the mid nineteenth century, so this kind of pressure for expansion should have been lower than ever in the 1880s and 1890s. Humanitarianism almost certainly had some effect on the conduct of British foreign policy, particularly in the Liberals' dealings with the Ottoman Empire; however, most leaders were unwilling to take the risks and pay the costs necessary to bring to an end the persecution of minority groups. As a result, humanitarianism had little effect on the broader grand-strategic picture.

The most plausible ideational explanation for the revival of British imperialism in the late nineteenth century is based on social Darwinism. Charles Darwin's *On the Origin of Species* was published in 1859, and his theory spread in popularity in the 1860s and 1870s—just prior to the rapid expansion of the empire. British elites had a vested interest in promoting social Darwinist ideology because it embraced the idea that their privileged status was the result of their inherent genetic superiority. For the sake of cognitive consistency, they should have subscribed to its foreign policy implications: that Britain needed to be aggressively imperialist to prove its competitive fitness vis-à-vis other European nations. Lord Salisbury, who was responsible for numerous additions to the empire in the 1880s and 1890s, was influenced by the theory. In 1868, he wrote that "'Eat and be eaten' is the great law of political as of animated nature. The nations of the earth are divided into the sheep and the wolves—the fat and defenceless against the hungry and strong."[8] Joseph Chamberlain and Lord Rosebery, both major figures in the expansion of the empire, also justified their policies in naturalistic terms.[9]

These anecdotes are suggestive, but they do not hold up to systematic analysis. In a survey of various "respectable" journals (i.e., those read by the British policymaking elite) published between 1870 and 1900, Mark Francis finds that "there is little in the periodical literature to indicate that English scientific analysis of primitive people resulted in the justification of empire, nor that it legitimized particular policies such as assimilation or a reservation system on which indigenous peoples would be protected from Europeans."[10] Indeed, Paul Crook's research reveals that many prominent social Darwinists, including Herbert Spencer and W. G. Sumner, drew conclusions from their beliefs that "paralleled the cosmopolitan pacifism" of the

---

[8] Quoted in Roberts, *Salisbury*, 691.
[9] Langer, *Diplomacy of Imperialism*, 92–94.
[10] Mark Francis, "Anthropology and Social Darwinism in the British Empire: 1870–1900," *Australian Journal of Politics and History* 40 (1994): 206. See also Bernard Porter, *The Lion's Share: A Short History of British Imperialism, 1850–1983*, 2d ed. (London: Longman, 1983), 138–39; C. A. Bodelson, *Studies in Mid-Victorian Imperialism* (Copenhagen: Gyldendals, 1924), 24.

Manchester School.[11] Crook argues that contemporary scholars have been misled by early-twentieth-century liberal writers, particularly J. A. Hobson, who exaggerated the link between social Darwinism and the New Imperialism of the 1880s and 1890s for instrumental reasons.[12] Finally, it should be noted that the theory fails in comparative perspective. Social Darwinism was much stronger in the United States than in Britain, yet Britain was far more imperialist than the United States.[13]

Throughout history, empire builders have found a ready supply of racial, religious, cultural, and political ideologies to justify their behavior. Even if they feel a deep-seated need for consistency in their policy beliefs, they can obtain it from many different sources. For example, Salisbury's immediate successor as Conservative prime minister, Arthur Balfour, abhorred the idea of social Darwinism, yet he was equally, if not more, aggressively imperialist.[14] The most pertinent question, therefore, is not what individual statesmen believed, but rather what coalitional interests lay behind the selection of those leaders and their parties' strategic agendas.

POLITICAL ECONOMY

While ideational theories have found little traction in historical debates on British imperialism, political economy perspectives have occupied a central place in the literature. The most important contribution to this paradigm is Cain and Hopkins's masterwork, *British Imperialism*. In many ways, it represents the latest refinement of J. A. Hobson's *Imperialism*, which was first published in 1902.[15] Cain and Hopkins argue that the driving force behind

[11] Paul Crook, *Darwinism, War, and History: The Debate over the Biology of War from the 'Origin of Species' to the First World War* (Cambridge: Cambridge University Press, 1994), 44–47, 94–97. On the connection between liberalism and Darwinism, see also Greta Jones, *Social Darwinism and English Thought: The Interaction between Biological and Social Theory* (Sussex: Harvester, 1980), chap. 3.

[12] Paul Crook, "Historical Monkey Business: The Myth of a Darwinized British Imperial Discourse," *History* 84, no. 276 (October 1999): 633–57.

[13] P. D. Marchant, "Social Darwinism," *Australian Journal of Politics and History* 3, no. 1 (November 1957): 47.

[14] Jason Tomes, *Balfour and Foreign Policy: The International Thought of a Conservative Statesman* (Cambridge: Cambridge University Press, 1997), 22–27.

[15] Cain and Hopkins, *British Imperialism*, vol. 1; P. J. Cain and A. G. Hopkins, *British Imperialism: Crisis and Deconstruction, 1914–1990*, vol. 2 (London: Longman, 1993); J. A. Hobson, *Imperialism: A Study*, 3d ed. (London: Allen and Unwin, 1938). See also Anthony Webster, *Gentlemen Capitalists: British Imperialism in South East Asia, 1770–1890* (London: Tauris, 1998); Raymond E. Dumett, ed., *Gentlemanly Capitalism and British Imperialism* (New York: Longman, 1999). Marxists have also focused on the role of finance, but their influence on the mainstream debate over the causes of British imperialism has been marginal in recent decades. On Marxist theories and their flaws, see Anthony Brewer, *Marxist Theories of Imperialism: A Critical Survey*, 2d ed. (London: Routledge, 1990).

the growth of the empire was the preferences of London-based investors and financial service-sector professionals. This sectoral group, which the authors dub the "gentlemanly capitalists," was well connected in the country's sociopolitical power structure and therefore was able to ensure that successive governments, Conservative and Liberal alike, protected British property throughout the world. As British finance penetrated deeper into the periphery, the empire naturally expanded. Manufacturers play little part in this story; unlike gentlemanly capitalists, they were unable to penetrate the upper echelons of the policymaking elite.

The finance-based explanation of Cain and Hopkins has not been uncontroversial, even among scholars who believe that there is a fundamental connection between imperialism and domestic economic interests. Another interpretation, which is best represented by William G. Hynes's *The Economics of Empire*, asserts that manufacturers' preferences were of critical importance.[16] After 1860, the rapid industrialization of France, Germany, and the United States, combined with the global increase in tariffs in the 1880s, put great competitive pressure on British manufacturers. Their loss of economic hegemony forced them to look for new markets in the periphery, and their governments—which, though dominated by financial interests, could not ignore such a large constituency—backed them up with military interventions, diplomatic support, and the extension of the empire. These steps would have been taken even if Britain had no imperial competitors; however, as it happened, the continental European powers began at the same time to seize colonies of their own, thereby threatening to cut off export markets that Britons wanted for themselves. As a result, the impulse for expansion became even more urgent.

In the following pages, I draw on both the financial and manufacturing explanations for British imperialism. As I will argue, the preferences of gentlemanly capitalists were a key determinant of the extension of the empire in the late nineteenth century. However, the London-based financial service sector was not the only powerful group in the British political economy. It is impossible to understand why the Liberal and Conservative Parties

---

[16] William G. Hynes, *The Economics of Empire: Britain, Africa, and the New Imperialism, 1870–95* (London: Longman, 1979). See also D. C. M. Platt, *Finance, Trade, and Politics in British Foreign Policy, 1815–1914* (Oxford: Clarendon, 1968), 359–68; Damodar R. SarDesai, "British Expansion in Southeast Asia: The Imperialism of Trade in the Nineteenth Century," in *The Man on the Spot: Essays on British Empire History*, ed. Roger D. Long (Westport, Conn.: Greenwood, 1995), 7–20; Porter, *Lion's Share*, 77–79, 139–51. Critiques of the "gentlemanly capitalist" theory that stress the political power of manufacturers and other economic groups include M. Daunton, "'Gentlemanly Capitalism' and British Industry, 1820–1914," *Past and Present* 122 (February 1989): 119–58; B. W. E. Alford, *Britain in the World Economy since 1880* (London: Longman, 1996), 102–5; C. W. Newbury, "The Tariff Factor in Anglo-French West African Partition," in *France and Britain in Africa: Imperial Rivalry and Colonial Rule*, ed. Prosser Gifford and William R. Louis (New Haven: Yale University Press, 1971), 221–59.

diverged over grand strategy in the 1860s and 1870s, or why there arose a "Liberal Imperialist" position in the 1880s and 1890s, without reference to manufacturing interests. The question of which and when each of the two economic interest groups was most influential can be answered only by examining the sectoral composition of Britain's political parties. Once it is revealed how coalitional interests were connected to partisan variation in grand strategy, it becomes possible to reconcile the financial and manufacturing interpretations of British imperialism.

Specifically, I argue that the two parties adopted different positions over the periphery in the late nineteenth century because their societal coalitions had divergent interests in the international economy. The Conservatives' primary constituency until the 1880s, the gentry, depended on income from employment in Britain's military-colonial institutions, including the army, navy, and foreign service. Then, from the 1880s onward, the party came to be dominated by the financial services sector of southeast England, which increasingly struggled to maintain its advantage over foreign competitors in finding profitable opportunities for investment in the periphery. Consequently, the Conservative Party and its sectoral coalition pursued an imperialist grand strategy throughout 1868–1939.

The Liberals, in contrast, represented merchandise exporters in the manufacturing and coal sectors. From 1868 to 1880, British manufacturers were highly competitive in peripheral markets, so they had no need for imperialism. Instead, their preferred strategy was interventionism, which would adequately protect their interests in the periphery at a far lower cost. After 1880, however, they faced rising competition from other industrializing great powers, so they and their party became increasingly imperialist. Even Labour, which took over the Liberals' electoral constituency in the interwar period, sought to hold on to the empire for as long as possible. Merchandise exporters' interests were divided between peripheral and core markets, so the Liberals and Labour never became as aggressively imperialist as the Conservatives. However, the fierce debates between interventionism and imperialism in the 1870s and 1880s were essentially resolved by the end of the century, when both parties' constituents needed their government to help them maintain their competitive position in the periphery.

I divide the case into six intervals, each spanning approximately one decade: 1868–80, 1880–92, 1892–1905, 1905–14, 1918–31, and 1931–39. This periodization serves two purposes. First, it makes the long stretch of history from 1868 to 1939 more analytically tractable. In four of the six intervals, both major parties (Liberals and Conservatives to 1922, Labour and Conservatives thereafter) were in power, so their governments' policies can easily be compared. Second, I have selected cut points in which there were changes in either the independent variable, sectoral interests, or the intervening variable, international and domestic constraints. This helps demonstrate how the theory predicts shifts in the dependent variable, grand strategy.

1868–80: ECONOMIC HEGEMONY

The international environment imposed few constraints on British grand strategy toward the periphery in 1868–80. German Chancellor Bismarck was not yet interested in colonies, France was preoccupied with Germany, and the United States confined itself to the Western Hemisphere. Thus, Britain had a free hand in much of the periphery. On the domestic side, however, funding for overseas adventures was in short supply. Annual charges on the debt, a legacy of the Napoleonic and Crimean Wars, consumed more than a third of the government's budget and 2.4–2.7 percent of the national income (see figure 6.1). This burden should not have altered the type of strategy hypothesized for each party; however, it should have limited the level of aggressiveness with which each pursued its strategy.

Figure 6.1. Government Spending, as Share of National Income

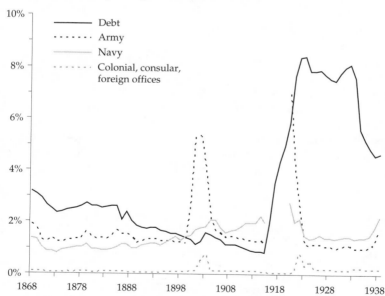

SOURCE: B. R. Mitchell and P. Deane, *Abstract of British Historical Statistics* (London: Cambridge University Press, 1962), 367–68, 397–99, 403.

Liberals

In 1868, the Liberals' primary economic constituency, manufacturers, occupied a dominant position in the global economy. They were more productive, technologically advanced, and capital-rich than their competitors in any other country. As a result, their products were sold at healthy profit margins in nearly every corner of the world. Manufacturers had little interest in territorial expansion as long as they could "conquer" peripheral markets on their own initiative. Imperialism would squander scarce resources on defense, necessitating higher taxes while providing only marginal benefits.

To balance manufacturers' interest in both the expansion of commerce and the reduction of the national debt, Liberal governments should have pursued an interventionist grand strategy. Their ambitions should have been limited to opening markets, enforcing property rights, controlling potential bottlenecks in trade routes, and responding to local threats. None of these tasks required additional colonies; Britain's global network of naval bases and army garrisons, acquired through three centuries of exploration and conflict in the periphery, would suffice. Indeed, Britain's geopolitical position was so secure that even manufacturers who exported to the periphery should have been willing to entertain the prospect of a partial withdrawal. Much as American peripheral interests accepted a partial disengagement from Latin America after World War I, British peripheral interests in 1868–80 should have been willing to undertake strategic retrenchment for the sake of fiscal parsimony.

The Liberal government of Prime Minister William E. Gladstone in 1868–74 confirms this prediction.[17] On the one hand, it was clearly interventionist, using force or the threat thereof on several occasions to protect British commercial interests overseas. Yet, it also attempted to cut costs, reduce existing responsibilities, and avoid taking on new ones. To that end, it pushed the colonies of settlement to provide for their own security and government. Gladstone hoped that they would remain in the empire, but he expected, and consequently prepared for, a cordial separation at some point in the

---

[17] See H. C. G. Matthew, *Gladstone, 1809–1898* (Oxford: Clarendon, 1997), 182–93; Paul Knaplund, *Gladstone and Britain's Imperial Policy* (London: Allen and Unwin, 1927), chap. 4; Paul Knaplund, *Gladstone's Foreign Policy* (London: Cass, 1935), chap. 3; Susan H. Farnsworth, *The Evolution of British Imperial Policy during the Mid-Nineteenth Century: A Study of the Peelite Contribution, 1846–1874* (New York: Garland, 1992), chaps. 6–7. Also useful are C. C. Eldridge, *England's Mission: The Imperial Idea in the Age of Gladstone and Disraeli, 1868–1880* (Chapel Hill: University of North Carolina Press, 1973), chaps. 3–6; C. C. Eldridge, *Victorian Imperialism* (London: Hodder and Stoughton, 1978), 86–101; Agatha Ramm, "Granville," in *British Foreign Secretaries and Foreign Policy: From Crimean War to First World War*, ed. Keith M. Wilson (London: Croom Helm, 1987), 85–94; Richard Shannon, *Gladstone: Heroic Minister, 1865–1898* (London: Allen Lane, 1999), 75–76, 86–91, 103–4, 108–9, 113–15.

future. In 1881, he summarized his party's view perfectly: "While we are opposed to imperialism, we are devoted to the empire."[18]

The Liberal government undertook only two limited forays into imperialism. First, it agreed to annex Griqualand West to protect British diamond prospectors. However, it did so only because it expected (mistakenly, as it turned out) that the territory would be administered by the Cape Colony, not the Colonial Office. Second, it proposed a voluntary federation between the Cape Colony, Natal, and the Boer republics of Transvaal and the Orange Free State. This measure would have significantly enlarged the empire, but not for the sake of expansion; rather, the Liberals believed that they could wean the two British colonies from their dependence on aid from London if they were unified with the Boer states. Thus, the government stipulated "that the extension of the British Sovereignty so as to include the republics must not bring new charges upon the imperial exchequer."[19] The Boers demurred, and the Liberals were not willing to press the issue, so the plan died. In short, even the imperialist exceptions to the Liberals' grand strategy were advanced under the principles of interventionism.

William E. Gladstone (December 1868–February 1874)

Interventionism

Partial retreats

- Induced the Cape Colony to assume greater powers of self-government.
- Removed troops from Canada despite ongoing diplomatic tensions with the United States and cross-border raids by Irish nationalists.
- Removed troops from New Zealand despite continuing hostilities between British settlers and the Maori.

Political intervention

- Sent a punitive expedition to the Gold Coast against the Ashanti; took control of the town of Elmina from the Netherlands.

Diplomatic settlement

- Proposed to trade possession of British Gambia for French Sierra Leone to consolidate Britain's sphere of influence in West Africa.

---

[18] Quoted in D. M. Schreuder, *Gladstone and Kruger* (London: Routledge and Kegan Paul, 1969), 47. See also ibid., 45–52; Eldridge, *Victorian Imperialism*, 94–101; Knaplund, *Gladstone and Britain's Imperial Policy*, 95–101; R. L. Schuyler, "The Climax of Anti-Imperialism in England," *Political Science Quarterly* 36, no. 4 (December 1921): 537–60; Farnsworth, *Evolution of British Imperial Policy*, 292, 330.

[19] Quoted in Knaplund, *Gladstone and Britain's Imperial Policy*, 131–32.

Imperialism

Landmass annexation

- Annexed Griqualand West under the mistaken assumption that the Cape Colony would assume control over it.
- Promoted the unification of the British territories of Cape Colony and Natal with the independent republics of Transvaal and the Orange Free State.

Conservatives

The Conservative Party's primary socioeconomic constituency in 1868–80 was Britain's elite upper class, the landed gentry. Many members of this group, particularly the "second sons" of aristocrats, depended on income from employment in the upper echelons of the civil service and military, giving them strong military-colonial interests. To protect their privileged position and provide them with opportunities to advance their standing, Conservative leaders should have followed an imperialist grand strategy. However, the extent of their strategic aggressiveness should have been limited by a major domestic constraint, the national debt. Faced with loan payments that consumed more than a third of the annual budget, Conservatives should have seen the virtues of discretion and restraint. They should not have sought to take as much territory as possible, but neither should they have been as adamantly opposed to annexing new colonies as the Liberals. By being selectively, cost-consciously imperialist, they could serve the economic interests of the gentry without having to raise their taxes.

As expected, the Conservatives' rise to power in 1874, led by Prime Minister Benjamin Disraeli, produced a visible shift in British grand strategy toward the periphery.[20] Whereas the Liberals were reluctant to assume control over territory without the consent of their prospective subjects, the

---

[20] See Richard Shannon, *The Age of Disraeli, 1868–1881: The Rise of Tory Democracy* (London: Longman, 1992), chaps. 11, 13; Eldridge, *England's Mission*, chaps. 6–8; Marvin Swartz, *The Politics of British Foreign Policy in the Era of Disraeli and Gladstone* (New York: St. Martin's, 1985), chaps. 1–5. Also useful are Eldridge, *Victorian Imperialism*, 106–19; Sarah Bradford, *Disraeli* (New York: Stein and Day, 1982), 322–29, 335–53; P. J. V. Rolo, "Derby," in *British Foreign Secretaries and Foreign Policy: From Crimean War to First World War*, ed. Keith M. Wilson (London: Croom Helm, 1987), 102–118; Richard W. Davis, *Disraeli* (Boston: Little, Brown: 1976), chap. 8; Freda Harcourt, "Disraeli's Imperialism, 1866–1868: A Question of Timing," *Historical Journal* 23, no. 1 (March 1980): 88–109; W. P. Morrell, *Britain in the Pacific Islands* (Oxford: Clarendon Press, 1960); W. David McIntyre, *The Imperial Frontier in the Tropics, 1865–75: A Study of British Colonial Policy in West Africa, Malaya, and the South Pacific in the Age of Gladstone and Disraeli* (London: Macmillan, 1967); Eric A. Walker, *A History of Southern Africa* (London: Longmans, Green, 1968); R. W. Seton-Watson, *Disraeli, Gladstone, and the Eastern Question: A Study in Diplomacy and Party Politics* (London: Macmillan, 1938).

Conservatives had no such scruples. First, they annexed Fiji. Native islanders wanted to maintain their independence, but the white settler minority and colonial lobby held sway over Disraeli. Second, the Conservatives revived the plan to federate British possessions in South Africa with the two independent Boer republics, the Orange Free State and Transvaal. Once again, the Boers resisted. With voluntary accession ruled out, the Conservatives decided to annex Transvaal by fiat. Despite strenuous opposition from the Boers, Conservative parliamentarians ratified a declaration "confirming the will and determination of the Queen's Government that the territory should continue for ever an integral part of her dominions in South Africa."[21] Third, the Conservatives invaded Afghanistan. Fearing an increase in Russian influence over the country, and therefore the loss of a strategic buffer between Russia and India, they made it an unofficial protectorate. Finally, Disraeli acquired Cyprus, a strategic outpost for British trade routes in the Eastern Mediterranean. For Conservatives, it was a plum catch; however, as one parliamentarian reported, the Liberals did not welcome the news of another imperial commitment: "Gladstone is rabid, and looks as if he must tear something or somebody in pieces or expire with rage."[22]

Benjamin Disraeli (February 1874–April 1880)

Interventionism

Political intervention

- Accepted a treaty with the Malaysian state of Perak that gave Britain a resident adviser in the government and two small territories to be used by the navy to fight piracy. Subsequently authorized a punitive expedition in response to the murder of a British official.
- Fought the Zulus over their conflicts with the Transvaal Boers; established predominant influence over Zululand.
- Sent a punitive expedition to Afghanistan in response to its formation of ties with Russia. Subsequently installed a British mission in Kabul, took territory near the Khyber Pass, and forced the Amir to accept British control over Afghan foreign policy. Sent a second punitive expedition after the mission was slaughtered.

Overseas bases

- Purchased the Egyptian Khedive's shares in the Suez Canal, 44 percent of the total.

[21] Quoted in Brian Bond, "The South African War, 1880–81," in *Victorian Military Campaigns,* ed. Brian Bond (New York: Praeger, 1967), 204.
[22] Quoted in Shannon, *Age of Disraeli,* 306.

- Annexed Cyprus for its strategic location near the Suez Canal and the Levant.
- Annexed Fiji on behalf of white settlers.

Imperialism
Landmass annexation
- Allowed the Cape Colony to annex Walvis Bay (initially administered by the Colonial Office), Griqualand East, and Fingoland.
- Offered to federate Transvaal and the Orange Free State with the Cape Colony and Natal. When refused, summarily annexed Transvaal.

Aside from Cyprus, Disraeli was not particularly systematic about which territories he chose to annex, nor did he act aggressively to take as much territory as possible. To be an imperialist, however, he did not need to seek out new colonies. Instead, he had only to consent to demands that arose from below. If he had ignored these demands, he would have alienated the imperialist interests of his coalition; if he had actively sought to expand the empire, he would have found it difficult to balance the budget without raising taxes. The bottom line of this strategy was not a vast territorial grab, but rather a moderate, cost-conscious imperialism, very much in line with the theory's prediction.

1880–92: COMPETITION AND DECLINE, PART 1

The relatively tranquil environment in which Britain conducted its peripheral affairs in 1868–80 did not last into the final decades of the nineteenth century. France, Germany, and Belgium began to carve off parts of Africa and Southeast Asia for themselves, while Russia continued its inexorable expansion into Central Asia. Yet, while external pressures mounted, Britain's domestic constraints remained tight. The national debt loomed large into the 1880s, consuming 26–36 percent of the annual budget and 1.9–2.6 percent of the national income (see figure 6.1).

The rise of competition over territories coveted by British businessmen and military planners presented successive British governments with a major new strategic dilemma. Britain could claim every scrap of potentially desirable land for itself, using the formidable resources of the empire wherever possible to preempt other states' attempts at expansion; or, it could allow its counterparts to take their fair share, avoiding costly new commitments and developing peaceful relationships with them. How each party responded to this combination of domestic and international constraints would depend on the changing economic interests of its sectoral coalition.

Liberals

The British economy was entering a period of transition in 1880. More than a decade had passed since the peak of its global dominance, and manufacturers were beginning to suffer from foreign competition in export markets that they had once dominated. At the same time, global protectionism was on the rise, creating barriers to British commerce not only in great powers such as Germany, France, and the United States, but also in Britain's own self-ruled colonies of settlement, particularly Australia and Canada. Consequently, the economic interests behind the Liberal Party were changing, even though the coalition itself retained its sectoral identity. Core markets were no longer as hospitable as they had once been, and Britain's competitive position therein could only continue to erode. In the periphery, in contrast, British manufacturers could use their centuries-old expertise in international trade, their global network of connections and contacts, and the backing of the Royal Navy and Colonial Office to tap into new, undeveloped markets, where competition would be minimal and profits would be high. In short, the base constituency of the Liberal Party was both becoming more dependent on peripheral trade and beginning to feel the need for its government to provide it with competitive advantages. In response, the party should have begun to transition from interventionism to imperialism.

William E. Gladstone and the Liberals returned to power in December 1880, and, with a brief interruption in the summer and autumn of 1885, remained in office until July 1886.[23] During this period, the rate at which they took on new peripheral commitments and colonies was measurably greater than in their previous government. However, not all Liberals were ready to embrace imperialism. Gladstone and many of his colleagues remained reluctant to add to their responsibilities, so Liberals continued to act less aggressively than Conservatives. The difference between 1868 and

---

[23] See Knaplund, *Gladstone and Britain's Imperial Policy*, chap. 5; Knaplund, *Gladstone's Foreign Policy*, chaps. 4–8; Matthew, *Gladstone*, chap. 6. Also useful are Shannon, *Gladstone*, chaps. 7–9; Eldridge, *Victorian Imperialism*, 154–71; Ramm, "Granville," 94–101; Swartz, *Politics of British Foreign Policy*; Schreuder, *Gladstone and Kruger*; Walker, *History of Southern Africa*; A. N. Porter, ed., *Atlas of British Expansion* (London: Routledge, 1991); Thomas Pakenham, *The Scramble for Africa* (London: Weidenfeld and Nicolson, 1991); John D. Hargreaves, *Prelude to the Partition of West Africa* (London: Macmillan, 1963); F. H. Hinsley, "International Rivalry in the Colonial Sphere, 1869–1885," in *The Cambridge History of the British Empire*, vol. 3, ed. E. A. Benians, Sir James Butler, and C. E. Carrington (Cambridge: Cambridge University Press, 1967), 95–126; R. E. Robinson, "Imperial Problems in British Politics, 1880–1895," in *The Cambridge History of the British Empire*, vol. 3, ed. E. A. Benians, Sir James Butler, and C. E. Carrington (Cambridge: Cambridge University Press, 1967), 127–80; H. H. Dodwell, "Central Asia, 1858–1918," in *The Cambridge History of the British Empire*, vol. 5, ed. H. H. Dodwell (Cambridge: Cambridge University Press, 1932), 403–31; Cecil Headlam, "The Race for the Interior, 1881–1895," in *The Cambridge History of the British Empire*, vol. 8, ed. J. Holland Rose, A. P. Newton, and E. A. Benians (Cambridge: Cambridge University Press, 1936), 507–38.

1880 was not that Gladstone altered his views on empire, but rather that he confronted ever-increasing pressures for imperialism within his party.

The more cautious side of this grand strategy is evident in the Liberals' decision to reverse the Conservatives' annexation of Transvaal. At first, Gladstone was reluctant to disrupt the status quo, but he changed his mind once the Boers began an armed revolt against British rule. Faced with a clear signal that Britain did not govern Transvaal with the consent of its subjects, he agreed to grant it independence, reserving only the right to veto its foreign treaties.

Gladstone also withdrew the force that the Conservatives had sent to Afghanistan. He believed that "Russian expansion in Central Asia was natural and, with respect to India, benign. There was, in his view, no Russian plan or intention to invade British India; an independent, unified, and guaranteed Afghanistan was therefore a sufficient bastion."[24] By the spring of 1885, however, Russia had reached the border of Afghanistan and threatened to continue southward. At that point, the prime minister responded decisively, securing a vote in Parliament for war credits of £11 million. Russia backed down and consented in principle to a proposal by Gladstone to have the dispute settled by a third-party arbitrator, the king of Denmark.[25] Before an agreement on the terms of the arbitration could be reached, however, the Liberal government fell.

The Liberals also tried to maintain a hands-off policy toward Egypt, which was beset with internal conflict over its status as a vassal to the Ottoman Empire.[26] Despite extensive trade and investment in the country, as well as Disraeli's acquisition of a near-controlling stake in the Suez Canal, Gladstone was unperturbed by reports of a growing tide of nationalist sentiment: "'Egypt for the Egyptians' is the sentiment to which I should wish to give scope: and could it prevail it would I think be the best, the only good solution of the 'Egyptian question.'"[27] The Colonial Office's men-on-the-spot, however, were hostile to Egyptian nationalism, and they biased their missives to make a case for intervention. With no better source of information, Gladstone had no choice but to conclude, as he was told, that Egypt was rapidly descending into disorder and violence.[28] In response, he asked France and Italy to join him in a multilateral intervention. When they refused, he acted unilaterally.

[24] Matthew, *Gladstone*, 381.

[25] Dodwell, "Central Asia," 424–25.

[26] Cain and Hopkins, *British Imperialism*, 1:363–64. See also A. G. Hopkins, "The Victorians and Africa: A Reconsideration of the Occupation of Egypt, 1882," *Journal of African History* 27, no. 2 (1986): 363–91; Swartz, *Politics of British Foreign Policy*, chap. 6.

[27] Quoted in Knaplund, *Gladstone's Foreign Policy*, 170–71.

[28] Matthew, *Gladstone*, 384; Alexander Schölch, "The 'Men on the Spot' and the English Occupation of Egypt in 1882," *Historical Journal* 19, no. 3 (September 1976): 773–85.

At no point did Gladstone contemplate the annexation of Egypt.[29] To lay the groundwork for withdrawal, however, he decided that its government must be reformed. British administrators would restore order, strengthen liberal institutions, and set aright Egypt's disastrously mismanaged finances. As soon as they accomplished these goals, the occupation would end. In the meantime, Gladstone ceded control over Egypt's treasury to the Concert of Europe, making the administration of Egypt a truly multilateral endeavor. He tried hard to ensure that Egypt would not be treated as a de facto colony, avoiding the commitments and expenses of imperial expansion. F. H. Hinsley explains the significance of this decision: "When all the world was ready for Great Britain to declare annexation or a protectorate, he did not miss the opportunity to alter Egypt's status; he refused it."[30]

William E. Gladstone (December 1880–June 1885, January 1886–July 1886)

Interventionism

Partial retreats

- Granted independence to Transvaal but maintained a veto over its foreign policy.

Political intervention

- Sent troops to the Sudan to rescue British forces from the Mahdists, an Islamic group opposed to British and Ottoman rule. Withdrew after the mission failed.
- Removed troops from Afghanistan, but subsequently responded to the threat of a Russian invasion with preparations for war. Eventually negotiated to have the border fixed by a third-party arbitrator.
- Sought French and Italian participation in a joint intervention to protect foreign trade and investment in Egypt. When refused, sent in troops unilaterally. Eventually granted control over the financial administration of Egypt to the Concert of Europe.

Commercial expansion

- Participated in the Berlin West Africa Conference with the goal of maintaining free trade over the Congo River basin.
- Granted a royal charter to the North Borneo Company to control and exploit the island of Borneo.

[29] M. J. Williams, "The Egyptian Campaign of 1882," in *Victorian Military Campaigns*, ed. Brian Bond (New York: Praeger, 1967), 281–82; Knaplund, *Gladstone's Foreign Policy*, 121–27; Matthew, *Gladstone*, 390–94; Eldridge, *Victorian Imperialism*, 157–60; Shannon, *Gladstone*, 305; C. J. Lowe, *The Reluctant Imperialists: British Foreign Policy, 1878–1902* (London: Routledge and Kegan Paul, 1967), 52, 69.
[30] Hinsley, "International Rivalry in the Colonial Sphere," 113.

Imperialism
  Territorial settlement
  - Negotiated a treaty with France to delineate spheres of influence between French Guinea and British Sierra Leone.
  Landmass annexation
  - Invalidated Queensland's annexation of eastern New Guinea. Subsequently allowed Queensland to have the southern half of the territory to preempt its annexation by Germany.
  - Established a protectorate over Southern Bechuanaland to prevent the Boers from linking up to the German colony of Angra Pequena; annexed St. Lucia Bay (on the border of Natal) to preempt its annexation by Germany; permitted the Cape Colony to annex tribal lands on its eastern frontier.
  - Established a protectorate over the Niger River basin to prevent France from imposing preferential tariffs over the region; granted the National Africa Company a royal charter to control and exploit the territory.

The Liberal governments of 1880–85 and 1886 did annex territory in New Guinea, South Africa, and West Africa, but in general they were far less predisposed than Conservatives to counteract the increasingly aggressive imperialism of the other great powers. Gladstone's views in particular are revealing. In accordance with international legal principles, he believed that if Britain were to have colonies, the right of other states to the same could not be denied. In September 1884, shortly after Bismarck's annexation of Angra Pequena, he gave a public speech explaining that German imperialism should be welcomed, not feared, because it would "bring forth from the bosom of the land new resources for the comfort, advantage, and happiness of mankind. . . . Come what may, let every other country do what it will—it is for them to consider how far their political strength will be increased by it. Into that question I do not enter."[31]
In private communication with cabinet members, Gladstone went so far as to argue that German imperialism could benefit the British Empire: "I should be extremely glad to see the Germans become our neighbours in South Africa, or even the neighbours of the Transvaal. We have to remember Chatham's conquest of Canada, so infinitely lauded, which killed dead as a mutton our best security for keeping the British Provinces."[32] In short, Gladstone recognized that Britons abroad were apprehensive of having non-British colonies bordering their own and, under such circumstances,

---

[31] Quoted in Matthew, *Gladstone*, 376. See also ibid., 375–77, 403–4; Knaplund, *Gladstone's Foreign Policy*, 126.
[32] Quoted in Matthew, *Gladstone*, 404.

would want to maintain close ties with the metropole. An additional benefit of German imperialism was that it would set off-limits lands that tempted British colonists into further annexations and wars with native tribes.[33] Finally, the German Empire was more open to British trade than French colonies in the early 1880s.[34]

The Liberal governments of 1880–86 oversaw, and generally did not oppose, the rapid rise of non-British imperialism across the globe. Many of the territories acquired by other great powers bordered on British colonies and protectorates, so they could have been considered to be of strategic importance. The German sphere of influence in southwest Africa surrounded Britain's base in Walvis Bay and bordered on the Cape Colony; the German claim to Tanganyika threatened to cut off one of Britain's local allies, the Sultan of Zanzibar, from the African mainland; the French and Italian territories on the Red Sea stood at a critical choke-point on the main naval route to India; and France's seizure of Tunis brought it uncomfortably close to the British stronghold of Malta. Yet, security considerations did not play an important role in British foreign and colonial policy under the Liberals in 1880–85 and 1886. When the expansion of British influence did occur, it was motivated primarily either by local colonists' demands (in New Guinea), the breakdown of local government (in Egypt), or the desire to keep high-profit trade areas outside the tariff wall of other imperial powers (in the Niger River). Only in the annexation of Bechuanaland was security the dominant concern.

Every time another great power expanded its empire near British territory, some members of the cabinet offered a plan to repel or at least limit rival claims, while Gladstone and his fellow Radicals opposed them.[35] Out of their debates grew a compromise strategy. In some instances, such as in the declaration of protectorates over southeastern New Guinea, Bechuanaland, and the Niger River, it was imperialist. In other cases, such as in the Egyptian affair and the deannexation of the Transvaal, it was interventionist. This apparent schizophrenia is very much in line with the theory. The interests of the Liberal Party's coalition were changing in the mid 1880s; many manufacturers were looking to peripheral markets to avoid higher tariffs and increased competition in the core. However, nearly half of all British merchandise exports were still sold in the United States and Europe, leaving a sizable portion of the Liberals' constituency without a strong stake in the expansion of the empire. Thus, it would have been surprising if deep cleavages over foreign policy had not arisen within the party. As long as Gladstone

---

[33] Paul W. Schroeder, "Gladstone as Bismarck," *Canadian Journal of History* 15, no. 2 (August 1980): 187; Matthew, *Gladstone*, 404.

[34] S. E. Crowe, *The Berlin West Africa Conference, 1884–85* (London: Longman, Green, 1942), 37.

[35] Knaplund, *Gladstone's Foreign Policy*, 121; Matthew, *Gladstone*, 408–9; Pakenham, *Scramble for Africa*, 283–84; Robinson, "Imperial Problems in British Politics," 151–53.

was to lead the Liberals, he would have to compromise between its factions. It was not until 1894 that his personal convictions were stretched so far by his party's changing interests that he became unable to represent it. At that point, which I will discuss later in this chapter, he resigned.

Conservatives

The socioeconomic coalition of the Conservative Party was also changing in the 1880s. The Conservatives' core constituency, the landed gentry, began to invest their political, economic, and social resources in the financial service sector, forming an alliance of elites known as the "gentlemanly capitalists." These two groups shared the same strategic outlook, albeit for different reasons. First, the gentry had military-colonial interests due to the employment of their "second sons" in the military and civil service. Their optimal strategy was imperialism. Second, the financial service sector faced increasing competition in the international economy. No longer did Britain have a monopoly on choice investments in the periphery; all of the other industrializing great powers now had surplus capital and energetic entrepreneurs of their own. In response, British financiers pushed deeper into undeveloped peripheral markets in search of new investment opportunities. They were successful in doing so, but their incursions into native lands often created frictions that threatened their activities. Thus, they benefited directly from the extension of British imperial control.

Like in 1874–80, the Conservatives should not have been insensitive to the costs of imperial expansion. The national debt remained high, posing a significant constraint on their ability to take on new responsibilities. However, the government risked losing economically and strategically valuable territories to its imperial competitors if it did not act quickly. It is not possible to determine *ex ante* the exact relative weight of these conflicting domestic and international imperatives, but both of them should have factored into the strategic calculus of the gentlemanly capitalists and their representatives in the Conservative Party.

The Conservatives' peripheral strategy through the final two decades of the century was controlled by Prime Minister Lord Salisbury.[36] Serving as

---

[36] See Roberts, *Salisbury*, chaps. 22, 24–26, 27–34; Lady Gwendolen Cecil, *Life of Robert, Marquis of Salisbury, 1880–1886*, vol. 3 (London: Hodder and Stoughton, 1931), chaps. 7–8; Lady Gwendolen Cecil, *Life of Robert, Marquis of Salisbury, 1887–1892*, vol. 4 (London: Hodder and Stoughton, 1932). Also useful are David Steele, *Lord Salisbury: A Political Biography* (London: UCL, 1999); Richard Shannon, *The Age of Salisbury, 1881–1902: Unionism and Empire* (London: Longman, 1996); C. J. Lowe, *Salisbury and the Mediterranean, 1886–1896* (London: Routledge and Kegan Paul, 1965); David Gillard, "Salisbury," in *British Foreign Secretaries and Foreign Policy: From Crimean War to First World War*, ed. Keith M. Wilson (London: Croom Helm, 1987), 119–37; F. H. Hinsley, "International Rivalry, 1885–1895," in *The Cambridge History of the British Empire*, vol. 3, ed. E. A. Benians, Sir James Butler, and C. E. Carrington (Cambridge: Cambridge

his own foreign minister (from January 1887, after the resignation of Lord Iddesleigh), he vastly extended Britain's influence over the periphery. He annexed several important territories in Southeast Asia, including Upper Burma and parts of Malaysia, but he is best known for the enormous tracts of land he claimed in Africa. Unlike Gladstone, he saw fit to respond to nearly every French, German, and Portuguese incursion into territories in which British traders and investors had a defensible interest.

Lord Salisbury (June 1885–January 1886, July 1886–August 1892)

Interventionism

Partial retreats
- Negotiated unsuccessfully with the Ottoman Empire to trade withdrawal from Egypt for the right to intervene in it and to end the Concert of Europe's control over its finances.

Overseas bases
- Established protectorates over the Gilbert Islands and Cook Islands to prevent their annexation by France or Germany.

Commercial expansion
- Granted a royal charter to Cecil Rhodes to control and exploit territory in the interior of southern Africa (Rhodesia).
- Granted a royal charter to the Imperial British East Africa Company to control and exploit Uganda.
- Established a British resident adviser in Pahang, Malaysia.

Imperialism

Territorial settlements
- Negotiated a treaty with Germany to trade Heligoland for Zanzibar (an entrepôt for trade between Africa and India), Uganda (the headwaters of the Nile), and other territory in East Africa; also traded the Caprivi Strip and border claims between Togoland and the Gold Coast for Lake Ngami.
- Negotiated treaties with France to delimit common borders in Africa, establish joint control over the New Hebrides Islands, and neutralize the Suez Canal.

Landmass annexation
- Established protectorates over the Malaysian states of Brunei, North Borneo, and Sarawak to control the "freelance imperialism" of British charter companies.
- Established a protectorate over Northern Bechuanaland.

University Press, 1967), 255–76; Morrell, *Britain in the Pacific Islands*, chaps. 8–12; John M. Ward, *British Policy in the South Pacific, 1786–1893* (Sydney: Australian, 1948); Pakenham, *Scramble for Africa*; Robinson, "Imperial Problems in British Politics"; Headlam, "Race for the Interior."

- Established protectorates over British East Africa and Zanzibar after negotiating for them in a territorial settlement with Germany.
- Threatened war against Portugal in response to abuses against British commercial interests in Nyasaland; subsequently established the protectorate of British Central Africa over part of Nyasaland.
- Deposed the native ruler of Upper Burma in response to his efforts to establish ties with France; subsequently annexed the territory to British India.
- Annexed Zululand to prevent the Boers from gaining access to the sea.

As expected, the Conservatives' imperialism was not incautious; in fact, almost all of the territories claimed for Britain were either annexed to its existing colonies or taken as protectorates and administered by chartered companies, so that the Crown would not have to shoulder the full burden of rule. Furthermore, Salisbury often decided that the costs of action outweighed the benefits. For example, he was dismissive of Australians' demands to expel France from the New Hebrides Islands: "They want us to incur all the bloodshed and danger, and the stupendous cost of a war with France, of which almost the exclusive burden will fall on us, for a group of islands which are to us as valueless as the South Pole—and to which they are only attached by as debating-club sentiment."[37] Similarly, when the British Consul-General in Egypt advised Salisbury to prevent Turkey from upgrading its fortifications on the Red Sea, along the crucial Suez route to India, he was unconcerned: "I would not be too much impressed by what the soldiers tell you about the strategic importance of those places. It is their way. If they were allowed full scope, they would insist on the importance of garrisoning the Moon in order to protect us from Mars."[38] The result was an exquisite political-economic balance: rapid imperial expansion on a tight budget, all to the benefit of the Conservatives' sectoral constituency.[39]

1892–1905: COMPETITION AND DECLINE, PART 2

As the great powers brought more and more of the periphery under their control, competition for the few remaining unclaimed territories intensified.

---

[37] Quoted in Roberts, *Salisbury*, 464. On Samoa, see ibid., 463.

[38] Quoted in ibid., 532. On the Sudan, see Cecil, *Life of Robert*, 3:234; Steele, *Lord Salisbury*, 246, 259–60.

[39] A. N. Porter, "Lord Salisbury, Foreign Policy, and Domestic Finance, 1860–1900," in *Salisbury: The Man and His Policies*, ed. Lord Blake and Hugh Cecil (London: Macmillan, 1987), 148–84.

Each successive addition to the British Empire would cost more than the last in blood, treasure, or diplomatic resolve. Policymakers were not compelled to act, but if they wished to secure their desiderata, they would have to do so quickly.

At the same time, a major domestic constraint on grand strategy was loosening. Charges on the national debt fell from 1.8 percent of the national income in 1892 to only 1.1 percent in 1901. The burden began to rise again when the bill for the Boer War of 1899–1902 came due, but, until then, British governments were in a better position to pay for new international commitments and military engagements—such as the Boer War itself.

Liberals

Manufacturers continued to lose ground in the international economy as the century drew to a close. Protectionism escalated with the American McKinley Tariff of 1891 and the French Méline Tariff of 1892, leaving the British with little hope for advancement in core markets. Even if the other great powers could have been convinced to lower their tariffs, the problem of competitive decline would have remained, forcing exporters to turn to the periphery. Thus, the party that represented manufacturers, the Liberals, should have adopted an increasingly imperialist strategy.

Gladstone became prime minister once again in 1892, but this "Grand Old Man," by now an octogenarian, exerted less control over foreign policy than ever before. As manufacturers' focus shifted toward peripheral markets, the Liberal Party elite increasingly came to be constituted of men whose views on grand strategy conflicted with those of the Radical old guard.[40] Gladstone had clashed with these "Liberal Imperialists" on many previous occasions, but he had always been willing to compromise or give in, rather than threaten resignation, when outnumbered in the cabinet. By the 1890s, however, his personal views had become sufficiently out of step with the majority in the government that it makes little sense to speak of "Gladstone's strategy" in this period. Instead, Lord Rosebery, who served as foreign minister in the first two years of the government, had almost exclusive control over foreign policy.

This shift in the balance of power within the Liberal government of 1892 is not indicative of a breakdown in interest aggregation; quite to the contrary. If Gladstone had been able to retain power over foreign policy and conduct it according to the same principles he had followed in 1868, when his constituents' interests were very different, one would have to conclude that individual politicians' personalities matter more than political-economic

---

[40] A. J. Anthony Morris, *Radicalism against War, 1906–1914: The Advocacy of Peace and Retrenchment* (London: Longman, 1972), 4–5.

The Political Economy of Grand Strategy

variables. However, Gladstone did lose control, and eventually resigned, over a conflict with Rosebery over naval spending in 1894. The "changing of the guard" from Gladstone to Rosebery was not merely about a dispute between two men; instead, it represented the logical outcome of a long-developing change in the Liberal Party's position on imperialism, made inevitable by a long-developing change in the interests of the party's primary economic constituency, manufacturers.

The Liberal government's grand strategy in 1892–95 was definitely imperialist.[41] Indeed, Rosebery publicly promised before coming to office that he would follow the same policies as his Conservative predecessor, Salisbury. One of the first issues he had to deal with was the financial collapse of the Imperial British East Africa Company, which had achieved effective control over Uganda in 1891. Gladstone, who had no desire to take on this demonstrably unprofitable territory as a colony, advocated that it be evacuated. Rosebery, in contrast, was reluctant to give up on it. Uganda lay at the headwaters of the Nile, and many British military planners believed that Egypt would not be secure unless Britain controlled the entire length of the river. If the government did not take responsibility for Uganda, Germany or France might claim it. Thus, Rosebery stalled the evacuation while building support for his policy. In June 1894, not long after Gladstone resigned and Rosebery took over as prime minster, he made Uganda a British protectorate. A similar conflict played out over Egypt: Gladstone sought an agreement with France that would allow Britain to withdraw, but Rosebery refused to discuss it with the French ambassador.

William E. Gladstone and Lord Rosebery (August 1892–July 1895)

Interventionism
  Coercive diplomacy
  • Negotiated unsuccessfully with Belgium and Germany over territorial arrangements that would keep France out of the Sudan; subsequently declared that any French intrusion into the Sudan would be considered a cause for war.

[41] See Gordon Martel, *Imperial Diplomacy: Rosebery and the Failure of Foreign Policy* (Kingston: McGill-Queen's University Press, 1986). Also useful are *The Foreign Policy of Lord Rosebery* (London: Humphreys, 1901); Robert Rhodes James, *Rosebery: A Biography of Archibald Philip, Fifth Earl of Rosebery* (London: Weidenfeld and Nicolson, 1963), chaps. 8, 10; Robert Offley Ashburton Crewe-Milnes, *Lord Rosebery* (New York: Harper, 1931), chaps. 14–15; P. J. V. Rolo, "Rosebery and Kimberly," in *British Foreign Secretaries and Foreign Policy: From Crimean War to First World War*, ed. Keith M. Wilson (London: Croom Helm, 1987), 143–58; Langer, *Diplomacy of Imperialism*, chaps. 2, 4–6; Peter Stansky, *Ambitions and Strategies: The Struggle for Leadership in the Liberal Party in the 1890s* (Oxford: Clarendon, 1964), 5–78, 106–30; Hinsley, "International Rivalry"; John D. Hargreaves, *West Africa Partitioned: The Elephants and the Grass* (Madison: University of Wisconsin Press, 1985); Headlam, "Race for the Interior"; Morrell, *Britain in the Pacific Islands*; Walker, *History of Southern Africa*; G. J. Alder, *British India's Northern Frontier, 1865–95: A Study in Imperial Policy* (London: Longmans, 1963).

- Threatened France against invading Thailand, an important trading partner and strategic buffer between India and French Indochina.

Commercial expansion

- Granted an extension to the borders of Southern Rhodesia, to be administered by the British South Africa Company.

Imperialism

Territorial settlement

- Negotiated a treaty with Russia over the northern border of British India in the Hindu Kush.
- Agreed to talks with Germany over the prospective division of Portugal's empire in the event of its collapse.

Landmass annexation

- Established a protectorate over Uganda to prevent its annexation by Germany.
- Established protectorates over the southern Solomon and Ellice island groups.
- Allowed the Cape Colony to annex Pondoland.
- Annexed Northern Rhodesia, a territory that had been administered by the British South Africa Company.

Rosebery did not expand the empire on as spectacular a scale as Salisbury; however, his government fell after only three years in office. In that time, Rosebery's record was unambiguously imperialist. It was not simply that he hoped to preserve and protect the empire; interventionists such as Gladstone could make the same claim. What made him an imperialist was his willingness to pay for British influence in the periphery. In the face of the rising costs and competition, Rosebery advanced Britain's imperial position, whereas Gladstone would have pulled back.

Conservatives

The Conservatives' primary economic constituency, the service sector of southeast England, also faced rising foreign competition at the turn of the century. Investors and traders from the other great powers became increasingly aggressive in their search for new markets, and their governments proved to be more than willing to help them with the annexation of colonies. The periphery would soon be divided between the great powers, so British imperialists would have to act quickly to get what they wanted. Consequently, the Conservative Party should have become even more willing than before to annex marginal territory and stand firm against threats to the empire.

Salisbury once again became prime minister in 1895. Unlike in 1886, the government he formed was not exclusively a Conservative one; he also invited Liberal Unionists into the cabinet. Although this change had important implications for domestic policy, specifically the question of Irish home rule, it should have had little impact on grand strategy. First, as explained above, the strategic interests of Liberal manufacturers were already rapidly converging with those of the Conservative gentlemanly capitalists in the 1890s. No longer did the two parties debate whether to retain the empire or cut it loose; instead, they only quibbled over how quickly it should expand. Thus, the Liberal Unionists should have found themselves at home with the imperialist Conservatives. Second, the Liberal Unionists were clearly the junior partners in the government: only 70 members of Parliament were Liberal Unionists in 1895, as opposed to 341 Conservatives (versus 177 Liberals and 82 Irish Nationalists).[42] Salisbury wanted the Liberal Unionists' support because he thought it would make the Conservatives stronger in the long run (the two parties eventually merged), but he still would have had a majority in Parliament without them. Finally, Liberal Unionist politicians were more likely to be aristocrats than their counterparts in the rump Liberal Party, so they were more likely to represent "gentlemanly capitalists" than Liberals. Thus, there is no reason to think that the governments of Lord Salisbury (1895–1902) and Arthur Balfour (1902–5) should have followed any peripheral strategy other than imperialism.

This is exactly what they did.[43] Salisbury, who simultaneously served as prime minister and foreign minister until 1900, pursued a strategy that was

[42] Martin Pugh, *The Making of Modern British Politics, 1867–1939*, 2d ed. (Cambridge, Mass.: Blackwell, 1993), 69.
[43] See J. A. S. Grenville, *Lord Salisbury and Foreign Policy: The Close of the Nineteenth Century* (London: Athlone, 1964); Roberts, *Salisbury*, chaps. 36–38, 40–47; F. H. Hinsley, "British Foreign Policy and Colonial Questions, 1895–1904," in *The Cambridge History of the British Empire*, vol. 3, ed. E. A. Benians, Sir James Butler, and C. E. Carrington (Cambridge: Cambridge University Press, 1967), 490–535; Lord Newton, *Lord Lansdowne: A Biography* (London: Macmillan, 1929), chaps. 6–7, 8–10, 12–14; George Monger, *The End of Isolation: British Foreign Policy, 1900–1907* (London: Nelson, 1963), chaps. 4–8. Also useful are Langer, *Diplomacy of Imperialism*; Steele, *Lord Salisbury*, chaps. 13–14; Robert Taylor, *Lord Salisbury* (London: Allen Lane, 1975), chap. 10; Monger, *End of Isolation*, chaps. 1–3; A. L. Kennedy, *Salisbury, 1830–1903: Portrait of a Statesman* (London: Murray, 1953), chaps. 16–17, 19–20; Hinsley, "British Foreign Policy and Colonial Questions," 490–535; Denis Judd, *Balfour and the British Empire: A Study in Imperial Evolution, 1874–1932* (London: Macmillan, 1968), chaps. 4, 12, 15; Blanche E. C. Dugdale, *Arthur James Balfour*, vol. 1 (London: Hutchinson, 1936), chaps. 17–18; Keith M. Wilson, *Empire and Continent: Studies in British Foreign Policy from the 1880s to the First World War* (London: Mansell, 1987); Geoffrey Miller, *Straits: British Policy towards the Ottoman Empire and the Origins of the Dardanelles Campaign* (Hull: University of Hull Press, 1997); Morrell, *Britain in the Pacific Islands*, 279, 309; Cain and Hopkins, *British Imperialism*, vol. 1; Iain Smith, "The Origins of the South African War, 1899–1902: A Reappraisal," *South African Historical Journal* 22 (May 1990): 24–60; Shula Marks, "Scrambling for South Africa," *Journal of African History* 23, no. 1 (1982): 97–113; G. N. Sanderson, "The Nile Basin and the Eastern Horn, 1870–1908," in *The Cambridge History of Africa*, vol. 6, ed. Roland Oliver and G. N. Sanderson (Cambridge: Cambridge University Press, 1985), 592–679.

more aggressively imperialist than that of any of his predecessors, including his own in 1886–92. By 1895, most of the world had already been divided up between the European powers or was held by independent peripheral countries whose self-rule was commonly recognized (China, the Ottoman Empire, and Latin American states). Nevertheless, the Conservatives proposed, carried out, or lent their support to a number of schemes that were intended to extend the reach of the British Empire.

Lord Salisbury and Arthur Balfour (July 1895–December 1905)

Interventionism

Coercive diplomacy

- Forced Turkey to back out of an agreement to give France a coaling station in Muscat; accepted a treaty that gave Britain control over the foreign policy of Kuwait.
- Negotiated an agreement with Russia to set the Great Wall as the dividing line between the two countries' railway concessions in China; sought German support in opposing the expansion of Russian influence over China.
- Invaded the Sudan and defeated the Mahdists, an Islamic movement opposed to British and Ottoman rule in Egypt. With the same forces, induced France to recognize British predominance over the upper Nile.

Overseas bases

- Enlarged the colony of Hong Kong and leased the port of Weihaiwei in response to Russia's acquisition of Port Arthur and Talienwan.

Imperialism

Territorial settlements

- Proposed the partition of the Ottoman Empire between Britain (Syria, Mesopotamia), Russia (Asia Minor), Austria (Salonica), Italy (Albania), and France (Tripoli, Morocco).
- Negotiated a treaty with Germany to trade British rights over Samoa for Tonga, Niue, the northern Solomon Islands, and a strip of land between the Gold Coast and Togoland.
- Negotiated a treaty with Germany to delineate separate spheres of influence within the Portuguese Empire. Specified that any Portuguese concessions to one side required equivalent compensation to the other.

Landmass annexations

- Challenged France for control over the upper Niger River, resulting in the establishment of the British Northern Niger and Southern Niger protectorates.

[217]

- Provided covert assistance for an unsuccessful revolt in the Boer state of Transvaal. Subsequently demanded that British gold prospectors be given the right to vote in Transvaal, a change that would have resulted in the annexation of the country to the British Empire. When refused, fought a three-year war against the Boers and forcibly annexed both Transvaal and the Orange Free State.

Interestingly, this government experienced an internal conflict over grand strategy similar to that which played out between Gladstone and Rosebery in 1892–95. As the Conservative Party became more aggressively imperialist, Salisbury fell out of step with the rest of his cabinet, particularly Colonial Minister Joseph Chamberlain. Chamberlain, who believed that the government should do everything in its ability to promote British trade and investment in the periphery, found Salisbury's patient diplomacy to be frustratingly passive.[44] Against Salisbury's wishes, Chamberlain responded aggressively to France's attempt to establish control over the upper Niger River, tried to convince the cabinet to threaten war against France during a dispute over control of the Sudan (the Fashoda Crisis), and conspired to overthrow Boer rule in southern Africa (the Jameson Raid). In this last case, his actions contributed to the escalation of a conflict that culminated in the Boer War of 1899–1902. After the loss of much blood and treasure, the Conservatives defeated and reannexed Transvaal, as well as the Orange Free State, to the British Empire.

Chamberlain was not the only minister in the government who agitated for a more assertive strategy. In August 1898, Arthur Balfour overrode a bedridden Salisbury to negotiate a treaty that determined how the Portuguese Empire would be divided between Britain and Germany if Portugal gave it up. Lord Lansdowne, who took over the Foreign Office in 1900, was also more hawkish than Salisbury.[45] Over the course of the late nineteenth century, upstarts in both the Liberal and Conservative parties managed to force their longtime leaders to concede to an increasingly imperialist grand strategy. When coalitional imperatives butted against the ingrained preferences of independent-minded leaders, it was the latter that gave way—just as the theory predicts.

1905–14: THE PREWAR EQUILIBRIUM

By 1905, almost all of Africa and Asia had been carved up by the imperial powers. As long as the United States kept Latin America off-limits, the only

[44] Peter T. Marsh, *Joseph Chamberlain: Entrepreneur in Politics* (New Haven: Yale University Press, 1994), 366, 428, 434, 448–50; Richard Jay, *Joseph Chamberlain: A Political Study* (Oxford: Clarendon, 1981), 188–95, 208–10, 217.
[45] Monger, *End of Isolation*, 75–76.

major territories that remained were ones in which Great Britain already had a strong commercial presence, the Ottoman Empire and China. Britain could not annex territory from either of these states without provoking a sharp counterreaction from the other great powers, and it could not govern them without an expensive occupying force. For the time being, international constraints would make it impossible for British leaders to pursue further expansion on the same scale as they had in the late nineteenth century.

Liberals

When the Liberals returned to power in December 1905, international trade was on the upswing. Merchandise exports revived significantly in both core and peripheral markets, growing from less than 16 percent of the national income in 1894–1903 to over 20 percent in 1904–13. Yet, the revival of the international economy did not mean the end of high tariffs and stiff competition. To sustain their recovery, British manufacturers needed colonial markets as much as ever before. Consequently, their representatives in the Liberal Party should have remained imperialist, albeit still less so than the Conservatives. Liberals might not have found new territories to annex; as noted above, all the low-hanging fruit had already been picked. Unlike the interventionist Radicals of the 1860s and 1870s, however, they should have clung tightly to their existing holdings, even in the face of rising costs for repression and defense.

The Liberals' actual strategy, led by Foreign Minister Edward Grey under prime ministers Henry Campbell-Bannerman and Herbert Asquith, confirms this prediction.[46] Compared to his predecessors, Grey's record in the periphery was not particularly impressive, but, as a self-declared Liberal Imperialist, he was clearly devoted to the empire. Not only did Grey maintain all of the territory annexed by the previous government, but he also secured a major extension of Britain's commitments in Persia. To prevent the entire country from falling under Russian control, Grey negotiated to partition it into separate spheres of influence. The best evidence that Grey was an imperialist was not his record in the periphery, however; it was his willingness to enter into a catastrophic world war to protect the empire from Britain's strategic competitors, as I explain in chapter 7.

---

[46] See F. H. Hinsley, ed., *British Foreign Policy under Sir Edward Grey* (Cambridge: Cambridge University Press, 1977); Keith M. Wilson, *The Policy of the Entente: Essays on the Determinants of British Foreign Policy, 1904–1914* (Cambridge: Cambridge University Press, 1985); C. J. Lowe and M. L. Dockrill, *The Mirage of Power: British Foreign Policy, 1902–1914*, vol. 1 (London: Routledge and Kegan Paul, 1972); Keith Robbins, *Sir Edward Grey: A Biography of Lord Grey of Fallodon* (London: Cassell, 1971), chaps. 7–16; Zara S. Steiner, *Britain and the Origins of the First World War* (London: Macmillan, 1977); Max Beloff, *Britain's Liberal Empire, 1897–1921* (London: Methuen, 1969).

Henry Campbell-Bannerman, Herbert Asquith (December 1905–August 1914)[47]

Imperialism
Territorial settlements
- Negotiated a treaty with Russia to divide Persia into separate spheres of influence (de facto protectorates).
- Oversaw the union of Transvaal, Orange Free State, Cape Colony, and Natal into the British colony of South Africa.
- Agreed to renegotiate the Anglo-German Treaty of 1898, which specified the prospective division of Portugal's colonies, on terms that were moderately more favorable to Germany.

Conservatives

At the turn of the century, the Conservatives' primary economic constituency, the gentlemanly capitalists, enjoyed a revival of fortunes similar to that experienced by Liberal manufacturers. Exports of services rose from approximately 6.0 percent of the national income in 1894–1903 to 7.5 percent in 1904–1913, while income from overseas investment grew from 7.0 percent to 8.5 percent. Yet, also like manufacturers, the gentlemanly capitalists could not afford to relax their grip on the empire. All of the competitive pressures that had led to the New Imperialism of the late nineteenth century still existed in the early twentieth century; indeed, the acquisition of so many new colonial markets was partly responsible for the gentlemanly capitalists' continued prosperity. Consequently, the Conservatives should have remained fervently committed to the empire, even more so than the Liberals. Whereas the Liberals had to mediate between their constituents' interests in both the core and periphery, the Conservatives could focus single-mindedly on the latter.

The Conservatives failed to oust the Liberals from power at any point in 1905–1914, so it is not possible to evaluate their strategy in this period with absolute certainty. However, their policy positions and campaign rhetoric do support the theory, in that they took every opportunity to attack the Liberal government for being soft on the empire.[48] Most notably, they argued that it compromised the security of the colonies by limiting the

---

[47] Britain entered World War I in August 1914; Asquith formed a coalition government in May 1915 and resigned as prime minister in December 1916.

[48] Andrew S. Thompson, "The Language of Imperialism and the Meanings of Empire: Imperial Discourse in British Politics, 1895–1914," *Journal of British Studies* 36, no. 2 (April 1997): 147–77; Wilfried Fest, "Jingoism and Xenophobia in the Electioneering Strategies of British Ruling Elites before 1914," in *Nationalist and Racialist Movements in Britain and Germany before 1914*, ed. Paul M. Kennedy and Anthony J. Nicholls (Oxford: Macmillan, 1981), 171–89; Frans Coetzee, *For Party or Country: Nationalism and the Dilemmas of Popular Conservatism in*

construction of dreadnoughts in 1905–9. It is questionable as to whether the Conservatives could have done any better in office; after all, they had cut naval estimates in the budgetary crisis of 1905, and their call to boost revenues with tariff reform had proved to be disastrously unpopular in the election of 1906.[49] Nevertheless, they retained their essential identity as the party of the British Empire, and there is little reason to doubt the sincerity of their interest in its security.

1918–31: THE POSTWAR EQUILIBRIUM

During World War I, British and Dominion forces seized enormous swaths of land in the German and Ottoman Empires. Thus, the Allies' victory in 1918 gave Britain one final opportunity for grand imperial expansion. If the British government wanted to claim these territories for itself, it could quickly and easily secure its gains. The only major constraint on its peripheral strategy was domestic. In the early 1920s, charges on the war debt peaked at 8.4 percent of the national income, consuming approximately 40 percent of the annual budget. Thus, any new additions to the empire would have to be bought on the cheap.

National Coalition

World War I was a disaster for the Liberal Party. As the struggle ground on into 1915–16, Prime Minister Asquith came under increasing criticism from Conservatives and Liberals alike for his failure to mobilize the economy for total war.[50] Thus, the stage was set for a skilled politician to build a new coalition and usurp control from Asquith. David Lloyd George fit the role perfectly: he was energetic, charismatic, and ideologically flexible. Promising a more vigorous prosecution of the war, he won the support of approximately half of his fellow Liberal MPs and negotiated the formation of a new government with the Conservative Party. Lloyd George became prime minister, Arthur Balfour became foreign minister, and the rest of the cabinet was divided between thirteen Conservatives, seven Liberals, and

Edwardian England (New York: Oxford University Press, 1990), chaps. 3–5; Rhodri Williams, *Defending the Empire: The Conservative Party and British Defense Policy, 1899–1915* (New Haven: Yale University Press, 1991).

[49] David D'Lugo and Ronald Rogowski, "The Anglo-German Naval Race and Comparative Constitutional 'Fitness,'" in *The Domestic Bases of Grand Strategy*, ed. Richard Rosecrance and Arthur A. Stein (Ithaca: Cornell University Press, 1993), 65–95.

[50] John Turner, *British Politics and the Great War: Coalition and Conflict, 1915–1918* (New Haven: Yale University Press, 1992), chap. 3.

two Labourites.[51] Lloyd George also created an inner War Cabinet, which initially comprised himself, one Labourite, and three Conservatives.

The resulting government was well balanced. Control over key posts was divided, so policymaking required a significant degree of compromise. Conservative ministers were in the majority, but Lloyd George's position at the top of the pyramid provided a strong counterweight for the Liberals. In issue-areas in which the parties had divergent interests, key decisions would be highly contested.

Since Liberals had a much greater stake in European markets than Conservatives, the coalition government would be deeply divided over Britain's strategy toward the great powers (see chapter 7). In contrast, there was little reason for acrimony over Britain's strategy toward the periphery. The gentlemanly capitalists of the Conservative Party still had enormous holdings throughout the globe, and the manufacturers of the Liberal Party remained highly reliant on export to peripheral markets. Neither constituency's competitive position had improved enough since the late nineteenth century that it should have wanted to break with the imperialist consensus. The political economy of Great Britain dictated broad support for imperialism within the Lloyd George government, tempered only by a strong budgetary constraint.

These predictions are borne out closely by the facts.[52] Lloyd George extended British influence throughout the world, and he managed to do so at a low cost. At the San Remo Conference of 1920, he worked out an arrangement with France and Italy to divide up the Middle East between their respective empires, with the lion's share going to Britain. He then convinced Woodrow Wilson to sign off on this arrangement with a compromise, the Mandate System, which gave the League of Nations nominal authority over the captured colonies. The advance of empire was not entirely consistent; Lloyd George withdrew British troops from northern Persia and granted independence to Egypt, Iraq, and Transjordan once it became evident that nationalist opposition within these states would force Britain to fight costly wars of occupation to maintain the status quo. However, Britain remained

[51] David Butler and Gareth Butler, *British Political Facts, 1900–1985*, 6th ed. (New York: St. Martin's, 1986), 9–12.

[52] See David Gilmour, *Curzon* (London: Murray, 1994); Michael L. Dockrill and J. Douglas Goold, *Peace without Promise: Britain and the Peace Conferences, 1919–23* (Hamden, Conn.: Archon, 1981); Inbal Rose, *Conservatism and Foreign Policy during the Lloyd George Coalition, 1918–1922* (London: Cass, 1999), 239–41; G. H. Bennett, *British Foreign Policy during the Curzon Period, 1919–24* (London: Macmillan, 1995). Also useful are Harold Nicolson, *Curzon: The Last Phase, 1919–1925* (New York: Harcourt, Brace, 1939); F. P. Walters, *The History of the League of Nations* (London: Oxford University Press, 1960); John Darwin, "Imperialism in Decline? Tendencies in British Imperial Policy between the Wars," *Historical Journal* 23, no. 3 (September 1980): 657–79; Beloff, *Britain's Liberal Empire*, 297–302; Max Beloff, *Dream of Commonwealth, 1921–42* (London: Macmillan, 1989).

the preponderant power in the Middle East, with extensive economic and military influence even in the territories it gave up.

David Lloyd George (November 1918–October 1922)[53]

Interventionism

Partial retreats

- Granted independence to Egypt, which Britain had annexed during World War I; however, maintained military forces there without Egyptian consent.
- Removed troops from northern Persia, but maintained forces in the southern part of the country. Negotiated unsuccessfully with Persia for a treaty on trade, economic aid, and military assistance.
- Forced Turkey to accept Allied occupation forces, a heavy indemnity, and international control over the Dardanelles (Treaty of Sèvres). When Turkish nationalists successfully fought back, negotiated a withdrawal.

Overseas bases

- Made Iraq, Transjordan, and Palestine into de facto protectorates under the supervision of the League of Nations (Class A Mandates). In the face of nationalist resistance, granted partial independence to Iraq and Transjordan in exchange for oil concessions and military bases.

Imperialism

Landmass annexations

- Made German East Africa and parts of Cameroon and Togoland into de facto colonies under the supervision of the League of Nations (Class B Mandates).
- Allowed South Africa to annex German Southwest Africa, Australia to annex New Guinea, and New Zealand to annex Western Samoa (Class C Mandates).

Conservatives

The fall of the Lloyd George coalition in 1922 brought the Conservatives back into power, this time under Prime Minister Bonar Law. Neither he nor the government lasted long: Law died seven months later, and his successor, Stanley Baldwin, held office for only eight more months. During that time, Law and Baldwin were occupied almost exclusively with great power

---

[53] Lloyd George became prime minister in December 1916; World War I ended in November 1918.

politics. When Baldwin and the Conservatives returned to office in late 1924, however, several disturbances in the periphery demanded their attention. As in previous periods, they should have sought to shore up the empire as best as possible. Yet, the crushing war debt should also have forced them to consider making modest concessions to avoid costly conflicts.

This prediction characterizes the Conservatives' strategy fairly well.[54] They did not add any territory to the empire, but neither did they cede any. They were willing to negotiate over British troop deployments and commercial rights in Turkey, Egypt, Persia, and China, but they refused to give up anything of importance, such as control over the Suez Canal. The Conservatives had no intention of turning away from the periphery; rather, they sought to keep as much of their influence as possible without having to devote scarce resources to the suppression of nationalist movements.

A. Bonar Law and Stanley Baldwin (October 1922–January 1924, November 1924–June 1929)

Interventionism
Partial retreats
- Negotiated with Egypt over the deployment of British forces but rejected demands that they be removed from the Suez Canal zone.
- Negotiated with Persia over the deployment of British troops in the Persian Gulf but rejected demands that they be removed entirely.

Diplomatic settlement
- Paid Turkey £500,000 to grant Iraq ownership of Mosul.

Imperialism
Colonial entrenchment
- Maintained control over all of Britain's existing colonies in the face of growing nationalist opposition.

Labour

In December 1923, Conservative prime minister Baldwin decided to call an election in hopes of winning a mandate to reverse Britain's long-standing free-trade policy. The effort failed miserably: the Conservatives lost 88 seats, bringing their total down to 259. Though they were still the largest party in Parliament, they lacked a majority, and Baldwin rejected any possibility of a coalition with the 159 Liberal MPs. Thus, the second-largest party, Labour,

[54] See David Dutton, *Austen Chamberlain: Gentleman in Politics* (Bolton: Anderson, 1985); Richard S. Grayson, *Austen Chamberlain and the Commitment to Europe: British Foreign Policy, 1924–29* (London: Cass, 1997).

came to power with only 191 MPs of its own and the tenuous support of the Liberals.[55] With Ramsay MacDonald as the new prime minister and Arthur Henderson at the Foreign Office, Labour finally had the opportunity to prove that its polemics on foreign policy were more than just empty rhetoric.[56] Prior to the war, the party had made a number of pronouncements on the evils of imperialism and the desirability of self-determination. This sentiment carried through to the end of the war, when Labour opposed the annexation of German and Ottoman territory.[57] If ideology were the primary determinant of grand strategy, the Labour government of 1924 clearly should have begun the process of decolonization.

The theory guiding this study renders a very different prediction. As explained in the previous chapter, the Labour Party began its existence with a narrow base of support, confined almost exclusively to the coal mining sector. This constituency was more dependent on trade with the great powers, and less dependent on trade with the periphery, than any other major societal group in Britain. After 1900, when 20–30 percent of coal production was exported, approximately 80 percent of it was sent to continental Europe and the United States.[58] As long as Labour representatives were elected almost exclusively from coal mining districts, the party would have little interest in imperialism. Without any economic stake in imperial markets, it should have regarded the empire as a waste of budgetary resources. Thus, Labour's pre-1924 opposition to imperialism is entirely consistent with the theory.

In the early 1920s, when Labour experienced a dramatic increase in support, the sectoral basis of its electoral coalition changed. No longer was it confined to coal; instead, it expanded into the Liberals' primary constituency, manufacturing. Like coal, the manufacturing sector had an interest in core markets; yet, unlike coal, it had also become highly dependent on the periphery. Following the election of December 1923, Labour was flush with new voters and MPs who had a strong interest in imperialism. To maintain their support, and thereby remain a viable governing party, the party's leaders would have to reverse their long-standing position on the empire. They did not need to become as aggressively imperialist as the Conservatives, whose constituency in the financial service sector had a greater stake in the empire than either manufacturing or coal mining, but they would need to become as imperialist as the Liberals, whose coalition they were taking over.

[55] David Marquand, *Ramsay MacDonald* (London: Cape, 1977), 283, 296.
[56] On Labour's foreign policy positions before 1924, see William P. Maddox, *Foreign Relations in British Labour Politics* (Cambridge, Mass.: Harvard University Press, 1934).
[57] Partha Sarathi Gupta, *Imperialism and the British Labour Movement, 1914–1964* (London: Macmillan, 1975), chap. 2.
[58] Roy Church, *The History of the British Coal Industry, 1830–1913* (Oxford: Clarendon, 1986), 19, 35; Barry Supple, *The History of the British Coal Industry, 1913–1946* (Oxford: Clarendon, 1987), 174–75, 273, 292–93.

Labour's actual strategy toward the periphery in 1924 resoundingly confirms this prediction.[59] Once the party expanded its electoral coalition to include the manufacturing sector, its outlook changed:

> As Labour grew stronger and gradually took the place of the divided Liberals as the official Opposition, the unyielding certainties of an anticapitalist, anti-imperialist propaganda began to erode. . . . Proximity to power quickened the rupture between the pragmatic mainstream of the party and its more ideological left wing, not only on domestic issues but on foreign policy as well.[60]

On taking office, the new secretary of state for Colonial Affairs reportedly told his staff, "I've been sent here to see that there's no mucking about with the British Empire."[61] The Labour government not only maintained Britain's grip on the colonies, but also cracked down hard on nationalists in India.

J. Ramsay MacDonald (January 1924–November 1924)

Interventionism
Partial retreats
- Negotiated with Egypt over the redeployment of British troops but refused to withdraw from the Suez Canal zone.

Imperialism
Colonial entrenchment
- Granted the British Raj the authority to detain individuals without trial in India.
- Maintained control over all of the colonies in the face of growing nationalist opposition.

---

[59] See George Glasgow, *MacDonald as Diplomatist: The Foreign Policy of the First Labour Government in Great Britain* (London: Cape, 1924); David Carlton, *MacDonald versus Henderson: The Foreign Policy of the Second Labour Government* (London: Macmillan, 1970). Also useful are Henry R. Winkler, *Paths Not Taken: British Labour and International Policy in the 1920s* (Chapel Hill: University of North Carolina, 1994); Beloff, *Dream of Commonwealth*; Marquand, *Ramsay MacDonald*; Richard W. Lyman, *The First Labour Government, 1924* (London: Chapman and Hall, 1957); Gupta, *Imperialism and the British Labour Movement*, chaps. 3–4; Stephen Howe, *Anticolonialism in British Politics: The Left and the End of Empire, 1918–1964* (Oxford: Clarendon, 1993), 40–52; Daniel Silverfarb, *Britain's Informal Empire in the Middle East: A Case Study of Iraq, 1929–1941* (New York: Oxford University Press, 1986); Howard Brasted and Carl Bridge, "The British Labour Party 'Nabobs' and Indian Reform, 1924–31," *Journal of Imperial and Commonwealth History* 17, no. 3 (May 1989): 396–412.

[60] Winkler, *Paths Not Taken*, 193. The postwar influx of Liberal politicians into the Labour Party also strengthened its internationalist tendencies; see Catherine A. Cline, *Recruits to Labour: The British Labour Party, 1914–1931* (Syracuse: Syracuse University Press, 1963), chap. 4.

[61] Quoted in Darby, *Three Faces of Imperialism*, 123.

When Labour returned to power in 1929–31, it held fast to this position. It continued to resist local independence movements, seeking to retain metropolitan prerogatives over the colonies as long as possible. It conceded that India would require a new constitution; however, the one it proposed was intended to weaken nationalists (especially the Congress Party) in favor of regional interests that benefited from British rule. Despite its anti-imperialist ideology, Labour proved to be just as willing as the Liberals to swallow its principles and defend its new constituents' interest in the empire.

J. Ramsay MacDonald (June 1929–August 1931)

Interventionism
Partial retreats
- Granted independence to Iraq but reserved the right to maintain two airbases, transport armed forces across the country, and be the exclusive supplier of the Iraqi military.
- Negotiated with China over the revision of the "unequal treaties" but refused to relinquish Britain's special position in Shanghai and Tientsin.

Imperialism
Colonial entrenchment
- Denied the right of self-determination to India; instead, advocated that it should have a new constitution based on the principle of federalism, which would weaken nationalist cohesion by strengthening regional governments.
- Maintained control over all of Britain's existing colonies in the face of growing nationalist opposition.

1931–39: EMPIRE IN DEPRESSION

After carving up the German and Ottoman empires with its allies in World War I, Britain had nowhere left to expand. It annexed all of the land that it could easily control, and it made protectorates of many other territories that would have been too costly to pacify and govern directly. Any further advances could be won only at great cost to Britain's diplomatic relations and overburdened military. To make matters worse, the international environment was becoming increasingly dangerous in the 1930s. Imperial Japan threatened Britain's position in all of East Asia, while Nazi Germany diverted defense planners' attention from the empire to the home isles. Britain certainly could have withdrawn from the periphery, but it would have been hard-pressed to advance.

Domestic constraints were just as troubling as the international situation. After 1931, it was not simply the war debt that limited Britain's peripheral strategy; the Great Depression caused a collapse in government revenue at a time when it was needed most to protect the empire. Thus, the substantive implications of an imperialist strategy continued to change. No longer would imperialists be defined by their desire to extend the empire, as they had been in the late nineteenth century; instead, they would be distinguished by their willingness to pay the costs required to maintain the existing empire against nationalist uprisings and external threats.

Conservatives

As the Great Depression deepened, the Labour Party found itself increasingly unable to govern. The economic collapse made it impossible to balance the budget without radical tax increases or severe spending cuts, while pressure on the pound was rapidly draining Britain's gold reserves. Paralyzed by internal division, the government resigned in late August 1931. In its place, MacDonald formed a "National" coalition with the Conservatives, most Liberals, and a few Labourites. Initially, the National government was expected to be a short-term expediency, lasting just long enough to enact austerity measures and save the pound. However, each of its principals agreed that it was in their interest to maintain the arrangement through the upcoming election. For the Conservatives, this decision was a smashing success: in November 1931, they won an unprecedented 473 of 610 seats in Parliament.

Despite their overwhelming victory, the Conservatives maintained their commitment to coalition government, taking only eleven of twenty positions in the cabinet and keeping MacDonald as the prime minister. The Foreign Office was given to John Simon, leader of the "Liberal Nationals." Though this group identified as Liberal, its members tended to lean to the right of the political spectrum, even to the point of supporting imperial tariffs in 1932. At that point, the two "true" Liberals in the cabinet, Herbert Samuel and Archibald Sinclair, resigned. The Liberal Nationals never formally merged with the Conservatives, but they are considered by most historians to have been de facto Conservatives. Thus, the coalition was less "National" than initially appears: "Before the resignation of the Samuelite Liberals the government was a genuine, if unbalanced, coalition. After September 1932 it looked like a Conservative administration which happened to have a non-Conservative at its head and several other non-Conservatives among its adherents."[62]

[62] David Dutton, *Simon: A Political Biography of Sir John Simon* (London: Aurum, 1992), 161. See also Richard S. Grayson, *Liberals, International Relations, and Appeasement: The Liberal Party, 1919–1939* (London: Cass, 2001), 8; Chris Cook, *A Short History of the Liberal Party, 1900–1997,*

The last pretense that the National government was a true coalition ended in June 1935, when its principals traded positions: MacDonald became lord president of the council, while Baldwin became prime minister. Simon stayed in the government but was replaced at the Foreign Office by the Conservative Samuel Hoare. The balance of power within the cabinet was ratified by the elections of November 1935, in which 386 Conservatives and 45 other National candidates won seats in Parliament, against only 154 Labourites and 21 Liberals.[63]

Just like the Lloyd George coalition of 1916–22, the National government raises some complex analytic issues. On the one hand, members of the Labour and Liberal parties initially held the prime and foreign ministries, and their combined strength within the cabinet was not insignificant. On the other hand, the coalition's survival was entirely at the mercy of Conservative parliamentarians, who at any moment could have torn down the government and replaced it with their own. MacDonald was not nearly as strong of a leader as Lloyd George, and his health was steadily degenerating through 1931–35. Meanwhile, Simon was congenitally indecisive and frequently sought the advice of the cabinet in formulating foreign policy. The real political force behind the government was not MacDonald or Simon, but rather the leader of the Conservative Party, Stanley Baldwin. In light of these circumstances, I treat the National government after November 1931 not as a coalition but rather as de facto Conservative. MacDonald was not a Conservative puppet, but neither did the left have much independent influence over Britain's foreign policy.

In any case, the partisan balance of power within the cabinet should not have made much of a difference to its peripheral strategy in 1931–39. In the depths of the Great Depression and the collapse of international trade, manufacturers had to depend even more than usual on demand within the British Dominions. Not all of the colonies were equally helpful; for example, the combination of native industry, tariff increases, and Japanese competition had a devastating effect on British textile exports to India.[64] Nevertheless, the empire's share of Britain's total exports increased from 42 percent in 1925–29 to 49 percent in 1935–39.[65] As a result, the Liberal Party should have

---

5th ed. (London: Macmillan, 1998), 116–19, 122–23; Roy Douglas, *The History of the Liberal Party, 1895–1970* (London: Sidgwick and Jackson, 1971), 233–34. For a moderately dissenting view, see Nick Smart, *The National Government, 1931–40* (London: Macmillan, 1999), chaps. 1–2; Philip Williamson, *National Crisis and National Government: British Politics, the Economy, and Empire, 1926–1932* (Cambridge: Cambridge University Press, 1992), 483–87; John Ramsden, *The Age of Balfour and Baldwin, 1902–1940* (London: Longman, 1978), 325–30.

[63] Ramsden, *Age of Balfour and Baldwin,* 345.

[64] Arthur Redford, *Manchester Merchants and Foreign Trade, 1850–1939,* vol. 2 (Manchester: Manchester University Press, 1956), chap. 22.

[65] Michael Barratt Brown, *After Imperialism* (London: Heinemann, 1963), 111.

remained solidly imperialist. The same logic applied to the Conservatives' constituency of gentlemanly capitalists: in times of international economic and political turmoil, the empire became a safe haven for British investors.

This combination of preferences and constraints led to predicable results.[66] As war drew nearer, the National government became increasingly cautious about using the armed forces to put down nationalist uprisings in British colonies and client states. It was not willing to sacrifice any vital imperial interests, but it did seek to conserve its military and financial resources wherever possible. In Egypt, for example, it negotiated a treaty in which it renounced the right of intervention and granted Egyptians control over their foreign and defense policy. In return, Britain retained a garrison at the Suez Canal and most of its influence over the Sudan.

In India, the National government was unable to convince nationalists to make the concessions it wanted, so it simply imposed its own solution, a decentralized federal constitution. It allowed extensive powers of self-rule, but it did not go so far as to grant dominion status to India. Parliament retained ultimate authority over the country, with emergency powers delegated to an appointed British governor-general. According to John Darwin, "the new arrangement was based not upon a strategy of slow unending retreat but on what appears in retrospect a bold attempt to destroy that facet of Indian nationalism—the all-India operations of the Congress—which threatened to turn India away from full participation in the imperial system."[67] International and domestic constraints forced the Conservative-led coalition to be more circumspect than usual, but it did not alter their imperialist outlook.

J. Ramsay MacDonald, Stanley Baldwin, Neville Chamberlain (August 1931–September 1939)[68]

Interventionism
   Partial retreats
   • Negotiated a treaty with Egypt in which Britain renounced the right of intervention and granted local control over

[66] British grand strategy in the 1930s is far too complex to be addressed adequately by general sources. On specific peripheral issues, see Laila Morsy, "The Military Clauses of the Anglo-Egyptian Treaty of Friendship and Alliance, 1936," *International Journal of Middle East Studies* 16, no. 1 (March 1984): 67–97; Steven Morewood, "Appeasement from Strength: The Making of the 1936 Anglo-Egyptian Treaty of Friendship and Alliance," *Diplomacy and Statecraft* 7, no. 3 (November 1996): 530–62; John Darwin, "An Undeclared Empire: The British in the Middle East, 1918–39," *Journal of Imperial and Commonwealth History* 27, no. 2 (May 1999): 159–76; Smart, *National Government*, chap. 3; Paul Knaplund, *Britain, Commonwealth, and Empire, 1901–1955* (London: Hamish Hamilton, 1956); R. J. Moore, *The Crisis of Indian Unity, 1917–1940* (Oxford: Clarendon Press, 1974); Darwin, "Imperialism in Decline?"
[67] Darwin, "Imperialism in Decline?" 677.
[68] Britain entered World War II in September 1939; Chamberlain resigned as prime minister in May 1940.

foreign and defense policy in return for a garrison at the Suez Canal and influence over the Sudan.

Imperialism

Colonial entrenchment

- Created a tariff wall around the British Empire at the Ottawa Conference of 1932 to promote imperial economic integration and exclude foreign goods.
- Refused the right of self-determination to India; imposed a new constitution that weakened nationalist cohesion by strengthening regional governments.
- Maintained control over all of Britain's existing colonies in the face of growing nationalist opposition.

Labour

Ramsay MacDonald's decision to defect from his party and form the National government had a devastating effect on Labour. Shorn of its leadership and discredited by its inability to deal with the economic crisis, it suffered severe losses in the election of November 1931. Despite winning 30.6 percent of the vote, it managed to secure only 52 seats in Parliament.[69] Of all of the senior ministers who served in the Labour government of 1929–31, the only one to retain his seat was George Lansbury, a septuagenarian pacifist. For lack of a better alternative, Lansbury was appointed party leader, and a relatively unknown former junior minister, Clement Attlee, became deputy leader. Labour did not begin to recover until 1935, when Attlee replaced Lansbury and the party increased its parliamentary delegation to 154 seats.

The disaster of 1931 had critical implications for the party's strategic interests. Nearly all of the manufacturing districts that Labour had captured from the Liberals in 1924 elected a Conservative, leaving Labour with little more than the coal mining districts that constituted its base prior to World War I. The result was another dramatic shift in the party's political-economic coalition. The manufacturing sector was highly dependent on peripheral markets, whereas coal was not. Since Labour's delegation in Parliament no longer represented a large number of manufacturing districts, it lost a great deal of its interest in imperialism.

The extent of this change should not be overstated. Most of the voters who had switched their affiliation to Labour in the 1920s remained loyal to their new party, so it retained a strong interest in imperialism at the

---

[69] Robert Pearce, *Attlee* (London: Longman, 1997), 49.

grassroots level. Even if only coal districts elected Labour representatives to Parliament in 1931, the continued support of manufacturing districts would be critical for the eventual revival of the party. Its new leaders could not ignore the imperialist tendencies of the manufacturing sector without consigning themselves to permanent minority status. On the balance, the Labour Party should not have become as stridently anti-imperialist as it had been prior to World War I; however, it very well could have become less imperialist than it had been in 1924–31.

Labour never held power in 1931–39, so it is difficult to determine what strategy it would have adopted if it had. It did, however, take a clear position on the most important peripheral issue confronting the National government, the reform of the Indian constitution, and its position does support the theory. Whereas MacDonald's National coalition resolved on an open-ended transition to dominionhood, limited self-government, and the exclusion of Congress from the constitutional reform process, Attlee called for an explicit timetable for dominionhood, substantial self-government, and broad-based Indian participation in the design of the new constitution.[70] The parties shared the underlying objective of keeping India in the Commonwealth, but they clearly disagreed over the pace and extent of reform.

CONCLUSION

British grand strategy toward the periphery in 1868–1939 was initially marked by a deep partisan cleavage. The Conservatives' socioeconomic coalition comprised two groups: the gentry, which had strong military-colonial interests, and, from the 1880s onward, the London financial services sector, which had an enormous stake in peripheral markets and faced sharp competitive pressures from the other great powers. Both constituencies benefited from the acquisition of colonies. Thus, the Conservatives were consistently imperialist, albeit modulating their strategy to be more or less aggressive in response to domestic and international constraints. In 1874–80, they annexed Transvaal, Cyprus, and Fiji, but, with the Treasury heavily burdened by debt, they did not expand indiscriminately. They did not begin to add huge swaths of undeveloped territory to the British Empire

---

[70] Mesbahuddin Ahmed, "The British Parliamentary Labour Party Stand on India, 1932–1935," *Journal of Indian History* 62, no. 1–3 (1984): 227–46; Howard Brasted and Carl Bridge, "The British Labour Party and Indian Nationalism, 1907–1947," *South Asia* 11, no. 2 (1988): 69–99; John Swift, *Labour in Crisis: Clement Attlee and the Labour Party in Opposition, 1931–40* (Basingstoke: Palgrave, 2001), chap. 3.

until the debt declined and the other great powers began to compete for colonies in the 1880s and 1890s. After World War I, Conservatives were once again constrained by debt and declining government revenue, so they focused on protecting their existing possessions from rising nationalist sentiment and the predation of other great powers.

In contrast, the Liberals' socioeconomic coalition, merchandise exporters, initially had little interest in imperialism. British manufacturers were highly competitive in world markets through the 1860s and 1870s, so they saw no need for their government to undertake costly new commitments in the periphery. Consequently, the Liberal Party adopted a strategy of interventionism. It maintained Britain's global network of military bases and used force when necessary to protect British trade and investment, but it firmly opposed the annexation of new territory. For example, it began preparing for a withdrawal from Egypt shortly after intervening, it allowed the Transvaal Boers to secede from the empire, and it welcomed progress toward self-government in the colonies of settlement.

The decline of the manufacturing sector in the 1880s and 1890s brought about major changes in the Liberals' strategic outlook. Hurt by rising tariff barriers and foreign competition, British exports began losing ground in Europe and the United States. In response, manufacturers became increasingly dependent on less-developed countries to buy their exports. To open new markets and prevent others from being closed off by rival powers, the Liberal Party transitioned from interventionism to imperialism. Merchandise exporters never became as wholly dependent on the periphery as the gentlemanly capitalists, so Liberals never became as aggressively imperialist as the Conservatives. However, the difference between the two parties was not great. By the turn of the century, most Liberals had abandoned any thought of giving up the territories whose annexation their party had opposed in the 1860s, 1870s, and 1880s.

Labour went through a similar transition. Before World War I, it was still a minor party with a very narrow base of support in the coal mining sector. Since almost all of Britain's coal exports were sent to Europe and the United States, Labour voters and politicians had little use for the empire. At the time, they railed against imperialism and called for the independence of any colony that desired it. After World War I, however, they became a major party by winning over the Liberals' manufacturing constituency. Since the long-suffering manufacturing sector was deeply dependent on peripheral markets, Labour shifted its strategy. By the time it rose to power in 1924, it had become just as imperialist as the Liberals. Only when the party was reduced to its coal mining base in the catastrophic election of November 1931 did it become more willing to relax control over the British Empire.

In conclusion, the theory has an excellent predictive record over British grand strategy in the periphery in 1868–1939. All of the governments in this period acted as expected, with each party consistently adapting to changes in its constituents' economic interests. In the next chapter, I consider whether the theory fares as well in explaining an even more complex subject, British grand strategy toward the great powers.

[7]

British Grand Strategy toward
the Great Powers

By any objective standard, British grand strategy toward the great powers from 1868 to 1939 was badly dysfunctional. In 1870–71, Britain stood on the sidelines as Prussia defeated France and unified Germany, creating a dangerous concentration of power at the heart of Europe. The unexpected speed and decisiveness of the war excuses Britain's failure to intervene, but the same cannot be said for its unwillingness to balance the continued rise of German power over the next thirty-five years. Not until 1905 did Britain finally begin to align with France against Germany. However, it refused to commit to a full-fledged alliance until after the outbreak of World War I, forgoing any chance it might have had to deter the conflict.

After World War I, Britain continued to underreact to changes in its external environment. Germany took advantage of every opportunity to challenge the postwar settlement, yet Britain did not oppose it with the threat of force until 1939. Even then, with national survival at stake, Britain failed to form a robust coalition against Germany. Instead, it dithered over negotiations with Soviet Russia, giving Stalin every incentive to make a separate peace with Hitler. Britain also tried to appease Italy and Japan, but it succeeded only in giving its adversaries more time to arm and expand unchecked.

Britain's grand strategy casts serious doubt on the realist claim that states balance against either power or objectively defined threats. To try to account for the anomalies in this case, realists have explored how various second-order factors can affect strategic choice, including offense-defense balance, buck-passing, regime type, intra-alliance bargaining dynamics, and economic interdependence.[1] Though valuable, this literature still falls short of explaining decision makers' underlying goals. British grand strategy responded not only to changes in the international system but also shifts in political control over policymaking.

A clear pattern of partisanship was evident throughout 1868–1939. First, in the mid to late nineteenth century, Conservatives focused on Russia, seeking to check the growth of its power at every opportunity; then, at the beginning of the twentieth century, they reversed their position on Russia and turned against Germany. In contrast, Liberals sought to avoid taking sides in continental politics until the outbreak of World War I. Second, new cleavages arose after the war. The Conservatives supported a harsh indemnity against Germany and refused to recognize the new Soviet regime, while Liberals and Labourites sought to reduce reparations on Germany and foster closer ties with the Soviets. The League of Nations was also a major point of contention: Liberals and Labourites advanced measures that would strengthen international law and collective security, while Conservatives opposed them. Finally, in the mid 1930s, the debate shifted yet again. Conservatives appeased Hitler, while Liberals and Labourites advocated using the League of Nations and an alliance with the Soviet Union to check German expansion. In short, how Britain reacted to changes in its external environment was a function of the partisan composition of its government. Only a theory of societal preferences can account for this variation.

IDEAS AND CULTURE

From an ideational perspective, there are two potential explanations for the recurrent pattern of partisanship in British grand strategy. First, some scholars argue that states' alignment policies are dictated by ideological affinities. Viewed in this light, British diplomacy in the interwar period was less about the pursuit of security than domestic legitimacy.[2] Labour

---

[1] Thomas J. Christensen and Jack Snyder, "Chain Gangs and Passed Bucks: Predicting Alliance Patterns in Multipolarity," *International Organization* 44, no. 2 (spring 1990): 137–68; Randall L. Schweller, "Bandwagoning for Profit: Bringing the Revisionist State Back In," *International Security* 19, no. 1 (summer 1994): 72–107; Robert G. Kaufman, "To Balance or Bandwagon? Alignment Decisions in 1930s Europe," *Security Studies* 1, no. 3 (spring 1992): 417–47; Glenn H. Snyder, *Alliance Politics* (Ithaca: Cornell University Press, 1997); Patricia A. Weitsman, *Dangerous Alliances: Proponents of Peace, Weapons of War* (Stanford: Stanford University Press, 1997); Paul A. Papayoanou, *Power Ties: Economic Interdependence, Balancing, and War* (Ann Arbor: University of Michigan Press, 1999).

[2] Sandra Halperin, "The Politics of Appeasement: The Rise of the Left and European International Relations during the Interwar Period," in *Contested Social Orders and International Politics*, ed. David Skidmore (Nashville: Vanderbilt University Press, 1997), 128–64; Mark L. Haas, *The Ideological Origins of Great Power Politics, 1789–1989* (Ithaca: Cornell University Press, 2005), chap. 4.

supported its socialist brethren in Russia, while the Conservatives appeased Nazi Germany to balance against the threat of communism. Each party believed that the world was engaged in a titanic struggle between rival ideologies and that the fate of foreign regimes would have a major impact on its own prospects for success.

Though intuitively appealing, this interpretation suffers from a number of serious empirical anomalies. First, domestic cleavages over alignment policy in the late nineteenth century directly contradict the theory. The aristocratic Conservatives were ideologically closer to Tsarist Russia than the Liberals, yet the Liberals were far more sanguine about the growth of Russian power in Central Asia and the Balkans. The parties' positions toward Germany prior to World War I are similarly problematic. The Conservatives should have sided with the German constitutional monarchy, while the progressive Liberals should have backed the French republic. In fact, the reverse occurred: Conservatives strongly supported France, while the Liberals sought rapprochement with Germany.

The ideological affinity perspective also underplays a critical fact about Labour in the interwar period: its leadership was openly hostile to British communists and purged them completely from the party's ranks in the mid 1920s.[3] Labourites had a somewhat higher opinion of the Soviet Union than the Comintern or the Communist Party of Great Britain, but they were far from enamored with the Soviet regime. For the Liberals, the ideological gap was even wider. Their laissez-faire principles were in direct opposition to communism, yet the party shared Labour's desire for diplomatic alignment with the Soviet Union. Ideological affinities may have had some influence on the domestic debate over foreign policy, but they could not have been the determining factor.

The other possibility is that ideologies affect policymakers' overarching vision of world order and fundamental international objectives. The Conservatives were the party of nationalism, tradition, and hierarchy, as demonstrated by their devotion to the Anglican Church and the monarchy. In the international sphere, their values were embodied by the British Empire. Therefore, Conservatives should have aligned against whatever countries posed the greatest threat to the empire. In contrast, Liberals and Labourites believed in equality, progressive institutions, and social welfare, as manifested by their support for unemployment insurance and other domestic reforms. In debates over international politics, their ideals were represented in proposals for collective security and the

[3] Stephen White, *Britain and the Bolshevik Revolution* (London: Macmillan, 1979), 214–16; David Carlton, *MacDonald versus Henderson: The Foreign Policy of the Second Labour Government* (London: Macmillan, 1970), 144–47; Andrew J. Williams, *Labour and Russia: The Attitude of the Labour Party to the USSR, 1924–34* (Manchester: Manchester University Press, 1989), 9–10, 213–14.

[237]

advancement of international law. Consequently, Liberals and Labourites should have sought to strengthen the institutions and principles of legitimate international order.

These hypotheses correspond well to partisan cleavages over British grand strategy. However, a closer analysis casts doubt on their explanatory power. First, a sizeable minority of Liberals in the late nineteenth and early twentieth centuries were both domestic progressives and international imperialists. If political ideology were the key determinant of foreign policy preferences, such a pairing should not have been possible. Second, historians have focused overwhelmingly on economic and strategic motives, not ideology, as the driving force behind the expansion of the British Empire. In the face of this scholarly consensus, it is difficult to justify basing a theory of grand strategy on the ideology of imperialism. Finally, the argument falls apart completely in comparative perspective: in the United States, support for collective security and international law was strongest in the South, which was the least liberal, least progressive part of the country. In both the United States and Great Britain, ideological inconsistencies troubled societal actors far less than threats to their economic interests.

POLITICAL ECONOMY

The pattern of partisanship in Britain's grand strategy toward the great powers can be traced directly to cleavages in its domestic political economy. The Liberals' main constituencies, the manufacturing and coal mining sectors, were highly dependent on exports to Europe. Consequently, Liberal governments pursued internationalism, a strategy designed to promote peaceful, cooperative relations among the great powers. Rather than picking favorites among their many commercial partners in Europe, Liberals sought to ensure that all states observed the norms of a stable international order. Only if a state posed a clear threat to that order did they align against it.

Conservatives had no such interest in norm-based cooperation. The only sectors in Britain that had close economic ties to Europe, manufacturing and coal, overwhelmingly supported the Liberals. The Conservatives' main constituencies, military-colonial interests and gentlemanly capitalists, had a far greater stake in the periphery. For them, Britain's military and diplomatic resources were better spent on the defense of the empire than the advancement of international law. Thus, Conservative governments followed a strategy of realpolitik.

Political-economic cleavages created a clear and consistent partisan divide over British grand strategy throughout 1868–1939. However, the specific content of each party's policies depended on changing constraints and opportunities in its strategic environment. To control for these factors, I divide the case into six periods: 1868–80, 1880–92, 1892–1905, 1905–14, 1918–31, and 1931–39. I begin each section by considering how shifting internal and external pressures should have affected each party's hypothesized strategy, then I test the theory by examining Britain's actual strategy in that period.

1868–80: BETWEEN CONCERT AND CONFLICT, PART 1

In 1868, Britain was near the peak of its relative power, both economic and military, in the international system. None of the other great powers could challenge the Royal Navy, either alone or in any plausible combination. The country's sole constraint was budgetary, as charges on the debt consumed more than 2 percent of the national income in every year until 1889 (see figure 6.1). Otherwise, British leaders were free to pursue whatever strategic goals best suited the parochial interests of their societal coalition.

Liberals

As noted above, Britain did not face any imminent threats in 1868–80; however, the international environment was far from ideal for the Liberals' hypothesized strategy, internationalism. Britain's dominant navy, extensive empire, and easily defensible borders gave it strong advantages in the periphery but little leverage in Europe. Furthermore, the pivotal actor on the continent was the very embodiment of modern realpolitik, Otto von Bismarck. With a deeply ingrained hostility to liberalism, the German chancellor never would have subordinated his foreign policy to the dictates of international law.

Consequently, the Liberals had to limit their ambitions over the short term. Rather than make impossible proposals for the sweeping reform of international politics, they should have focused on lesser measures, such as the promotion of legal norms and bilateral cooperation, that would have had some chance of success. Above all, they should have avoided making the international environment more tense by seeking gains at the expense of other great powers. If they aligned against any other country, it should have been only for the sake of defending the international order, not for the aggrandizement of their own power.

The Liberals' actual grand strategy corresponds well to these predictions. Led by Prime Minister William E. Gladstone, the Liberal government of 1868–74 consistently prioritized legalistic, norm-based cooperation over power-based realpolitik.[4] Gladstone did not attempt a systematic program for the codification and institutionalization of international law, but he did pursue internationalist solutions to each of the diplomatic disputes that arose over his term in office. The most serious crisis was the Franco-Prussian War of 1870–71. On the outbreak of hostilities, Gladstone presented identical treaties to France and Prussia in which he promised to ally against whichever power violated Belgium's neutrality. He then offered Britain's good offices to the belligerents, hoping to end the war through peaceful negotiation.[5]

Once it became apparent that Belgium was safe and France would be defeated, Gladstone turned his attention to Germany's claim on Alsace-Lorraine. Surprisingly, he paid little heed to the power-political implications of France's loss to the newly united German state:

> The talk about not ceding any territory he termed extravagant; the idea of punishing France as a disturber of peace he disregarded; nor did he think the cession by France and the acquisition by Germany of Alsace and Lorraine would upset the balance of power in Europe. Gladstone was more concerned with the ethical principle involved in the trafficking in people as if they were chattel, with the effects of such an action on the prospect of settling various disturbing European questions, and, above all, with whether a peace on such terms would promote tranquility and stability in Europe.[6]

Gladstone's prescient diplomacy failed to sway the victorious Germans, however, and the cabinet refused to take more decisive action. His last real hope, that concerted pressure from the great powers would convince Germany to back off its claim, was lost when Russia refused to help.

Another concern was Russia's unilateral abrogation of the 1856 Treaty of Paris. This treaty, which had been signed by all of the major European powers at the end of the Crimean War, imposed severe restrictions on

---

[4] On the general principles of Gladstone's policies toward Europe, see W. N. Medlicott, *Bismarck, Gladstone, and the Concert of Europe* (London: Athlone, 1956), 17–33; F. R. Flournoy, "British Liberal Theories of International Relations, 1848–1898," *Journal of the History of Ideas* 7, no. 2 (April 1946): 195–217; K. A. P. Sandiford, "Gladstone and Europe," in *The Gladstonian Turn of Mind: Essays Presented to J. B. Conacher*, ed. Bruce L. Kinzer (Toronto: University of Toronto Press, 1985), 177–96; Maureen M. Robson, "Liberals and 'Vital Interest': The Debate on International Arbitration, 1815–72," *Bulletin of the Institute of Historical Research* 32, no. 85 (May 1959): 41–42, 51–55; D. M. Schreuder, "Gladstone and the Conscience of the State," in *The Conscience of the Victorian State*, ed. Peter Marsh (Syracuse: Syracuse University Press, 1979), 95–98; D. M. Schreuder, *Gladstone and Kruger* (London: Routledge and Kegan Paul, 1969), 43–45; A. J. P. Taylor, *The Trouble Makers: Dissent over Foreign Policy, 1792–1939* (London: Hamish, 1957), chap. 3.

[5] Richard Shannon, *Gladstone: Heroic Minister, 1865–1898* (London: Allen Lane, 1999), 88.

[6] Paul Knaplund, *Gladstone's Foreign Policy* (London: Cass, 1935), 54–55. See also Schreuder, "Gladstone and the Conscience of the State," 98; D. M. Schreuder, "Gladstone as 'Troublemaker': Liberal Foreign Policy and the German Annexation of Alsace-Lorraine, 1870–1871," *Journal of British Studies* 17, no. 2 (spring 1978): 106–35.

Russian naval strength in the Black Sea. With the support of Bismarck, Tsar Alexander II renounced the treaty while the rest of Europe was focused on the Franco-Prussian War. Gladstone had opposed the naval restrictions when they were imposed in 1856, but he was deeply troubled by the implications of Russia's actions for the integrity of international law. Thus, he sought to make sure that Russia's *fait accompli* was ratified through proper procedures. He convened a conference in London, where the signatories to the Treaty of Paris asserted as an "essential principle of the law of nations that no Power can liberate itself from the engagements of a treaty, nor modify the stipulations thereof, unless with the consent of the contracting Powers by means of an amicable agreement."[7] Gladstone was thereby able to win a small victory for internationalist principles.

Gladstone's internationalism also governed his relations with the United States. Since the end of the Civil War, the United States had demanded compensation for the sale of three commerce-destroying ships from British shipyards to the Confederacy. In 1865–68, Prime Minister Lord Palmerston brushed off American calls for arbitration, asserting that Britain had acted in good faith and that it alone was responsible for interpreting and enforcing its neutrality laws.[8] Gladstone, in contrast, had no compunction about subjecting British foreign policy to the judgment of an arbitration tribunal: "He saw the process as exemplifying the means by which two civilized nations could settle differences, without either having to admit being wrong."[9]

This decision was not dictated by international pressures or relative power. Gladstone could, like Palmerston, have ignored the matter entirely, hoping that passions on the other side of the Atlantic would subside over time. American resentment did not pose any particular danger, since the United States disarmed rapidly after the Civil War and made no indication that it would threaten Britain's one weak spot, the long border with Canada. Even if Gladstone worried that the affair would poison Anglo-American relations over the long term, he might have proposed a direct settlement rather than bind Britain to the ruling of an international court. Instead, he agreed to arbitration, the terms of which were set in the 1871 Treaty of Washington. The result, he believed, had broad implications for the prospects of international law: "Both the Treaty of Washington and the arbitration could be offered to the world as a path for the future."[10]

[7] Quoted in Paul Hayes, *The Nineteenth Century: 1814–1880* (London: Black, 1975), 60. See also Marvin Swartz, *The Politics of British Foreign Policy in the Era of Disraeli and Gladstone* (New York: St. Martin's, 1985), 27.

[8] H. Lauterpacht and R. Y. Jennings, "International Law and Colonial Questions, 1870–1914," in *The Cambridge History of the British Empire*, vol. 3, ed. E. A. Benians, James Butler, and C. E. Carrington (Cambridge: Cambridge University Press, 1967), 689–91; Robson, "Liberals and 'Vital Interest,'" 48–51.

[9] H. C. G. Matthew, *Gladstone, 1809–1898* (Oxford: Clarendon, 1997), 188.

[10] Quoted in ibid., 188. See also Shannon, *Gladstone*, 75.

The Conservatives, whose constituency of military-colonial interests had little at stake on the continent, should have had a very different view of Britain's "national interests." Their strategic imperative was to align against the state that posed the greatest threat to the British Empire. Throughout the late nineteenth century, Russia best fit that description. Britain had colonial disputes with nearly every great power, but only Russia had both the capacity and the desire to endanger the empire. The United States could have invaded and annexed the Canadian provinces at any time it pleased; however, it showed little interest in doing so after the 1850s, and there was nothing that the British army could have done to stop it if it had. France was jealous of many of Britain's possessions, but its warships were no match for the Royal Navy. Germany's fleet was even less powerful, and it did not begin to seek colonies until the mid 1880s. Russia, in contrast, had been rapidly expanding into Central Asia, drawing closer to the crown jewel of the British Empire, India, with every passing year. The Hindu Kush was a formidable defensive barrier, but British defense planners still feared an overland invasion through Afghanistan. Thus, Conservatives should have used coercive realpolitik to limit Russia's territorial expansion, military power, and diplomatic influence. In contrast to the Liberals, who treated Russia as a potential partner for cooperation, the Conservative government of 1874–80 should have been thoroughly Russophobic.

This strategy would be far easier to carry out than internationalism. Whereas the Liberals sought to reduce diplomatic tensions in Europe, the Conservatives benefited from long-standing rivalries on the continent. As long as the great powers remained locked in a balanced, competitive dynamic, they would be highly sensitive to changes in each other's relative power. Thus, Conservatives could exert an inordinate amount of influence by offering limited support to one side or another. By skillfully manipulating the game of power politics on the continent, they would be able to protect their vast peripheral empire long after Britain's relative economic decline should have rendered their position untenable.

The grand strategy of the Conservative government of 1874–80, which was led by Prime Minster Benjamin Disraeli, confirms these expectations. Disraeli's diplomacy with the great powers was occupied by the "Eastern Question"—that is, the problems arising from the collapse of the Ottoman Empire in the Balkans. In the spring of 1876, Bulgarian Christians rose up against their Turkish rulers, who responded with brutal atrocities. A few months later, Serbia and Montenegro declared war against Turkey, turning the affair into a full-fledged international crisis. In Britain, as in Russia and Austria-Hungary, there was a strong public reaction against the Ottoman Empire's human rights violations. Gladstone contributed to the uproar by publishing a pamphlet, *The Bulgarian Horrors and the Question of the East,* which argued in favor of self-determination for European populations subjugated by the Turks. He cared little for the geopolitical implications of this policy; instead, he called for the great powers to come to the aid of their fellow Christians and support the creation of a unified Bulgarian nation. Gladstone emphasized values that brought the great powers together in common cause, regardless of their strategic position in the crisis.

In contrast, Disraeli focused on Britain's parochial imperial interests. He recognized that the Ottoman Empire occupied a unique position, straddling Europe and Asia Minor, that blocked Russian access to the Eastern Mediterranean and limited Russian influence in the Balkans. As long as the Ottoman Empire remained strong and independent, Britain could ensure the security of the naval approach to the all-important Suez Canal.[11] Thus, Disraeli adopted a pro-Turkish stance in the Eastern Question. The "ruthlessly pragmatic" prime minister cared little for abstract normative principles or even the fate of the Bulgarians; he regretted only that the Turks could not act quickly enough to put down the rebellion.[12]

By late 1876, the Turks had beaten back the Serbian army, but the threat of Russian intervention forced them to accept an armistice. At that point, Disraeli proposed a conference at which the Ottoman Empire and the great powers could reach a mutually satisfactory solution to the Eastern Question. However, he put little stock in multilateral diplomacy. He regarded the Constantinople Conference as "mainly a means of throwing dust into the eyes of agitated public opinion and of preserving a degree of unity within the cabinet. His own preference was for a confrontation with Russia. . . . He never could quite understand why, with Britain's naval supremacy undisputed, there should be any difficulty about contemplating a military solution."[13] In other words, Disraeli used the Concert of Europe only to provide cover for his fundamentally uncooperative policy. He refused to join the concert powers in the coercion of the Turks, thereby dooming the conference to failure.[14]

In April 1877, Russia declared war on the Ottoman Empire and sent an army through Romania into the Balkans. Fearing that it intended to seize the naval route to the Mediterranean, the Conservatives decided to send an additional three thousand troops to Malta and unanimously vowed to ask

---

[11] P. J. V. Rolo, "Derby," in *British Foreign Secretaries and Foreign Policy: From Crimean War to First World War,* ed. Keith M. Wilson (London: Croom Helm, 1987), 110; Richard W. Davis, *Disraeli* (Boston: Little, Brown, 1976), 201–2.

[12] Paul Smith, *Disraeli: A Brief Life* (Cambridge: Cambridge University Press, 1996), 190–91; P. J. Durrans, "A Two-Edged Sword: The Liberal Attack on Disraelian Imperialism," *Journal of Imperial and Commonwealth History* 10, no. 3 (May 1982): 274.

[13] Rolo, "Derby," 110.

[14] Richard Shannon, *The Age of Disraeli, 1868–1881: The Rise of Tory Democracy* (London: Longman, 1992), 288–94.

the queen for a declaration of war if Russia occupied Constantinople. In February 1878, a renewed Russian advance led the government to secure an emergency military appropriation of £6 million and order the fleet into the Dardanelles.[15] Disraeli also sought an alliance with Austria-Hungary, the purpose of which would be to force Russia to retreat from Constantinople and Gallipoli, but the Austrians rejected his terms. They did, however, propose a meeting of the Concert of Europe as a means to resolve the Anglo-Russian conflict. The Conservatives accepted, but imposed conditions that Russia could not accept, so an impasse resulted.

Russia's military campaign soon forced the Turks to give up the game. Sultan Abdul Hamid II signed a treaty that stripped his empire of nearly all of its European possessions and created a large, independent Bulgarian state. The Ottoman Empire would retain Constantinople, but it would never again be secure from Russian pressure because the tsar would have a powerful client state within striking distance. Disraeli found this unacceptable, so he escalated the dispute by mobilizing British army reserves and sending seven thousand Indian troops to the region. Two months later, Anglo-Russian negotiations at last defused the crisis. Russia conceded to a smaller Bulgaria in return for a guarantee that no Turkish troops would be allowed in the territory restored to the Ottoman Empire. The sultan also agreed to implement domestic reforms, protect the rights of Christians, and give Cyprus to Britain, in return for which Britain promised to protect the Turks' Asiatic possessions from Russia.

Only after securing this agreement did Disraeli consent to attend a meeting of the Concert of Europe, the Congress of Berlin, in June 1878. At the congress, Britain and Russia hammered out the final details of their accord, and for the most part the other powers concurred. The Treaty of Berlin, which put a European "seal of approval" on the concessions that Disraeli had obtained primarily through military escalation and bilateral negotiations, was signed by the assembled concert on July 13. Despite the imprimatur of multilateralism, it was little more than a façade on the Conservatives' fundamentally realpolitik grand strategy.

1880–92: BETWEEN CONCERT AND CONFLICT, PART 2

In the 1880s and 1890s, all of the great powers except Austria-Hungary sought to expand their overseas empires and deep-water navies. The New Imperialism of the late nineteenth century contributed greatly to the erosion of Britain's relative power. The shift, however, was a gradual one. By 1892, British policymakers had only just begun to consider how new rivalries in the periphery would affect their strategy in Europe. Britain's external

---

[15] R. W. Seton-Watson, *Disraeli, Gladstone, and the Eastern Question: A Study in Diplomacy and Party Politics* (London, 1938), 297–317.

environment in 1880–92 was not so constrained that it should have led societal coalitions to reconsider their positions. Liberal governments were free to devote their energies to promoting multilateral cooperation, while Conservatives could continue to focus on threats to the empire.

Liberals

The rapid decline of the manufacturing sector caused a major change in the Liberals' approach toward the periphery, as explained in the previous chapter. It should not, however, have had an immediate effect on the party's strategy toward the great powers. In the 1880s, exports to Europe and the United States still accounted for 8–10 percent of Britain's national income and were an enormously important part of the regional economies of northern England, Wales, and Scotland. Consequently, the Liberals should have remained internationalist. Their strategic imperative was to promote adherence to international law and shared norms of behavior, to foster multilateral cooperation and collective security through international institutions, to abjure self-interested gains for the sake of broader harmony, and to maintain neutrality in other powers' disputes unless confronted with a direct challenge to international order. Their ability to make progress on this agenda would be limited by Britain's declining power and continuing hostility between the continental powers, but their strategy nevertheless should have been clearly identifiable as internationalist.

Gladstone's strategy toward the great powers in 1880–86 was, in fact, consistent with this prediction. In a campaign speech in 1880, he made clear his intention "to strive to cultivate and maintain, aye, to the very uttermost, what is called the concert of Europe; to keep the powers of Europe in union together. And why? Because by keeping all in union together you neutralize, and fetter, and bind up the selfish aims of each."[16] Once the Liberals returned to office, Gladstone followed through on this promise. On three separate occasions, he attempted to use the concert to build consensus and organize joint action against third parties.

One such case was the occupation of Egypt, as discussed in chapter 6. Once Gladstone decided on the necessity of intervention, he appealed to France, Italy, and Turkey to join with him in a concerted, "internationalized" operation. However, he found no willing partners. Lacking a multilateral option, Gladstone resorted to unilateral action, declaring that "we are discharging single-handed an European duty."[17] His rhetoric might have

---

[16] W. E. Gladstone, "On Domestic and Foreign Affairs," in *Modern British Eloquence*, ed. David B. Strother (New York: Funk and Wagnalls, 1969), 329–30.

[17] Quoted in Shannon, *Gladstone*, 304. See also Agatha Ramm, "Great Britain and France in Egypt, 1876–1882," in *France and Britain in Africa: Imperial Rivalry and Colonial Rule*, ed. Prosser Gifford and William R. Louis (New Haven: Yale University Press, 1971), 100–102, 113.

seemed self-serving, but he did not forget his commitment to the Concert of Europe. When it became apparent that Egypt's military and financial position was so precarious that Britain could not withdraw in short order, Gladstone turned to the continental great powers for help. In May 1884, he convened a conference on Egypt, which, after many months of negotiations, ended in the creation of an international commission that would oversee the repayment of Egypt's debt to European investors.[18]

The implications of this agreement, the London Convention of March 1885, were far-reaching. As long as the concert controlled Egypt's treasury, British efforts to reform the Egyptian government, coerce its leaders, and deploy its army against Islamic revolutionaries in the Sudan would depend on the cooperation of the resentful French and manipulative Germans. Furthermore, the great powers' participation in the convention gave them a legal claim against any attempt by Britain to alter its political relationship with Egypt. These restrictions seriously constrained British grand strategy in the following decades—not just in Egypt, not just in the Sudan, but with spillover effects in many colonial disputes around the world. In short, Gladstone's devotion to concert diplomacy clearly amounted to more than just cheap talk, and it was "unrelated to power and power politics."[19]

The other two occasions on which Gladstone sought to involve the Concert of Europe in British foreign policy were motivated primarily by humanitarian concerns. In the 1878 Treaty of Berlin, the sultan of Turkey had agreed to certain territorial adjustments in the Balkans, not all of which he actually carried out. Gladstone, who already disliked the sultan for his role in the Bulgarian atrocities of 1875–78, decided that he must be made to honor his obligations. Shortly after coming to power, in June 1880, Gladstone convened the concert to force the cession of Turkish land to Montenegro and Greece. The sultan refused the concert's entreaties, so the British delegation advocated a joint naval demonstration off the Albanian coastline. The other great powers concurred, but none granted its navy the authority to use force, so again the sultan stood firm. Gladstone then proposed to blockade the port of Smyrna—ideally as a joint action, but one that he may have been willing to carry out unilaterally if the concert could not agree—and the sultan finally made concessions over Montenegro.[20]

The following year, continued diplomatic pressure led to the cession of Ottoman territory to Greece.[21] Still, the Greeks wanted more, so in the spring of

---

[18] R. Robinson and J. Gallagher, *Africa and the Victorians: The Official Mind of Imperialism* (London: Macmillan, 1961), 137–51.

[19] Ramm, "Great Britain and France," 113.

[20] Knaplund, *Gladstone's Foreign Policy*, 143.

[21] At one point, Gladstone even contemplated handing over Cyprus to Greece as part of a deal, but he decided that this would not sit well with public opinion so soon after the Liberals' retreat from Afghanistan and Transvaal. See Knaplund, *Gladstone's Foreign Policy*, 148.

1886, they mobilized their army along the frontier with Turkey and threatened war. Foreign Secretary Lord Rosebery, who was left to manage the problem while Gladstone tried to secure home rule for Ireland, brought together the Concert of Europe to condemn the Greek aggression and arrange for a joint naval blockade.[22] Greece drew down its military, and the crisis passed. In sum, the Liberal governments of 1880–85 and 1886 had some modest but important successes in their attempts to promote internationalism and enforce international law, an outcome that clearly confirms the theory's predictions.

Conservatives

While Liberal internationalists were relatively unaffected by gradual changes in international constraints in the 1880s, Conservative imperialists could not afford to be so sanguine. The empire remained reasonably secure, but its margin of safety was receding. Britain's diplomatic detachment was becoming a liability, forcing it to defend itself against every one of the powers with which it shared colonial borders. The Conservatives should have continued to focus on Russia as the primary threat to their interests, but they also had to concern themselves with the bigger picture of great power politics and its impact on the defense of the empire.

Lord Salisbury, who had previously served as foreign minister under Disraeli in 1878–80, became prime minister when the Conservatives came to office in 1885. Salisbury's relations with the great powers were, like Disraeli's, based on the realpolitik practices of shifting alliances, bilateral diplomacy, and veiled threat-making, rather than any sort of commitment to international law, norms of behavior, or moral precepts. This was clearly evident in many of his peripheral policies, as discussed in the previous chapter. For example, he attempted to reach an accommodation with the Ottoman Empire that would invalidate Gladstone's commitment to multilateral control over Egypt. Salisbury also withdrew Gladstone's preliminary agreement with Russia to bring the Afghanistan frontier question to arbitration, and he rejected Portugal's demand for the arbitration of a dispute over Nyasaland.

The Conservatives' record on arbitration was not entirely negative; Salisbury made use of it on several occasions for "low politics" disputes, and he agreed to submit to it in three minor disagreements with Germany over boundaries in East and Southwest Africa.[23] On the whole, however, he

[22] Gordon Martel, *Imperial Diplomacy: Rosebery and the Failure of Foreign Policy* (Kingston: McGill-Queen's University Press, 1986), 31, 45–46; *The Foreign Policy of Lord Rosebery* (London: Humphreys, 1901), 4–11.
[23] John Bassett Moore, *History and Digest of the International Arbitrations to Which the United States Has Been a Party*, vol. 5 (Washington, D.C.: Government Printing Office, 1898), 4940–47; A. M. Stuyt, *Survey of International Arbitrations, 1794–1970* (Dobbs Ferry, N.Y.: Oceana, 1972), 167; Jackson H. Ralston, *International Arbitration from Athens to Locarno* (Stanford: Stanford University Press, 1929), 232.

showed little interest in furthering the cause of international law for major "high politics" issues, and his diplomacy was devoid of any attempt to promote cooperation as a good in itself.[24] His overriding strategic imperative was the security of the empire, and Europe mattered only to the extent that changes in the balance of power affected his ability to protect the empire.[25]

Salisbury, like Disraeli, focused most of his attention on the Ottoman Empire and the defense of the Suez route to India.[26] In 1877–78, the Conservatives had sought to prevent Bulgaria from annexing the province of Eastern Roumelia from the Ottoman Empire. At the time, they feared that a greater Bulgarian state would help Russia gain access to the Dardanelles, thereby threatening Britain's naval control over the eastern Mediterranean. In 1885, however, Bulgaria's ruler, Prince Alexander, decided to rid his country of Russian influence. As a result, both the Conservatives and Russia reversed their positions.[27] Russia tried to undermine its former client, while Salisbury worked to strengthen it as a bulwark against Russian designs on Constantinople. In September of that year, Prince Alexander declared the unification of Bulgaria with Eastern Roumelia, and Salisbury gave it his blessing, despite the opposition of key members of the Concert of Europe. Then, in November 1885, when Serbia attacked Bulgaria, Salisbury worked on Bulgaria's behalf to prevent any of the surrounding countries from intervening.

Although Russia lost influence in Bulgaria, the Conservatives could not trust that its Black Sea fleet would forever be bottled up behind the Bosporus. If it broke through, it could join forces with the French and directly challenge the Royal Navy. Thus, Salisbury sought to strengthen Britain's position through diplomatic means. The result was the Mediterranean Agreements of 1887, in which he pledged with Italy and Austria-Hungary to preserve the status quo in the region.[28] No formal commitments were made, and the pact was kept secret, but Salisbury nevertheless accomplished his primary goal: to augment Britain's naval power in case France or Russia moved to threaten the Suez route. The Mediterranean Agreements were only a small step toward a continental commitment, but they were an augur of what was to come as the Conservatives sought to secure the British Empire in the face of relative decline.

---

[24] Andrew Roberts, *Salisbury: Victorian Titan* (London: Weidenfeld and Nicolson, 1999), 632; David Steele, *Lord Salisbury: A Political Biography* (London: UCL, 1999), 4, 125, 142–43, 151–52, 178.
[25] C. J. Lowe, *Salisbury and the Mediterranean, 1886–1896* (London: Routledge and Kegan Paul, 1965), 1–2; David Gillard, "Salisbury," in *British Foreign Secretaries and Foreign Policy: From Crimean War to First World War*, ed. Keith M. Wilson (London: Croom Helm, 1987), 126–27.
[26] J. A. S. Grenville, *Lord Salisbury and Foreign Policy: The Close of the Nineteenth Century* (London: Athlone, 1964), 24–28; Gillard, "Salisbury," 125–30.
[27] Martel, *Imperial Diplomacy*, 26–29; Roberts, *Salisbury*, 355–56; Steele, *Lord Salisbury*, 182, 249.
[28] Lowe, *Salisbury and the Mediterranean*.

1892–1905: DEALING WITH DECLINE

By the early 1890s, the race to carve up Africa and Asia was well underway. Britain remained the strongest power in the periphery, but it faced challenges on nearly all of its imperial frontiers. Meanwhile, Britain's two most dangerous rivals, Russia and France, formed a close-knit alliance in 1894, forcing defense planners to prepare to fight both simultaneously. This combination of factors increased diplomatic tensions and hardened the lines of conflict all across Europe. The deteriorating international order should not have deterred either Liberals or Conservatives from trying to advance their strategic goals, but their actions clearly should have been circumscribed by their constraints.

Liberals

While the external environment was changing, an equally important transformation was occurring in Britain's political economy. The Liberals' primary constituency, the manufacturing sector, was becoming increasingly dependent on peripheral markets. Within the party, the Radical majority remained devoted to an internationalist strategy, but the Liberal Imperialist minority was rapidly gaining influence. Most Liberal Imperialists shared the Radicals' interest in peace and stability in Europe, but they were also deeply concerned about the defense of the empire. If imperial security would benefit from a decision to abandon Britain's traditional neutrality and align with one or more of the continental powers, they were willing to accept the costs of doing so. On the whole, the Liberals should have remained internationalist, but the direction of their grand strategy should have become more contentious within the party.

This prediction is not borne out by the facts. Lord Rosebery, who controlled foreign policy in the Liberal government of 1892–95, did not act in a manner that could be considered even weakly internationalist, despite his coalition's heavy reliance on income from exports to Europe and the United States. Rosebery publicly promised before coming to power that his strategy would be the same as that of his Conservative predecessor, and he made good on his pledge.[29] Much of his great power diplomacy focused on Russia and France, whose combined forces posed the greatest threat to the empire. Rosebery believed that British naval power in the eastern Mediterranean would not only help secure the Suez route to India, but also protect India's northern border.[30] His reasoning was rather tortuous, but is worth explaining because it

---

[29] P. J. V. Rolo, "Rosebery and Kimberly," in *British Foreign Secretaries and Foreign Policy: From Crimean War to First World War*, ed. Keith M. Wilson (London: Croom Helm, 1987), 143.
[30] Martel, *Imperial Diplomacy*, 136–57, 175–76, 257; W. L. Langer, *The Diplomacy of Imperialism, 1890–1902*, 2d ed. (New York: Knopf, 1951), 45–46, 49, 53.

shows how his diplomacy with the European great powers was designed to serve peripheral interests. As long as Russia felt threatened by Germany and Austria-Hungary, it needed to concentrate its armies in Eastern Europe. Germany aligned against Russia because it was protected from a Franco-Russian combination by its Triple Alliance with Italy and Austria-Hungary. Italy's enthusiasm for the Triple Alliance was predicated on British support, since its long coastline was vulnerable to the superior French fleet. If Britain abandoned the Mediterranean or let France and Russia gain a decisive advantage over the Royal Navy, Italy would presumably leave the Triple Alliance to bandwagon with France. In all likelihood, Germany would then try to make peace with Russia to avoid a two-front war without Italy's support, and Russia would be free to shift its forces to the east to invade India.

Following this logic, Rosebery concluded that Salisbury's Mediterranean Agreements of 1887 must be maintained—though not extended, since any greater reliance on or commitment to the Triple Alliance might draw Britain into a continental war. To keep pace with the other great powers' naval construction programs, Britain's forces in the Mediterranean had to be enlarged, even if that meant taking ships away from the squadrons that defended the home isles. In response, the Admiralty Board demanded enormous new outlays for shipbuilding, which Rosebery championed in the cabinet. Gladstone, in contrast, favored rapprochement with both Russia and France, so he fought bitterly against the new naval estimates. In the end, Rosebery got his way, and Gladstone resigned.

Rosebery's strategy toward the great powers in 1892–95 was, like Salisbury's, devoted exclusively to the defense of the empire. He did not try to revive the concert, use arbitration to resolve major "high-politics" conflicts, or do anything to foster cooperation between the great powers.[31] Even a humanitarian crisis in Turkey, where Armenian Christians were being persecuted, interested him only for its potential impact on his delicate power-balancing act.[32] He proposed to Russia and France that they join with him to force reforms on the Turks, but he did so only for the sake of staying in step with Russia. In short, there is little evidence in his strategy of internationalism. The theory does predict some degree of convergence between the Liberals and Conservatives, since the Liberals' stake in the empire was gradually increasing, but Rosebery went further down this path than expected. Thus, the Liberal government's strategy toward the great powers in 1892–95 cannot be counted in favor of the theory.

---

[31] Rosebery did agree to the arbitration of a colonial border with Portugal in southeast Africa, but the dispute was too minor for its resolution to count as meaningfully internationalist. See Stuyt, *Survey of International Arbitrations*, 189; W. Evans Darby, *International Tribunals*, 4th ed. (London: Dent, 1904), 822.

[32] Martel, *Imperial Diplomacy*, 143, 247; Peter Stansky, *Ambitions and Strategies: The Struggle for Leadership in the Liberal Party in the 1890s* (Oxford: Clarendon, 1964), 126–27.

Conservatives

As the established party of the empire, the Conservatives were just as concerned as Rosebery about the relative decline of British power in the periphery. Moreover, they were not constrained by a pro-Europe, anti-alignment faction within their own party, as Rosebery was vis-à-vis the Radicals. Thus, as threats to the empire mounted, the Conservatives should have become increasingly willing to form alliances, ententes, and other arrangements with the great powers to protect their colonies and contain Russia. At the same time, they should have continued to oppose commitments to international law and collective security.

These predictions are largely, but not entirely, confirmed by the Conservative governments of 1895–1905. In two separate instances, Prime Minister Salisbury ventured into internationalism. The first followed several failed attempts to resolve the Eastern Question. Shortly after coming to office in July 1895, Salisbury proposed to Germany that the Ottoman Empire be partitioned between the great powers. Germany declined, so he sought to persuade Russia and France to work out a joint plan to coerce the Turks. Again, he was rebuffed, so he threatened a unilateral naval demonstration. The effort failed, and he was unable to convince either the Admiralty or the cabinet to consider stronger measures. Finally, Salisbury shifted tack: he proposed a meeting of the Concert of Europe to formulate demands for the reform of the Ottoman Empire. Remarkably, all of the great powers assented, and in February 1897, they agreed to create a "supreme council of state" to oversee the process. Before anything could be accomplished, however, Greece declared war against Turkey. The decision was ill-advised; the Greek armies were quickly overwhelmed. The concert then interceded, forcing Turkey to give up almost all of the land it had overrun.

Although the affair marked a departure from the Conservatives' long-standing disdain for the Concert of Europe, its significance should not be exaggerated. Whereas Gladstone had believed from the outset that the great powers should cooperate to reform Turkey, Salisbury saw multilateralism only as a last recourse when all else failed: "Had they been able to settle accounts with Russia and France they would have thrown overboard the concert and all the paraphernalia that went with it."[33]

The other instance in which Salisbury dabbled in internationalism was the Venezuelan Crisis with the United States. In July 1895, President Grover Cleveland caused a diplomatic row by asserting that Britain had violated the Monroe Doctrine in a dispute over territory on the border of British Guiana and Venezuela. Salisbury had no intention of backing down, but his colleagues were not so courageous. By January 1896, the cabinet decided that Britain could not afford a crisis with the United States while

---

[33] Langer, *Diplomacy of Imperialism*, 381.

simultaneously facing heightened Anglo-Boer tensions, continued problems with Turkey, and hostility from the continental powers. Thus, Salisbury, who was "highly skeptical about arbitrations in general and those involving America in particular," had no choice but to accept Cleveland's demand for the adjudication of the dispute.[34] After negotiating a *compromis* treaty in November 1896, he also reluctantly agreed to a treaty requiring that all future conflicts between Britain and the United States be submitted to arbitration.[35] Then, in March 1897, as the Fashoda crisis was approaching, Salisbury proposed to the French ambassador that the two countries enter into a general arbitration agreement of their own.[36] The French were not interested, and Salisbury did not pursue the matter.

The United States took advantage of British weakness in two other disputes. First, it demanded a revision of the Clayton-Bulwer Treaty of 1850, which gave Britain shared rights over a future isthmian canal. In February 1899, Salisbury preferred to let negotiations stalemate rather than make major concessions. A year later, however, pressures to settle were mounting. The Boer War was going poorly, and the United States seemed increasingly likely to abrogate the Clayton-Bulwer Treaty unilaterally. Thus, in February 1900, Salisbury agreed to give the Americans exclusive control over the prospective canal. The U.S. Senate rejected the treaty, so it was renegotiated and signed in November 1901.

The second issue was the unresolved Alaska-Canada boundary. Canada's legal claim to the territory under dispute was weak, but the Conservatives did not want to appear insensitive to King Edward's colonial subjects.[37] Thus, Lord Lansdowne, who had taken over the Foreign Office from the aging Salisbury, agreed to submit the case to a tribunal composed of six impartial judges, with three appointed by each side. President Roosevelt selected men who were neither judges nor impartial, so Lansdowne gave two of his slots to Canadians—but reserved the third for a British judge, who cast the deciding vote with the Americans. With this minor concession, the Conservatives completed a critical step in their strategic retrenchment: the appeasement of the most economically powerful country in the world.

In addition to constructing a de facto entente with the United States, Lansdowne attempted to align Britain more closely with several other great powers. At the turn of the century, Anglo-German relations were beginning to degrade, but they were far from being past the point of repair. Germany, which sought to strengthen its position on the continent, called for a

---

[34] Roberts, *Salisbury*, 632. See also Steele, *Lord Salisbury*, 332; Grenville, *Lord Salisbury*, 68.
[35] Nelson M. Blake, "The Olney-Pauncefote Treaty of 1897," *American Historical Review* 50, no. 2 (January 1945): 230–31, 233–34; Darby, *International Tribunals*, 390–99.
[36] A. L. Kennedy, *Salisbury, 1830–1903: Portrait of a Statesman* (London: Murray, 1953), 280–82.
[37] Grenville, *Lord Salisbury*, 372–73.

comprehensive understanding with Britain. Though Salisbury disapproved of the idea of a formal alliance with the Reich, Lansdowne pressed ahead with negotiations.[38] Nothing came of it, however. Lansdowne was unwilling to commit Britain to the Triple Alliance, as Kaiser Wilhelm II demanded, while the kaiser refused to help Britain against Russia in China, as Lansdowne required. Thereafter, Anglo-German relations steadily worsened and Germany accelerated its naval program.

Lansdowne was more successful in securing an alliance with Japan. His motives were simple: if Russia and France were to combine against Britain in the Far East, the British Navy would be at a severe numerical disadvantage. Thus, in January 1902, he signed an agreement with Japan in which each country pledged to come to the other's aid if it were attacked by any two powers. Not long thereafter, in February 1904, Japan went to war with Russia. This turned out to be a windfall for Britain: Japan annihilated the Russian fleet, eliminating the threat of Franco-Russian naval cooperation against Britain. Shortly before the war formally ended in September 1905, Britain and Japan renewed their alliance. It was set for a ten-year period, double that of the original pact; it was extended to India; and it would be triggered if either of the signatories were attacked by only one other power.

The Conservative government's last strategic initiative was a turn toward France, which began in early 1903. Contrary to popular misconception, it was not the fear of an imminent threat from Germany that set Lansdowne on this course.[39] Germany's battleship construction program, though troubling, did not yet bring it anywhere near equality with Britain. Prior to the Russo-Japanese War, the German Navy was only the fourth strongest in the world, and its army was held in check by the Franco-Russian alliance. Instead, the most important factor in the Conservatives' decision to seek an entente with France was the problem of Russia. If Anglo-French relations were to improve, France would be far less likely side with Russia against Britain. Indeed, France would have a strong incentive to promote rapprochement between its two partners, paving the way for a comprehensive settlement of Anglo-Russian conflict over Afghanistan, Persia, and China. Not until the Russo-Japanese War of 1904–5 and the Moroccan Crisis of 1905–6 did British strategy begin to shift in a clearly anti-German direction. Throughout 1902–5, Lansdowne's main concern was Russia, still the greatest threat to the empire.

---

[38] Robert Taylor, *Lord Salisbury* (London: Allen Lane, 1975), 176, 180–82; Roberts, *Salisbury*, 802, 812–14; Grenville, *Lord Salisbury*, 435–36.

[39] George Monger, *The End of Isolation: British Foreign Policy, 1900–1907* (London: Nelson, 1963), 109–11, 114, 163, 200–201, 205–6, 311–12; Pierre Guillen, "The Entente of 1904 as a Colonial Settlement," in *France and Britain in Africa*, ed. Prosser Gifford and William R. Lewis (New Haven: Yale University Press, 1971), 335–38.

The Anglo-French entente negotiations focused on North Africa. In late December 1902, the two sides settled on a plan to maintain the status quo in Morocco in the face of potential German intervention. This agreement laid the groundwork for a broader colonial settlement, the terms of which were finalized in April 1904. Each side made a number of trade-offs, the most important of which were British support for French claims to paramountcy in Morocco and French support for British efforts to end the Concert of Europe's role in Egypt. In an additional, secret convention, Britain and France recognized each other's right to annex Egypt and Morocco.

The Entente Cordiale soon became a pillar of British diplomacy. In April 1905, Germany challenged France over Morocco, and the cabinet responded with unqualified support for the French. Notably, the Conservatives' greatest concern in the crisis was not France's position in Europe. Rather, they feared that France would make colonial concessions to Germany that would threaten Britain's control over key naval lanes. Only when it became evident that the French would not back down did the threat of a Franco-German war come to dominate British thinking. As George Monger writes,

> The whole cast of mind of the government was imperial, and it was only slowly and reluctantly that they were coming to recognize their involvement in Europe. Indeed, this recognition grew in the first place out of their imperial interests; for they realized that the result of a war between Germany and the entente, although fought over imperial and naval issues, might well be decided by the battles between the French and German armies in Europe.[40]

Slowly but surely, the Conservatives were being drawn into continental affairs. However, it was not because they valued peace and cooperation, like the Gladstonian Liberals; instead, it was a necessary extension of their peripheral interests.

One important question remains: Why did this flurry of diplomatic activity come in 1902–5? British leaders could have entered into alliance negotiations with European powers at any point in the prior thirty years covered in this study, yet they did not. The answer is that the combination of increased naval competition and the unexpectedly difficult Boer War seriously constrained Britain's military budget. Without major new tax increases, which the Conservatives found to be politically unacceptable, it would not be possible for them to pursue all of their strategic goals at once.[41] Until the turn of the century, their studied detachment from

---

[40] Monger, *End of Isolation*, 207.
[41] Keith M. Wilson, *The Policy of the Entente: Essays on the Determinants of British Foreign Policy, 1904–1914* (Cambridge: Cambridge University Press, 1985), 4–7; Aaron L. Friedberg, *The Weary Titan: Britain and the Experience of Relative Decline, 1895–1905* (Princeton: Princeton University Press, 1988), chap. 3.

continental alliances had allowed them to avoid unwanted conflicts and maintain a free hand in the scramble for colonies. Yet, as Britain's relative power declined, this detachment became increasingly expensive, forcing the government to defend the empire from all comers. The Admiralty, War Office, and the Committee on Imperial Defence, which undertook a comprehensive reassessment of Britain's military readiness, could not resolve this difficulty simply by reshuffling its force deployments and scrapping obsolete vessels.[42] Thus, the government faced a straightforward choice: either maintain Britain's freedom of action and pursue a less aggressive, less costly strategy, or continue to defend and extend the empire aggressively while sacrificing "splendid isolation." Given that their gentlemanly capitalist coalition had become enormously reliant on investment in the periphery, it is unsurprising that the Conservatives chose imperial security over strategic independence.

1905–14: ENTENTE FOR EMPIRE

The Moroccan Crisis of 1905–6, in which Germany threatened war with France over a minor colonial dispute, signaled the beginning of a dangerous period of diplomatic brinkmanship in Europe. Conflict threatened at every turn, forcing British leaders to consider the conditions under which they would join a continental war. To make matters worse, the rapid growth of Germany's battleship fleet posed a direct challenge to the maritime supremacy of the Royal Navy. This presented Britain with another difficult choice: either enter into a naval arms race in which it would have to outspend its rival by a two-to-one ratio to keep its lead, or stand by as Germany steadily built up a force that might someday be used to seize control of the British Empire.

As Germany became more menacing, the problem of Russia temporarily receded. The Russian military had taken a beating in its war with Japan, so it no longer posed an immediate threat to the British Empire. However, Russia would eventually recover from its losses, and when it did, it would pose as great a threat as ever before. It had steadily been consolidating its gains in Central Asia, and it was building a railroad network that could quickly bring its forces close to the Indian frontier. Russia's ambitions in that part of the world had not diminished; to the contrary, its constant meddling in Persian affairs proved that it would continue to extend its influence whenever possible.

In sum, the British Empire was caught between two grave dangers: first, the short-term threat posed by the expansion of the German battleship navy

---

[42] Ruddock F. MacKay, *Balfour: Intellectual Statesman* (Oxford: Oxford University Press, 1985), chap. 9; Friedberg, *Weary Titan*, chaps. 4–5.

and, second, the long-term problem of the revival of Russian power. How Britain's leaders responded to this dilemma would depend very much on the strategic interests of their electoral coalition. As the world drew closer to war, the partisan composition of Britain's government would play a critical role in determining the course of world history.

Liberals

In the Liberal governments of 1905–14, there were two prime ministers, three elections, a constitutional crisis, and the beginnings of a major political realignment. Through all of this upheaval, however, there was one constant: British foreign policy was controlled almost exclusively by Edward Grey. The cabinet was not always united behind him, but he was given an exceptional degree of leeway from the prime ministers under whom he served, Henry Campbell-Bannerman (who died in 1908) and Herbert Asquith.[43] All major diplomatic initiatives originated with Grey, so the history of the grand strategy of the Liberal Party in 1905–14 centers on him.

As explained in chapter 5, British manufacturers grew increasingly dependent on export to the periphery in the 1880s and 1890s. Consequently, the imperialist faction of the Liberal Party gained greater influence over grand strategy. By the turn of the century, the Liberal Imperialists were still in the minority, but the party as a whole needed their support to win a majority in Parliament and maintain its always-precarious unity.[44] Thus, it should come as no surprise that the man selected to be foreign minister in the Liberal government of 1905, just like in 1892, would have been a Liberal Imperialist. Grey had sided with Rosebery against Gladstone in 1892–95 and supported the Boer War in 1899–1902, so he established a reputation among Conservatives as someone who could be trusted with the defense of the empire.[45]

That Grey was an imperialist does not mean that the Liberals should have pursued the same strategy as the Conservatives. To the contrary, their sectoral constituency still had an enormous stake in export to the great powers, giving them a clear interest in internationalism. The Liberals should have been concerned about protecting their growing trade with the periphery, but not to so great an extent that they should have converted to pure realpolitik. If Grey were no more internationalist than Rosebery had been in 1892–95, his actions would count as another disconfirmation of the theory.

In fact, the Liberals' grand strategy toward the great powers was, as expected, a compromise between the Radicals' internationalism and the

[43] Monger, *End of Isolation*, 307–10; Niall Ferguson, *The Pity of War: Explaining World War I* (New York: Basic Books, 1999), 58.
[44] Monger, *End of Isolation*, 258.
[45] Ferguson, *Pity of War*, 59; Wilson, *Policy of the Entente*, 29–32.

Liberal Imperialists' realpolitik. Grey himself was the strongest proponent of the latter paradigm. Like most Conservatives, he was committed to uphold the Entente Cordiale, even to the point of bringing Britain into a war with Germany. In the logic that led Grey to support the entente, the greatest threat by far was to the empire.[46] All of Britain's conflicts with the great powers pertained to its empire, not the security of the home isles or its European trade. If Grey had been willing to sacrifice parts of the empire, he could have appeased any foreseeable threats from a continental hegemon. Only if he insisted on maintaining the integrity of the empire would the entente be indispensable.

Grey was not troubled merely by the abstract idea of a shift in the European balance of power; he also had specific concerns about Britain's diplomatic position in the wake of a continental conflagration. If Britain were to stay neutral in a war between the Franco-Russian and German-Austrian alliances, the result could be disastrous. If the French and Russians triumphed, they would be resentful of Britain's nonparticipation and might proceed to combine their forces, defeat the British fleet, and divide the empire between themselves. On the other hand, if the Central Powers were to emerge victorious, Germany would be the master of all of Europe, more powerful than ever before. Since Kaiser Wilhelm II had been willing to rattle the saber toward Britain before the war, when he most needed Britain's support against France and Russia, he would surely be hostile after defeating them. The best scenario for the security of the empire would be the relaxation of tensions in Europe. However, if there were to be a war, Britain would have to side with France and Russia both to stay in their good graces and prevent a German victory.

Grey outlined this logic in a memorandum written less than two months after he came to office. If Britain did not adhere to the entente, he argued,

> [there would be] a general feeling in every country that we had behaved meanly and left France in the lurch. The United States would despise us, Russia would not think it worth while to make a friendly arrangement with us in Asia, Japan would prepare to re-insure herself elsewhere, we should be left without a friend and without the power of making a friend and Germany would take some pleasure, after what has passed, in exploiting the whole situation to our disadvantage. . . . The more I review the situation the more it appears to me that we cannot [stay out of a war] without losing our good name and our friends and wrecking our policy and position in the world.[47]

---

[46] Wilson, *Policy of the Entente*, chaps. 4–5; Zara S. Steiner, *Britain and the Origins of the First World War* (London: Macmillan, 1977), 242–47. Not all of the Liberal Imperialists were as enthusiastic about the entente as either Grey or the Conservatives; see Monger, *End of Isolation*, 259–60.

[47] Quoted in Wilson, *Policy of the Entente*, 94–95.

Grey was much more interested in collective security and international law than most Conservatives, but his position on France was very close to theirs.[48]

Despite its advantages, the Entente Cordiale was not universally popular. It forced Britain to align against one of its best trading partners, Germany, so it was viewed with great skepticism by the Europe-oriented Radical wing of the Liberal Party.[49] The Radicals argued that Germany's fleet-building program, though sizable, was not yet a serious threat: in 1905, Germany had only seventeen battleships to Britain's forty-six. Thus, an Anglo-German rapprochement would be possible if only Britain would retreat from its rigid support of France. The entente with France, as well as the alliance with Japan, divided the world into hostile, opposing camps and therefore endangered the peace. The idea that Britain had to choose between the two sides was a false dichotomy; the country would be better off maintaining a position of benevolent neutrality and "killing any German aggression with the kindness of concessions."[50] Many Radicals considered Britain's new colonies in Africa and Southeast Asia to be a costly, unnecessary burden and would happily have ceded to Germany its "fair share" of the spoils.

Moroccan Crises

Grey's devotion to the entente was tested from the moment he took office. At the Algeçiras Conference of January 1906, Germany provoked an international crisis by demanding that France cease its efforts to secure influence over Morocco. In the ensuing negotiations, much depended on the precise position that Grey took.[51] If he did not back France strongly enough, it would have no choice but to make concessions to Germany. In that case, the entente would likely dissolve, since the French would have no reason to help Britain if it would do nothing for them. Grey's hopes for reconciliation with Russia would be lost, and Britain would be left isolated in future disputes with the European powers. Even worse, France might be forced to cede strategically important colonies to Germany, directly endangering Britain's imperial security. On the other hand, if Britain supported

---

[48] Monger, *End of Isolation,* 280.

[49] Howard S. Weinroth, "The British Radicals and the Balance of Power, 1902–1914," *Historical Journal* 13, no. 4 (December 1970); A. J. Anthony Morris, *Radicalism against War, 1906–1914: The Advocacy of Peace and Retrenchment* (London: Longman, 1972).

[50] Wilson, *Policy of the Entente,* 26. See also J. E. Tyler, "Campbell-Bannerman and the Liberal Imperialists, 1906–1908," *History* 23, no. 1 (autumn 1983): 256; C. J. Lowe and M. L. Dockrill, *The Mirage of Power: British Foreign Policy, 1902–1914,* vol. 1 (London: Routledge and Kegan Paul, 1972), 32–37.

[51] This section follows Monger, *End of Isolation,* chap. 10. Also useful are S. L. Mayer, "Anglo-German Rivalry at the Algeçiras Conference," in *Britain and Germany in Africa: Imperial Rivalry and Colonial Rule,* ed. Prosser Gifford and William R. Louis (New Haven: Yale University Press, 1967), 215–44; Lowe and Dockrill, *Mirage of Power,* 1:21–28.

France too strongly, it might refuse to make any concessions at all, leading Germany to a declaration of war.

Grey's response was to engage in a delicate balancing act. In public, he backed France's position; behind the scenes, he refused to give French Ambassador Paul Cambon any formal guarantees of military support. Instead, he told Cambon that, if Germany attacked France, public opinion might push the Liberal government toward war. He did allow that British and French military attachés should consult on the possibility of joint action; however, this had to be done in a strictly unofficial capacity, so that he and Prime Minister Campbell-Bannerman could keep the meetings secret from their less Francophile colleagues. The implications of Grey's position were clear: he would be willing to come to France's rescue under certain circumstances, but not if it recklessly provoked Germany with outrageous demands. To maintain the sympathies of the British public and the Liberal cabinet, in which support for the entente was already shaky, France would have to act reasonably.

Relations with Germany remained tense for the next few years, so Radicals called on Grey to negotiate an Anglo-German entente. The talks centered on the question of whether Britain would enter a war between Germany and France. In return for Britain's neutrality, German chancellor Theobald von Bethmann-Holweg promised to slow down naval construction. This offer appealed to some Radicals, who already opposed intervention on the continent and wanted to trade guns for butter.[52] Grey, however, was unpersuaded. Any agreement with Germany would weaken the Anglo-French entente, which he considered vital for the security of the empire. Through much of 1909–10, he and Bethmann-Holweg exchanged various proposals on neutrality and arms control, but the differences between them were always too great. Grey would not abandon France, and Bethmann-Holweg was not willing to make concessions for anything less.

In the spring of 1911, a new diplomatic crisis further strained Anglo-German relations. A civil war broke out in Morocco, and France responded by sending troops to the capital. Germany then accused France of violating their prior agreement from the Algeçiras Conference and demanded compensation. In the ensuing negotiations, Grey followed the same balancing act as in 1905–6. He had to avoid three potential dangers: first, that France and Germany would negotiate an agreement that would be inimical to British colonial interests; second, that France would lose confidence in British support and give in to German demands; and third, that France would be so confident that it would refuse to make any significant concessions, thereby provoking Germany to war. To navigate between these perils,

[52] D. W. Sweet, "Great Britain and Germany, 1905–1911," in *British Foreign Policy under Sir Edward Grey*, ed. F. H. Hinsley (Cambridge: Cambridge University Press, 1977), 217, 229–30.

Grey supported France and warned Germany not to overreach, but he also worked to facilitate negotiations and persuade the French to accept reasonable proposals.[53] In November, the two sides finally cut a deal.

After the second Moroccan crisis was resolved, Grey agreed to reopen talks for an Anglo-German entente. However, the basic conflicts of interest between the two countries, as described above, had not changed.[54] More promising was the renegotiation of a secret treaty from 1898 that detailed how the Portuguese Empire should be divided if it were ever to dissolve. Grey approached the matter in a "pro-German spirit," hoping to demonstrate goodwill, and he eventually agreed to terms that were more favorable to Germany than before.[55] However, the treaty never became operative because of a last-moment dispute over whether it should be published. Like most internationalists, Grey found secret treaties to be unwise and immoral, and he wanted to make sure that the world knew that he had not violated Britain's existing alliance commitment to Portugal. The German government, in contrast, did not want to risk public criticism and chose to abandon the treaty rather than give in to Grey's "sentimental scruples."[56]

Balkans Crises

In 1907, Grey successfully negotiated an entente with Russia over Persia (see chapter 6). Subsequently, he hoped to use his newfound influence with Russia to settle matters in the Balkans, where conflict had broken out between Bulgarian-backed Macedonian nationalists, the Turkish army, and partisan militias of Serbs and Greeks. In this chaotic struggle, Macedonian Christians were being slaughtered en masse, and Turkish-Bulgarian relations were nearing the point of war, which might have pulled in the great powers. In response, Grey called for a meeting of the Concert of Europe, telling Parliament, "Our great object is to keep in step with the Powers, or to keep them in step with us, as the case may be."[57] He then made a number of proposals to speed up the reform of Turkish rule in Macedonia. However, both Austria-Hungary and Russia opposed any change in the status quo. Faced with their intransigence, Grey gave up.

---

[53] M. L. Dockrill, "British Policy during the Agadir Crisis of 1911," in *British Foreign Policy under Sir Edward Grey*, ed. F. H. Hinsley (Cambridge: Cambridge University Press, 1977), 271–87; Lowe and Dockrill, *Mirage of Power*, 1:37–48.

[54] Lowe and Dockrill, *Mirage of Power*, 1:48–52.

[55] Quoted in R. T. B. Langhorne, "Great Britain and Germany, 1911–1914," in *British Foreign Policy under Sir Edward Grey*, ed. F. H. Hinsley (Cambridge: Cambridge University Press, 1977), 311.

[56] Quoted in ibid., 312. See also Lowe and Dockrill, *Mirage of Power*, 1:124–27; Max Beloff, *Britain's Liberal Empire, 1897–1921* (London: Methuen, 1969), 125–26.

[57] Quoted in F. R. Bridge, "Relations with Austria-Hungary and the Balkan States," in *British Foreign Policy under Sir Edward Grey*, ed. F. H. Hinsley (Cambridge: Cambridge University Press, 1977), 168.

In early October, a far more serious crisis emerged. First, Bulgaria asserted its complete sovereignty from the Ottoman Empire; then, two days later, Austria annexed another Turkish dependency, Bosnia-Herzegovina. Though Turkish prestige was hurt, these changes had no effect on the balance of power or governing authority in the Balkans. Under the terms of the Treaty of Berlin, which had been negotiated under the auspices of the Concert of Europe and signed by all of the great powers in 1878, Austria had administrative control over Bosnia-Herzegovina and Bulgaria was functionally autonomous from Turkey. Grey was not particularly interested in the fate of either territory, since their de facto status had long since been decided. Instead, in classic Gladstonian fashion, he focused on the legal issue at stake in the crisis: Austria's unilateral abrogation of the Treaty of Berlin. Upon hearing of the annexation of Bosnia, Grey argued that

> engagements into which any Power has entered can only be broken or modified with the full assent of the Contracting Parties, and after a friendly agreement has been arrived at. A deliberate violation or alteration of the Berlin Treaty, undertaken without previous consultation with the other Powers, of which in this case Turkey is most affected, could never be approved or recognized by His Majesty's Government.[58]

As Grey later wrote, Austria had "struck at the root of all good international order."[59] There was little he could do about it, however. Austria refused to take part in a conference on the issue, much less reconsider its decision.

The failure of multilateral diplomacy in the Bosnian affair did not lead Grey to give up on it. In 1911, he sought to convene the Concert of Europe to avert the coming conflict in the Balkans, but again key states refused to participate. Grey's fears were soon realized: in October 1912, the small Balkan states declared war on Turkey and, in so doing, smashed the Treaty of Berlin. The disruption of the status quo was a clear threat to peace across Europe, so at last the great powers heeded the call to work together. Given this opportunity, Grey was able to play a critical role in the management of the crisis. As Lowe and Dockrill write, "The Concert of Europe, never a particularly harmonious or united instrument to promote peaceful change, had enjoyed a brief, if frail, renaissance under his leadership."[60]

Much of Grey's efficacy was due to self-restraint. He refused to take advantage of the situation to improve Britain's position in Egypt, made no attempt to create or exploit divisions within the Triple Alliance, and opposed Russian proposals that might have alienated Austria. Furthermore, he insisted that the other powers adhere to the same standard: "The

[58] Edward Grey, *Twenty-Five Years: 1892–1916* (New York: Stokes, 1925), 170.
[59] Ibid., 169.
[60] Lowe and Dockrill, *Mirage of Power*, 1:117.

terms of the peace must not contain any condition that would be specifically injurious to the interests of any one of the Powers: otherwise the unity of the Powers could not be preserved." In short, everything was to be subsumed to the "paramount urgency of preserving the Concert of Europe."[61] The only sense in which his approach was not purely internationalist was that he rejected calls for an official meeting of the concert powers. Instead, he believed that an informal conference of ambassadors would be most likely to produce satisfactory results.

With Grey guiding it, the conference of ambassadors managed to reach compromises over a number of territorial conflicts resulting from the Balkans wars. Grey even managed to persuade the assembled powers to participate in a multilateral naval blockade of Montenegro, which had defied their will by seeking to annex the Albanian town of Scutari. However, the concert ultimately failed to stabilize the Albanian situation, and the status of many Aegean islands remained in dispute. The fundamental problem was that, once the danger of a general European conflagration had passed, Austria and Italy were unwilling to forgo the opportunity for self-interested gains, and Germany would not act to restrain them. With time, Grey became increasingly disillusioned with the efficacy of his role as "honest broker" in the crisis.[62] If the members of the Triple Alliance were colluding to subvert the concert, then there was little point in sacrificing British interests for the sake of promoting unity. Grey did not give up on the concert entirely, but he did take a more self-serving position in it henceforth. He would act as a neutral arbitrator as long as the Triple Alliance was willing to play by the rules, but he reverted to his alignment with the Entente Cordiale once it became clear that the Triple Alliance powers were acting in bad faith.

Other Initiatives

Though the series of crises in Europe took most of Grey's attention, he did undertake two internationalist initiatives outside of the concert. First, at the Hague Conference of 1907, Grey signed off on the International Prize Court Convention, which established a centralized system for the adjudication of claims over the maritime seizure of contraband. For Britain, the convention represented an important commitment to international law. Britain was more likely than any other country to impose a naval blockade in a time of war, so the Liberals' decision to cede sovereign authority from their national prize courts to an international body could have had a serious

---

[61] Quoted in R. J. Crampton, "The Balkans, 1909–1914," in *British Foreign Policy under Sir Edward Grey*, ed. F. H. Hinsley (Cambridge: Cambridge University Press, 1977), 262, 264.

[62] M. B. Hayne, "Great Britain, the Albanian Question, and the Concert of Europe, 1911–1914," *Balkan Studies* 28, no. 2 (1987): 341–49.

impact on their national security. They fought hard for the ratification of the treaty in the House of Commons, but the opposition of the Admiralty led the House of Lords to reject it. Second, in 1911, Grey negotiated a partially binding arbitration treaty with the United States (see chapter 4). Pleased by the result, he averred that "the effect of such agreements upon disarmament and the *morale* of international politics should be considerable."[63] However, the U.S. Senate emasculated the treaty with reservations, and it was abandoned.

Relations with Japan were more conflictual. The country's continuing efforts to enlarge its colonial sphere of influence inevitably brought it into conflict with the British Empire. Grey would not give Japan free rein to expand at Britain's expense, but he also valued its cooperation. The Anglo-Japanese alliance, originally signed in 1902, had served Britain well, allowing the Admiralty to focus its attention on Germany and the North Sea without overburdening the Treasury. Thus, Grey negotiated an extension to the treaty in 1911, though not without altering its terms to reflect changes in the international environment. Russia no longer threatened India, so the clause covering the defense of India was deleted; Britain recognized Japan's annexation of Korea; and an exception was made to prevent the alliance from coming into effect in the event of war with any power with which one of the signatories had concluded an arbitration treaty. This last provision was intended to give Britain a legal escape in the event that Japan and the United States came into conflict. Grey had no intention of fighting the United States on Japan's behalf, regardless of the circumstances.[64]

Sarajevo Crisis

On the other hand, Grey proved to be willing to fight Germany on France's behalf. On June 28, 1914, a Serbian nationalist shot Austria's Archduke Ferdinand in Sarajevo, sparking the fourth major European crisis of the period. Each time before, Grey had played a delicate balancing act between the Franco-Russian and Austro-German alliances, trying to keep the peace without abandoning the Entente Cordiale. This time was no different.[65] Had Grey realized that Austria and Germany would be unwilling

---

[63] Quoted in Edmund Ions, *James Bryce and American Democracy, 1870–1922* (London: Macmillan, 1968), 235.

[64] I. H. Nish, "Great Britain, Japan, and North-East Asia, 1905–1911," in *British Foreign Policy under Sir Edward Grey*, ed. F. H. Hinsley (Cambridge: Cambridge University Press, 1977), 367.

[65] Michael G. Ekstein and Zara Steiner, "The Sarajevo Crisis," in *British Foreign Policy under Sir Edward Grey*, ed. F. H. Hinsley (Cambridge: Cambridge University Press, 1977), 401, 409–10; Keith Robbins, *Sir Edward Grey: A Biography of Lord Grey of Fallodon* (London: Cassell, 1971), 288–89; M. Ekstein, "Sir Edward Grey and Imperial Germany in 1914," *Journal of Contemporary History* 6, no. 3 (1971): 121–31; M. Ekstein, "Some Notes on Sir Edward Grey's Foreign Policy in July 1914," *Historical Journal* 15, no. 2 (June 1972): 321–24; Lowe and Dockrill, *Mirage of Power*, 1:138–39.

to compromise, he might have acted more decisively to oppose them; however, given his prior experience with European crises, the diplomatic position he adopted was by no means unreasonable. Grey was simply trying to tread the line between neutrality and alignment—specifically, between the internationalist concert and the empire-oriented, realpolitik entente—just as he had always done.

Only in the final days of July, when Austria became entirely unyielding, did Grey consider throwing his full support to the entente. He did not do so, however, at least in part because there was a serious split in opinion within the Liberal Party.[66] Though it had become increasingly imperialist in aggregate, it still had a large faction of pure internationalists. These Radicals had a Gladstonian dislike of balance-of-power realpolitik and were unwilling to go to war merely to widen the margin of security for imperial defense planners. They could not hold Germany blameless for the crisis, but neither did they see any particular principle at stake in the dispute that would necessitate intervention. As long as Germany fought for limited aims, as it had in 1870–71, and comported itself according to the strictures of international law, it should not be Britain's enemy. Indeed, some Liberals blamed tensions on Russia, whose rapid rearmament program, aggressive Balkans diplomacy, and mobilization against Austria had needlessly provoked Germany.[67] If Grey had taken a stronger stand against Germany early in the crisis, the Radical wing of the party might have revolted, leading to the fall of the government.

Grey did not make an explicit declaration of intent to defend France from Germany, nor did he give up hope that a diplomatic solution to the crisis could be found. However, he was firmly set on the need for intervention if war broke out.[68] To rally support in the cabinet, he argued that Britain was morally obliged to come to the aid of France because, after ten years with the entente, France had come to rely on Britain for its defense.[69] This argument may have helped to sway a few ministers, but it begs the underlying question: Why should Britain have followed the policy of the entente at all, thereby incurring a "moral obligation" to France? The reason was quite the same as it had been since 1905, when Grey supported France in the first Moroccan crisis: only by fighting on the side of the entente could Britain hope to secure the empire in a postwar world order. If Germany

---

[66] Robbins, *Sir Edward Grey*, 290–91, 294; Lowe and Dockrill, *Mirage of Power*, 1:145–52; Morris, *Radicalism against War*.

[67] Michael G. Ekstein, "Russia, Constantinople, and the Straits, 1914–1915," in *British Foreign Policy under Sir Edward Grey*, ed. F. H. Hinsley (Cambridge: Cambridge University Press, 1977), 425.

[68] Wilson, *Policy of the Entente*, 138.

[69] Robbins, *Sir Edward Grey*, 295–97.

won a general war on the continent while Britain waited on the sidelines, it would become the dominant power in Europe and therefore would be free to challenge Britain over peripheral issues. Germany had long coveted the British Empire and would at last be in position to wreak havoc against it. On the other hand, if France and Russia won a general war on the continent without Britain's help, they would be inclined to collaborate against Britain to expand their own empires. Russia would advance in Central Asia and China; France would move forward in Southeast Asia and Africa. There was little hope that these two powers could be played off each other; their joint interest in making gains at Britain's expense would outweigh any points of friction between them once they defeated Germany. Only by siding with them against Germany could Grey ensure that Britain would have a place at the bargaining table in a postwar settlement. In short, Grey considered the security of the empire to be a sufficient cause to bring Britain into a general war.

Though the Liberal Imperialists were ready for war, the Radicals dominated both the party and the cabinet, and Grey could do nothing without their consent. When Germany declared war on Russia, leading France to follow suit by declaring war on Germany, the Radicals refused to take sides. Instead, they decided that, provided the German navy stayed out of the English Channel, the integrity of Belgium would be Britain's sole *casus belli*. Only if Germany were to send its forces through Belgium would Britain enter the war.

Many scholars have puzzled over why the neutrality of Belgium should have mattered more to the cabinet than the fate of France. Finding no answer to this question, they surmise that the Radicals' position was merely a façade over a narrowly defined conception of the national self-interest.[70] In this view, the Radicals were far more concerned about the prospect of German control over the gateway to the English Channel than Belgium's sovereign rights. I find this interpretation to be unlikely. First, Belgium was not vital to the defense of the English Channel. As long as Britain had naval superiority, it could destroy any invasion fleet while it gathered in port. Even as die-hard a realist as Lord Salisbury had wanted to abandon Britain's guarantee of Belgian neutrality back in 1887.[71] Of course, Germany posed more of a threat to Britain in 1914 than in 1887, but the distribution of power in Europe had not changed enough to invalidate Salisbury's logic. If the leader of the Conservative Party could envision permitting German armies to pass through Belgium and defeat France in 1887, then the far less hawkish Radicals should have had no difficulty doing the same in 1914.

---

[70] Ekstein and Steiner, "Sarajevo Crisis," 407; Morris, *Radicalism against War*, 401–2; Steiner, *Britain and the Origins of the First World War*, 235–37.
[71] Roberts, *Salisbury*, 438–40.

Second, if Germany were to conquer France, it could take all of the ports it wanted on the English Channel and the Atlantic Ocean. Alternatively, if it did not want to annex northern France, it could easily secure Belgium after defeating France. If the integrity of Belgium really was a vital national interest for Britain, then the integrity of France was an equally vital national interest. Since the Radicals were willing to go to war for Belgium, but not for France, one must conclude either that they were stupendously irrational or that their concern for Belgium was not military in nature.

The answer to this puzzle lies in the logic of internationalism. Edward Grey was an internationalist, but he was also an imperialist; thus, he was willing to go to war for France even if no internationalist principles were at stake. The Radicals, on the other hand, were pure internationalists, representing the many manufacturers and coal miners who had never developed a strong interest in peripheral markets. What concerned them was not the prospect that Germany would grow powerful at France's expense; after all, it had done the same in 1870–71. Rather, the greatest danger in their minds was that Germany would not respect recognized norms of international behavior once it defeated France. The Belgian question served as a litmus test of German intentions: if Germany observed the rights of neutral states while in the midst of a war for its national survival, it could be trusted to act with reasonable self-restraint if it should emerge victorious. If it invaded Belgium, however, there was no telling how else it might violate international law. It might annex parts of France, Belgium, all of their colonies, and any other countries it desired, as Asquith emphasized in his war speech to Parliament.[72] Though the Radicals were surely concerned about the specific legal question of the violation of Belgian neutrality, the broader question of German intentions was far more important. Thus, the Radicals, no less than the Liberal Imperialists, based their position on their expectations about the postwar order. The difference was that the Radicals cared most about the prospects for stability and cooperation in the European core, whereas the Liberal Imperialists were most concerned about the future security of the empire. It was simply luck that these two imperatives converged on the defense of Belgium, giving the cabinet an unambiguous *casus belli*.

---

[72] Herbert H. Asquith, *Speeches by the Earl of Oxford and Asquith, K. G.* (New York: Doran, 1927), 195. This speech made a very favorable impression on at least one of the Radical members of the cabinet who voted for the war, Herbert Samuel; see Bernard Wasserstein, *Herbert Samuel: A Political Life* (Oxford: Clarendon, 1992), 164. Another cabinet Radical, John Simon, reported feeling "entirely deceived" by Germany and changed his mind about noninvolvement on reaching the conclusion that its leaders had provoked the war. See David Dutton, *Simon: A Political Biography of Sir John Simon* (London: Aurum, 1992), 31.

Conservatives

The Conservatives' motive for creating the Entente Cordiale in 1904 was to reduce the fiscal burdens of defense. Over time, however, with the rise of German navalism and the succession of crises on the continent, concerns about how to protect the empire in the event, and aftermath, of a war between the great powers weighed heavily on them.[73] Faced with the same dilemma as Grey, the quintessential Liberal Imperialist, the Conservatives and their gentlemanly capitalist constituency should have reached the same conclusion: that, to safeguard the empire both over the short term and in a postwar world order, they would have to align with France and Russia against Germany.

When the Conservatives left office in 1905, they were already the most vocal supporters of the entente. Over the next several years, they became ever more adamantly committed to defending France and reconciling with Russia. In 1912, Conservative leader Bonar Law proposed to Grey that Britain should enter into a formal military alliance with France. In 1914, on the outbreak of hostilities on the continent, Law and Lord Lansdowne, the former Conservative foreign minister, offered to Asquith "the assurance of the united support of the Opposition in all measures required by England's intervention in the war."[74] In short, as Rhodri Williams writes, "The Unionists' support for the dispatch of the British Expeditionary Force to France in a future Franco-German war was unswerving from 1911 to 1914."[75] If the Conservatives had been in power during the crisis of July 1914, they almost certainly would have

---

[73] Keith M. Wilson, "British Power in the European Balance, 1906–14," in *Retreat from Power*, vol. 1, ed. David Dilks (London: Macmillan, 1981), 21–41; Wilson, *Policy of the Entente*, 29–32, 135, 138; Rhodri Williams, *Defending the Empire: The Conservative Party and British Defense Policy, 1899–1915* (New Haven: Yale University Press, 1991), 196–98, 228; Monger, *End of Isolation*, 207; K. G. Robbins, "The Foreign Secretary, the Cabinet, Parliament, and the Parties," in *British Foreign Policy under Sir Edward Grey*, ed. F. H. Hinsley (Cambridge: Cambridge University Press, 1977), 6–7, 14, 18–19.

[74] Quoted in Austen Chamberlain, *Down the Years* (London: Cassell, 1935), 99.

[75] Williams, *Defending the Empire*, 198. See also ibid., 195–99, 228. Many prominent financiers in the City of London initially opposed British intervention in the war. Their response is not consistent with the theory, but it is not entirely surprising either. In the days leading up to and following the outbreak of war on the continent, there was widespread panic and collapse in European securities markets, so bankers naturally focused on the short-term costs of intervention. See Luigi Albertini, *The Origins of the War of 1914*, trans. Isabella M. Massey, vol. 3 (London: Oxford University Press, 1953), 370, 376–77; David Kynaston, *The City of London: Golden Years, 1890–1914*, vol. 2 (London: Chatto and Windus, 1995), 609–10; Ferguson, *Pity of War*, 195. Following the decision to intervene, there is countervailing evidence of pro-war preferences in London. Before the institution of conscription in February 1916, 40.1 percent of those employed in finance and commerce volunteered to fight, as opposed to 29.2 percent in industry and 24.7 percent in mining and quarrying. See J. M. Winter, *The Great War and the British People* (Cambridge, Mass.: Harvard University Press, 1986), 34.

proclaimed their unambiguous support for the French in a final attempt to deter Germany from initiating World War I.[76]

1918–31: NEGOTIATING THE PEACE

The surrender of Germany on November 11, 1918, marked the beginning of a new era in international politics. The fledgling peace raised a whole new slate of issues over which British interest groups and the political parties that represented them had reason to disagree. The stakes were enormous; the priorities that the government adopted at the Paris Peace Conference and subsequent negotiations would determine Britain's position in the world for the foreseeable future.

Under normal conditions, the potential differences between the two parties' hypothesized strategies would make the theory easy to test. However, this task is complicated by the fact that the postwar government was a coalition until 1922. The Liberals held approximately two-fifths of the seats and the prime ministry, while the Conservatives occupied three-fifths of the seats and the foreign ministry. The balance of power within the cabinet was so evenly divided that the coalition cannot be identified as strictly Conservative or Liberal. To determine whether domestic cleavages over security policy correspond to the theory's expectations, I first examine how each party initially laid out its strategic vision for the postwar era. I then address the actual strategy of the coalition government, showing how its often erratic behavior was the product of Prime Minister David Lloyd George's attempts to reconcile the two very different strategic paradigms of his political partners.

Postwar Cleavages

Liberals and Labourites, whose societal coalition of manufacturers and coal miners had a strong stake in trade with Europe, should have been concerned above all about the reconciliation of the great powers. If the terms of the peace settlement were too harsh, the defeated Germans would devote their energies to trying to overthrow the new world order. At best, this would make it difficult to reestablish a normal trading relationship; at worst, it would result in the redivision of Europe into hostile blocs seeking autarchy from each other. The same logic applied to Russia, which had been diplomatically isolated since its communist revolution. To reintegrate

---

[76] On the prospects of deterrence, see Sean M. Lynn-Jones, "Détente and Deterrence: Anglo-German Relations, 1911–1914," *International Security* 11, no. 2 (fall 1986): 121–50; Dale C. Copeland, *The Origins of Major War* (Ithaca: Cornell University Press, 2000), 63–66.

Germany and Russia into the international community, and to take advantage of the postwar window of opportunity for reform, the Liberal and Labour parties should have advanced an ambitious internationalist agenda: the limitation of demands for reparations, adherence to the principle of self-determination, multilateral reductions in armaments, and the creation of strong institutions for arbitration and collective security.[77]

Liberal opinion closely followed these prescriptions. The League of Nations, for example, was originally a Liberal idea; both during and after the war the strongest support for the league came from Liberal politicians, constituents, and newspaper editorialists.[78] The first intimation of the party's interest in such a project came on September 25, 1914, when Asquith gave a speech calling for "a real European partnership based on the recognition of equal right, and established and enforced by a common will."[79] Not long thereafter, in January 1915, Grey began trying to persuade Woodrow Wilson of the need for a postwar collective security organization—that is, "some League for preservation of Peace, to which the United States were a party and which could effectively discourage an aggressive policy or breach of treaties by anybody."[80]

The Liberals' enthusiastically pro-league position was seconded by the Labour Party.[81] Indeed, once a draft of the actual League Covenant was published, Labour criticized it for not being internationalist enough. For most members of both the Liberal and Labour parties, the essence of the

---

[77] See C. J. Lowe and M. L. Dockrill, *The Mirage of Power: British Foreign Policy, 1914–1922,* vol. 2 (London: Routledge and Kegan Paul, 1972), 340–41, 352, 356–57; G. H. Bennett, *British Foreign Policy during the Curzon Period, 1919–24* (London: Macmillan, 1995), 61–62; Peter Rowland, *Lloyd George* (London: Barrie and Jenkins, 1975), 497.

[78] George W. Egerton, *Great Britain and the Creation of the League of Nations: Strategy, Politics, and International Organization, 1914–1919* (Chapel Hill: University of North Carolina Press, 1978), 52–53, 142–43; Henry R. Winkler, *The League of Nations Movement in Great Britain, 1914–1919* (New Brunswick: Rutgers University Press, 1952), chap. 6; J. A. Thompson, "The League of Nations Union and the Promotion of the League Idea in Great Britain," *Australian Journal of Politics and History* 18, no. 1 (April 1972): 58–59.

[79] Herbert H. Asquith, *Memories and Reflections, 1852–1927,* vol. 2 (Boston: Little, Brown, 1928), 47. See also Egerton, *Great Britain and the Creation of the League of Nations,* 24.

[80] Quoted in C. M. Mason, "Anglo-American Relations: Mediation and 'Permanent Peace,'" in *British Foreign Policy under Sir Edward Grey,* ed. F. H. Hinsley (Cambridge: Cambridge University Press, 1977), 471–72. Grey's insistence was surely not without ulterior motives. The league proposal reinforced the Anglo-American relationship in a time of great stress; it gave Wilson an incentive to ensure that Britain did not lose the war; it helped deflect Edward House's proposal for mediation, which Russia and France would not have accepted; and it persuaded Wilson to make a commitment to uphold the postwar settlement, which could deter future wars. However, Grey sincerely believed in the viability of collective security, as demonstrated by his prewar efforts to revive the Concert of Europe, and he almost certainly would have pursued a similar course on the league without the Americans. See Mason, "Anglo-American Relations," 481; Egerton, *Great Britain and the Creation of the League of Nations,* 25; Robbins, *Sir Edward Grey,* 341.

[81] Egerton, *Great Britain and the Creation of the League of Nations,* 53–57; Winkler, *League of Nations Movement,* chap. 7.

league was its binding collective security provisions. If all nations would commit themselves to resisting aggression and enforcing international law, there would be less danger that the world would be drawn into war by an opposing system of alliances, and commerce would triumph over militarism. A critical element of this program was that Germany and the Soviet Union must be rehabilitated and admitted to the league; otherwise, the new organization would simply perpetuate wartime rivalries.[82] In short, the Liberal and Labour parties were clearly committed to constructing a new world order based on internationalist principles.

Conservatives had very different strategic concerns, demanding very different policy responses. Their constituency of gentlemanly capitalists was hit hard by the war (see chapter 5). If the financial sector were to recover, the British government would need to adhere to fiscal and monetary orthodoxy as closely as possible. To this end, charges on the war debt, which consumed nearly 8 percent of the national income throughout the 1920s and early 1930s, were a serious concern.[83] They hurt both the balance of payments and international confidence in the pound, making a return to the gold standard all the more difficult. The sooner the debt could be paid off, the better.

The easiest way to accomplish this, the Conservatives found, was to exact tribute from Germany. For their coalition, reparations were a convenient alternative to Labour's proposal that the war be paid for with a tax on capital.[84] As Lloyd George pointedly noted, "[the] English workman has no desire to overwhelm the German people with excessive demands. It is rather in the upper classes that an unbridled hatred of the German will be found."[85] Conservatives insisted on a high indemnity, higher even than that which France initially proposed, and were reluctant to make concessions in subsequent negotiations over its revision.[86] Reparations might hurt European economic recovery, but they offered a clear solution to the problems of the British financial sector without necessitating massive tax increases on the wealthy.

Conservatives had two additional reasons to be unsympathetic to Germany.[87] First, most wanted to exclude it from the League of Nations. In their view, the purpose of the league was to preserve Allied unity and

[82] Inbal Rose, *Conservatism and Foreign Policy during the Lloyd George Coalition, 1918–1922* (London: Cass, 1999), 55.

[83] B. R. Mitchell and P. Deane, *Abstract of British Historical Statistics* (London: Cambridge University Press, 1962), 367–68, 397–99, 403.

[84] Bruce Kent, *The Spoils of War: The Politics, Economics, and Diplomacy of Reparations, 1918–1932* (Oxford: Clarendon, 1989), 18, 28–40, 374, 390.

[85] Quoted in Lowe and Dockrill, *Mirage of Power*, 2:347.

[86] On Conservative opinion, see Rose, *Conservatism and Foreign Policy*, 10, 34–35; Michael L. Dockrill and J. Douglas Goold, *Peace without Promise: Britain and the Peace Conferences, 1919–23* (Hamden, Conn.: Archon, 1981), 51–53. On the renegotiation of the indemnity, see Richard S. Grayson, *Austen Chamberlain and the Commitment to Europe: British Foreign Policy, 1924–29* (London: Cass, 1997), 132; Kent, *Spoils of War*, 199–205.

[87] Rose, *Conservatism and Foreign Policy*, 31–32, 37, 40–41, 54.

enforce a punitive peace against Germany, not to foster consensus-building and reconciliation among the great powers. Second, many Conservatives did not feel constrained by the principle of self-determination. They argued that the territorial boundaries of Europe should, above all, be designed to prevent Germany from posing a threat to its neighbors. German resentment and irredentism were only secondary concerns. As long as Germany paid reparations and refrained from initiating another war, Conservatives had no reason to be dissatisfied with the postwar settlement in Europe.

Soviet Russia, on the other hand, was a serious concern.[88] Though its army was weakened by the devastating world war and its subsequent civil war, it still hung menacingly over Britain's possessions in Central Asia. Even worse, the Soviet government routinely used communist propaganda to stir up anti-imperial sentiment. The Comintern's activities in India were particularly troubling in light of the colony's growing independence movement and violent campaigns of civil disobedience. As a result, Russia returned to its pre-1905 status as the primary threat to the empire, and the Conservative press and politicians once again became hostile to it.

Conservatives also felt unease about the League of Nations, particularly the provisions that bound its signatories to enforce collective security and submit to international arbitration.[89] To keep the United States involved in European security and maintain good relations with Woodrow Wilson, they could accept some lesser arrangement that facilitated consultation and coordination, but not much more. In place of the League of Nations, the Conservatives countered with proposals to create a kind of formalized Concert of Europe, which would be dominated by the great powers and would not require any commitment to collective security. Thus, Britain's political parties entered the interwar period with clear differences in opinion over grand strategy, consistent with earlier cleavages but magnified by the opportunity to construct a new international order.

National Coalition

As noted above, the unusual composition of the Lloyd George coalition makes its postwar grand strategy difficult to predict. If the majority party in the cabinet had held both the prime and foreign ministries, that party's preferences should have dominated the conduct of grand strategy. In 1916–22, however, control over these posts was divided. Liberal internationalists

[88] Ibid., 205–6. See also Max Beloff, *Dream of Commonwealth, 1921–42* (London: Macmillan, 1989), 253–59; Zafar Imam, *Colonialism in East-West Relations: A Study of Soviet Policy towards India and Anglo-Soviet Relations, 1917–1947* (New Delhi: Eastman, 1969), chaps. 2–8; Chattar S. Samra, *India and Anglo-Soviet Relations (1917–1947)* (London: Asia, 1959), chaps. 2–5.

[89] Egerton, *Great Britain and the Creation of the League of Nations*, 34–36, 69–72, 121–25, 141–42; Rose, *Conservatism and Foreign Policy*, 56–63; Winkler, *League of Nations Movement*, chap. 5; Thompson, "League of Nations Union," 58–61.

could win out on some issues, but Conservative adherents of realpolitik might dominate others. In such a situation, it is possible to make only one safe prediction: that the strategy of the coalition government should have reflected some sort of compromise, quite likely one that would not be internally consistent.

International Organization

British grand strategy after the war did, in fact, vacillate between internationalism and realpolitik. Lloyd George's approach toward the League of Nations illustrates this dynamic clearly. To represent Britain in negotiations over the League Covenant at the Paris Peace Conference, Lloyd George appointed two stridently pro-league activists, Jan Smuts and Lord Robert Cecil. These men were selected because Lloyd George wished to promote Anglo-American unity and satisfy public opinion, not because they represented the collective will of his ministers.[90] In late January and early February of 1919, when talks over a draft version of the covenant were reaching a critical stage, the cabinet became increasingly restive over the direction in which Cecil was taking them. Lloyd George therefore instructed Cecil to scale back on Wilson's proposal for collective security, replacing it with the simple requirement that the great powers should convene whenever there was a breach of the peace. Cecil, who favored a strong league, ignored Lloyd George. Despite Conservative objections, he continued to act on his own ideals in negotiations over the final draft of the covenant.

Lloyd George accepted this internationalist outcome, but he made no attempt to carry out the mission of the League of Nations. To represent Britain on the League Council, he appointed a former Conservative prime minister, Arthur Balfour, who thought that the league was good for little more than "delay and publicity."[91] Balfour did resolve several issues through the council, but most of these involved patching holes in the Versailles Treaty rather than settling conflict between member-states. The league was made responsible for the governance of the Saar and Danzig, the apportionment of Upper Silesia between Germany and Poland, and the rescue of Austria's failing economy. It also appointed an arbitration panel to resolve a minor territorial dispute between Sweden and Finland. Balfour tried to keep the league from addressing, much less acting on, most other international crises, including the Polish-Russian war, the Turkish invasion of Armenia, and the Greco-Turkish War.[92] The council did attempt to

[90] Dockrill and Goold, *Peace without Promise*, 57–61; Egerton, *Great Britain and the Creation of the League of Nations*, 101–9. Lloyd George was more skeptical of the league than most Liberals, but he supported it in his public statements. See ibid., 171, 177.

[91] Quoted in Sydney H. Zebel, *Balfour: A Political Biography* (London: Cambridge University Press, 1973), 265. See also Bennett, *British Foreign Policy*, 10.

[92] F. P. Walters, *The History of the League of Nations* (London: Oxford University Press, 1960), chaps. 9–11, 13–15, 17.

mediate a territorial dispute between Poland and Lithuania, but it did not take decisive action to end the conflict. Only once, to compel Yugoslavia to withdraw from Albania in 1921, did Britain threaten to impose sanctions through the league.

The same ambivalence could be seen in the government's stance on the Permanent Court of International Justice. In negotiations over a draft of the PCIJ charter, Balfour blocked a provision that would have required member states to accept binding arbitration in their disputes. Thus, the coalition government opted out of one of the most critical elements of the internationalist agenda. It could tolerate the league as it currently existed but would make no effort to rely on or develop it:

> Lloyd George remarked to some friends at this time that he was impressed with the way that "A. J. B. [Balfour] was dominating the League of Nations." Winston Churchill responded with laughter that "if you wanted nothing done, A. J. B. was undoubtedly the best man for the task. There was no one equal to him."[93]

Such was the nature of Lloyd George's compromise: the League Covenant was made internationalist enough to satisfy the Liberals, but Balfour's realpolitik would keep the League Council from overcommitting or endangering British imperial interests.

Western Europe

Lloyd George also made compromises over the treatment of Germany. To represent Britain on the reparations commission at the peace conference, he selected Australian prime minister William Morris Hughes, Lord Sumner, and Lord Cunliffe, a former governor of the Bank of England. These men, who embodied the interests of the British Empire, aristocracy, and finance, were known to support a heavy indemnity.[94] As they negotiated in Paris, however, Lloyd George tried to sway the British public to support a moderate settlement. In the Fontainebleau Memorandum of March 1919, he argued that harsh terms would only encourage Bolshevism and German revanchism, not secure a lasting peace in Europe.[95] This caused great consternation among Conservative backbenchers, who demanded that Germany pay for as much of the war as possible.[96] Nor did it persuade the reparations commissioners

---

[93] Zebel, *Balfour*, 267. See also Walters, *History of the League of Nations*, 93, 116, 125.

[94] Kent, *Spoils of War*, 68; Marc Trachtenberg, "Reparation at the Paris Peace Conference," *Journal of Modern History* 51, no. 1 (March 1979): 32, 36.

[95] Martin Gilbert, *The Roots of Appeasement* (New York: New American Library, 1966), appendix 1, 189–96. Lloyd George also advocated bringing Germany into the League of Nations; see ibid., 86, 195.

[96] Rose, *Conservatism and Foreign Policy*, 34–35; Lowe and Dockrill, *Mirage of Power*, 2:347.

to change their minds. Three days before the memorandum was published, Lloyd George indicated that an indemnity of 100 billion marks would be "quite acceptable," if only Cunliffe and Sumner agreed. (He wanted their assent for his own "protection and justification," as he put it.)[97] Yet, on the day that the memorandum was published, they were still demanding 220 billion marks. Faced with a revolt of his coalition partners' base, Lloyd George deferred to his appointed experts. The British delegation's demands went so far beyond the French and American proposals that no compromise was possible; instead, the issue was deferred to a Reparations Commission, which was charged with producing a report in January 1921.

The Reparations Commission did not fix the final amount, but it did set preliminary guidelines for future negotiations over the schedule of repayment. Germany balked at these proposals, so France retaliated by seizing three Rhineland cities. Lloyd George was unenthusiastic about the French response, but he believed in the need for Allied unity, so he secured the cabinet's support for British participation in the operation. Then, in the spring of 1921, the London Reparations Conference convened to determine the exact amount of the indemnity: 132 billion gold marks, to be paid at a rate of two billion marks per year plus 26 percent of the value of German exports.[98] Germany accepted these terms, but soon thereafter the mark crashed. Faced with the collapse of the German economy in the winter of 1921–22, Lloyd George pressed France to grant the suspension of repayment and a 50 percent or greater reduction of the total amount owed.[99] At the Cannes Conference of January 1922, France made a few concessions, but Lloyd George could not offer it enough in terms of military security for it to be willing to take a substantially softer line toward Germany. Another repayment crisis at the end of summer that year was also resolved by short-term measures; it was all that Lloyd George could do to dissuade France from invading the Ruhr.

Lloyd George was also troubled by the prospect of German irredentism. If Poland were given a port on the Baltic, as the French wanted, millions of Germans would come under Polish sovereignty. Instead, Lloyd George secured a compromise solution in which Danzig would be a "free city," self-governed under league supervision but nominally within Polish sovereignty. He also convinced France and the United States to support a plebiscite in Upper Silesia, so that Germans living there would not be forced to live in Poland; he kept the Saar from being annexed by France; and he fought

[97] Quoted in Trachtenberg, "Reparation at the Paris Peace Conference," 38. What Lloyd George actually wanted has been subject to debate; see ibid., 32, 52–53; Charles S. Maier, "The Truth about the Treaties?," *Journal of Modern History* 51, no. 1 (March 1979): 59–60; Kent, *Spoils of War*, 39–40, 374.

[98] Bennett, *British Foreign Policy*, 18–20.

[99] Gilbert, *Roots of Appeasement*, 76–84.

Marshal Ferdinand Foch's plan to create a new Rhineland state in western Germany. In return, Lloyd George agreed to a defensive alliance with France. The offer was tempered by the condition that the alliance would not be operative unless the United States joined it. The expected costs of a tripartite alliance were low, since the combined power of these countries should have sufficed to deter Germany from another war, and the expected benefits were high, considering that Germany likely would have chosen to resume the war rather than accept partition. Lloyd George did make a few concessions for the French, who insisted that the Allies occupy parts of western Germany for up to fifteen years and that a buffer zone on the German side of the Rhine be permanently demilitarized. However, he secured his fundamental goal of keeping the Rhineland in Germany.

Unfortunately, the U.S. Senate refused to ratify the alliance, so Britain was not technically bound to it. In December 1921, Lloyd George offered a bilateral accord to France, but with several new conditions: a joint settlement of the problems of Turkey and Tangiers, the reduction of the French submarine program, the revision of the indemnity, the creation of a conference over European reconstruction, and the reopening of trade relations with Russia. In response, French foreign minister Raymond Poincaré "indicated that he would not regard the terms of the treaty as worth paying for since they added nothing to what Britain would have to do in her own interest."[100] Lloyd George refused to offer any greater commitments, such as joining the Franco-Polish alliance, so negotiations collapsed in July 1922.

Soviet Russia, Pacific Rim

The cabinet was intensely divided over British policy toward Russia. Most Liberals and Labourites, including Lloyd George, wanted to encourage Anglo-Russian trade, asserting that it could benefit both the British economy and the recovery of continental Europe.[101] Conservative foreign minister Lord Curzon, on the other hand, had long considered Russia, whether communist or not, to be a grave threat to the empire. He not only opposed diplomatic dialogue with the Soviet government but also sought to keep British troops in the Caucasus, so as to prevent Russia from retaking the newly independent buffer states of Azerbaijan, Armenia, and Georgia.[102]

Lloyd George won this debate within the cabinet. First, he withdrew British forces from the Caucasus, albeit more for the sake of budgetary parsimony than pro-Soviet sentiment.[103] He then negotiated an Anglo-Soviet

---

[100] Quoted in Anne Orde, *Great Britain and International Security, 1920–1926* (London: Royal Historical Society, 1978), 33. See also ibid., chap. 1; Bennett, *British Foreign Policy*, 19–25.
[101] On the Liberals, see Bennett, *British Foreign Policy*, 62–63, 75; Lowe and Dockrill, *Mirage of Power*, 2:331–32; Rose, *Conservatism and Foreign Policy*, 207–8. On Labour, see below.
[102] David Gilmour, *Curzon* (London: Murray, 1994), 513–14.
[103] Beloff, *Dream of Commonwealth*, 32.

trade agreement in March 1921. However, Curzon did manage to include in the treaty a provision that forbade either side from "hostile action or undertakings against the other and from conducting outside its own borders any official propaganda direct or indirect against the . . . British Empire or the Russian Soviet Republic."[104] To many Conservatives, the expansion of trade had little value unless it could be used as leverage against Russian misbehavior. Against their wishes, Lloyd George continued to seek rapprochement with the Bolsheviks: in the spring of 1922, he took the highly controversial move of inviting them to his Genoa Conference on European reconstruction.[105]

Meanwhile, British strategy in the Pacific was complicated by mutual antagonism between the United States and Japan. At the Washington Conference of 1922, Balfour sought to create a "triple alliance" with them, but neither took an interest in it. Instead, he had to settle for the weak Four-Power Treaty, in which the three countries plus France pledged to consult each other in the event of aggression. The Washington Conference also produced a major naval arms reduction agreement. President Harding's proposal for massive cutbacks in both future construction and existing ships came as a surprise to the British delegation, but it was not unwelcome, given the burden of the war debt.[106]

Overall, the coalition government's grand strategy toward the great powers was an incoherent hodgepodge of Liberal internationalism and Conservative realpolitik. Throughout his tenure as prime minister, Lloyd George made numerous compromises between the two factions. He signed on to the internationalist League Covenant, but he rejected the binding arbitration provision of the PCIJ and kept the League Council from taking meaningful action on Europe's most serious conflicts; he prevented France from dividing up German territory and opposed burdening Germany with a harsh indemnity, but he appointed hawkish reparations commissioners and maintained that Britain should get its fair share of the spoils; and he embraced trade with Soviet Russia as a means to spark Europe's postwar economic recovery, but he allowed the Conservatives to impose political conditions on the Anglo-Soviet trade agreement. With all of these turnabouts, Lloyd George clearly deserves his reputation as one of the most dexterous politicians in British history. As one Conservative newspaper reported, his "ideas are in a state of constant flux according to the exigencies of the domestic situation."[107] The "Welsh wizard," as he was called, did not always manage

---

[104] Quoted in Bennett, *British Foreign Policy*, 69. See also ibid., 66–67, 73; M. V. Glenny, "The Anglo-Soviet Trade Agreement, March 1921," *Journal of Contemporary History* 5, no. 2 (1970): 63–82.

[105] Rose, *Conservatism and Foreign Policy*, 217–20.

[106] Zebel, *Balfour*, 267–68; Bennett, *British Foreign Policy*, 169–71; Rose, *Conservatism and Foreign Policy*, 169–71.

[107] Quoted in Rose, *Conservatism and Foreign Policy*, 136.

to please his coalition partners, but his consistent inconsistency somehow kept them in line through turbulent times.

Conservatives

In October 1922, the Conservatives abandoned Lloyd George and formed a government of their own. Foreign Minister Lord Curzon, free at last from the yoke of coalitional politicking, took full responsibility over grand strategy. The Conservatives then lost the election of December 1923, but they were not out of power long; Labour's first government fell after only nine months. In November 1924, the Conservatives returned to office with a new foreign minister, Austen Chamberlain, and remained in control until June 1929. Following the logic of postwar partisanship, both Conservative governments, which are treated together below, should have reverted to an unqualified strategy of realpolitik, with the goal of protecting the interests of finance and maintaining the security of the empire.

International Organization

The Conservatives did indeed adhere to a strategy of realpolitik, and this approach was clearly evident in their dealings with the League of Nations. The internationalist Lord Robert Cecil was appointed to be Britain's representative on the League Council, but he was kept on a short rein, and his colleagues in the government squelched every attempt to extend or strengthen international law. First, they rejected the Draft Treaty of Mutual Assistance, a league proposal to reduce global armaments and commit members to oppose international aggression with military means.[108] (The League Covenant required only the imposition of economic sanctions.) Second, they refused to join the Optional Clause of the PCIJ, which would have bound Britain to the arbitration of its disputes with other signatories.[109] Finally, when Italy invaded the Greek island of Corfu, a classic interstate dispute of the type that the league was designed to resolve, Curzon initially granted that the council should consider the question but henceforth worked against efforts to enforce the covenant on Greece's behalf.[110]

Chamberlain was less dismissive of the league than Curzon, but he nevertheless withdrew two internationalist initiatives that Labour had put on the agenda in 1924. First, like Curzon, he rejected the Optional Clause of the PCIJ; and second, he refused to sign the Geneva Protocol of the League

---

[108] Walters, *History of the League of Nations,* 225–27.
[109] Lorna Lloyd, *Peace through Law: Britain and the International Court in the 1920s* (Suffolk: Boydell, 1997), 18–20.
[110] Harold Nicolson, *Curzon: The Last Phase, 1919–1925* (New York: Harcourt, Brace, 1939), 368–73; Gilmour, *Curzon,* 589.

of Nations, a comprehensive program for arbitration, disarmament, and the designation of aggressor states.[111] He also declined to seek British accession to the General Act of 1928, an adjunct to the Optional Clause.[112] Even more limited forms of internationalism were deemed unacceptable. In late 1925, he resisted Egypt's attempt to bring a dispute with Italy before the League of Nations.[113] Though Egypt was nominally independent, Chamberlain was unwilling to tolerate league jurisdiction over any issue pertaining to British imperial interests. The council could deal only with questions of "third-rate importance" in which Britain had no stake; the Conservatives actively opposed its involvement in more weighty affairs. Their disdain for collective security and disarmament so discouraged Lord Robert Cecil, Britain's ambassador to the council, that he resigned in 1927.

Western Europe

In the autumn and winter of 1922, Germany spiraled into economic and financial crisis. France refused to make concessions on the reparations schedule; instead, it threatened to invade the Ruhr. In response, the Conservatives drew back temporarily from their harsh position on the indemnity. First, they recognized that the collapse of the German economy made the existing reparations agreement unsustainable.[114] If Britain were ever to see the sums pledged to it, the Allies would have to defer payment in the short term. Second, France would make matters worse by invading the Ruhr. The region was Germany's industrial heartland; if it were occupied by French troops, the Weimar government would be unable to earn enough revenue to fulfill its obligations. Finally, France still harbored ambitions to create an independent state in the Rhineland and was building up its military to levels far beyond what was needed to suppress Germany. According to G. H. Bennett, "France seemed to have adopted the outlook of Prussian militarism, and her domination of continental Europe was regarded as an accomplished fact by late 1923. By contrast, the British government no longer saw Germany as their chief

---

[111] Austen Chamberlain, *Peace in Our Time* (London: Allan, 1928), 182; Lloyd, *Peace through Law*, 46–51, 61–65, 103–4. In 1926, Chamberlain had a change of heart about the Optional Clause, but he found little support for it in the cabinet, so he gave up on it. Lloyd argues that the government was moving toward acceptance of the Optional Clause before it lost the election of 1929, but she admits that "whether they would have signed the Clause, and what reservations they might have attached to their signature, is one of history's unknowns." See ibid., 166–96, 249–51 (quote on 251).

[112] Ibid., *Peace through Law*, 115–19.

[113] Grayson, *Austen Chamberlain*, 60, 105; Walters, *History of the League of Nations*, 289.

[114] Bennett, *British Foreign Policy*, 31–32; Nicolson, *Curzon*, 363–67.

European rival."[115] Thus, when French and Belgian forces invaded the Ruhr in January 1923, the Conservatives declined to join them. The government could not directly oppose France without creating a dangerous rift in the postwar settlement, but neither did it have an interest in dismembering Germany.

The Conservatives' rejection of the Geneva Protocol of the League of Nations aggravated the growing rift in Anglo-French relations. The French had hoped that the protocol would strengthen Britain's commitment to continental security, so the defeat of the agreement came as a serious blow to them. If Britain offered nothing as a substitute, France's fears of Germany would continue to destabilize western Europe.[116] Consequently, the Conservatives renewed their earlier offer of a defensive alliance, and in October 1925, the British, French, Belgian, and German governments signed the Locarno Pact. Britain agreed to guarantee the Franco-German border, Germany joined the League of Nations, the Rhineland was neutralized, and Germany agreed that any disputes over its eastern border would be resolved by arbitration.

The Locarno Pact achieved a number of Conservative strategic goals at once. It calmed Franco-German tensions, thereby reducing the danger that Britain would be drawn into another European war; it reconciled Germany to making reparations payments; and it prevented France from attempting to separate the Rhineland from Germany and establish de facto hegemony over the continent.[117] It also met with the approval of the Liberal and Labour parties, since it reassured the French without creating an exclusionary, polarizing alliance.[118] At the same time, however, the Locarno Pact did nothing to advance the cause of international law. Indeed, it committed Britain to little more than that to which it would have agreed in a bilateral Anglo-French alliance. As Chamberlain told the House of Commons, "I do not think that the obligations of this country could be more narrowly circumscribed to the vital national interest than they are in the Treaty of Locarno."[119] The pact stood apart from the league system of collective security, and Britain refused to join any of its provisions for arbitration.

---

[115] Bennett, *British Foreign Policy*, 38–39. See also Nicolson, *Curzon*, 375–76; Orde, *Great Britain and International Security*, 170–72.

[116] Orde, *Great Britain and International Security*, 71–73; David Dutton, *Austen Chamberlain: Gentleman in Politics* (Bolton: Anderson, 1985), 238–39; Grayson, *Austen Chamberlain*, 44–48.

[117] Walters, *History of the League of Nations*, 285.

[118] Dutton, *Austen Chamberlain*, 250. Liberals and Labourites did, however, have some misgivings about making security arrangements outside of the League of Nations. See Lloyd, *Peace through Law*, 199; Orde, *Great Britain and International Security*, 151.

[119] Quoted in Dutton, *Austen Chamberlain*, 250.

Soviet Russia

Germany posed no threat to the empire until the mid 1930s, so the Conservatives took no further action against it. By contrast, Soviet Russia's use of propaganda, subversion, and aid for nationalist movements in the British Empire was a serious concern. In the spring of 1923, Curzon decided to take action. He drew up a list of complaints and stated that the Anglo-Soviet trade agreement would be canceled in ten days if the Russians did not reform their behavior. As G. H. Bennett explains, "Bolshevik propaganda in Asia was the note's (and Curzon's) principal concern. . . . Curzon cared little for the trade agreement and he had few qualms about using it as a lever with which to gain concessions from the Soviet government."[120] The Soviets relented, but relations remained strained. The situation did not improve until 1924, when Labour came to power and granted recognition of the Soviet regime.

After the Labour government fell, the status quo held for only two years. The new Conservative foreign minister, Austen Chamberlain, was less perturbed by Soviet misdeeds than Lord Curzon had been. However, he could not ignore them for long, as the Soviets' continued meddling in British domestic and imperial affairs exacerbated strong anticommunist sentiment within the Conservative Party. In 1926–27, evidence was found that the Soviets had incited mob violence in China, spied on the British legation in Peking, supported strikers in Britain, and stolen a British signal book. Concerned by this trend, the Committee for Imperial Defense began planning in July 1926 for a potential war in Afghanistan. Lord Milne, Britain's chief of the Imperial General Staff, believed that Soviet intrigues in China were part of a broader plan, "namely, the overthrow of British interests in the Far and Middle East with the ultimate object of undermining our supremacy in India."[121] As suspicions escalated, Chamberlain could not resist the pressure within his party for a breach. In May 1927, the government announced that police investigations had "conclusively proved that both military espionage and subversive activities against the British Empire were directed and carried out" in the offices of the Soviet Trade Delegation in London.[122] Against Chamberlain's advice, the cabinet voted in May 1927 for a complete rupture in relations, including the expulsion of Soviet representatives and the cancellation of the 1921 trade agreement.[123] Official Anglo-Soviet contacts

---

[120] Bennett, *British Foreign Policy*, 73.

[121] Quoted in Grayson, *Austen Chamberlain*, 266. See also Orde, *Great Britain and International Security*, 178–179; Curtis Keeble, *Britain and the Soviet Union, 1917–89* (London: Macmillan, 1990), 99–108.

[122] Quoted in Keeble, *Britain and the Soviet Union*, 106.

[123] Robert D. Warth, "The Arcos Raid and the Anglo-Soviet 'Cold War' of the 1920's," *World Affairs Quarterly* 29, no. 2 (July 1958): 122–24; Gottfried Niedhart, "British Attitudes

ceased completely, and British merchandise exports to the Soviet Union fell by more than half.[124]

Pacific Rim

Britain's relations with the United States were far less acrimonious, though not unproblematic. The Geneva Naval Conference of 1927 foundered, as did subsequent attempts to reach an agreement on belligerent maritime rights. Nevertheless, the Americans offered two new proposals in 1928: the Kellogg-Briand Pact to outlaw war and a new bilateral arbitration treaty. Neither met with enthusiasm from the Conservative government. The cabinet ratified the Kellogg-Briand Pact, but only once Chamberlain sent a letter to the United States and members of the League of Nations with the assertion that the agreement would not restrict Britain's freedom of action in "certain regions of which the welfare and integrity constitute a special and vital interest to our peace and safety."[125] As discussed in chapter 4, the pact amounted to little more than a public relations gimmick. Even without Chamberlain's informal reservation, the cabinet's decision to accept the agreement would not have been indicative of a meaningful commitment to internationalism.

The arbitration treaty was more problematic. It would restrict not only Britain's diplomatic freedom of action but also the Royal Navy's ability to blockade American shipping in wartime. The Conservatives had no desire to sacrifice British imperial interests on the altar of arbitration, but they could not oppose it without aggravating existing tensions in Anglo-American relations.[126] After months of tortured discussions, Chamberlain finally concluded that the best course of action would be to sign the treaty without a reservation for maritime belligerency. However, most Conservatives remained unpersuaded. According to the First Lord of the Admiralty, "If it were known that we had cast our belligerent rights upon the waters, there would be a split in the Conservative Party from top to bottom."[127] With an election pending, Prime Minister Stanley Baldwin put off discussion of the treaty, and the Conservatives were voted out of office.

---

and Policies towards the Soviet Union and International Communism, 1933–39," in *The Fascist Challenge and the Policy of Appeasement*, ed. Wolfgang J. Mommsen and Lothar Kettenacker (London: Allen and Unwin, 1983), 288. Both authors argue that the most likely cause of the rupture was Soviet misconduct in China, not agitprop in the home isles.
[124] Keeble, *Britain and the Soviet Union*, 108.
[125] Quoted in B. J. C. McKercher, *The Second Baldwin Government and the United States, 1924–1929* (Cambridge: Cambridge University Press, 1984), 126. See also Grayson, *Austen Chamberlain*, 159; Dutton, *Austen Chamberlain*, 278; Lloyd, *Peace through Law*, 129.
[126] McKercher, *Second Baldwin Government*, chaps. 6, 8; Lloyd, *Peace through Law*, chap. 6.
[127] Quoted in Lloyd, *Peace through Law*, 148.

Labour

Labour came to power for the first time for nine months in 1924, then returned to office in 1929–31. As the party took over the Liberals' constituency of manufacturers and coal miners, it should also have assumed the Liberals' mantle as the champion of internationalism. The centerpiece of its strategy should have been the League of Nations. If strengthened, the league could assuage French fears of invasion while simultaneously promoting the integration of Germany into the new world order, thereby ending the poisonous cycle of reparations crises and encouraging closer Anglo-French relations.[128]

Despite its short stays in office, Labour had ample opportunity to take a stand on internationalism. In 1924, one proposal to revise the League Covenant was already under consideration, the Draft Treaty of Mutual Assistance. Prime Minister Ramsay MacDonald disagreed with some of its specifics, so he called on the league to produce a major new initiative that would rectify its problems. The resulting agreement, negotiated by Foreign Minister Arthur Henderson and the League Council, was titled the Geneva Protocol on the Pacific Settlement of International Disputes. It featured three components that were intended to be mutually reinforcing.[129] First, it created a system of arbitration that would be applicable to all interstate disputes. If one state refused arbitration, it would be deemed an aggressor unless the council unanimously voted otherwise. Thus, the league would no longer be burdened with identifying which side was at fault in the particular circumstances of any given conflict. Second, sanctions would be imposed automatically against aggressors that resorted to force. Third, once the protocol had been ratified by the majority of the council and ten other member-states, the league would generate a plan for the reduction of armaments and hold an international conference on the issue. If that conference succeeded, the arbitration and collective security provisions of the protocol would come into force.

MacDonald also ordered a review of Britain's position on the Optional Clause of the Permanent Court of International Justice, which allowed states to commit themselves to the compulsory arbitration of all of their disputes with fellow signatories. The Geneva Protocol required its members to sign on to the Optional Clause, but the PCIJ existed independently of the protocol, so a decision to join the clause would bind Britain to arbitration even if the protocol failed. By the time the Labour government of 1924 fell,

---

[128] Michael R. Gordon, *Conflict and Consensus in Labour's Foreign Policy, 1914–1965* (Stanford: Stanford University Press, 1969), 49; Elaine Windrich, *British Labour's Foreign Policy* (Stanford: Stanford University Press, 1952), 32–33.

[129] Walters, *History of the League of Nations*, 272–74; Windrich, *British Labour's Foreign Policy*, 40; Orde, *Great Britain and International Security*, 68–69; P. J. Noel Baker, *The Geneva Protocol* (London: 1925).

it had not yet acceded to the Optional Clause, but every indication was that it was planning to do so.[130] The Geneva Protocol died for the same reason: MacDonald simply did not have enough time to get it to a vote in Parliament. He had reservations about its collective security provisions, so he may not have been able or willing to ratify the treaty without amendments.[131] Nevertheless, the internationalist principles underlying the treaty were clearly an important element of his government's grand strategy. He implored Parliament, "Give us ten years of the working of the Protocol, and we will have Europe with a new habit of mind."[132]

When Labour regained power in 1929, it immediately returned to some of the unfinished projects of its first government. By this point, Prime Minister MacDonald was reluctant to make further commitments to collective security and international arbitration, but his view was in the minority. Foreign Minister Henderson managed to persuade the cabinet to support the majority of his internationalist initiatives, even when MacDonald objected. Most important, Labour acceded to the Optional Clause of the PCIJ.[133] The Admiralty insisted that reservations be made to establish a "British Monroe Doctrine" and exclude issues pertaining to belligerent maritime rights, but Henderson refused to back down. In the end, he accepted only three minor reservations, the most limiting of which made an exception for disputes between the Dominions. The government also signed the General Act of Arbitration, Conciliation, and Judicial Settlement, which filled in a gap in the Optional Clause by requiring the adjudication of "non-justicable" disputes (i.e., those in which no definite international legal principle was in question).[134] In the parliamentary debate over each of these treaties, Conservative amendments to restrict the scope of Britain's commitment were defeated by a united coalition of Labourites and Liberals.

Germany

One of the first Labour government's greatest foreign policy successes came in the normalization of relations with Germany. In 1924, the international

---

[130] Lloyd, *Peace through Law*, 24–29, 34–51.

[131] Ibid., 37–45; Catherine A. Cline, *Recruits to Labour: The British Labour Party, 1914–1931* (Syracuse: Syracuse University Press, 1963), 89–97; Richard W. Lyman, *The First Labour Government, 1924* (London: Chapman and Hall, 1957), 176–80; Carlton, *MacDonald versus Henderson*, 73–74; David Marquand, *Ramsay MacDonald* (London: Cape, 1977), 355–56; Orde, *Great Britain and International Security*, 69–70.

[132] Quoted in Gordon, *Conflict and Consensus*, 53.

[133] Carlton, *MacDonald versus Henderson*, 75–78; Kenneth E. Miller, *Socialism and Foreign Policy: Theory and Practice in Britain to 1931* (The Hague: Nijhoff, 1967), 208–10; Lloyd, *Peace through Law*, chap. 8.

[134] Carlton, *MacDonald versus Henderson*, 93; Miller, *Socialism and Foreign Policy*, 211; William R. Tucker, *The Attitude of the British Labour Party towards European and Collective Security Problems, 1920–1939* (Geneva: University of Geneva, 1950), 146–47.

environment was changing in ways that created a window of opportunity for a settlement. France had begun to accept that its occupation of the Ruhr was an abject failure, its hard-line president was replaced by a moderate, and the United States agreed to prop up Germany's economy with the Dawes Plan. Under these favorable circumstances, MacDonald managed to convince France to accept two critical changes in policy: to link reparations payments to German economic recovery and to resolve disputes through arbitration. Force would be used only when Germany was in "flagrant default" and when all of the Allies agreed to it. Then, in 1929, Henderson worked with Germany to prevail upon France to make the most important concession of all: to withdraw the last of the Allied forces from the Rhineland by June 1930.[135] Finally, in January 1930, the powers met again to address unresolved issues pertaining to repayment, at which point Henderson persuaded France that if Germany were to make a willful default, the Allies would have to present their case to the PCIJ before taking military action.[136]

Soviet Russia

The last major goal of Labour's grand strategy was to normalize relations with Soviet Russia. Before the party came to power in 1924, both the Lloyd George coalition and the subsequent Conservative government had concluded that de jure diplomatic recognition of the Bolshevik regime should be the last step in a comprehensive settlement of Anglo-Soviet disputes. In contrast, MacDonald decided to grant recognition as one of his first acts in office. He and his fellow Labourites disliked the Soviet Union's domestic brutality and international propaganda, but they were more concerned about promoting exports to revive the depressed industries of northern England, Scotland, and Wales. The linkage between economics and alignment was made explicit in Labour's campaign manifestos:

> [Russian] orders for machinery and manufactures, which would have found employment for thousands of British workers, have been lost to this country. . . . A Labour Government, whilst opposed to the interference of the Russian Government with the domestic politics of other nations, would at once take steps to establish diplomatic and commercial relations with it, would settle by treaty or otherwise any outstanding differences, and would make every effort to encourage a revival of trade with Soviet Russia.[137]

---

[135] Most Conservatives shared this goal, but they were not willing to put serious pressure on the French to obtain it. See Carlton, *MacDonald versus Henderson*, 33.

[136] Ibid., 61; Tucker, *Attitude of the British Labour Party*, 120.

[137] Labour Party, *Labour and the Nation*, rev. ed. (London: Labour Party, 1928), 49. See also White, *Britain and the Bolshevik Revolution*, 224–33; Williams, *Labour and Russia*, 77–82, 85–86, 88, 110–15, 128; Carlton, *MacDonald versus Henderson*, chap. 7.

Labour failed to resolve the thorniest of disputes between the two countries, the Soviets' refusal to repay loans subscribed by the tsar. However, it did sign two treaties: a standard trade agreement, and a general settlement of Anglo-Russian affairs that was designed to become operative when the outstanding loans question was settled.[138]

After the first Labour government fell from power, the Conservatives undid much of its diplomatic handiwork. In 1927, they dealt a serious blow to Anglo-Russian relations by ordering a complete and immediate diplomatic breach. For the next two years, the two countries had no official contacts and bilateral trade fell precipitously. Labour made the resulting economic losses a major issue in the next election campaign, citing a group of northern English industrialists who had recently visited the Soviet Union and returned with glowing reports on prospects for export.[139]

When the party returned to power in 1929, the normalization of Anglo-Soviet relations was high on its agenda.[140] Henderson initially took a hard line against Soviet propaganda, but he settled for empty promises once it became evident that this was all that Stalin was willing to offer. Once again supported by the Liberals, the Labour government secured the ratification of an Anglo-Soviet diplomatic recognition treaty in November 1929 and temporary trade and fisheries agreements in April and May of 1930. Comintern activity subsequently increased, but Henderson held fast to his policy of forbearance. Through its attempts at reconciliation with the USSR and Germany, as well as its devotion to the League of Nations and PCIJ, Labour (and the Liberals) demonstrated that its strategic goals diverged dramatically from those of the Conservative Party—and, in so doing, conformed closely to theoretical expectations.

1931–39: Appeasement in Hard Times

After little more than a decade of peace, the new world order began to crumble. The Great Depression shook the system to its core: international trade collapsed, budgets imploded, unemployment surged, conflicts flared, and moderate regimes fell. In Japan, Italy, and Germany, nationalist leaders focused their discontent on the postwar settlement, seeking to overthrow

---

[138] Liberals initially supported the negotiations, but they disagreed with the specifics of the latter deal and sided with the Conservatives to vote it down. See Marquand, *Ramsay MacDonald*, 363–64.

[139] E. Remnant, "The British Industrial Mission to Russia," *English Review* 49 (July 1929): 27–41.

[140] Donald M. Lammers, "The Second Labour Government and the Restoration of Relations with Soviet Russia (1929)," *Bulletin of the Institute of Historical Research* 37, no. 95 (1964): 60–72; Carlton, *MacDonald versus Henderson*, chap. 8; Williams, *Labour and Russia*, chaps. 7–9; Miller, *Socialism and Foreign Policy*, 201–4; Keeble, *Britain and the Soviet Union*, 108–11.

treaties that limited their military strength and territorial boundaries. For Britain, the economic crisis climaxed in the summer of 1931, leading it to withdraw from the gold standard and slash public spending. Whatever grand strategy it followed, its behavior would be severely circumscribed by both international and domestic constraints. In these trying times, governments could afford to pursue only their most critical priorities. As a result, the 1931–39 period provides one of the most analytically clear-cut and historically important illustrations of the logic of the theory.

As explained in chapter 6, Conservatives were the dominant force in British politics from November 1931 through the beginning of World War II. They invited Liberals and Labourites to join them in a national coalition, but they controlled policymaking. Even in 1931–35, when Ramsay MacDonald was prime minister, the real power lay with Conservative party leaders Stanley Baldwin and Neville Chamberlain. Thus, I treat the National government of 1931–39 as de facto Conservative. Neither the Liberal nor Labour Parties held power in this period, so for them I test the theory on policies advocated while in opposition.

Conservatives

The Great Depression had a disastrous effect on the Conservatives' primary economic constituency, the already weakened financial services sector. In September 1931, a currency crisis forced the government to abandon the gold standard. The depression also brought an end to German reparations, eliminating the Treasury's foreign source of revenue. Meanwhile, annual charges on the debt remained over 4.5 percent of the national income. After December 1932, the government finally suspended the repayment of its foreign loans. The imposition of tariffs in 1931 and the creation of the Imperial Preference system at the Ottawa Conference of 1932 helped to ease the crisis, but the government still had to adopt harsh austerity measures to balance the budget.[141] If Britain were ever to return to the gold standard, it would need to adhere strictly to fiscal and monetary orthodoxy, despite continuing economic hardship.[142]

These considerations did not alter the Conservatives' essential strategic imperative, as dictated by the interests of London-based investors and

---

[141] Several scholars have noted that these Conservative policies prioritized the interests of finance and the empire over trade with Europe. See David E. Kaiser, *Economic Diplomacy and the Origins of the Second World War: Germany, Britain, France, and Eastern Europe, 1930–1939* (Princeton: Princeton University Press, 1980), chap. 4; Scott Newton, *Profits of Peace: The Political Economy of Anglo-German Appeasement* (Oxford: Clarendon, 1996), 38–40; P. J. Cain and A. G. Hopkins, *British Imperialism: Crisis and Deconstruction, 1914–1990*, vol. 2 (London: Longman, 1993), 83–93.

[142] Robert P. Shay, *British Rearmament in the Thirties: Politics and Profits* (Princeton: Princeton University Press, 1977), 11–18; Newton, *Profits of Peace*, 114–22.

traders: to maintain Britain's predominant position in the periphery, align against the greatest threat to the empire, and avoid entangling commitments to international law and multilateral institutions. Nevertheless, the Great Depression presented an enormous constraint on the conduct of this strategy. The Conservatives wanted desperately to keep taxes low, balance the budget, and prepare for a return to the gold standard. They could not accomplish any of these goals if Britain were to enter into a full-scale arms race with all of its competitors. Thus, party leaders were under great pressure to adopt a form of strategic triage similar to that of 1895–1905. The home isles and the empire would have to take strict precedence in defense planning and alignment decisions; the situation within Europe should have become a priority only if it posed an imminent threat to the first two theaters of concern.

Japan

Shortly after coming to power in August 1931, the Conservative-dominated National government faced a major diplomatic crisis in the Far East.[143] In mid September, Japan invaded Manchuria, and China called on the League of Nations for assistance. Although Japan had clearly violated the League Covenant, Foreign Minister John Simon argued that it would be unwise for Britain to respond. Britain would shoulder most of the costs of any action taken by the league, and its position in East Asia was far too precarious to risk a war with Japan. It was not until early 1933, when Japan began to extend its control into the neighboring province of Jehol, that the government finally felt obliged to act. Against Simon's counsel, it imposed an embargo on British arms exports to both China and Japan. Other countries declined to join in the effort, so it was rescinded after only two weeks.

Over the next year, Britain experienced a rapid deterioration in its security environment. With the rearmament of Italy and Germany, Britain's potential adversaries increased in both number and strength. In 1934, the Defence Requirements Committee reported that the Royal Navy was stretched too thin to deal with all of them and asked for a major rearmament program. The Conservatives did not comply; instead, they lowered income taxes, much to the benefit of their wealthy constituents. Rather than increase spending on arms, they turned to diplomacy.[144]

---

[143] Walters, *History of the League of Nations*, chap. 4; Dutton, *Simon*, chap. 5; Paul Haggie, *Britannia at Bay: The Defence of the British Empire against Japan, 1931–1941* (Oxford: Clarendon, 1981), 18–43; Christopher Thorne, "The Quest for Arms Embargoes: Failure in 1933," *Journal of Contemporary History* 5, no. 4 (1970): 129–49.

[144] Kevin Narizny, "Both Guns and Butter, or Neither: Class Interests in the Political Economy of Rearmament," *American Political Science Review* 97, no. 2 (May 2003): 209–11.

Japan was to be the linchpin of British strategy in the Far East.[145] The United States was too isolationist to be a reliable partner, and Soviet Russia had repeatedly proved itself to be hostile to the British Empire. Japan, in contrast, shared the Conservatives' antipathy toward the USSR. Against the advice of the Foreign Office, which argued that an entente with Japan would alienate China and the United States, the Treasury insisted on moving forward with negotiations, and the cabinet agreed. In return for an offer to recognize Japanese gains in Manchuria, Britain sought concessions over naval arms limitations and a guarantee of Chinese sovereignty south of the Great Wall. Japan declined these terms, but talks continued intermittently through June 1937, when full-scale war broke out between Japan and China.

Far more than the occupation of Manchuria, the Sino-Japanese war had a disastrous effect on Britain's position in the Far East.[146] Japan attacked cities in Britain's traditional sphere of influence, interfered with British commercial rights, demanded that British authorities cooperate in its efforts to capture Chinese resisters, and even sank a British gunboat. Yet, by that point, there was little that Britain could do in response. Without the support of the United States, and with war looming in Europe, it dared not provoke Japan. It gave limited financial support to the Chinese Nationalists but otherwise stood by passively as the Japanese military advanced.

Italy

The National government's reaction to Italian aggression was marked by a similar ambivalence.[147] In early 1935, Mussolini began preparations for the conquest and annexation of Abyssinia, an independent member of the League of Nations. The Manchurian crisis had already weakened the league; another failure of collective security would shatter it. With an election scheduled for mid November, the Conservatives would lose critical swing votes if they did not take action. On the other hand, the party had no economic or

[145] Stephen L. Endicott, *Diplomacy and Enterprise: British China Policy, 1933–1937* (Vancouver: University of British Columbia Press, 1975), chap. 3; Ann Trotter, "Tentative Steps for an Anglo-Japanese Rapprochement in 1934," *Modern Asian Studies* 8, no. 1 (1974): 59–83; Gill Bennett, "British Policy in the Far East, 1933–1936: Treasury and Foreign Office," *Modern Asian Studies* 26, no. 3 (July 1992): 545–68.
[146] Peter Lowe, *Great Britain and the Origins of the Pacific War: A Study of British Policy in East Asia, 1937–1941* (Oxford: Clarendon, 1977), chaps. 1–3.
[147] J. A. Cross, *Sir Samuel Hoare, a Political Biography* (London: Cape, 1977), 193–265; James C. Robertson, "The Origins of British Opposition to Mussolini over Ethiopia," *Journal of British Studies* 9, no. 1 (November 1969): 122–42; A. R. Peters, *Anthony Eden at the Foreign Office, 1931–1938* (New York: St. Martin's, 1986), 165–69, 196–206; R. A. C. Parker, "Great Britain, France, and the Ethiopian Crisis, 1935–1936," *English Historical Review* 89, no. 351 (April 1974): 293–332; Richard Davis, "Mésentente Cordiale: The Failure of the Anglo-French Alliance," *European History Quarterly* 23, no. 4 (October 1993): 513–27.

strategic interest in opposing Italy. The Admiralty initially believed that it was capable of defeating the Italian fleet, but it estimated that victory could cost three to four battleships, a loss that it could ill afford given the possibility of war with Japan and Germany.[148] Furthermore, cooperation with Italy was vital if Hitler were to be contained and spending on rearmament limited. Faced with these conflicting imperatives, Simon's successor at the Foreign Office, Samuel Hoare, tried to finesse the problem. He pacified public opinion by calling for sanctions, but he expected not to have to follow through with imposing them. In all likelihood, France would object to such measures, and Hoare could give up without taking the blame.

The Italian army finally invaded Abyssinia in October 1935. To Hoare's surprise, the French agreed to sanctions, so he was obliged to make good on his promise. With Britain leading the charge, the League of Nations voted to cut off all loans to Italy, refuse Italian exports, and prevent the export of certain raw materials to Italy. Hoare's actions constitute a clear instance of internationalism and therefore violate the prediction that the government's strategy should have been strictly realpolitik. However, as noted above, it represented a short-term election strategy gone awry rather than the optimal response of sincere internationalists. France soon decided to appease Italy, and Hoare followed suit. Only a few weeks after asking the league to impose sanctions, Hoare and French prime minister Pierre Laval offered Mussolini a settlement that would have required Abyssinia to make enormous territorial and economic concessions to Italy.

When the details of the Hoare-Laval Plan were revealed to the British public, the response was near-universal condemnation. The cabinet asked Hoare to recant; instead, he resigned. He was replaced by Anthony Eden, who was somewhat more optimistic about the success of a league policy. Rather than make further concessions to Italy, he hoped to tighten the screws by adding oil to the list of sanctioned goods. Though the cabinet resisted, Baldwin stood behind Eden, arguing that "a refusal to impose an oil sanction would have a disastrous effect both now and at the next General Election."[149] However, the French were reluctant to antagonize Mussolini further, and they were soon preoccupied by Germany's reoccupation of the Rhineland. Unwilling to act alone, Eden gave up the fight. Indeed, he even contemplated proposing a radical restructuring of the League Covenant to replace its collective security provisions with a network of regional security pacts.[150] Once Abyssinia capitulated, Britain voted to lift sanctions on Italy.

[148] Rosaria Quartararo, "Imperial Defence in the Mediterranean on the Eve of the Ethiopian Crisis (July–October 1935)," *Historical Journal* 20, no. 1 (March 1977): 186.
[149] Quoted in Peters, *Anthony Eden*, 168.
[150] Ibid., 199–200.

Over the next few years, Eden became increasingly isolated within the cabinet over the issue of Anglo-Italian relations.[151] He believed that Mussolini's ultimate goal was to revive the Roman Empire, a path that would inevitably bring Italy into conflict with Britain. Consequently, the most that he was willing to concede was the Gentlemen's Agreement of January 1937, in which the two countries publicly asserted their desire to uphold the territorial status quo in the Mediterranean. Chamberlain, in contrast, became increasingly convinced of the need to appease Italy. After he became prime minister in May 1937, he pushed Eden to open negotiations and even met with the Italian ambassador himself. In February 1938, Eden resigned in frustration. His replacement, Lord Halifax, was a close ally of Chamberlain, and the cabinet stood behind their policy of appeasement. This paved the way for the Easter Agreement of April 1938, in which Britain recognized the Italian conquest of Abyssinia in return for an Italian promise to withdraw its forces from the civil war in Spain.

Germany

The rise of Hitler and the German military severely complicated the Conservatives' strategic calculus. For Britain to respond in proportion to this new threat would require either enormous tax increases or massive borrowing, both of which were unacceptable to the financial community. Of particular concern were the potential for inflation, which would necessitate the imposition of controls over consumption and capital investment, and the conversion of export-oriented manufacturing to the production of arms, which would have a negative impact on the balance of payments.[152] Even worse, rearmament would increase imports. This would further weaken the pound, drain gold reserves, and necessitate the sale of British investors' overseas assets.[153] Finally, the creation of an expeditionary force for Europe would take precious funds from the expansion of the navy, which was needed to defend the empire against Japan.[154]

---

[151] William C. Mills, "The Chamberlain-Grandi Conversations of July–August 1937 and the Appeasement of Italy," *International History Review* 19, no. 3 (August 1997): 594–619; Roy Douglas, "Chamberlain and Eden, 1937–1938," *Journal of Contemporary History* 13, no. 1 (January 1978): 97–116; Norman Rose, "The Resignation of Anthony Eden," *Historical Journal* 25, no. 4 (December 1982): 911–31; Robert Mallett, "Fascist Foreign Policy and Official Italian Views of Anthony Eden in the 1930s," *Historical Journal* 43, no. 1 (March 2000): 157–87.

[152] Shay, *British Rearmament*, 75–79; Newton, *Profits of Peace*, 66–73, 116–17; G. C. Peden, *British Rearmament and the Treasury, 1932–1939* (Edinburgh: Scottish Academic, 1979), chap. 3; Cain and Hopkins, *British Imperialism*, 2:93–99.

[153] Newton, *Profits of Peace*, 99, 115; Peden, *British Rearmament and the Treasury*, 62–63.

[154] D. C. Watt, "The Anglo-German Naval Agreement of 1935: An Interim Judgment," *Journal of Modern History* 28, no. 2 (June 1956): 165–66; G. A. H. Gordon, "The Admiralty and Appeasement," *Naval History* 5, no. 2 (summer 1991): 44–48.

In the face of all of these concerns about the impact of rearmament on the financial sector, Conservatives looked for an alternative to confrontation with Germany. Given that their constituents' economic interests lay in the periphery, not the core, appeasement was an appealing option. After all, Germany posed far less of a threat to the empire in the mid 1930s than it did in the early 1910s. Unlike the Soviet Union, it did not seek to undermine Britain's rule over its colonies. In 1937, Hitler sympathetically advised Lord Halifax, the former viceroy of India, that Britain should "shoot Gandhi and if that did not suffice to reduce them to submission, shoot a dozen leading members of Congress, and if that did not suffice, shoot 200 until order is established."[155] In fact, the Fuhrer had little interest in either naval expansion or the annexation of territory outside Europe. He occasionally asked for the return of Germany's prewar colonies, but he never pressed the point. His views on Anglo-German relations were plainly stated in *Mein Kampf*, in which he argued that the separation between the two countries' natural spheres of influence—the periphery for Britain and continental Europe for Germany—made them natural allies.[156]

Throughout the 1930s, a succession of British foreign ministers sought to entice Germany into negotiations over arms control, offering various revisions in the Versailles Treaty as an inducement. Each time, Germany ignored, rejected, or superseded their proposals through unilateral action. The one exception, however, was absolutely critical to the Conservatives' interests. In 1935, Hitler offered to limit his surface navy to 35 percent of the size of the combined forces of the British Commonwealth. As D. C. Watt writes, "England was to be placated by the sacrifice of the German fleet into leaving Germany a free hand for the moral and political conquest of Europe."[157] The National government accepted the agreement, and Hitler kept his promise until April 1939. With its navy in check, Germany could harm Britain only if it managed to defeat France and establish military hegemony over the continent. Only then, once it was flush with power, might its ambitions turn toward the British Empire.

None of this persuaded British leaders that German behavior was innocuous. To the contrary, the Defence Requirements Committee reported in February 1934 that Germany was the "ultimate potential enemy against whom our 'long range' defence policy must be directed."[158] It advised a massive rearmament program for the army, prioritizing the creation

[155] Quoted in Michael Dockrill, "Defending the Empire or Defeating the Enemy: British War Aims, 1938–47," in *Britain and the Threat to Stability in Europe, 1918–45*, ed. Peter Catterall and C. J. Morris (London: Leicester University Press, 1993), 112.

[156] Adolf Hitler, *Mein Kampf*, trans. Ralph Manheim (Boston: Houghton Mifflin, 1943), 618–21.

[157] Watt, "Anglo-German Naval Agreement," 160.

[158] Quoted in Paul Doerr, *British Foreign Policy, 1919–1939* (Manchester: Manchester University Press, 1998), 164–65. See also Shay, *British Rearmament*, 30–42.

of a "Regular Expeditionary Force" that could be sent to Europe within a month after the outbreak of war. Yet, the cabinet did not act on this recommendation. Instead, as Robert Shay notes, it adopted the position of the Treasury, which argued that "the financial and political dangers that were inherent in the increased spending suggested by the D.R.C. were a far more serious threat to the national security than the foreign menaces that the D.R.C. report sought to deal with."[159]

Satisfied by Hitler's accommodation of the British Empire, the Conservative-dominated government chose to forgo the advice of its military experts in favor of the "national security" interests of its primary economic constituency, the financial services sector. Britain began to rearm slowly in 1936, but only as a minimalist response to the threat posed by German bombers to its cities. The Inskip Report of December 1937 and the "limited liability" doctrine, which asserted that Britain would not commit its army for use in a war against Germany, reflected the Conservatives' fundamental strategic priorities: protect the home isles and the empire, not Europe.[160] It took until February 1939, five years after the Defense Requirements Committee called for the urgent creation of a Regular Expeditionary Force, for the government to begin planning a continental deployment.

Given their priorities, it was only natural for Conservative leaders to settle on a policy of appeasement. In March 1936, they passively accepted the remilitarization of the Rhineland by the German Army. They refused to consider either a military response, economic sanctions, or closer cooperation with France, leaving their erstwhile ally alone after the loss of its best defense against invasion. Then, in March 1938, Germany annexed Austria. Not only did Britain acquiesce to this violation of the Versailles Treaty, but it also refused a Soviet demand for an international conference to confront the issue. The next capitulation came at the infamous Munich Conference of September 1938, when the Conservatives agreed to allow Germany to annex the Sudeten region of Czechoslovakia. Confronted with the danger of war, they chose to sacrifice the sovereign territory of a small democratic state and to turn their back on French pleas for help in the hope that Hitler's ambitions would at last be satiated. Finally, in March 1939,

---

[159] Shay, *British Rearmament*, 42.
[160] Peden, *British Rearmament and the Treasury*, 10, 143; Reinhard Meyers, "British Imperial Interests and the Policy of Appeasement," in *The Fascist Challenge and the Policy of Appeasement*, ed. Wolfgang J. Mommsen and Lothar Kettenacker (London: Allen and Unwin, 1983), 339–51; Brian Bond, *British Military Policy between the Two World Wars* (Oxford: Clarendon, 1980), chaps. 8–9; Michael Howard, *The Continental Commitment: The Dilemma of British Defence Policy in the Era of the Two World Wars* (London: Temple Smith, 1972), chaps. 5–6. The government also feared that a strong continental commitment would allow France to draw it into another war. See Dutton, *Simon*, 194; Robert J. Young, *In Command of France: French Foreign Policy and Military Planning, 1933–1940* (Cambridge, Mass.: Harvard University Press, 1978), 213–15, 221–29.

they stood by idly as Germany conquered the remainder of Czechoslovakia, despite having guaranteed its survival at the Munich Conference.

The invasion of Czechoslovakia revealed, beyond all shadow of doubt, that Hitler's intentions were not limited to the annexation of German-speaking populations. All of Europe was at risk, including Britain itself. Thus, the National government decided at last to abandon its strategy of appeasement and shift to deterrence. On the last day of March 1939, it promised to defend the independence of Poland, then extended the guarantee to Romania two weeks thereafter.[161] Germany invaded Poland on September 1, 1939, and two days later Britain declared war.

Colonial Appeasement

Though committed to the empire, Conservative leaders had always taken a flexible approach toward its defense. Rather than cling indiscriminately to every last scrap of territory, they had offered modest concessions to obtain long-term security for their most valuable possessions. Such was the case in the 1890s, so it was again in the 1930s. One attempt at colonial appeasement came in June 1935, when Foreign Minister Hoare sought to dissuade Italy from invading Abyssinia.[162] Britain had no significant economic or security interests in the region, so Hoare proposed to resolve the matter by ceding land on the border of British Somaliland. Mussolini opposed all of Hoare's entreaties, however, and eventually went on to invade and annex Abyssinia.

Hitler, unlike Mussolini, had little interest in the periphery, and he reassured British leaders of this to demonstrate his benign intentions toward their empire.[163] After March 1936, however, he made a tactical decision to call for the return of Germany's prewar colonies. At no point did he threaten the British Empire; he used the issue only as a bargaining chip to obtain his desiderata in Europe. In response, the National government considered various schemes for territorial transfers and economic concessions. It was loathe to give up anything of value, but neither could it ignore the possibility that Britain might be able to resolve the crisis in Europe with only a minor sacrifice in its peripheral interests.[164] In March 1938, it finally made an offer: in exchange

---

[161] Even in the guarantee to Poland, Chamberlain left some room for interpretation over the circumstances under which Britain would declare war. See Alan J. Foster, "An Unequivocal Guarantee? Fleet Street and the British Guarantee to Poland, 31 March 1939," *Journal of Contemporary History* 26, no. 1 (January 1991): 33–47; A. J. Prazmowska, "War over Danzig? The Dilemma of Anglo-Polish Relations in the Months Preceding the Outbreak of the Second World War," *Historical Journal* 26, no. 1 (March 1983): 177–83.

[162] Cross, *Sir Samuel Hoare*, 196–97; Robertson, "Origins of British Opposition."

[163] Andrew J. Crozier, *Appeasement and Germany's Last Bid for Colonies* (London: Macmillan, 1988), 58–62, 140–41, 232–33; A. Edho Ekoko, "The British Attitude towards Germany's Colonial Irredentism in Africa in the Inter-War Years," *Journal of Contemporary History* 14, no. 2 (April 1979): 290–91.

[164] Crozier, *Appeasement*, chaps. 6, 8; Ekoko, "British Attitude."

for compromises over Austria, Czechoslovakia, and arms control, Germany would be given control over parts of the Belgian Congo and Portuguese Angola, regain the British mandate of Togoland and the French mandate of Cameroon, and receive part of British Nigeria and French Equatorial Africa. Britain did not reveal these terms to the other powers on whose largesse the plan depended, but it did not matter; Hitler refused the deal.

Russia

Even in the 1930s, Soviet Russia still posed a serious threat to the British Empire. The danger was not primarily military in nature; the Red Army rated relatively low on British defense planners' list of immediate concerns. Yet, there did remain an "obsessive fear of Russian pressure through Afghanistan to India," the most important part of the dependent empire.[165] Furthermore, Comintern propagandists continued to agitate for the revolt of oppressed peoples against their capitalist overlords, undermining the integrity of the empire in general and India in particular. To defend the Indian subcontinent and suppress native rebellions, approximately fifty-five thousand British regulars were stationed there in 1938, a force of more than half the size of the home army.[166] As long as the Conservatives believed that they might be able to appease Germany, they had little interest in cooperating with the Soviets, who remained the more clear-cut long-term enemy of the empire. Anthony Eden, who served as foreign secretary between 1935 and 1938, made this point directly in his memoirs:

> I often considered our relations with Russia and the possibility that her power might be put into the scales in resistance to the demands of Germany, Italy and Japan. . . . Yet reports constantly arrived on my desk about the Comintern's world-wide activities against the British Empire. It was not possible to work in confidence with a power which pursued such methods.[167]

Ideological differences doubtless contributed to the Conservatives' antipathy toward the Soviet Union, but their policies were ultimately based on a hardnosed calculation of imperial interests.

Shortly after the Ottawa Conference of 1932, which created a system of tariff preferences within the British Empire, the National government gave notice of its decision to terminate the Anglo-Soviet trade agreement of 1930. According to Curtis Keeble, this move "was seen by the Government as a

---

[165] Keeble, *Britain and the Soviet Union*, 126. See also Bond, *British Military Policy*, 107–11; Imam, *Colonialism in East-West Relations*, chaps. 9–10; Niedhart, "British Attitudes and Policies," 288.

[166] Bond, *British Military Policy*, 118.

[167] Anthony Eden, *Facing the Dictators: The Memoirs of Anthony Eden, Earl of Avon* (Boston: Houghton Mifflin, 1962), 589. See also Keeble, *Britain and the Soviet Union*, 129–40.

necessary consequence of Ottawa rather than a major move in British-Soviet relations."[168] Nevertheless, it signaled that trade with the Soviet Union had little value to the ruling coalition. Britain agreed to renegotiate, but only if offered much more favorable terms. Not long thereafter, several British citizens working in the Soviet Union were arrested for espionage. The cabinet halted negotiations in protest and imposed a complete embargo on Soviet imports. The accused were convicted, but given light sentences, so the embargo was rescinded and talks were reopened. Faced with the hard-line tactics of Britain and the threat of Nazi Germany, Stalin softened his approach and reined in the Comintern. This, in turn, allowed the National government to accept a temporary trade agreement in February 1934 and to vote for Soviet membership in the League of Nations in September 1934.

The decline of Soviet agitation against British interests led to an uneasy truce between the two countries, but little more. Conservative leader Stanley Baldwin's view of continental affairs was typical: "If there is any fighting in Europe to be done, I should like to see the Bolsheviks and the Nazis doing it. . . . If he [Hitler] moves East, I shall not break my heart."[169] It was not until May 1939, more than two months after German tanks rolled into Prague, that the government decided to open alliance talks with the Soviet Union. It did not do so with any sense of urgency; instead, it dickered over terms, refused to make concessions critical to Soviet interests, and left a great deal of doubt as to its willingness to declare war in the event that Germany invaded Poland. After several months without progress, Stalin gave up on the negotiations and made a separate peace with Germany.[170] Thus, the Conservatives' balancing policy came too little and too late, and they lost any chance they might have had to deter Hitler from war.

Labour

Labour's interest in the stability of Europe took it on the opposite policy arc as the Conservatives. In the 1920s and early 1930s, the party argued that Germany had been wronged by the Treaty of Versailles and advocated its revision. However, Hitler gave them increasing reason to reevaluate their pro-German position. His withdrawal from the League of Nations in

---

[168] Keeble, *Britain and the Soviet Union*, 112. See also ibid., 111–16; Dutton, *Simon*, 174, 184.
[169] Quoted in Keeble, *Britain and the Soviet Union*, 120.
[170] Geoffrey Roberts, "The Alliance That Failed: Moscow and the Triple Alliance Negotiations, 1939," *European History Quarterly* 26, no. 3 (July 1996): 383–414; Michael Jabara Carley, "End of the 'Low, Dishonest Decade': Failure of the Anglo-Franco-Soviet Alliance in 1939," *Europe-Asia Studies* 45, no. 2 (1993): 303–41. Even if Stalin never intended to side with Britain in 1939, as some historians aver, the point remains that the Conservatives took diplomatically uncompromising and militarily unreasonable positions in the negotiations (e.g., their reluctance to compel Poland to host Soviet forces).

October 1933, unilateral repudiation of the Versailles Treaty in March 1935, interference in the Spanish Civil War, *Anschluss* with Austria, and coercion of Czechoslovakia made it increasingly clear that his foreign policy was incompatible with the creation and maintenance of a cooperative, stable international order in Europe, even if he did not make a bid for continental hegemony.

Equally critically, Hitler was also undermining the basis of Europe's trading system. The Nazis' economic policies, including the New Plan of 1934 and the Four Year Plan of 1936, made Germany more autarchic and deepened its dominance over Eastern Europe.[171] These programs had a mixed effect on German industry, but they were unambiguously harmful to British merchandise exporters. The coal sector, which was the bedrock of Labour's electoral support, was particularly hard-hit. Between 1933 and 1939, Britain's export of coal dropped by 20 percent while Germany's rose by 33 percent.[172] In early 1939, the British government secured a commitment from the Nazis to limit their coal exports, but only after threatening a subsidy war. Hitler's diplomatic and trade policies constituted a deep threat to the economic interests of Labour's electoral coalition, and evidence for this was steadily mounting throughout the 1930s.

In response, Labour gradually shifted its position on Germany.[173] In the early 1930s, the party advocated disarmament and collective security based on economic sanctions. The first break with this policy came in the fall of 1935, when Labour's annual meeting produced a resolution that the use of force might be necessary to counter violations of the League Covenant. Another major change occurred in October 1937, when the party accepted the necessity of rearmament. By September 1938, its transformation was complete. In the midst of the international crisis over the Sudetenland, Labourites took a militantly anti-German stance. They were outraged not only by Germany's coercion of Czechoslovakia, but also because "its provocative mobilizations and untruthful Press campaigns impede the recovery of industry and trade, and poison international relationships." In response, they resolved that "whatever the risks involved, Great Britain must make its stand against aggression. There is now no room for doubt or hesitation."[174] Just like the Liberal Party in 1914, the Labour Party in 1938 decided to act forcefully once Germany's disregard for the sovereign rights of a small state

[171] Newton, *Profits of Peace*, 55–57; William Carr, *Arms, Autarky, and Aggression: A Study in German Foreign Policy, 1933–1939* (London: Arnold, 1972), 58–63.

[172] Newton, *Profits of Peace*, 97. See also Kaiser, *Economic Diplomacy*, 184–88.

[173] Gordon, *Conflict and Consensus*, 68–82; John F. Naylor, *Labour's International Policy: The Labour Party in the 1930s* (London: Weidenfeld and Nicolson, 1969). On the Liberals, see Richard S. Grayson, *Liberals, International Relations, and Appeasement: The Liberal Party, 1919–1939* (London: Cass, 2001).

[174] Labour Party, *Report of the 38th Annual Conference* (London: Labour Party, 1939), 14.

provided a direct indication of its willingness to do violence to the legal foundations of the international political and economic order in Europe.

Also telling is Labour's response to the demands of German nationalists for the return of their prewar colonies. In August 1936, the party published a lengthy pamphlet in which it rejected outright the idea of a territorial transfer.[175] The ideal solution, it argued, would be for all of the colonial powers to hand over control of their empires to the League of Nations, but this was conveniently impracticable. Instead, Labour proposed that the League of Nations take a supervisory role in the administration of colonies in tropical Africa. The colonial powers would have to promise to promote self-government, refrain from building fortifications, and accept the oversight of the League, but they would retain functional control over their possessions. Labour also demanded that the colonial powers adhere to the "open door" principle within their dependent empires. This position was not appeasement but rather a natural extension of the party's advocacy of free trade and opposition to the Imperial Preference System.

While Germany grew increasingly belligerent, the Soviet Union undertook a strikingly internationalist realignment of its foreign policy.[176] First, Soviet and French negotiators sought to create the Eastern Pact for the Guarantee of Mutual Security, an analogue to the Treaty of Locarno for the states lying between Germany and the Soviet Union. Second, after years of disdaining the League of Nations, the Soviet Union applied for membership and was finally seated at the League Council in September 1934. The following year, when the league confronted the Italian invasion of Abyssinia, the Soviets unwaveringly supported the use of sanctions and called for the strengthening of the covenant's collective security provisions. They also sought to cooperate with Britain over the civil war in Spain, though they decided to pursue an independent line once they saw that the British policy of nonintervention was failing to prevent German and Italian interference. In March 1938, they called for an international conference to respond to the *Anschluss* but were rebuffed by Britain; then, in the Sudeten crisis of September 1938, they insisted that they would go to war on Czechoslovakia's behalf if only the French would join them.

Labour had sought to foster ties with the Soviet Union throughout the 1920s and early 1930s, even when Soviet foreign policy was at its most anti-British. Thus, Labourites responded quite positively to this turnabout after 1933. Not only had the Soviet Union's strategic interests aligned with theirs;

---

[175] Labour Party, *The Demand for Colonial Territories and Equality of Economic Opportunity* (London: Labour Party, 1936), 47–52. See also Crozier, *Appeasement*, 167.

[176] F. S. Northedge and Audrey Wells, *Britain and Soviet Communism: The Impact of a Revolution* (London: Macmillan, 1982), 51–63; Keeble, *Britain and the Soviet Union*, 122–40; Jonathan Haslam, *The Soviet Union and the Struggle for Collective Security in Europe, 1933–39* (London: Macmillan, 1984).

Stalin had also chosen to pursue his goals through their preferred means, the League of Nations and collective security (rather than pure realpolitik alliances). While the Conservatives kept at arm's length from the Soviet Union, Labour called for Britain to work with it to resist German and Italian aggression. In its annual conference of September 1938, the party announced that "the British Government must leave no doubt in the mind of the German Government that they will unite with the French and Soviet Governments to resist any attack on Czechoslovakia."[177] If Labour had been in power, not the Conservatives, it almost certainly would have ended the policy of appeasement in 1938, prior to the Munich Agreement, and aligned with the Soviets to try to stop Hitler's threat to the European international order.[178]

CONCLUSION

The history of British grand strategy toward the great powers in 1868–1939 reveals a pronounced pattern of partisanship. The Liberal and Labour parties, whose electoral support came from industries that were highly dependent on export to Europe, consistently sought to establish a stable, cooperative international order on the continent. They did not attempt to prevent war at all costs, but rather sought to defend the status quo against states that threatened the future of the European trading system. In 1870–71, for example, when war broke out between France and Prussia, their primary goal was to ensure that both sides respected the sovereignty of neutral Belgium and limited their territorial demands. The Liberals did not direct their strategy against any country in particular; instead, they sought to promote good relations among all of the great powers. To this end, they used arbitration to resolve the *Alabama* claims dispute with the United States, handed control over Egypt's treasury to the Concert of Europe, and used multilateral diplomacy to address problems in the Balkans.

By the end of the nineteenth century, manufacturers had developed such a strong interest in peripheral markets that the Liberals' strategic preferences began to bifurcate. While Liberal Imperialists pushed for close alignment with France to protect the empire, internationalist Radicals tried to

---

[177] Labour Party, *Report of the 38th Annual Conference*, 14.

[178] On this counterfactual, see Naylor, *Labour's International Policy*, 257–60. On the military implications of going to war in 1938, see Bond, *British Military Policy*, 277–86. In a Gallup poll conducted in the spring of 1939, 84 percent of respondents answered "yes" to the question, "Do you favour a military alliance between Britain and Russia?" See R. A. C. Parker, *Chamberlain and Appeasement: British Policy and the Coming of the Second World War* (New York: St. Martin's, 1993), 233.

preserve Britain's formal neutrality in continental affairs. In 1911–14, the Radicals refused to balance against Germany because they had little reason to believe that it would act less moderately on defeating France than it had in 1871. It was not until Germany invaded neutral Belgium, too late to attempt deterrence, that they had a clear sign that it would endanger their long-term interests.

After the war, Liberals and Labourites demanded that the new world order be founded on internationalist principles. They advocated a strong League of Nations, accession to the binding arbitration clause of the PCIJ, reconciliation with Germany and Russia, and the strict enforcement of collective security. Throughout the 1920s, they tried to foster peaceful cooperation among the great powers; then, in the 1930s, they took an increasingly firm stand against German, Italian, and Japanese violations of international law. Unlike in the years leading up to World War I, they had good reason to be unyieldingly hostile to Germany by 1938. Even before it was certain that Hitler would initiate a war for continental hegemony, his repeated efforts to undermine political and commercial relationships throughout Europe gave Labour a clear imperative to align with the Soviet Union against Nazi Germany.

The Conservative Party, whose electoral coalition was based on the financial services sector, had a far greater stake in the periphery than Europe. Its strategic imperative was to use realpolitik to align against whatever state posed the gravest threat to the empire. Throughout the late nineteenth century, that state was Russia. Its steady advance into Central Asia brought it menacingly close to India, and its designs on Constantinople endangered Britain's imperial line of supply through the Suez Canal. In response, the Conservatives resisted Russian expansion through every means possible, including high-stakes crisis bargaining over the borders of Afghanistan and Bulgaria, a defensive alliance with Japan, and ententes with France, Italy, and Austria-Hungary. They did not shy from conflicts with other countries when imperial interests were at stake, but their grand strategy clearly focused on the overarching problem of Russia.

By 1905, changes in the external environment had begun to dictate a shift in the Conservatives' strategic calculus. Germany embarked on a massive naval construction program to try to achieve parity with Britain, while Japan annihilated the Russian fleet. Consequently, Germany quickly replaced Russia as the primary threat to the empire. The Conservatives' new alignment imperative, to balance against Germany, was reinforced by the situation in Europe. If one of the opposing continental alliances defeated the other, the empire would be vulnerable to the victor. The Conservatives therefore argued that Britain must adhere to the less dangerous of the two sides, the Franco-Russian alliance, either to prevent war from occurring or to be certain of being in the winning coalition.

Finally, in the 1930s, a very different strategy was needed to protect the interests of investors. Germany had lost its colonies and voluntarily limited its naval construction, so it posed far less of a threat to the empire than it had in 1914. Meanwhile, the financial sector was badly shaken by the Great Depression, and its recovery would have been severely compromised by a major rearmament program. In response, the Conservatives opted for appeasement. They offered only modest opposition to Japanese and Italian violations of the League Covenant, and they did almost nothing to resist the expansion of German influence in Europe. It was not until Germany invaded Czechoslovakia that they concluded that Hitler could not be satiated, by which time it was too late to respond effectively.

[8]

Conclusions

In the first chapter of this book, I proposed to address two critical puzzles in the diplomatic history of the United States and Great Britain: the irregular rate of growth in their overseas commitments and the pattern of partisanship in their grand strategies. These phenomena pose a major challenge to realism, the dominant paradigm in the study of international security. In the following pages, I review the key elements of my analysis, consider what can be learned from the few disconfirming observations, and reexamine the question of nonmaterial preferences. I then discuss the broader implications of the theory, focusing on its applicability to the study of foreign economic policy, cases other than the United States and Great Britain, and contemporary American grand strategy.

Realism should be well equipped to explain variance in the expansion and contraction of states' foreign commitments. There are two realist schools of thought on the subject, offensive and defensive. Offensive realists assert that states try to expand as far as their capabilities allow. When a great power is rising, it will seek greater influence in the international system; conversely, when its economy is declining relative to its competitors, it will undertake a strategic retrenchment.

Offensive realism has a dismal predictive record over the two cases in this study. First, the United States never developed its international power in proportion to its domestic resources. Its engagement in international politics was particularly limited in 1865–96, a period of enormous industrial growth. At the turn of the century, it began to expand at a faster pace, but it did not maintain its advance. In 1918–29, the United States was so far ahead of its rivals in war-ravaged Europe that it could have exercised leadership throughout the international system; instead, it withdrew. Britain, in turn, is no less problematic. In the late 1860s and early 1870s, at the peak of its relative economic power, it sought to devolve authority to its colonies. It then entered a long period of relative decline, yet it did not continue to retrench. Instead, it embarked on a massive enlargement of its empire.

Defensive realism, in contrast, claims that states normally seek to expand only when threatened. This argument can plausibly be applied to the revival of British imperialism in the late nineteenth century, but it has trouble with the United States. While the European great powers clashed over territory in Africa and Asia, they generally respected the Monroe Doctrine. Only in the brief periods preceding its entry into the two world wars did the United States need to take action to maintain its defensive perimeter in the Western Hemisphere. Furthermore, much of its geopolitical maneuvering was directed at East Asia, where it had no real security interests.

Realists are broadly correct in asserting that states' relative power limits their material capacity for expansion. What they fail to explain, however, is what motivates expansion within those limits. I argue that the critical factor is the weight of peripheral and military-colonial interests within the executive's electoral coalition. Politicians who represent constituencies that rely on export to or investment in weak, undeveloped states in the periphery, or that profit from government spending on defense and foreign policy, tend to be more expansionist than those who do not. Policymakers also take into account factors that affect the marginal returns and opportunity costs of budgetary outlays on grand strategy, such as domestic debt and international adversaries. As intervening variables, these constraints do not alter coalitions' underlying goals; instead, they determine the level of resources devoted to those goals.

This theory yields a straightforward explanation for variance in American and British grand strategy toward the periphery. In the first two decades following the Civil War, few Americans were involved with peripheral markets, and the high national debt put downward pressure on military spending. Consequently, the impulse to expand was weak. Not until the end of the century, when exports surged and the debt declined, was there a change in course. The United States developed its international influence rapidly in the 1890s and early 1900s, continuing through the end of World War I. At that point, with its gains secure, it initiated a modest retrenchment to help pay off its new war debt.

In Britain, every major socioeconomic group had a stake in foreign markets, so none advocated true isolationism. Yet, sectoral interests did change over time. First, in the 1880s and 1890s, Britain grew much more dependent on trade and investment in the periphery, and its firms suffered from intense competitive pressures, so it became much more aggressively imperialist in those decades. Second, the constraints on the conduct of its strategy changed over time. The impulse for expansion in the 1880s and 1890s was heightened by imperial rivalries and facilitated by a decline in the national debt. In contrast, in the periods of 1868–80 and 1918–29, Britain had a high national debt and faced few challenges in the periphery, so it acted with greater moderation.

PATTERN OF PARTISANSHIP

The second empirical puzzle addressed by this study is partisanship. If grand strategy is dictated by unitary "national interests," as realists assert, it should not change substantially when a new political coalition comes to power. Variance in individual decision makers' personalities might have a marginal impact on strategic choice, but it should not produce a consistent pattern of partisanship in foreign policymaking.

In reality, debates over grand strategy in the United States and Great Britain were often intensely partisan, and many elections resulted in momentous shifts in policy. The question of internationalism was particularly divisive. Democrats, Liberals, and Labourites made binding commitments to legal mechanisms of dispute resolution; Republicans and Conservatives opposed them. Similar cleavages appeared over some of the most vital security issues confronting each country. In Britain, Liberals and Labourites generally supported rapprochement with Germany in 1905–14, whereas Conservatives took a hard line against it and instead favored France. Conservatives were also more enthusiastic about imperialism than Liberals and Labourites, though this difference became less pronounced after the turn of the century. Meanwhile, in the United States, Democrats were consistently less interventionist than Republicans.

This study offers a clear explanation for these differences. Just like in domestic policy, partisanship over foreign policy originates in the imbalanced distribution of economic interests across political parties. In the United States, the Republican coalition was composed primarily of northeastern businesses, particularly the manufacturing sector. This group had almost no concern for the international economy until the 1880s and 1890s, when its interest in peripheral markets began to grow. Consequently, most Republicans were isolationist before 1880, then increasingly interventionist thereafter.

Democrats also needed the support of northeastern businesses, but their primary constituency was southern farmers. Farmers had little stake in the periphery; instead, they were highly dependent on exports to Europe. To balance between these two groups' interests, Democratic presidents

ation, rendering infeasible any attempt to deter Germany from initiating the

adopted a two-track strategy: interventionism toward the periphery and internationalism toward the great powers. Since Democrats were more fundamentally the party of farmers than business, however, they never pursued interventionism with as much vigor as their Republican counterparts. Nearly every time a Democrat became president, he would scale back on Republican commitments in the periphery while attempting to advance the cause of international cooperation.

In Britain, the Conservative coalition was initially dominated by the landed gentry, whose privileged position in the civil service and military gave them a clear interest in imperialism. As the franchise expanded, the gentry co-opted the London-based financial service sector to form an alliance of "gentlemanly capitalists." This group relied heavily on income from investments in the periphery, which came under increasing pressure from foreign competition toward the end of the nineteenth century and through the interwar period. As a result, the Conservatives were consistently imperialist throughout 1868–1939.

The Liberal and Labour coalition comprised manufacturers and coal miners in northern England, Wales, and Scotland. In the 1860s and 1870s, these sectors were highly competitive in international markets, both in the periphery and the core. Thus, Liberal governments initially adopted a two-track strategy of interventionism and internationalism. Thereafter, British industry declined, becoming more dependent on the periphery in general and the empire in particular. In response, Liberal and Labour leaders shifted to a two-track strategy of imperialism and internationalism. Since they were divided between two conflicting strategic imperatives, however, they remained less aggressively imperialist than Conservatives.

The theory also explains partisan disagreement over Britain's diplomatic alignments. In the late nineteenth century, the greatest threat to the empire was Russia's advance into Central Asia, toward India; in the early twentieth century, it was Germany's fleet-building program. To deal with both, the unequivocally imperialist Conservatives sought closer relations with France. Meanwhile, the Liberals, whose constituents' interests were divided between core and peripheral markets, had to balance two contradictory goals: protect the empire, but avoid exacerbating tensions in Europe by "picking sides" against Germany. Tensions within the party came to a head in 1914, when Liberal Imperialists clashed with Radicals over the terms under which Britain would enter World War I. The result was equivocation, rendering infeasible any attempt to deter Germany from initiating the conflict.

After winning the war, Conservatives had no reason either to balance against or appease Germany. Instead, they forced it to make enormous reparations payments to help pay off Britain's massive debt. For the defense of the empire, Soviet Russia's support for national independence movements was a far greater concern. Thus, Conservatives refused to normalize ties with the Bolshevik regime. The Liberal and Labour parties, in contrast, prioritized the restoration of trade with Europe, so they opposed the harsh indemnity on Germany and supported the diplomatic recognition of Russia. Finally, the two parties divided over Nazi Germany. Hitler never directly threatened the British Empire, and rearmament would have hurt the London financial sector, so Conservatives sought to appease the Third Reich for as long as possible. Labour was more sensitive to Hitler's violations of international law and disruptions of intra-European trade, so it demanded that Britain make its final stand at the Munich Conference of 1938.

EXPLAINING THE OUTLIERS

Not all observations in this study confirm the theory. To understand why, it is necessary to return to the theory's deductive roots. One of its most fundamental assumptions is that individuals act according to their own economic interests. If they are not competent to do so, or if they prioritize noneconomic goals, their behavior will disconfirm its predictions. In the cases of Andrew Johnson, Ulysses Grant, and William Taft, this assumption may have been violated. These men are considered by historians to have been among the least adept politicians ever to have become president in the United States. Johnson, who came to power only because of the assassination of Lincoln, offended so many members of Congress that they impeached him and nearly secured a conviction. Grant was far more popular, but he was a general, not a politician, and he is universally considered to have been a poor president. The same goes for Taft, who had never sought elected office before his successful run at the presidency, and who played the game of politics so badly that he nearly caused the destruction of the Republican Party. Every time these leaders strayed from the predictions of the theory, their own party repudiated their strategic initiatives.

It does not suffice, however, to wave off these aberrations as the product of individual decision makers' character flaws. The theory points to a more fundamental question: Why were these men selected to lead their parties in the first place? In fact, each one at least partially circumvented the political processes by which unsuitable candidates are normally weeded out. Johnson was never elected president, Grant was chosen only because he was a war hero, and Taft was handpicked by his enormously popular predecessor. None of these men was subject to the intense scrutiny of his party, so none was disqualified from leadership by his eccentric opinions on grand strategy.

Three other disconfirmations remain to be explained. In each one, the decisions that violated the theory's predictions were not major or were influenced by unique circumstances. With a few ad hoc departures from the simple hypotheses laid out in chapter 1, these anomalies fit well with the logic of the theory. First, Democratic president Grover Cleveland, whose primary constituency was southern farmers with core interests, failed to undertake any internationalist initiatives in his first term in office. He did, however, have political incentives to downplay foreign affairs. His coalition consisted not only of southern core interests but also a substantial contingent of northeastern peripheral and domestic interests. Since the two sides had opposing views on grand strategy, Cleveland could "play it safe" by avoiding controversy. During his second term, in contrast, an ongoing economic crisis created pressure for him to be more proactive.

Second, the Liberal Lord Rosebery, whose coalition of manufacturing and coal also had strong core interests, made no attempt to promote norm-based cooperation through either international arbitration or the Concert of Europe. This should not come as a great surprise: opportunities for internationalism were scarce at the height of the imperial "scramble" in the 1890s. Rosebery's tenure as foreign minister and prime minister lasted only three years, so the possibility remains that he would have changed course had he been able to hold office for a longer term.

Finally, Conservative prime minister Lord Salisbury dabbled in multilateral diplomacy and international arbitration toward the end of his career, even though his coalition of gentlemanly capitalists had little interest in internationalism. Again, there were mitigating circumstances. The Concert of Europe was a last resort for Salisbury, used only after he had exhausted every other unilateral, bilateral, and trilateral alternative to accomplish his goals in the Balkans. As for arbitration, he consented to it not because he thought it was beneficial, but because rejecting it would have caused serious tensions with the United States. The two countries had just gotten over the Venezuelan crisis, and Britain was occupied with the Boer War, so Salisbury and his fellow Conservatives reluctantly accepted a treaty that they thought was far too strong.

Given that no theory of international relations could hope to have a perfect predictive record over so many observations, these aberrations seem relatively innocuous. Overall, the political economy perspective offers a consistent explanation for all of the major historical features of each of the two cases. For the United States, it accounts for the shift from isolationism to interventionism in the late nineteenth century, the decision to enter World War I, the creation of the League of Nations, the strategic inactivity of the 1920s, and the events leading up to World War II. For Great Britain, it accounts for the shift from interventionism to imperialism in the 1880s, the formation of the Entente Cordiale, the decision to enter World War I, the imposition of a harsh indemnity on Germany, and the policy of appeasement in the 1930s. Furthermore, its errors seem to be distributed randomly throughout the cases. The only potentially significant "trend" that it fails to predict is the weak imperialism of Johnson and Grant in 1865–77.

NONMATERIAL PREFERENCES

In each of the cases, I found that material interests consistently trumped culture and ideology. However, I do not discount the possibility that ideas influence grand strategy under certain conditions. Ethnic and religious affinities, in particular, can cause individuals from all socioeconomic backgrounds to act in common cause with their brethren overseas. In the United States, diaspora groups lobby intensely for policies favoring their home countries, often with great success.[1] None was so strong as to impose its preferences on either national party in 1865–1941; however, at least one group, German-Americans, was able to influence the votes of individual members of Congress in debates over intervention in World Wars I and II.[2] If I had focused on legislative politics rather than executive strategy, such factors would have warranted greater attention.

Another important nonmaterial preference is humanitarianism. The desire to help individuals suffering from extreme persecution or deprivation can play an important role in the making of foreign policy. In this study, it was most evident in Gladstone's support for Bulgarian independence and McKinley's decision to expel Spain from Cuba. Its influence, however, was sporadic. Typically, humanitarian intervention occurs only under special circumstances: when the costs of intervention are low and the public is well informed about atrocities, or when intervention promises to increase the country's power and influence internationally. Thus, it is not a systematic component of grand strategy.

The nonmaterial source of preferences with the broadest potential explanatory power is political ideology. In this view, the critical variable is individuals' beliefs about the efficacy of social engineering. Liberals, who

---

[1] Tony Smith, *Foreign Attachments: The Power of Ethnic Groups in the Making of American Foreign Policy* (Cambridge, Mass.: Harvard University Press, 2000).

[2] Samuel Lubell, "Who Votes Isolationist and Why," *Harper's Magazine* 202 (April 1951): 29–36. It is difficult to assess whether a shared culture of Anglo-Saxon Protestantism generated goodwill between the United States and Great Britain. Though allies in World Wars I and II, the two countries fought each other in the Revolutionary War and the War of 1812, and they had numerous diplomatic disputes throughout the nineteenth century. More revealing is the fact that their strategic cooperation has been negatively correlated with their ethnic similarity. Anglo-American relations were most conflictual in the late eighteenth and early nineteenth centuries, when most American citizens had familial ties to England, and most cooperative in the mid-late twentieth and early twenty-first centuries, after numerous waves of immigration and the enfranchisement of southern blacks made the American electorate much more diverse.

trust in the creation of new institutions to advance human welfare, tend to be internationalist, whereas conservatives, who are skeptical of change, see no viable alternative to the unilateral use of force. What motivates strategic choice, therefore, is not a cost-benefit analysis of specific policies but rather a deep-seated need for cognitive consistency between domestic and international philosophies.

This argument is intuitively appealing, but it does not hold up to the evidence. In the case of the United States, the most internationalist section of the country, the South, was the least liberal. Britain is a better fit, since liberal northern England, Wales, and Scotland were more internationalist than conservative southeast England. However, if the analysis had begun in 1815, this pattern would have been reversed. After the Napoleonic Wars, a multilateral, norm-based international institution, the Concert of Europe, served as a bulwark of monarchical rule again the forces of reform; thus, the advocates of internationalism were conservatives. Not until the mid nineteenth century, after the Revolutions of 1848 and the collapse of the "old diplomacy," did liberals begin to latch onto the concert as a multilateral forum for the creation of international law.[3] In this case and most others, grand strategies are chosen not for ideological consistency but rather because they are instrumental to material interests.

FOREIGN ECONOMIC POLICY

Throughout this study, I have argued that domestic groups' preferences over grand strategy are a function of their position in the world economy. In so doing, I have drawn from the insights of E. E. Schattschneider and others scholars' research on the sectoral politics of tariff policy. Given the common roots and resemblances between their work and mine, it is worth considering the extent to which our dependent variables, foreign economic policy and grand strategy, are correlated. If there is a strong relationship between them, it will not only corroborate the argument of this book but also provide testament to the broad explanatory power of sectoral interests in state behavior.

Before pursuing this question, however, a note of caution is in order. I do not argue that preferences over foreign economic policy map directly onto preferences over grand strategy. Sectors' interests in grand strategy center on their geographic source of income (core, peripheral, or domestic) and reliance on government spending (for military-colonial interests). Sectors' interests in foreign economic policy, in contrast, derive primarily from their

---

[3] Carsten Holbraad, *The Concert of Europe: A Study in German and British International Theory, 1815–1914* (Harlow: Longmans, 1970).

competitiveness with imports. The difference between these independent variables can cause divergence in policy preferences. Protectionist import-competing firms are rarely able to export to the core, so they are unlikely to be internationalist; however, whether they should favor imperialism or iso-lationism remains an open question until their market orientation is known. Free-trading competitive firms' interests over grand strategy are even more indeterminate: whether they export to the core, periphery, or not at all de-pends on exogenous factors like foreign demand and tariff barriers. More-over, many attributes of sectors other than competitiveness can affect their position on trade policy, including their import dependence, asset speci-ficity, factor abundance, and capacity for collective action. Finally, societal support for tariffs may depend on distributional conflicts that cut across sec-tors. For example, leftist coalitions might oppose tariffs because alternative forms of revenue collection, such as income taxation, are more progressive.

Despite these limitations, clear correspondences in trade policy and grand strategy can be seen in both cases in this study. In the United States, the agrarian South was both internationally competitive and intensely re-liant on exporting to Europe. For the Democratic Party, therefore, trade liberalization and internationalism were closely linked.[4] Each of the three Democrats elected as president in 1865–1941 ran on a platform of tariff re-form, and each followed through on his promise to push for broad rate cuts while in office. Meanwhile, the industrial Northeast had a mix of com-petitive and uncompetitive firms, but even the former were excluded from European markets by tariffs on manufactures. As a result, the Republican Party favored a combination of protectionism at home and the promotion of its exports in the periphery, where weak states could be coerced to open their markets through interventionism and demands for trade "reciprocity." Democrats enacted all of the major tariff reductions of the period (e.g., the Underwood Act of 1913, the Reciprocal Act of 1934), while Republicans delivered all of the major increases (e.g., the McKinley Act of 1890, the Fordney-McCumber Act of 1922, the Smoot-Hawley Act of 1930).[5]

The Democrats were not a true free-trade coalition. Legislators often worked at cross-purposes from party leaders, allying with Republicans in a logroll to protect their individual districts' interests. If the voting popula-tion of the South had matched that of the Northeast, the Democrats might have been able to develop a more cohesive position on tariffs. However, as

[4] Peter Trubowitz, *Defining the National Interest: Conflict and Change in American Foreign Policy* (Chicago: University of Chicago Press, 1998), chaps. 2–3.

[5] Tom E. Terrill, *The Tariff, Politics, and American Foreign Policy, 1874–1901* (Westport, Conn.: Greenwood, 1973); Edward S. Kaplan and Thomas W. Ryley, *Prelude to Trade Wars: American Tariff Policy, 1890–1922* (Westport, Conn.: Greenwood, 1994); Edward S. Kaplan, *American Trade Policy, 1923–1995* (Westport, Conn.: Greenwood, 1996), 1–50.

detailed in chapter 2, they could not win national elections without reaching out to urban voters in the Northeast—voters who often had the same interest in industrial tariffs as Republicans. Thus, the Democratic Party made compromises over trade for precisely the same reason that it compromised between internationalist and interventionist grand strategies.

In a notable exception to their support for tariff reductions, southerners opposed the reciprocity treaties that Republican presidents Arthur and Harrison foisted on Latin American states in the 1880s and 1890s. The agreements, which were designed to boost the exports of northeastern manufacturers, encouraged target countries to pay for their imports by increasing their exports of subtropical agricultural goods to the United States. This, in turn, threatened southern farmers. Thus, southern Democrats' resistance to these treaties was consistent with their sectoral interests. As such, it is an exception that proves the rule.

Britain was also internally divided over trade, though not consistently, and not only for sectoral reasons.[6] After the repeal of the Corn Laws in 1846 and the Navigation Acts in 1849, the country became a paragon of economic openness. The strongest support for this policy came from the Liberal Party and northern English textile manufacturers, as represented by the "Manchester School" of political economy. In the 1860s and 1870s, at the height of Britain's export dominance, their interest in free trade was straightforward: it lowered the cost of factors of production, which added to manufacturers' already considerable competitive advantages. Furthermore, it encouraged other countries to reciprocate with the opening of their own markets to British exports, as France did in the Cobden-Chevalier Treaty of 1860.

Toward the end of the nineteenth century, the relative decline of British industry and global rise of protectionism weakened this logic, but other considerations came to the fore. First, not all industries in Liberal constituencies suffered equally; for example, exports of coal increased dramatically. Second, by the turn of the century, the Liberals had become a leftist party, making increasingly explicit appeals to the distributional interests of the lower classes.[7] To that end, they and Labour attacked tariffs as a particularly

[6] Aaron L. Friedberg, *The Weary Titan: Britain and the Experience of Relative Decline, 1895–1905* (Princeton: Princeton University Press, 1988), chaps. 2–3; Tim Rooth, *British Protectionism and the International Economy: Overseas Commercial Policy in the 1930s* (Cambridge: Cambridge University Press, 1993), chaps. 1–3.

[7] H. V. Emy, "The Impact of Financial Policy on English Party Politics before 1914," *Historical Journal* 15, no. 1 (March 1972): 105–13. In the United States, the Democrats did not become a class-based party until the 1930s; see James L. Sundquist, *Dynamics of the Party System: Alignment and Realignment of Political Parties in the United States*, rev. ed. (Washington, D.C.: Brookings, 1983), chaps. 7–10. On the relationship between class interests, forms of taxation, and grand strategy, see Kevin Narizny, "Both Guns and Butter, or Neither: Class Interests in the Political Economy of Rearmament," *American Political Science Review* 97, no. 2 (May 2003): 203–20.

regressive form of taxation. Whatever protection it might provide to factory workers, they argued, it would do far greater harm by raising the price of consumer goods. Even in the depths of the Great Depression, many Liberals and Labourites remained steadfastly opposed to tariffs.

For the gentlemanly capitalists of the Conservative Party, free trade was a mixed blessing.[8] On the one hand, as the capital of the international economy, London had a powerful stake in an open trading system. If Britain were to raise barriers to foreign commerce, the financial services and trade sector would lose a key element of its comparative advantage. On the other hand, tariffs did have three offsetting benefits. First, the creation of a tariff wall around the empire, an "imperial preference system," would produce greater economic and political integration between Britain and its colonies. While fearful of retaliation from other countries, the gentlemanly capitalists had to be mindful of their far greater, and proportionally increasing, stake in the British Empire. Second, rising imports put pressure on the balance of payments. By stanching the outflow of sterling, tariffs would help keep Britain on the gold standard, a critical consideration for financiers. Finally, as noted above, the burden of indirect taxation fell disproportionately on the lower classes. In the face of periodic budget crises, produced in part by the growing burdens of imperial defense, Conservatives strained to find new sources of government revenue. Rather than raise income taxes on their affluent constituents, they turned to proposals for a broad-based system of tariffs. The party campaigned for protectionism three times: 1905–6, 1923, and 1931–32. On the first two occasions, it met with crushing defeats at the polls. Only once the Great Depression hit Britain in full force did the Conservatives finally succeed in enacting an imperial tariff.

In sum, partisan cleavages over trade policy and grand strategy followed the same pattern in both Great Britain and the United States. The more core-oriented coalitions (Liberals, Labour, and Democrats) supported internationalism and freer trade, while the less core-oriented coalitions (Conservatives and Republicans) did not. This correlation cannot be attributed to sectoral interests alone, however; a different configuration of class interests in Britain, for example, could have muddied this result. Sectoral interests are an excellent starting point for the analysis of both trade policy and grand strategy, but it would be an oversimplification to see them as an all-encompassing "master variable" for the political economy paradigm.

---

[8] P. J. Cain and A. G. Hopkins, *British Imperialism: Innovation and Expansion, 1688–1914*, vol. 1 (London: Longman, 1993), chap. 7; P. J. Cain and A. G. Hopkins, *British Imperialism: Crisis and Deconstruction, 1914–1990*, vol. 2 (London: Longman, 1993), chap. 5.

Great Britain and the United States had more influence over the shaping of international order than any other great powers in the nineteenth and twentieth centuries. This fact alone makes it vital for political scientists, policymakers, and historians to understand the sources of their behavior in 1865–1941. Nevertheless, one might argue that these countries are also the "most likely" cases for this study. In this view, the theory is able to explain their actions only because they had special characteristics that cannot be generalized to other strategic environments. If so, it may be of limited value as a general perspective on international relations. This critique centers on two commonalities between the United States and Great Britain in the period under consideration: democracy and abundant security. I consider the merits of each argument below.

Democracy

One reason for skepticism about the broader implications of this study is that both of its cases were liberal democracies. Democracies are designed to aggregate societal interests in a reliable and consistent manner; autocracies are not. In the absence of regular, competitive elections, state leaders may be able to conduct foreign policy according to their personal whims. For example, the Nazis' elimination of political opposition in Germany allowed Adolf Hitler to initiate a war that offered few material benefits to his people. Even in less tightly centralized authoritarian states, like Wilhelmine Germany and Tsarist Russia, unelected leaders have had substantial freedom of action in international affairs.

I find no fault with the logic of this point: it is entirely consistent with the coalitional view of interest aggregation on which the theory is based. Indeed, it was incorporated into my hypotheses from the outset. In the first chapter, I argued that none of the four broad-based sectoral groups under consideration (domestic, core, peripheral, and military-colonial interests) could expect to benefit from a strategy of supremacism. It is telling, therefore, that the most supremacist regimes in modern history, Napoleonic France and Nazi Germany, ruled through the repression and reorganization of their domestic interest groups. In such cases, the theory will have limited explanatory leverage. It should be noted, however, that most perspectives on international relations, including realism, struggle with the same problem: neither Napoleon nor Hitler consistently acted according to standard definitions of the "national interest."

Despite these limitations, I do not accept the charge that the theory applies to liberal democracies alone. The world is not neatly divided between democratic states, in which leaders are accountable to socioeconomic coalitions, and authoritarian states, in which leaders are free to disregard domestic preferences entirely. In fact, most nondemocratic governments have well-defined constituencies on whose support they depend. These "selectorates" are typically composed of some combination of military officers, high-level bureaucrats, business elites, landowners, and trade union leaders—that is, actors who could use their power, wealth, and organization to destabilize the regime. In some states, they influence the selection and replacement of leaders in a ruling party; in others, they exercise a tacit veto over policy-making through the threat of a coup. In either case, their preferences should have a predictable impact on grand strategy.

A brief scan of the historical literature on nondemocratic great powers makes this point abundantly clear. Beginning with Eckart Kehr, numerous scholars have argued that Germany's strategic aggressiveness prior to World War I can be traced to the economic interests of the ruling coalition of "iron and rye."[9] Jack Snyder, a political scientist, draws extensively from this research in his own work, in which he attributes strategic "overexpansion" to pathologies of interest aggregation in Wilhelmine Germany, Imperial Japan, and the Soviet Union, as well as the United States in the Cold War and Britain in the mid to late nineteenth century.[10] There are important differences between Snyder's views and mine; in particular, I argue that parochial interests and political contestation always lie at the root of state behavior, not just in exceptional cases in which "logrolling coalitions" of avaricious elites "hijack" the state to their own ends. The essential point, however, remains that political-economic preferences play a vital role in the strategy of authoritarian great powers.

Abundant Security

Another potential critique of this study is that both of the countries on which I tested the theory enjoyed abundant security. The United States did not face a serious threat to its national survival at any point in the period under consideration, and the borders of the British Isles were more secure than those of any other European great power. Consequently, American and British leaders had broad leeway in their conduct of grand strategy. Commitments to internationalist institutions could seriously hamper their

---

[9] Eckart Kehr, *Economic Interest, Militarism, and Foreign Policy: Essays on German History*, trans. Grete Heinz, ed. Gordon A. Craig (Berkeley: University of California Press, 1977). For overviews of more recent work on the subject, see Gordon Martel, ed., *Modern Germany Reconsidered, 1870–1945* (London: Routledge, 1992); Roger Chickering, ed., *Imperial Germany: A Historiographical Companion* (Westport, Conn.: Greenwood, 1996).

[10] Jack Snyder, *Myths of Empire: Domestic Politics and International Ambition* (Ithaca: Cornell University Press, 1991). On Japan, see also James H. Nolt, "Business Conflict and the Origin of the Pacific War" (Ph.D. diss., University of Chicago, 1994).

peripheral policies but would not put their homelands at risk. They also had a reasonable degree of freedom to choose which, if any, alignments and alliances they formed. Among the other great powers, only Japan was similarly unconstrained. France, Germany, Russia, Austria-Hungary, and Italy all had to confront the possibility of losing territory, or even their national independence, in a war with a bordering state.

Furthermore, both the United States and Great Britain held a privileged position in the periphery. Throughout 1865–1941, the supremacy of the United States over Central and South America was never seriously challenged. The country would face difficulties in dealing with East Asia, but it had a free rein within the Western Hemisphere. Having this "inside track" in the periphery, like having a secure homeland, gave the United States considerable strategic flexibility. In particular, it was free to expand at its leisure. It was not forced into the game by European competition; there would be no penalty for procrastination as long as its ambitions were limited to its backyard. The vast oceans separating the Americas from Eurasia ensured that the United States could face down any challenge in its sphere of influence, even when it was militarily weak and politically isolated.[11]

Britain did not have an exclusive sphere of influence on any continent other than Australia, but it did have a "first mover" advantage in the game of imperialism. Beginning in the mid 1880s, its empire in Africa and Asia came under pressure from the other great powers, but it still had a far greater capacity to expand than any of its competitors. Not only did it have a dominant fleet, a global network of military bases, and control over most strategic naval lanes, but it also had major colonies in each of the regions that would be divided up in the New Imperialism of the 1880s and 1890s. Australia, India, and the Cape Colony served as jumping-off points from which Britain could expand into Oceania, South Asia, and Southern Africa, respectively. Britain could afford a lackadaisical grand strategy in the 1860s, 1870s, and 1880s because it already had regional spheres of influence throughout the periphery. As with the United States, the timing of its decision to expand was relatively unconstrained by the international environment.

Part of this "abundant security" critique of my case selection is indisputably correct: the United States had exceptional freedom of action in its grand strategy. Even in 1941, when it was attacked by surprise in a conflict for which it was not well prepared, it never had to cede an inch of its homeland territory. It had to abandon the Philippines, but no president ever considered the islands to be an indispensable part of a permanent "American Empire." In short, the United States in 1865–1941—before ballistic

---

[11] Robert J. Art, "The United States, the Balance of Power, and World War II: Was Spykman Right?" *Security Studies* 14, no. 3 (spring 2005): 365–406.

missiles and transnational terrorism brought the possibility of devastation to its interior—may indeed be a special case. A monograph on the domestic sources of its behavior in this period would be informative but not necessarily generalizable.

For Great Britain, however, it would be facile to dismiss the enormity of the country's strategic challenges simply because it was separated from the continent by a narrow stretch of water. Even if a serious threat to its homeland did not emerge until the rise of Hitler's *Wehrmacht*, its armed forces were in constant danger. At first they faced the possibility of war with the Franco-Russian alliance in India and at sea, then they had to scramble to keep ahead of Kaiser Wilhelm II's fleet-building program, and finally they were nearly overwhelmed by the combined air and maritime power of the Axis Powers. Britain had far more international commitments than any other country, yet its relative economic power was rapidly declining. It managed to maintain its hegemony over the periphery through two world wars, but this was due to a combination of diplomatic skill and good fortune, not an unconstrained international environment.

Other studies reinforce the point that socioeconomic interests are critical in cases of high international constraint. For example, Benjamin Fordham examines American grand strategy in the first few years of the Cold War, at the height of fears of conflict with the Soviet Union.[12] He finds that the Democrats' decisions to launch the Marshall Plan and intervene in the Korean War were influenced by their constituents' stake in foreign markets. Similarly, Peter Trubowitz addresses the late Cold War, when a seemingly declining United States faced the threat of Soviet advances on multiple fronts.[13] He shows how congressional support for the Reagan defense buildup depended on districts' exposure to international trade and reliance on military spending. Finally, Christopher Layne demonstrates that American grand strategy since 1940 has been motivated less by the need for security than the desire to create an "Open Door World" for trade and investment.[14] At every level of threat, structure of polarity, and shift in relative power, the study of grand strategy must begin with societal preferences.

AMERICAN GRAND STRATEGY REVISITED

If sectoral interests have motivated the behavior of great powers throughout the nineteenth and twentieth centuries, they should be no less relevant

---

[12] Benjamin O. Fordham, *Building the Cold War Consensus: The Political Economy of U.S. National Security Policy, 1949–51* (Ann Arbor: University of Michigan Press, 1998).

[13] Trubowitz, *Defining the National Interest.*

[14] Christopher Layne, *The Peace of Illusions: American Grand Strategy from 1940 to the Present* (Ithaca: Cornell University Press, 2006).

to American grand strategy in the twenty-first century. Peter Trubowitz's study of congressional politics in the 1980s provides an excellent jumping-off point for analysis. He argues that partisan conflicts over the Reagan defense buildup were the product of sectional economic differences.[15] In the northeastern "rust belt," older industries suffered from inefficiency and import competition and were losing ground in international markets. Consequently, the Democratic Party, which had represented northeastern labor since the Great Depression, sought to reduce American commitments overseas and substitute social welfare programs for defense spending. In contrast, the "sun belt" states of the South and West increased their exports through a boom in agriculture and the development of high-technology, military-oriented industries. As a result, the Republican Party, which drew on the South and West for much of its electoral support, pushed for a more aggressive, costly grand strategy.

Since the late 1980s, the political economy of the United States has been transformed. Parts of the Northeast still suffer from industrial decline, but most have diversified out of traditional manufacturing.[16] Advances in information technology, investment in human capital, and innovation in business practices have made the service sector the engine of the new "knowledge economy." From this base, American firms have taken full advantage of their flexible labor market, permissive regulatory environment, and open financial system to seize the opportunities offered by globalization. Though merchandise exports have fluctuated over the past twenty-five years, exports of services and income from overseas investment have grown steadily (see figure 8.1). The Asian financial crisis of 1997–98 and the destruction of the World Trade Center in 2001 put a dent in this growth, but the fundamentals appear to be solid. Barring a catastrophic shock, the United States will almost certainly continue its integration into the international economy through the 2010s.

It is more difficult to discern a trend in the geographic distribution of American exports and overseas investment (see figure 8.2). Exports to Canada and Mexico increased dramatically in 1988–2000, fueled in part by the Canada-U.S. Free Trade Agreement in 1989 and the North American Free Trade Agreement in 1994. It seems improbable, however, that American businesses will be content to focus on North America, or even the Western Hemisphere, as long as they remain competitive enough to have opportunities elsewhere. More likely, they will expect their government to continue to press for economic liberalization and political stabilization throughout the world. In this view, NAFTA does not portend the regionalization

[15] Trubowitz, *Defining the National Interest*, chap. 4.
[16] John B. Judis and Ruy Teixeira, *The Emerging Democratic Majority* (New York: Scribner, 2002), 88–108.

Figure 8.1. U.S. Income from Exports and Overseas Investment, as Share of Gross Domestic Product

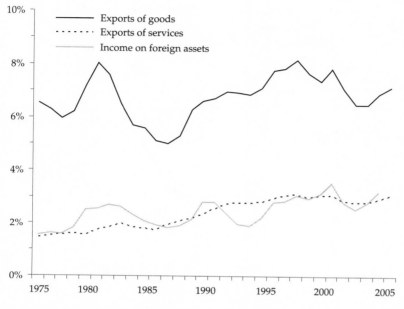

SOURCE: United States Department of Commerce, *Statistical Abstract of the United States* (Washington, D.C.: Government Printing Office, various years).

of American strategic interests; rather, it is a platform for their ongoing globalization.

American businesses should be most interested in developing markets, where they have a comparative advantage in information technology and organizational expertise. In such countries, they can export high value-added merchandise like software and biotechnology, sell financial and other services, invest in local firms, and contract out low-wage manufacturing. Advanced economies, in contrast, have less to offer. In the turmoil of the late 1990s and early 2000s, they were a safe haven for skittish capital; the share of American foreign direct investment in Europe increased from 48.8 percent in 1997 to 55.2 percent in 2003.[17] By 2005, however, it had declined to 51.2 percent. Once the international economic environment stabilizes, the highest rates of return on trade and investment will be found, as usual, on the frontier.

[17] United States Bureau of Economic Analysis, Interactive Tables, "U.S. Direct Investment Abroad on a Historical-Cost Basis," http://www.bea.gov/bea/di1.htm (last accessed July 2006).

Figure 8.2. U.S. Merchandise Exports, as Share of Gross Domestic Product

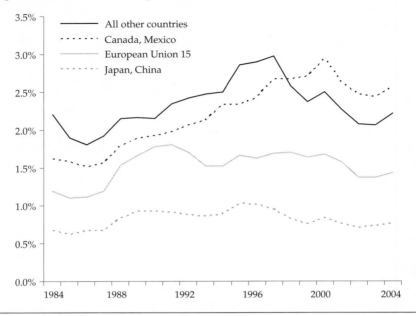

SOURCE: United States Department of Commerce, International Trade Administration, "Foreign Trade Highlights," http://www.ita.doc.gov/td/industry/otea/usfth/aggregate/H03t26.html (last accessed July 2006).

If these trends hold, the strongest of the four sectoral groups specified by the theory will be internationally competitive peripheral interests. Their hypothesized strategy, interventionism, should hold sway over American party politics well into the twenty-first century. Specifically, I expect the United States to continue to extend its influence throughout the globe, threaten force to advance its economic interests, and maintain its military primacy. Contrary to what some analysts suggest, it will not be tempted to withdraw into isolationism, no matter what is the outcome of its current adventures in the Middle East.[18] Indeed, it would be a mistake to expect the Iraq War of 2003 to produce a shift in public opinion comparable to that of the Vietnam War. In the 1960s and 1970s, the economic decline of the Northeast fueled opposition to interventionism; in the 2010s, the revival of the Northeast should sustain, and even enhance, support for it. Perhaps

[18] Charles A. Kupchan, *The End of the American Era: U.S. Foreign Policy and the Geopolitics of the Twenty-First Century* (New York: Knopf, 2003), 204–15, 236–44; John J. Mearsheimer, *The Tragedy of Great Power Politics* (New York: Norton, 2001), 386–92.

the growing national debt will induce caution, but not a wholesale shift in strategy.

Equally unlikely is a turn toward internationalism. No political coalition has a stake in the core comparable to that of the Democrats, Liberals, or Labour in 1865–1941; thus, neither the rise of transnational threats nor challenges from rival great powers should suffice to persuade Americans to accept major new commitments in collective security, binding arbitration, or international law over "high politics" issues. Instead, the United States will probably limit its involvement in multilateral cooperation to ad hoc measures in which it is able to dominate the agenda and preserve its freedom of action. This does not mean that it will renounce its existing internationalist treaties and practices; after all, the approximately 2.5 percent of its GDP that is derived from merchandise exports to the European Union, Japan, and China is highly significant in absolute terms. However, the stronger growth potential of trade and investment in the periphery means that diplomatic, political, and military capital invested in interventionism will pay greater dividends than if spent on internationalist initiatives.

What, then, of partisanship? Since the 1970s and 1980s, the revival of the northeastern "rust belt," combined with the continuing prosperity of southern and western states, has removed much of the conflict of interest between Democratic and Republican constituencies over the international economy. Furthermore, there is no longer a close correspondence between the economic and political geographies of the United States. Prior to 1941, the production of goods was highly segregated by region: raw materials came from the South and West, while manufactures came from the Northeast. Since then, and especially since the 1990s, sectors have become much more diffusely distributed. For example, software is created in Boston, San Francisco, Provo, and Austin, while automobiles are assembled in both Michigan and Alabama.

Yet, differences do remain. In the close election of 2004, Democratic candidate John Kerry won two-thirds of his Electoral College votes in the Northeast, whereas Republican candidate George W. Bush won two-thirds of his Electoral College votes in the South. These regions are clearly the political base of their respective parties. If their locus of interest in the international economy were the same, the theory would predict that the two parties' strategic preferences would converge completely. However, this is not the case (see figure 8.3). Of all of the merchandise exported from northeastern states that voted for Kerry (i.e., the entire region but Indiana and Ohio), 28.0 percent was sent to Europe. In contrast, only 20.2 percent of merchandise exports from the solidly Republican South was sent to Europe. Furthermore, approximately half of American foreign direct investment is held in Europe. Since the American financial services sector is concentrated in such northeastern cities as New York, Chicago, and Boston, it contributes

Figure 8.3. U.S. Merchandise Exports Sent to Europe, as Share of Total, by Originating Region, 2004

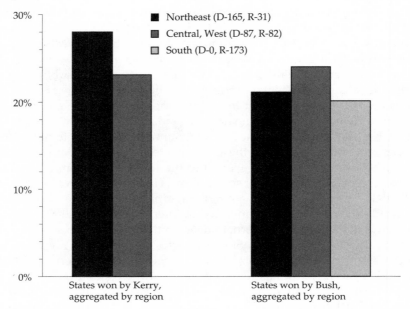

Source: United States Department of Commerce, TradeStats Express, "State-by-State Exports to a Selected Market," http://tse.export.gov/SEDMapState.aspx (last accessed July 2006). Note: The figures in parentheses represent the regional distribution of electoral votes in the election of 2004.

significantly to the regional imbalance. Absent a radical realignment in the party system, Democrats will continue to have a stronger interest than Republicans in Europe, and therefore internationalism, well into the twenty-first century.

These differences, while important, should not be exaggerated. American politics are as regionally polarized as ever, but, as noted above, the economy is less geographically segmented. Compared to the late nineteenth and early twentieth centuries, neither party has a strong base of core interests. In the most core-oriented subsection of the country, New England, the share of merchandise exports sent to Europe was only 38.4 percent in 2004. What this means, as I have already suggested, is that not even Democratic leaders should be definitively internationalist. Rather, I expect that, for any given issue on which there is a continuum of strategic choice, the Democratic position will be moderately *more* internationalist than that of Republicans.

Recent history provides some support for this prediction. In the election of 2000, for example, Democratic candidate Al Gore advocated the use of NATO as a collective security organization, with American participation in multilateral interventions to stabilize the Balkans, while Republican candidate George W. Bush took a more unilateralist line, seeking to draw down American commitments to peacekeeping. Furthermore, in a striking parallel to debates over the Soviet Union in the interwar period, a new cleavage arose over China: Gore called for it to be integrated into the "international community" through economic interdependence and institutionalized cooperation, whereas Bush was more concerned about balancing the threat that it posed to American power in the East Asian periphery. Finally, the two parties diverged sharply over the Middle East. Republicans favored the unilateral use of force to expand their influence in the region, while Democrats were more concerned about the consequences of breaking ranks with their diplomatic partners in NATO and the United Nations Security Council.

As I have emphasized throughout this study, the theory is not equipped to predict every foreign policy decision. It has particular difficulty with the invasion of Iraq in 2003, one of the most salient issues in American grand strategy at the time of this writing (August 2006). It helps account for the partisan pattern of disagreement over the war; however, it does not explain the decision for the war itself. Indeed, the conflict came as a surprise to nearly every theoretical perspective on international relations: neither constructivists nor institutionalists expected the United States to violate prevailing norms against preventive war and, in so doing, to create a deep rift in the transatlantic security community, while realists decried the idealistic Bush Doctrine as contrary to American "national interests."

What, then, can be made of these events? According to administration insiders, Bush and his foreign policy team came to the White House in January 2001 with designs for regime change in Iraq that were far more ambitious than outside observers could have anticipated.[19] If this is correct, it has critical implications for the use of this case to test the theory. Coalitional interests should be able to explain Bush's pre-9/11 approach to foreign policy; however, they cannot be expected to account for all aspects of Bush's response to 9/11. During the election of 2000, no reporters, voters, campaign contributors, special interest groups, or political competitors asked Bush what he would do in the event that the United States was subject to a catastrophic terrorist attack; the issue simply did not enter into the calculations

[19] Ron Suskind, *The Price of Loyalty: George W. Bush, the White House, and the Education of Paul O'Neill* (New York: Simon and Schuster, 2004), 72–75, 85–87, 96–97, 129; Richard A. Clarke, *Against All Enemies: Inside America's War on Terror* (New York: Free Press, 2004), 244–46, 264–74.

of any of the major actors involved in the process of interest aggregation. Thus, the crisis opened a wedge for political agency, and the administration took full advantage of it. The post-9/11 Bush presidency might count as a disconfirming observation for the theory, but like the outliers discussed earlier in this chapter, it does not upset the theory's underlying logic.

Whatever the future may hold for American grand strategy, the implications of this study are far-reaching. That state leaders are wont to attach the word *national* to "security policy" does not alter the fact that, like any other program on which governments spend large sums of money, it can create acute distributional conflicts. Whether the result is sharp partisan conflict, cross-party cleavages, or short-term consensus depends on the content and configuration of domestic preferences at the time. The theory does not explain merely partisanship; rather, it uses partisanship as analytic leverage into the underlying motives of state behavior. With this leverage, it is able to account for broad patterns of continuity and change in grand strategy without resorting to ad hoc auxiliary hypotheses. The political economy paradigm does not encompass every cause of foreign policy, but its deductive logic, sound methodology, and predictive power make it a solid challenger to realism as a foundational perspective on international relations.

Index

Abyssinia, 152–53, 288–89, 290, 293, 297
Afghanistan, 203, 206, 207, 247, 294
Alabama claims, 118–19, 241
Alaska, 81, 82, 95, 129, 252
Albania, 246, 262, 273
Algeçiras Conference, 258–59
Anglican Church, 160, 163 n13
Angra Pequena, 208
appeasement, 252–54, 259, 291–94, 295–96
arbitration, 92, 93, 110, 118–19, 123–24,
    128–30, 140–41, 143, 144, 206, 207,
    241, 247, 252, 262–63, 271, 273, 277,
    279, 281, 284. *See also* conciliation;
    internationalism; Permanent Court of
    International Justice
arms control, 132, 139, 142–43, 146, 147, 259,
    275, 276, 277, 278, 281, 282, 291, 294, 296
army
    British, 70, 162, 254, 267, 280, 290, 291–92,
        294, 296
    U.S., 70, 127, 149, 150, 153, 156
Arthur, Chester A., 87–88, 121, 123
Ashanti, 178, 201
Asquith, Herbert H., 219–20, 221, 266, 269
Atlantic Charter, 154
Attlee, Clement R., 231–32
Australia, 109, 110, 177, 180, 208, 212, 223
Austria, 272, 292, 294, 296, 297. *See also*
    Austria-Hungary
Austria-Hungary, 132, 242, 244, 248, 250,
    257, 260–62, 263–64

Baldwin, Stanley, 223–24, 229–31, 281, 286,
    289, 295

Balfour, Arthur J., 196, 217–18, 221, 272–73,
    276
Baltic states, 155. *See also* Lithuania
Beard, Charles A., 4, 77, 116
Bechuanaland, 208, 209, 211
Belgium, 133, 151, 192n2, 214, 240,
    265–66, 279
beliefs. *See also* preferences: ideational
    about economic conditions, 37, 47
    about national interests, 2, 26, 30,
        31–32, 37
    cognitive consistency, 27
Bennett, George H., 278, 280
Bensel, Richard F., 78, 117
Berlin Conference, 88, 91, 207
Bismarck, Otto von, 14, 239. *See also*
    Germany, Wilhelmine
Blaine, James G., 56, 87
Bodelson, Carl A., 180–81
Boers. *See also* Orange Free State; Transvaal
    first war with Britain, 206
    second war with Britain, 171, 178, 218
Borneo. *See* Malaysia
Brazil, 92, 93, 101, 102, 131
Bright, John, 163, 183 n65
Britain. *See also* England; Scotland; Wales
    in U.S. grand strategy, 85, 88, 89, 93, 98,
        104, 110, 118–20, 123–24, 126, 128–30,
        131–39, 141, 142, 143, 144–45, 147, 148,
        149, 151, 153–54, 156
    mid Victorian, 159–60, 163, 179, 310, 313
British Central Africa, 212
British East Africa, 212
British South Africa Company, 215

Bryan, William J., 57–58, 66, 101, 115, 131
Bulgaria, 242–44, 248, 260–61
Burma, 211, 212
Bush, George W., 28, 319, 321–22

Cain, Peter J., 193–94, 196–97
Cameroon, 223
Campbell, Charles S., 47, 94
Campbell-Bannerman, Henry, 219–20
Canada, 84, 129, 177, 180, 201, 208, 252, 316
canal diplomacy. *See* Clayton-Bulwer
    Treaty; Nicaragua, canal; Panama,
    canal; Suez Canal
Cape Colony, 201, 202, 203, 204, 208, 209,
    215, 220
case selection, 32–33, 312–15
Cecil, Lord Robert, 184, 272, 277, 278
Chamberlain, A. Neville, 286, 290, 293 n161
Chamberlain, J. Austen, 144, 277–80, 281
Chamberlain, Joseph, 195, 218
Chile, 89
China, 96, 98, 99, 102, 131, 142, 280. *See also*
    Open Door policy
    railroad concessions, 101, 104, 217
    unequal treaties, 224, 227
    war with Japan, 146–47, 155–56, 287, 288
Churchill, Winston L. S., 273
Clausewitz, Carl von, 9
Clayton-Bulwer Treaty, 88, 98, 252
Cleveland, Grover, 56, 57, 90–93, 101,
    123–25, 251, 306
coal (British sector), 166, 174, 176, 225, 296
Cobden, Richard, 183n65
collective security. *See* internationalism;
    Concert of Europe; League of Nations;
    United Nations
Colombia, 82, 84, 88, 99
Communist International, 154, 276, 280, 284,
    285, 294, 295
Concert of Europe, 207, 211, 243, 244,
    245–47, 251, 254, 260–62, 271, 308
conciliation, 101, 102, 110, 131–32
Congress, U.S. *See* House of Representa-
    tives; Senate
Conservative Party
    internal divisions, 218
    political economy, 159–62
    strategic interests, 172–73
Constantinople Conference, 243
constraints. *See* grand strategy: constraints
constructivism, 3, 4, 38, 321
Cook Islands, 211
Coolidge, J. Calvin, 106–7, 143–45
core (of the international system), 12

core interests, 19, 23
    British, 175–76, 182–85
    U.S., 51, 54, 59–61, 319–21
cotton. *See* farming (U.S. sector): southern
Crook, D. Paul, 195–96
Cuba, 81, 82, 83, 84, 88, 91, 93, 94–95,
    97–99, 106
Culebra, 82
culture. *See* preferences: ideational
Curzon, Lord, 275–76, 277, 280
Cyprus, 203, 204, 244
Czechoslovakia, 292–93, 294, 296, 297

Darby, Phillip, 179, 182
Dardanelles, 223, 248
Darwin, Charles R. *See* social Darwinism
Darwin, John, 230
Davis, Lance E., 165
Dawes Plan, 144, 284
debt, government, 24
    British, 169, 199, 204, 213, 221, 227–28,
        239, 270, 286–87, 290
    U.S., 79, 83, 86, 103, 107, 118, 139, 142, 145,
        319
Defence Requirements Committee, 287,
    291–92
defensive realism, 6–7, 74–75, 84, 302
deflation, 62, 91, 92, 181
democracy. *See* interest aggregation:
    democratic
Democratic Party
    internal divisions, 57–58, 124–25
    political economy, 55–59, 319–20
    strategic interests, 63–64, 320–21
Denmark, 82, 99, 102, 206
Depression of 1893–97, 44, 57, 62, 91, 124, 125
Dewey, Thomas E., 150
Disraeli, Benjamin, 202–4, 242–44
Dobson, John M., 97
Dockrill, Michael L., 261
dollar diplomacy, 100, 101
domestic interests, 19, 23
    U.S., 42, 51–52
Dominican Republic, 83, 84, 88, 89, 98–99,
    100, 101, 102, 106, 107
Draft Treaty of Mutual Assistance, 277, 282
Dulles, Foster R., 52

Easter Agreement, 290
Ecuador, 101, 102, 131
Eden, R. Anthony, 289–90, 294
Egypt, 206–7, 209, 211, 214, 222, 223, 224,
    226, 230–31, 245–46, 247, 254, 278.
    See also Suez Canal

El Salvador, 88
Ellice Islands, 215
England
    northern, 172, 173, 174, 183, 184
    southeast, 160–61, 165–67, 170–71, 172, 173, 267 n75
Entente Cordiale. *See* France: entente with Britain
Ershkowitz, Herbert, 52
Ethiopia. *See* Abyssinia
evidentiary standards, 31–32, 36–38

farming (U.S. sector), 62
    southern, 59–61, 132, 135–36, 148, 151, 154
    western, 40, 41–42, 57–58, 64–67
Ferguson, Thomas, 117
Fiji, 203, 204
finance (British sector), 160–61, 165–66, 168–72, 197, 267 n75, 286
finance (U.S. sector), 317, 319–20
Finland, 155, 272
Five-Power Treaty, 142
Fontainebleau Memorandum, 273
Fordham, Benjamin O., 315
Four-Power Treaty, 142, 146, 276
Fourteen Points, 139
France, 129, 131, 132, 141, 142, 143, 144, 150, 153–54, 156, 248, 249–50, 251, 252, 254, 274, 275, 276, 278–79, 284, 289, 292, 298
    alliance with Russia, 249, 257–60
    entente with Britain, 253–55, 257–59, 262, 263–65, 267
    Napoleonic, 13, 312
    peripheral policies, 82, 98, 104, 126, 201, 206, 207, 208, 209, 214, 215, 217, 218, 222, 254
    tariffs and trade, 151, 179–80, 181, 209, 213, 310
    war with Prussia, 240

Gallagher, John, 193–94
Gambia, 201
Garfield, James A., 87–88, 121, 123
Geneva Disarmament Conference, 147
Geneva Naval Conference, 143, 147, 281
Geneva Protocol, 277–78, 279, 282–83
Genoa Conference, 276
gentlemanly capitalists, 160–61, 197. *See also* finance; gentry
Gentlemen's Agreement, 290
gentry, 159–65, 173
German East Africa, 223
German Southwest Africa, 223

Germany, Nazi, 13, 148, 150, 153–54, 155, 156–57, 289, 290–94, 295, 296–97, 312
    peripheral policies, 293–94, 297
    tariffs and trade, 150, 151, 296
Germany, Weimar, 141, 143, 144, 270–71, 272, 273–75, 278–79, 283–84
Germany, Wilhelmine, 127, 129, 132–39, 148, 240, 250, 251, 252–53, 254–55, 257–60, 262, 263–66, 312, 313
    peripheral policies, 83, 85, 89, 91, 96, 98, 99, 122, 123, 208–9, 212, 214, 215, 217, 220, 247, 254
    tariffs and trade, 132, 179
Gilbert Islands, 211
Gladstone, William E., 183 n65, 200–202, 205–10, 213–15, 239–41, 242–43, 245–47, 250
Gold Coast, 201, 211, 217
gold standard, 57–58, 62, 169, 270, 286–87
Good Neighbor Policy, 109
Gore, Albert A., 321
grand strategy, 8–16, 22, 70
    constraints, 23–24, 68–71, 302. *See also* debt; monetary crises; recessions; threat; House of Lords; House of Representatives; Senate
Grant, Ulysses S., 83–85, 119–20, 305
Great Depression, 107–8, 145, 149, 150–51, 228, 231
Greece, 246–47, 251, 260–61, 277
Greeley, Horace, 80
Greenland, 81, 82, 154
Grey, Edward, 219–20, 256–66, 269
Griqualand, 201, 202, 204
Guam, 95, 97–98
Guiana, 92, 93, 251
Guinea, 208

Hague Peace Conferences, 128, 262
Haiti, 89, 101, 102, 106, 108, 109, 110
Halifax, Lord, 290, 291
Harding, Warren G., 105–6, 115, 142–43
Harrison, Benjamin, 89, 121–22, 123
Hawaii, 82, 84, 88, 89, 90, 91–92, 97–98, 109, 110
Hay, John M., 126
Hayes, Rutherford B., 85–86, 120
Heligoland, 211
Henderson, Arthur, 225, 282–85
Hinsley, Francis H., 207
Hitler, Adolf, 291. *See also* Germany, Nazi
Hoare, Samuel J. G., 229, 289, 293
Hobson, Charles K., 168
Hobson, John A., 3, 170, 196

Hofstadter, Richard, 76
Holbraad, Carsten, 165
Honduras, 106
Hong Kong, 217
Hoover, Herbert C., 108–9, 146–47
Hopkins, Anthony G., 193–94, 196–97
House of Lords, 263
House of Representatives, 56, 70–71, 94,
    121, 131, 137, 148–49, 152, 154
House, Edward M., 132, 135, 269n80
Hughes, Charles E., 115, 127
Hull, Cordell, 153, 156
humanitarianism, 77, 95, 102, 195, 240, 242,
    246, 307
Huttenback, Robert A., 165
Hynes, William G., 181, 197

Iceland, 154
ideology. *See* liberalism; preferences:
    ideational; social Darwinism
Imperial British East Africa Company,
    211, 214
imperialism (grand strategy), 13, 20–21, 22
    predicted in Britain, 163–64, 168–71,
        179–82, 187
India, 177, 180, 212, 215, 229
    external defense, 206, 249, 253, 263, 294
    internal control, 226, 227, 230, 231, 232,
        271, 291, 294
inflation, 290
Inskip Report, 292
institutionalism, 4, 321
Inter-American Conferences, 106, 110,
    123, 130
Inter-American Court of Justice, 110
interest aggregation, 7–8, 25–30, 31–32, 37,
    85, 103. *See also* preferences
    agential, 25–27
    authoritarian, 313
    coalitional, 27–30, 312
    democratic, 32, 312–13
    failures, 29–30, 83, 130–31, 305–7, 321–22
international law. *See* internationalism
international political economy,
    2–3, 308–11
International Prize Court Convention,
    128–29, 262
internationalism (grand strategy), 15, 19, 20
    predicted in Britain, 182–85, 187
    predicted in the United States, 54, 55,
        61–62, 63–64, 65–67, 320–21
interventionism (grand strategy), 14, 16,
    20–21
    predicted in Britain, 177–79

predicted in the United States, 52, 54–55,
    64, 318–19
investment. *See* finance
Iran. *See* Persia
Iraq, 222, 223, 224, 227
    war with the United States, 18, 318, 321
isolationism (grand strategy), 11, 19
    predicted in the United States, 51, 54,
        63–64, 65–67
Italy, 152–53, 157, 248, 250, 262, 277,
    288–90
    peripheral policies, 152, 206, 207, 222,
        288–89, 293
    tariffs and trade, 179

Japan, 142, 147, 150, 155–56, 263, 276,
    288, 313
    alliance with Britain, 253, 257, 263
    peripheral policies, 98, 104, 126, 263
    war with China, 146–47, 155–56,
        287, 288
    war with Russia, 126, 253
Johnson, Andrew, 81–83, 84–85, 118–19,
    305

Keeble, Curtis, 294
Kehr, Eckart, 4, 313
Kellogg, Frank B., 144
Kellogg-Briand Pact, 144, 146, 281
Kerry, John F., 319
Knox, Philander C., 130
Korea, 87, 88, 263
Kuehl, Warren F., 67
Kuwait, 217

Labour Party
    internal divisions, 283
    political economy, 186–87, 231–32
    strategic interests, 182, 187
LaFeber, Walter, 43, 77–78
Landon, Alfred M., 149, 150
Lansbury, George, 231
Lansdowne, Lord, 218, 252–53, 267
Law, A. Bonar, 223–24, 267
Layne, Christopher, 315
League of Nations, 104, 138, 140–41,
    143, 144, 146, 152, 222, 223, 269–71,
    272–73, 277–78, 287, 288–89, 295, 296,
    297–98. *See also* Draft Treaty of Mutual
    Assistance; Geneva Protocol
    Mandate System, 104, 222, 223
League of Nations Union, 184
Lend-Lease Act, 149, 154, 155
Liberal National Party, 228

Liberal Party
   internal divisions, 173, 209–10, 213–14,
      221–22, 228, 249, 250, 256–57, 259,
      264, 265–66
   political economy, 160, 173–74
   strategic interests, 185–86
Liberal Unionist Party, 173, 216
liberalism, 116, 196n11, 237–38, 307–8. *See
   also* Moravcsik, Andrew
Liberia, 100
Lithuania, 155, 273
Lloyd George, David, 221–23, 270, 271–77
Locarno Pact, 279
Lodge, Henry C., 115, 124, 127
London. *See* England: southeast
London Convention, 246
London Naval Conference, 147
London Reparations Conference, 274
Lowe, Cedric J., 261
Lusitania, 136, 138

MacDonald, J. Ramsay, 225–27, 228–31,
   282–85, 286
Macedonia, 260–61
Madagascar, 87, 88
Mahan, Alfred T., 121–22
Malaysia, 203, 207, 211
Manchester School, 183, 196
Mansergh, Nicholas, 191
manufacturing (British sector), 167n24, 169,
   173–85, 197, 225
manufacturing (U.S. sector), 41–51, 57–59,
   316–17, 319
Maori, 177, 178, 201
Martinique, 82
Marxism, 4n3, 196n15
May, Ernest R., 76
McCain, John S., 28
McCormick, Thomas J., 96
McKinley, William, 40, 58, 93–98, 122,
   126, 127
Mediterranean Agreements, 248, 250
merchant marine, 135–39
Merk, Frederick, 75–76
Mexico, 82, 84, 88, 102
   war with the United States, 85
Midway Islands, 82
Midwest (U.S. region), 64–67
military doctrine, 15
military-colonial interests, 21–22, 23
   British, 162
monetary crises, 24
   British, 169, 228, 267n75, 286, 290
   U.S., 91, 94–95

Monger, George W., 254
Monroe Doctrine, 84, 86, 90, 93, 98, 99, 104,
   144, 251
Montenegro, 242, 246, 262
Moravcsik, Andrew, 7
Morocco, 254, 258, 259
motives (of decisionmakers). *See* beliefs
multilateralism. *See* internationalism
Munich Conference, 153, 292, 298

Natal, 201, 202, 203, 204, 220
National Africa Company, 208
national interests, 1–2, 6, 25, 27, 35–36, 78,
   157, 303, 312
navy
   British, 142, 143, 147, 162–63, 178, 248,
      249–50, 253, 255, 257, 258, 262–63,
      276, 281, 287, 289, 290, 291
   U.S., 95, 121–22, 124–25, 127, 128–29, 142,
      143, 147
neoclassical realism, 5–6
Netherlands, 151, 201
Neutrality Acts, 148–49, 152–54, 155
New Guinea, 208, 209, 223
New Hebrides Islands, 211, 212
New Zealand, 177, 180, 201, 223
Nicaragua, 82, 85, 86, 88, 91, 92, 93, 100, 102,
   106, 107, 108, 109
   canal, 81, 82, 88, 91, 93, 128, 252
Niger, 208, 209, 217, 218
Nine-Power Treaty, 142, 146
Ninkovich, Frank A., 114–15
Niue, 217
North American Free Trade Agreement, 316
North Atlantic Treaty Organization, 321
North Borneo Company, 207
Northeast (U.S. region), 39–51, 56–57, 316,
   319
Nyasaland, 212, 247

offensive realism, 73–74, 84, 301–2
Olney, Richard, 123
Olney-Pauncefote Treaty, 62
Open Door policy, 96, 98, 99, 100, 126, 134,
   139, 142, 146, 150, 155, 297, 315
Orange Free State, 201, 202, 203, 204, 218, 220
Ottawa Conference, 231, 286, 294
Ottoman Empire, 206, 211, 212, 217, 242–44,
   245–47, 248, 250, 251, 260–61. *See also*
   Turkey
overproduction, 42, 44, 182

Palestine, 223
Palmerston, Lord, 241

Panama, 82, 84, 88, 99
  canal, 83, 84, 87, 88, 99, 128, 130, 131, 252
Pan-American Conferences.
  See Inter-American Conferences
Pan-American Pact, 101, 102
Paris Peace Conference. *See* Treaty of
  Sèvres; Treaty of Versailles
parsimony, 4, 7, 11, 16, 17, 38
partisanship, 1–4, 25–30, 35–36, 75, 114,
  115–16, 157–58, 191–92, 236, 303–5, 322
Payne-Aldrich Act, 45
Peace Ballot, 184
peripheral interests, 19–21, 23–24
  British, 165–71, 175–82
  U.S., 45–51, 52–53, 316–19
periphery (of the international system), 12
Permanent Court of International Justice,
  141, 143, 144, 152, 273, 284
  General Act, 278, 283
  Optional Clause, 273, 277, 278, 282–83
Persia, 219, 220, 222, 223, 224, 260
Philippines, 95–98, 99, 101, 102, 106, 108,
  109, 110
Platt Amendment, 97, 109
Poland, 141, 155, 272, 273, 274, 293, 295
Polk, James K., 85
Populist Party, 57
Portugal, 212, 215, 217, 218, 220, 247, 260
Pratt, Julius W., 75–76
preferences, 1, 3, 4, 7–8, 31, 322. *See also*
  beliefs; interest aggregation
  class, 18, 270, 287, 309, 310–11
  ideational, 26–27, 75–77, 95, 114–16, 194,
    236–38, 307–8
  sectoral, 18–23, 308–11
Prussia, 14
  war with France, 240
psychic crisis. *See* Hofstadter, Richard
Puerto Rico, 82, 88, 91, 97

race. *See* social Darwinism
Reagan, Ronald W., 316
realism, 4–8, 9, 31, 33–36, 38, 70–71, 73–75,
  78, 84, 113–14, 157, 191–94, 235–36,
  301–5, 312, 321, 322. *See also* defensive
  realism; offensive realism; neoclassical
  realism
realpolitik (grand strategy), 14
  predicted in Britain, 164–65, 171–72
  predicted in the United States, 53
recessions, 24. *See also* Depression of
  1893–97; Great Depression
Reciprocal Trade Agreements Act, 151
Reform Act, 159

reparations, 144, 270–71, 273–74, 278–79,
  284
Republican Party
  internal divisions, 40, 55
  political economy, 39–41, 319–20
  strategic interests, 54, 320–21
Rhodes, Cecil J., 211
Rhodesia, 211, 215
Robinson, Ronald E., 193–94
Romania, 293
Roosevelt Corollary, 99
Roosevelt, Franklin D., 58, 116, 149, 150,
  151, 152–57
Roosevelt, Theodore, 40, 98–100, 116, 126,
  127, 130–31, 252
Rosebery, Lord, 195, 213–15, 249–50, 306
Russia, Soviet, 153, 155, 156, 270, 275–76,
  292, 294–95, 297–98, 313
  peripheral policies, 271, 280–81, 294
  tariffs and trade, 143, 144, 151, 154–55,
    276, 280, 284–85, 294–95
Russia, Tsarist, 131, 240–41, 242–44, 248,
  249–50, 251, 253, 261, 264, 312
  alliance with France, 249, 257
  entente with Britain, 219, 257, 258, 260
  peripheral policies, 82, 98, 126, 203, 206,
    207, 215, 217, 219, 220, 242, 247
  war with Japan, 126, 253

Salisbury, Lord, 123–24, 192 n2, 195, 210–12,
  215–18, 251, 265, 306
Samoa, 84, 85, 89, 91, 93, 98, 217, 223
Samuel, Herbert L., 228, 266 n72
San Remo Conference, 222
Schattschneider, E. E., 2, 4, 308
Schumpeter, Joseph A., 194
Scotland, 172, 173, 174, 184
security, 3, 4, 9. *See also* realism; threats
Senate, 62, 66, 70–71, 84–85, 90, 94, 121,
  124, 129, 130, 131, 137, 143, 144,
  148–49, 152, 153, 154, 252, 263, 275
Senegal, 181
Serbia, 242, 243, 260–61
Seward, William H., 81
shipping. *See* merchant marine; trade
Sierra Leone, 201, 208
Simon, John A., 228–29, 266 n72, 287
Snyder, Jack, 313
social Darwinism, 75–76, 194–96
Solomon Islands, 215, 217
South (U.S. region), 55–56, 116, 132,
  316, 319
  Confederate, 118
  Reconstruction, 41, 80, 119

Index

South Africa, 177, 203, 204, 220, 223. *See also* Cape Colony; Natal; Orange Free State; Transvaal
Soviet Union. *See* Russia, Soviet
Spain, 82, 83, 88, 91, 93, 94–98, 120, 131
civil war, 153, 290, 296, 297
war with the United States, 94–95, 98, 122, 126
St. Bartholomew, 82
St. John. *See* Virgin Islands
St. Lucia Bay, 208
St. Thomas. *See* Virgin Islands
state-centered realism. *See* Zakaria, Fareed
Stimson Doctrine, 147, 153
Stimson, Henry L., 146–47
Stone, Ralph A., 66
Sudan, 207, 214, 217, 218, 230–31, 246
Suez Canal, 203, 206, 211, 224, 226, 230–31, 243, 248
supremacism (grand strategy), 13, 14, 22
Sweden, 82, 272

Taft, Robert A., 149
Taft, William H., 40, 100, 115, 126, 127, 129–30, 305
Taft-Katsura Agreement, 126
Tanganyika, 209
tariffs, 3, 44, 50, 179–80, 209, 229, 308–11. *See also* trade agreements
British, 221, 224, 286, 294, 310–11
U.S., 86, 179, 213, 309–10
terrorism, 315, 321
Thailand, 215
threats, 23–24, 313–15. *See also* realism; security
tobacco. *See* farming (U.S. sector): southern
Togoland, 211, 217, 223
Tonga, 217
Tracy, Benjamin F., 121
trade (British sector), 160, 165, 166–67
trade agreements. *See also* tariffs
British, 151, 276, 280, 284–85, 294–95, 310
U.S., 82, 84, 87, 88, 89, 90, 91, 151, 156, 309–10
Transjordan, 222, 223
Transvaal, 201, 202, 203, 204, 206, 207, 209, 212, 218, 220
Treaty of Berlin, 244, 261

Treaty of Paris, 240–41
Treaty of Sèvres, 223
Treaty of Versailles, 104, 143, 272, 291, 292, 296
Treaty of Washington, 119, 241
Trubowitz, Peter, 78, 117, 315, 316
Tunis, 209
Turkey, 223, 224. *See also* Ottoman Empire
Turner, Frederick J., 103

Uganda, 211, 214, 215
United Kingdom. *See* Britain
United Nations, 321
United States
Cold War strategy, 10–11, 14, 313, 315
contemporary, 315–22
in British grand strategy, 201, 222, 241, 251–52, 257, 263, 269, 275, 276, 281, 284

Venezuela, 83, 92, 93, 99, 251
Virgin Islands, 82, 99, 102

Wake Island, 97–98
Wales, 172, 173, 174, 184
Walvis Bay, 209
Washington Conference, 142–43, 146, 147, 156, 276
West (U.S. region), 40, 41–42, 57–58, 316, 319. *See also* Midwest
wheat. *See* farming (U.S. sector): western
Williams, Rhodri, 267
Williams, William A., 43, 77–78
Willkie, Wendell L., 150
Wilson, T. Woodrow, 15, 58, 101–3, 104, 115, 116, 127, 131–42, 222, 269
World Court. *See* Permanent Court of International Justice
World War I, 93, 127, 132–39, 148, 161, 221, 257, 265–66, 267
World War II, 149–50, 293, 295

Yugoslavia, 273

Zakaria, Fareed, 6, 8, 70, 73–74, 84–85
Zanzibar, 209, 211, 212
Zimmerman Telegram, 137
Zulus, 178, 203, 212